Managing Sustainable Development

Second Edition

Michael Carley and Ian Christie

EARTHSCAN

Earthscan Publications Ltd, London and Sterling, VA

Second edition first published in the UK and USA in 2000 by
Earthscan Publications Ltd

First edition 1992

A catalogue record for this book is available from the British Library

ISBN: 1 85383 440 8 paperback
1 85383 445 9 hardback

Typesetting by PCS Mapping & DTP, Newcastle upon Tyne
Printed and bound by Creative Print and Design (Wales), Ebbw Vale
Cover design by Susanne Harris
Cover photo courtesy of GST Technology Ltd (Greenstreet), www.gstsoft.com/

For a full list of publications please contact:

Earthscan Publications Ltd
120 Pentonville Road
London, N1 9JN, UK
Tel: +44 (0)20 7278 0433
Fax: +44 (0)20 7278 1142
Email: earthinfo@earthscan.co.uk
http://www.earthscan.co.uk

22883 Quicksilver Drive, Sterling, VA 20166–2012, USA

Earthscan is an editorially independent subsidiary of Kogan Page Ltd and publishes in association with WWF-UK and the International Institute for Environment and Development

This book is printed on elemental chlorine-free paper

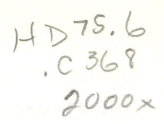

Contents

Part V – Case Studies in Innovation Management

List of Figures

List of Tables

Preface

The argument of this book is straightforward. We believe that, unwittingly, our unequivocal acceptance of industrial growth and expansion has brought us to the threshold of the earth's ability to absorb pollution and exploit its scarce resources. These resources include air, fresh water, the seas, the land and many human cultures and languages which have become vulnerable. There is nothing new in this observation and we do not intend to dwell on it in the book. Following the oft-cited report of the Brundtland Commission,[1] the need for change is discussed in terms of 'sustainable' development, but there is still substantial disagreement on what this means and how to achieve it.

Our ability to affect the environment is matched by an inability to assess the consequences of our actions, as we come to realize that natural and human processes are inextricably intertwined. To what end, we no longer know. We must now develop some realistic guidelines on the means of achieving genuine sustainable development and enhancing the quality of our relationship with the planet. What is required is good environmental management on a global scale, which means on national, regional and community scales as well. The issue is complicated by the fact that environmental problems have arisen largely because of the cumulative effects of industrial development in and by the 'developed' countries. The North in general, and the West in particular, have become rich at the expense of the planet. Therefore the newly industrializing countries of the developing world are insisting, with justification, that they are owed economic and technological recompense for this unfair situtation. This intensifies the North–South debate.

The situation is also complicated by rapid world population growth. By the end of the 21st century world population will have doubled from its present 5 billion to between 8 and 12 billion. The growth will be mostly in the developing countries. But the population of the United States will also grow by 50 per cent – an important point given that Americans currently consume around a quarter of all the world's resources each year. Taken together, the developed countries consume between 60 per cent and 85 per cent of key resources per year, even though the residents of these developed countries make up about one-fifth of the world's population. It is inconceivable that the many billions of people living outside the developed, Organization for Economic Co-operation and Development (OECD) countries could enjoy the intensely consumerist lifestyle of the rich one-fifth, without precipitating spiralling environmental decline. A wholly different development paradigm is required which joins North and South in a common endeavour.

All this suggests that environmental management is about far more than biophysical manipulation and control – it concerns the mutually beneficial management of the humankind–nature interaction to ensure environmental and social equality for future generations. This kind of environmental management begins with a sense of collective vision about the future, and continues with difficult decisions about the appropriate balance between industrial production, consumption and environmental quality. The nature of these decisions means that the realization of sustainable development, however it is defined and on whatever scale, is an intensely political process involving continual trade-offs between economic, social and biophysical needs and objectives. It is a political process of mediation in which old Right–Left thinking is largely irrelevant. This is the fascinating human dimension in environmental management.

The challenge of sustainable development is also made more complex by three recent developments in the world's political economy. The first is the rapid demise of the socialist experiment, and the spread of what the World Bank likes to call 'market-friendly' policies, under terms such as structural adjustment. Market-friendly policies imply a reduced role for the public sector in countries of all political hues and new freedoms from state control for entrepreneurs, ranging from those in multinational corporations to what in Malaysia are called 'backyard' industries. While such freedoms make a proven contribution to economic growth and may help to redistribute growth to the world's poorer regions, they may not be compatible with sustainable development. The question remains to be answered.

A second development is that the spread of economic liberalism is being accompanied by a Westernization of the world, in terms of the adoption of Western science and technology and, in some cases, the spread of liberal democratic ideas. Democratic notions are deeply attractive for many reasons, but it is dangerous to conflate political and economic liberalism. At the extreme, one recent and popular form of liberalism is *laissez-faire* capitalism, which is incompatible with sustainable development.

A third development is that both economic and political liberalization are accompanied by what can be called the ideology of consumerism, or 'Coca-Cola/Sony culture', spread by word of mouth and by advances in communication, such as the rapid spread of television following rural electrification, satellite television and new global linkages over the Internet and global telephone systems. Increase in the worldwide flow of advertising has led to a heightened awareness in developing countries of how the rich world lives, and legitimate desires to share in those lifestyles and standards of living. For example, it is likely that increased prosperity will double the number of automobiles in the world in the next 30 years (from the current 500 million vehicles), with dramatic environmental consequences. A world of well over a billion vehicles, reproducing on a planetary scale many of the developmental errors committed by the West and the Communist states, is heading for unsustainability.

The result of these trends is that just when many of the world's leaders and people are accepting the dominance of capitalist industrialism as the means to economic growth, we also need to question the fundamental assumptions behind this dominant mode of social organization, in terms of its implications for sustainable development. We are not implying, of course, that answers to all these grand questions emerge from this book. As will be seen, the tension between individualist entrepreneurialism and the need for social control in pursuit of the greater public good has been a focus of unresolved debate since the 17th century. We are no closer to a resolution. On the contrary, we suggest that there are no grand answers and that, instead, environmental managers will continue to need to 'muddle through', but in a much more sensitive and reflective manner than has been the norm. Sustainable development will be an ongoing, cumulative process, rather than an 'end-product', based on millions of right decisions at all levels of management from the global to the local.

Constructive responses to environmental crisis are threefold. The first requirement is continuing philosophical and moral debate about the appropriate nature of sustainable development, North–South relations, and the need to empower local communities to manage their own futures. The second is for the development of human resources and organizational capacity for environmental management, linking governments, business and community groups in a sense of common purpose. The third requirement is for fundamental research and development, especially in energy, agriculture and manufacturing processes.

This book makes its contribution to the first two requirements. Our focus is on the constraints to improved human resource management and organizational capacity, and the means to improve that capacity. We believe that improvements in environmental management skills, encompassing the human–environment interaction, are not only possible, but that they are beginning to surface in many different countries. This book is intended to help to promote better practice in environmental management. We have drawn partly on recent thinking in business management, public administration and organizational development, but mostly on our knowledge of, and involvement in, some notable existing innovations in environmental management. These innovations in practice, from around the world, are documented in the fifth part of the book.

It is these case studies which illustrate what we call the action network approach to environmental management. As we will show, such networks focus on tangible challenges of environment and development. They work at a number of levels: as growing constituencies for sustainable development, seen as an ongoing political process of mediation and consensus; as new partnerships between government, business and non-governmental or community groups; and as groups of natural and social scientists and public administrators with a commitment to mutual learning to develop new management skills.

As the case studies in Part V show, the network approach works by turning constraints on environmental management into opportunities for sustainable development. It also involves a substantially revised definition of management. This replaces the idea of control by a few people with that of negotiation and organizational learning. In this model, many relevant participants, or stakeholders, attempt to arrange their mutual affairs in a manner which is in harmony with nature and with each other. In this definition, management is teamwork, based on a continually evolving consensus on the direction towards sustainable development. This more egalitarian, participative approach to management is fundamental to the idea of an action-centred network. It also renders obsolete some common but divisive distinctions, such as the idea of 'developed' and 'developing' countries, for reasons set out in Chapter 2.

Welcome to the Revised Edition

The first edition of this book was published in 1992. At that time, mainly from our own experience in various types of development projects, we perceived that there was a type of organizational framework which seemed particularly suited to resolving difficult environmental problems and contributing to the complex, dynamic challenges of sustainable development. We called this type of approach an 'action-oriented network', since shortened to an action network. These are more than information networks and are characterized by a systematic drive to positive achievement and review, and what is called in the book horizontal integration. This integration is between objectives in the economy and for the environment and social development, and mutual involvement of the skills of public, private and voluntary sectors working in partnership.

What we found particularly exciting about action networks was that a similar approach seemed equally applicable in linking bottom-up and top-down efforts at various spatial levels: village or neighbourhood, city, bioregion, national, regional and international levels. Achieving mutually reinforcing effort at all levels seems to us essential for sustainable development. This we defined as vertical integration. Action networking also offered the potential for what we call 'networks of networks' to emerge, thus broadening the scope of the linkage between the bottom-up and the top-down and increasing what the book calls a constituency for sustainable development. Vertical integration remains one of the most pressing challenges of sustainable development as we move into the next, fateful millennium for the earth's people and environment.

In the eight years since the first edition, the United Nations Conference on Environment and Development (UNCED) at Rio in 1992 has come and gone, as have international conferences at Istanbul, Kyoto and Buenos Aires among others. In those years, sustainable development has gone from being a cry in the wilderness to become the objective of most governments, in name if not in action. But an enormous and long-lasting task of moving sufficiently towards sustainability remains in front of us.

A steady, positive response to the first edition over the years encouraged the authors finally to accede to our publisher's increasingly desperate pleas for a revised edition. Fortunately it has not proved as difficult as anticipated, since we seemed to have got much the right way around the first time. But in this revised edition we have done three things. First, we have updated the text in the entire book to take into account the many changes in world events and the global economy. Yet the basic principles remain the same. Second, we have updated the case studies in Part II, following up on the good beginnings of these action networks to document their achievements and difficulties, and the learning generated, between 1991 and 1999. The case study of the National Environmental Policy Plan (NEPP) of The Netherlands is a good example brought up to date on the Third NEPP, presented in 1998. Finally, we have added an additional chapter to broaden the range of the case studies, all of which are on action networks which work at international, national and local levels simultaneously, thus fostering vertical integration.

Outline of the Book

The book consists of five parts. Part I looks at the main trends in the world over the next 50 years and their likely environmental consequences. These include: population growth, industrialization and urbanization, changes in land use and ground-cover, and what we call globalization effects. Chapter 2 looks at the nature of sustainable development; whether it is compatible with economic growth, the idea of carrying capacity and the limitations of market economics. The chapter goes on to consider the relationship of world trends, particularly the momentum of industrialism, to political change on a world scale: the collapse of Communism, the 'market revolution' and the rise of a world culture of consumerism. The implications for the notion of sustainable development are considered.

Part II looks at the patterns of thought and action that are deeply ingrained within the Western industrial model of development. Sources from the Enlightenment onwards are examined to help us to understand the relationship of individuals with industrial societies, and that of humankind with nature and its embodiment in our economic systems. Factors considered include our perceptions of nature, our ambivalent relationship with science and technology, and the emerging perceptions of humankind and nature which are likely to be influential in the next century.

This section also looks at the political assumptions of Westernization and so-called market-friendly policies, and their implications for the management of sustainable development. We consider the possible damage of 'excessive individualism', the relationship between the individual and the state, and the implications of neo-conservativist thought.

Part III turns to the present organization of world business and finance, the emerging global culture of industrial consumption and consumerism, and the implications of these for sustainable development. Factors considered include: the globalization of the industrial economy, the nature of consumerism and advertising, and North–South inequalities in trade and other resource flows.

In Chapter 6, these top-down economic arrangements are contrasted with a growing need for bottom-up local participation, both to fulfil democratic aspirations and for effectiveness in developing and implementing policy in environmental management. The tension between centralization and decentralization is indentified as a major challenge to sustainable development and environmental management. Proposals that radical decentralization could foster sustainable development are analysed.

Part IV turns to the potential of innovative management approaches which contribute to sustainable development. Chapter 7 reviews the main institutional and organizational constraints on integrated environmental management. Chapter 8 considers management in conditions of endemic turbulence and uncertainty, and the role of action networks in environmental management, including policy, issue, professional and producer networks. These are contrasted with the action network, which links government, business and voluntary organizations in problem solving and the mobilization of resources. In this approach, conflict is seen as the opportunity for innovation, based on 'action learning' strategies within networks. Chapter 9 describes the assumptions and methods of working in action networks.

Part V comprises five chapters of case studies in environmental management which illustrate the action-network approach in the industrialized and developing worlds. The projects and methods these case studies describe work at different geographic levels: local or neighbourhood (the Groundwork Trusts in Britain); regional (watershed management in Ghana, Zambia and Zimbabwe, waste management in Lagos and Kuala Lumpur, and resource management in Mauritius and Guyana); provincial or state (the California Growth Management Consensus Project); national (the National Environmental Policy Planning process in The Netherlands); and international (Homeless International, the Global Action Plan, the African Energy Policy Research Network and the Sustainable Europe Campaign).

Michael Carley
Professor of Planning and Housing
Centre for Environment and Human Settlements
Heriot-Watt University, Edinburgh

Ian Christie
Associate Director
Local Futures Group, London
January 2000

Acknowledgements

We would like to thank the many people who provided inspiration and assistance in the preparation of this book. They are not responsible, of course, for the views advanced in this book, and any errors are entirely our own.

For the assistance with this revised edition, thanks to Tony Hawkhead, Chief Executive, and Ian Thorn, Communications Director, both at Groundwork, Birmingham, UK; Judy Jones, journalist and author, Malmesbury, UK; Dr Susan Sherry, California Center for Public Dispute Resolution; Dr Stephen Karekezi, Director, African Energy Policy Research Network, Nairobi; Marilyn Mehlmann, General Secretary, Global Action Programme, Sweden; Dr H J Staats, Centre for Energy and Environmental Research, Leiden University, The Netherlands; Teo Wams, Director, and Philippe Spapens, Campaigns Co-ordinator, Vereniging Milieudefensie, The Netherlands; and John Walton, Deputy Chief Executive, Homeless International, Coventry.

For assistance with the first edition, thanks to: Dr Mayer Hillman, London; John Davidson, Groundwork Foundation, Birmingham; Dr Martin Odei, Institute of Aquatic Biology, Ghana; Professor E E Okun and Dr W Odofin, Ministry of Science and Technology, Nigeria; Dr S Silangwa and Chris Mwasile, National Council for Scientific Research, Zambia; Dr Andrew Mathuthu, Chemistry Department, University of Zimbabwe; Professor J Manrakhan, Vice-Chancellor, and Dr Kishor Baguant, School of Engineering, University of Mauritius; Dr Abu Bakar Jaafar and Hasmah Harun, Department of Environment, Malaysia; Dr Walter Chin, Guyana Agency for Health Sciences Education, Environment and Food Policy; Dr S Varadarajan, Consultancy Development Centre, India; Dr Ray Zammit, Office of the Parliamentary Secretary for the Environment, Malta; Michaela Smith, Commonwealth Consultative Group on Technology Management, London; Dr Alexander King, past President, Club of Rome; Dr Dominique Levieil of the fisheries management section of the European Community; the late Dr Jaap Rodenberg, Greenpeace, Amsterdam; Professor Bill Rees, School of Community and Regional Planning, and Professor Brahm Wiesman, Centre for Human Settlements, both at the University of British Columbia; Professor Keith Banting, Queens University, Ontario; Patricia Carley, Washington; Dr Susan Sherry, Growth Management Consensus Project, California State University; Dr Joan Wilson Anderson, Southern California Water Committee; Dr Christopher Moore, CDR Associates, Boulder, Colorado; and Michael Chapman, San Francisco.

We would also like to thank our families: Sarah, Nicholas, Thea and Caroline, who are not only 'green' but also very patient.

Michael Carley and Ian Christie
Edinburgh and London
January 2000

List of Acronyms and Abbreviations

AIDS	acquired immune deficiency syndrome
AFREPEN	African Energy Policy Research Network
BTCV	British Trust for Conservation Volunteers
C&C	command and control
CAP	Common Agricultural Policy
CFC	chlorofluorocarbon
CPTM	Commonwealth Partnership for Techology Management
DETR	Department of the Environment, Transport and the Regions
EIA	environmental impact assessment
EPA	Environmental Protection Agency
EU	European Union
FEPA	Federal Environmental Protection Agency
FMST	Federal Ministry of Science and Technology
GAHEF	Guyana Agency for Health Education, Environment and Food Policy
GAP	Global Action Plan
GATT	General Agreement on Tariffs and Trade
GBC	Groundwork Black Country
GDP	gross domestic product
GMCP	Growth Management Consensus Project
GNP	gross national product
HIPC	highly indebted poor country
HIV	human immunodeficiency virus
ICLEI	International Centre for Local Environmental Initiatives
IDEA	Innovations in Development for Environmental Action
IIED	International Institute for Environment and Development
IMF	International Monetary Fund
IPCC	International Panel on Climate Change
LA21	Local Agenda 21
LSWDB	Lagos State Waste Disposal Board
MAI	Multilateral Agreement on Investment
NCC	Nature Conservancy Council
NEPP	National Environmental Policy Plan
NGO	non-governmental organization
NIC	newly industrialized country
NWT	Northwest Territories
OECD	Organization for Economic Co-operation and Development
OPEC	Organization of Petroleum Exporting Countries
PCB	polychlorinated biphenyl
RIIA	Royal Institute of International Affairs
SAHPF	South Africa Homeless People's Federation
SAP	structural adjustment programme

SEC	Sustainable Europe Campaign
TNC	transnational corporation
UK	United Kingdom
UN	United Nations
UNCED	United Nations Conference on Environment and Development
UNDP	United Nations Development Programme
UNEP	United Nations Environment Programme
US	United States
USDA	United States Department of Agriculture
WTO	World Trade Organization
WWF	World Wide Fund For Nature

Part I

Introduction

1

The Ecology of an Industrial Planet

... there is no 'natural habitat', in the sense of a terrestrial ecosystem that has evolved without the presence of a human element. There is only the choice between different methods and forms of human involvement in the habitat.

T Swanson and E Barbier[1]

In the life of the earth, 200 years is a mere flicker of time. Yet within the past two centuries the rise of industrialism has transformed the planet in ways that natural processes and previous civilizations would have taken millennia to achieve. In this short era of 'modernity' we have wrought dramatic changes to the environment, the most far-reaching being our effect on the chemistry of the atmosphere and the genetic diversity of the planet. These changes have given rise to fear of a global environmental crisis, and to calls for a shift from exploitative industrialism – 'business-as-usual' – to something called 'sustainable' development.

In Chapter 2 we consider what kind of development can be defined as sustainable. Here, we review the global social trends and negative environmental consequences that are likely to lead to unsustainable development in the next half century. These constitute the first of a series of constraints on sustainable development that are explored in this book.

This chapter can do no more than provide a brief overview of global environmental issues: many comprehensive sources are available.[2] Our purpose is to explore the scale of major challenges to sustainable development, to give some idea of their interactions and to set the stage for discussion about how we might improve environmental management. This book is about the processes of environmental decision-making and implementation, the assumptions and values that underlie these processes, and how they can be improved to lead to sustainable development.

Figure 1.1 outlines some major world trends and their consequences. The trends are not necessarily malign in themselves, whereas the consequences we have listed always are. So, for example, we do not immediately interpret as negative population increase, industrialization, the growth of cities, the shift of land from forestry to agriculture, or the increased mobility offered by the automobile or global air transport. Population growth can be accommodated easily in some ecosystems; many countries need industrialization to alleviate poverty; for many people an urban life-style is preferable to the limitations of rural life; almost everybody wishes to travel; and so on. On the face of it, there is nothing intrinsically wrong with these facts and aspirations.

The key issue for sustainable development is the magnitude of the changes induced by the trends listed above. There is a 'technocentric' school of thought which suggests that the negative consequences of these trends can be overcome or managed; and that human technological prowess will allow indefinite economic growth, will help

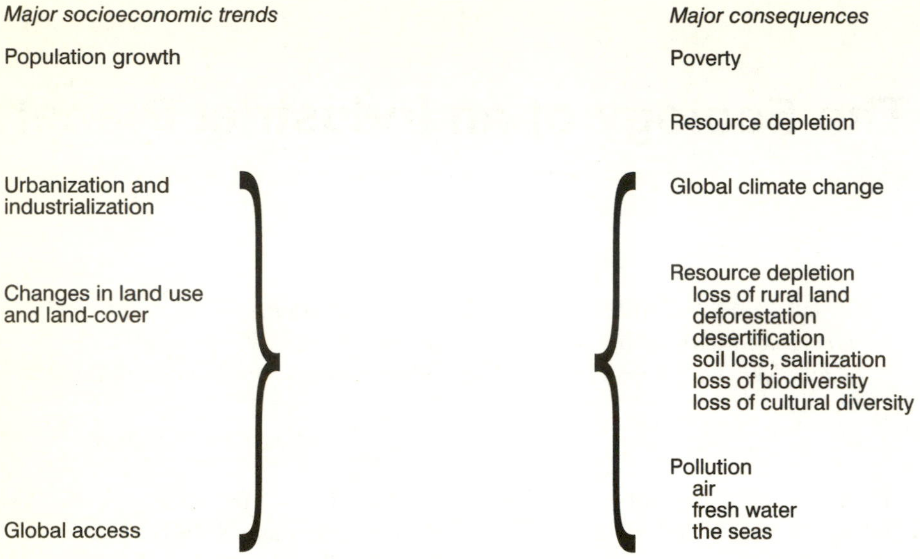

Figure 1.1 *Major world socioeconomic trends and sustainable development*

to manage and eventually contain global population increase, and will deliver ever higher living standards.[3]

However, this perspective fails to take sufficient account of the delicate balance of complex ecosystems and the possibility of dynamic negative changes being triggered by excessive human growth. For example:

- The current world population growth of some 80 million people per year – although down from the peak of 87 million in 1990 – virtually ensures poverty, undernourishment and resource depletion in many ecosystems.
- Industrialism on the current fossil-fuel burning model is unsustainable in atmospheric terms.
- A certain amount of rapid urbanization is manageable, but not with the growth rates seen in cities such as Lagos, which grew by 10.2 million people in 1975–2000 at an average annual rate of 5.8 per cent.[4]
- The 501 million cars in use worldwide are not only precipitating local crises of congestion and pollution, but adding to wider problems of environmental impact: the billion-strong fleet forecast for 2020 will contribute greatly to global pollution problems as well as to a growth in traffic across the world of some 60 per cent in the period 2000–2020.
- Deforestation and carbon dioxide generation on a massive scale are eroding the earth's built-in adjustment mechanisms in many areas.
- Our use of global fresh water and marine resources has grown hugely: freshwater withdrawals have nearly doubled since 1960, such that humanity uses more than half the planet's accessible freshwater run-off – great rivers such as the Colorado and the Yellow River now fail to reach the sea much of the time as so much water is diverted for agriculture and industry; marine fish consumption doubled between 1960 and the early 1990s, such that some 60 per cent of the world's sea fish resources are overfished or at the limit of sustainable harvesting.[5]

Similarly, at the local level, the scale of new development is tipping many economies and ecosystems into crisis. A small number of tourists on a Greek or a Caribbean island can be a boon to local life and even provide an economic basis for sustainable development. But when tourists outnumber local people by ten to one, and foreign travel companies package both local economy and local culture for sale, a threshold has been exceeded and negative effects begin to pile up for all concerned. In every case, the magnitude of change is too great. Critical, if unknown, thresholds have been exceeded and the situation is no longer amenable to beneficial local management. Usually, thresholds for sustainability – carrying capacities – are substantially exceeded even before we become aware of the nature of the problem.

The situation is made more complex and intractable because the trends and their consequences are highly interactive in a manner that is difficult to identify and measure, and sometimes even difficult to imagine. So, for example, urbanization is partly a result of, and partly a cause of, migration from countryside to city. The urbanization process itself generates economic activities which raise income levels, draw in resources from the countryside and even from faraway savannahs and rainforests, and generate enormous amounts of waste which end up as pollution of air, water and land. The increased income generates more consumption, more industry, more pollution, more automobility, urban sprawl, endemic traffic congestion, and so on. Urban sprawl results in the loss of prime farmland which, when combined with rural population growth, contributes to lowland forest loss due to agricultural expansion in the countryside well away from the city, thus completing a cycle of interaction. These processes are unfolding rapidly, but our responses to date fail to match the size of the problem.

Relationships between such trends and their consequences are not merely distinctions on a continuum of 'good' to 'bad' environmental effects: they are the very stuff of debate over the nature of sustainable development and the future of the planet. They go to the heart of our values and assumptions about how much of the earth's finite resources we are individually entitled to consume, and to our views on how much resource depletion is allowable in a sustainable framework. They are also important because there has been little public debate about the meaning of sustainable development. It is perhaps most important to acknowledge that, given the political and economic constraints on environmental policy, progress towards sustainability will have to be incremental rather than revolutionary. This means that the best time to start doing something, and then to learn from what we are doing, is now.

The Major Trends and Consequences

Population growth and poverty

Between 1850 and 1950 the world's population doubled from 1.25 billion to some 2.5 billion. By 1987 it had doubled again. A further billion people were added in the following decade. The global population at the turn of the millennium is 6 billion: in June 1999 the United Nations (UN) forecast that the 6 billionth person was due to be born in October 1999. Estimates for the next 100 years range from a total population of 8 to 14 billion before the rise levels off and some time in the 22nd or 23rd century stabilization or a fall occurs. We can hope that the stabilization will be a result of more countries passing through a 'demographic transition' in which average family size falls as agricultural productivity rises, contraception becomes more available and cultur-

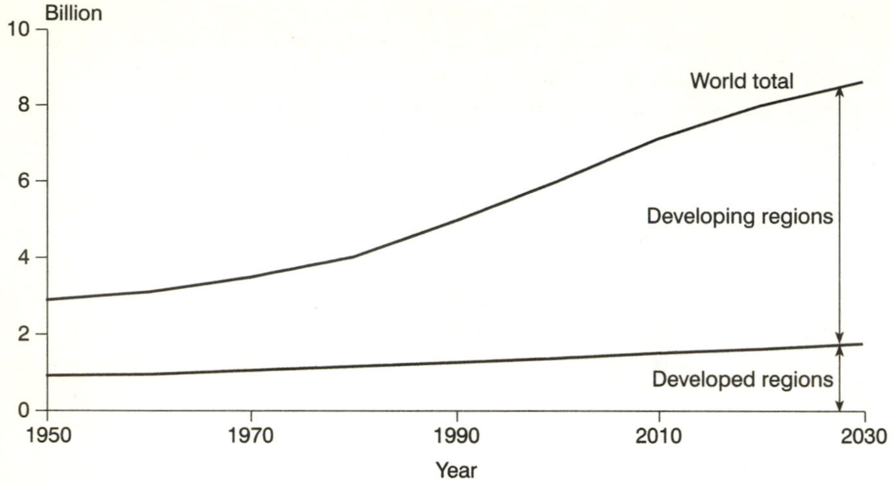

Source: Mannion, A M, *Global Environmental Change: A Natural and Cultural Environmental History*, Longman Scientific and Technical, London, 1991

Figure 1.2 *World population growth, 1950–2030*

ally acceptable, women gain better access to education and enter the labour market in larger numbers, and urban populations rise. But rising mortality rates could also play a part, reflecting the spread of diseases such as acquired immune deficiency syndrome (AIDS)/human immunodeficiency virus (HIV), extreme weather from climate change and pollution-related illness.

This rapidly rising population reflects progress in the form of increased life expectancy and improved health care. It also means that more skills, ideas and labour are available to add to economic and social resources: more people are not intrinsically a 'burden' on families or societies, and having children makes sense to people everywhere. But although warnings about the 'population explosion' are out of fashion, there can be no doubt that the high rates of increase in population in many areas mean a significant increase in pressure on the earth's resources and food-producing systems. In some industrialized countries population is set to stabilize or decline, but in parts of the developing world, which accounts for the majority of the global population (Figure 1.2), big increases are yet to come: some countries will double or triple their population by 2050 on current trends (Table 1.1). By 2050 the population of Nigeria will have risen from 122 million in 1998 to 339 million – more than the total African continent supported in 1950.[6] In the same period, the population of India is predicted to surpass China as the most populous country, adding 600 million people to reach over 1.5 billion.

Approximately one-fifth of the world's population (about 1 billion people) lives in absolute poverty, with some 841 million undernourished and some 1.2 billion without access to safe drinking water. Population growth, environmental degradation and poverty are closely related, and the quality of conditions for agricultural production is the decisive influence on the development of rural poverty. The relationship is indicated in Table 1.2. The shrinkage of the land available for grain harvesting as a result of land lost to housing, alternative crops, urban development, erosion and other factors is set to be most acute in the developing countries with the biggest population

Table 1.1 *The 20 largest countries ranked according to population size, 1998, with projections for 2050*

	1998		*2050*	
Rank	*Country*	*Population (million)*	*Country*	*Population (million)*
1	China	1255	India	1533
2	India	976	China	1517
3	United States	274	Pakistan	357
4	Indonesia	207	United States	348
5	Brazil	165	Nigeria	339
6	Russia	148	Indonesia	318
7	Pakistan	147	Brazil	243
8	Japan	126	Bangladesh	218
9	Bangladesh	124	Ethiopia	213
10	Nigeria	122	Iran	170
11	Mexico	96	The Congo	165
12	Germany	82	Mexico	154
13	Vietnam	78	Philippines	131
14	Iran	73	Vietnam	130
15	Philippines	72	Egypt	115
16	Egypt	66	Russia	114
17	Turkey	64	Japan	110
18	Thailand	62	Turkey	98
19	France	60	South Africa	91
20	Ethiopia	59	Tanzania	89

Source: United Nations, *World Population Prospects: The 1996 Revision*, New York, 1996, cited in Worldwatch Institute, *State of the World 1999*, Washington, DC, 1999 (www.worldwatch.org)

increases; and these countries also have high proportions of underweight children and other indices of extreme poverty and malnutrition. It is true that some significant improvements in agricultural production and technology have led to increased agricultural productivity in many nations. But this has not been sufficient to prevent a rise in the absolute number of people living in poverty, despite a fall in the proportion of people in poverty.

Population growth, combined with land and soil degradation, means that the situation is not likely to improve in the foreseeable future for many poor parts of the world, even though birth rates have been falling in countries such as India and Bangladesh since the 1970s and mortality rates have gone up in areas such as parts of Africa and the former Soviet Union. According to the United States Department of Agriculture (USDA), the grain-harvested area per person worldwide fell from 0.23 hectares to 0.12 hectares between 1950 and 1998. New land will be brought into production, but much of this land will be of poor quality and only briefly useful because it comes from deforestation or the cultivation of hillsides. Millions of hectares of crop land are lost to soil erosion each year.

If the effects of soil erosion, salinization (salt intrusion), overgrazing and water shortages are added, USDA projects that there will be a further shrinkage in grain area per person by 2050 to 0.07 hectares; in a country such as Egypt, with very little fertile land and huge population growth in prospect, average grain land per person will shrink to as little as 0.02 hectares.[7] By mid-century there will be little or no new high quality crop land available. There will be immense pressure in the coming decades to rethink some current crop selection, land use policies and the use of land for livestock rather than grain, and also to adopt new biotechnological

Table 1.2 *Grain-harvested area per person in selected countries in 1950, with projections for 2000 and 2050 (hectares)*

Country	*1950*	*2000*	*2050*
United States	0.41	0.23	0.19
Brazil	0.34	0.11	0.08
India	0.28	0.10	0.07
Bangladesh	0.29	0.10	0.06
China	0.16	0.07	0.06
Iran	0.61	0.13	0.06
Nigeria	0.52	0.13	0.05
Indonesia	0.18	0.07	0.04
Ethiopia	0.39	0.11	0.03
Pakistan	0.31	0.08	0.03

Source: US Department of Agriculture, *Production, Supply, and Distribution, electronic database*, Washington DC, updated October 1998; United Nations, *World Population Prospects: The 1996 Revision*, New York, 1996, cited in Worldwatch Institute, *State of the World 1999*, Washington, DC, 1999 (www.worldwatch.org)

approaches to raising crop productivity in the light of the emerging scarcity of crop lands in many of the poorest countries.

In many rural areas of the developing world, rapidily increasing populations put pressure on limited natural resources. Demand for wood for fuel, and slash-and-burn cultivation, often alongside new roads, have resulted in deforestation, deterioration of soil quality, erosion and downstream flooding.[8] The pressure extends out to sea, with extensive overfishing and destruction of coral reefs. To compound the problem, large farms producing export crops such as coffee, sugar, bananas, cotton and cattle, destined for industrial countries, have in many places displaced small farmers growing food for local consumption.

The implications of these trends are profoundly disturbing in what they imply about our approach to ecological and social limits to growth as it has been known. Sir Crispin Tickell (former UK Ambassador to the UN) notes that the distribution of world population corresponds less and less to the distribution of the earth's resources.[9] In the industrial countries we label as 'developed', industrialization has been sustained by an agricultural revolution which greatly increased food production, and those countries had substantial natural resources. The same cannot be said for much of the industrializing world: in many cases, despite the achievements of agricultural technology, there has been no agricultural revolution sufficient to sustain a newly industrialized and highly populous society, and urban poverty is growing as urban populations expand through migration by the poor from the countryside.

Land conversion and degradation

Deforestation

Living forests are in many cases net absorbers or 'sinks' for carbon dioxide from the atmosphere, locking up carbon and thus reducing the the build-up of greenhouse gases that contribute to global climate change. The loss of temperate and tropical forests is a growing source of concern not only in relation to the quality of local environments and economies, but also to the ecological security of all the globe as a whole. Industrial timber cutting is potentially sustainable if it is managed well, but where it is uncontrolled it can be a major cause of primary forest destruction in both temperate and tropical ecosystems.[10] Between 1970 and 1995 the value of legally harvested forest products almost tripled, reaching US$142 billion.

The expansion has taken place not only in the South but also in the North: while during the 1990s forest cover has increased in parts of Europe and North America, much logging of old growth and planted woodlands continues with damaging effects on the flora and fauna as shown in Table 1.3. The growth of logging in developing countries has accompanied the clearance of land for agriculture and housing, resulting in massive loss of forest cover in countries such as Brazil, the Russian Far East, Indonesia and Malaysia. Logging in Latin America, for example, degrades nearly 58,000 square kilometres annually but also opens up woodlands to clearing by ranchers and farmers, which is a major direct cause of forest loss. When forests are burned, they release carbon, thus accelerating the build-up of greenhouse gases in the atmosphere; the process also contributes to the risks of soil erosion and desertification.

Tropical forests account for half of the world's forested land. In their natural state, tropical forests are the most productive of the earth's ecosystems. They harbour the widest diversity of plant and animal species and produce two or three times as much organic matter as temperate forests.[11] In an area of 10 hectares in Sarawak, Malaysia, 780 tree species have been found.[12] Tropical forests also supply many products, including fruits, vegetables, bush meat, nuts, oils, spices, medicines, fibres, resins, tannins, honey, firewood and building materials.[13] The full long-term economic value of these sustainable resources is rarely considered in decisions about logging. The most rapid rates of deforestation in the tropics are in the rainforests: some 15 million hectares of tropical forest are lost each year. There is also significant deforestation in savannah woodlands in the tropics.

The loss of temperate woodlands should not be forgotten in the midst of concern over tropical deforestation; the immense appetite of Northern consumers for wood products – accounting for three-quarters of world demand – fuels large-scale logging in the broadleaf and mixed forests of North America, Europe, Russia and Chile as well as in the tropics. In Asia, some 70 per cent of the original forest cover has gone; some 60 per cent of temperate forest has gone; and some 70 per cent of the original cover of tropical dry forest has been lost. The *Living Planet Report* of 1998 from the World Wide Fund For Nature (WWF), the New Economics Foundation and the World Conservation Monitoring Centre comments, 'Today, largely intact tracts of undisturbed forest remain only in the Russian Federation, Canada and the Amazon and Congo basins'.[14] In Russia, the Amazon and the Congo the forests are under severe pressure; in Canada, the loss of old growth woods has been substantial.

Estimates of the rates of regional deforestation vary, but by any measure there is cause for concern about the local and global implications. Table 1.3 shows estimates for deforestation during the period 1990–95. Mannion comments that 'the area already affected is immense and the average rates of deforestation in these regions are sufficiently high that there is a real danger that the forests will disappear altogether in the next 200 years'.[15] The implication of continued deforestation is that perhaps 1.2 million species – a quarter of all those existing in the 1980s – will disappear by the year 2020; tens of thousands of so far undocumented plant species are thought to be in the at-risk tropical forests and their loss could rob humanity of many benefits.

In addition to habitat loss and species extinction, the environmental effects of deforestation include soil degradation, water run-off and erosion. Loss of forest cover and the accompanying erosion may accentuate the harm done to people by the

Table 1.3 *Deforestation rates in the 1990s*

Annual deforestation rates 1990–95, 000s of square km	
East Asia and Pacific	29.8
Europe and Central Asia	- 5.8
Latin America and the Caribbean	57.8
Middle East and North Africa	0.8
South Asia	1.3
Sub-Saharan Africa	29.4
High income countries	–11.6

Source: World Bank Atlas 1999, World Bank, Washington DC, 1999, p29

extremes of the weather and natural disasters. The catastrophic forest fires of 1997 in Indonesia and in 1997–99 in the Russian Far East, Mexico, Florida and the Amazon, highlighted the risks to public health, life and property as well as to biodiversity and the local climate. The diversity of causes of the fires – local or regional drought, the impact of El Niño on global weather systems, uncontrolled land clearance, arson, high temperatures – underlined the weakened state of forest protection and forest ecosystems in many areas.[16] The factors feed on each other: deforestation in the Amazon has contributed to local reductions in rainfall, accentuating dryness in the remaining forests which makes fires more likely and more damaging.

The most significant reasons for deforestation, in addition to industrial logging, are plantation agriculture (with crops such as oil palm); large-scale cattle ranching; mineral extraction; road and dam construction; and shifting small-scale agriculture and fuelwood collection. The exact contribution of each factor is debatable.

In Amazonia and Central America the establishment of large-scale cattle ranches to meet North American demand for beef has made a significant contribution to deforestation. Prance suggests that it is by far the largest cause of forest loss in Amazonia.[17] In Amazonia during 1965–83, the establishment of 470 cattle ranches of an average size of 23,000 hectares accounted for 30 per cent of the total deforestation.[18] The schemes resulted in the rapid loss of soil fertility. The government subsidy regime at the time encouraged further clearance rather than investment in land maintenance. Ranching is also linked to road building and mineral extraction, in what can amount to a subsidized industrialization package for the rainforest. Figure 1.3 shows the relationship between road building and deforestation in Rondonia, Brazil.

The European Commission's Joint Research Centre has concluded that the pressure from farmers and loggers on the tropical forests of South East Asia, Central Africa and the Amazon is so great that there is no prospect of saving much old growth forest.[19] Instead, policy should focus on identifying and protecting areas of high biodiversity in the central Amazon, New Guinea and the Congo basin. This pessimistic conclusion, based on satellite mapping of deforestation as well as fieldwork in rainforest 'hotspots' of logging and clearance, reflects an analysis that the pressures of poverty, economic development and the inadequate enforcement of environmental policies combine to make large-scale deforestation, as occurred in the North long ago, inevitable. In South East Asia land is taken for commercial plantations; in the Amazon, most of the forest is cleared for pasture; in Central Africa logging is increasingly intensive.

Although tropical deforestation is now highly controversial in the West and has aroused public alarm, it is important to note two points. First, the tropical countries are

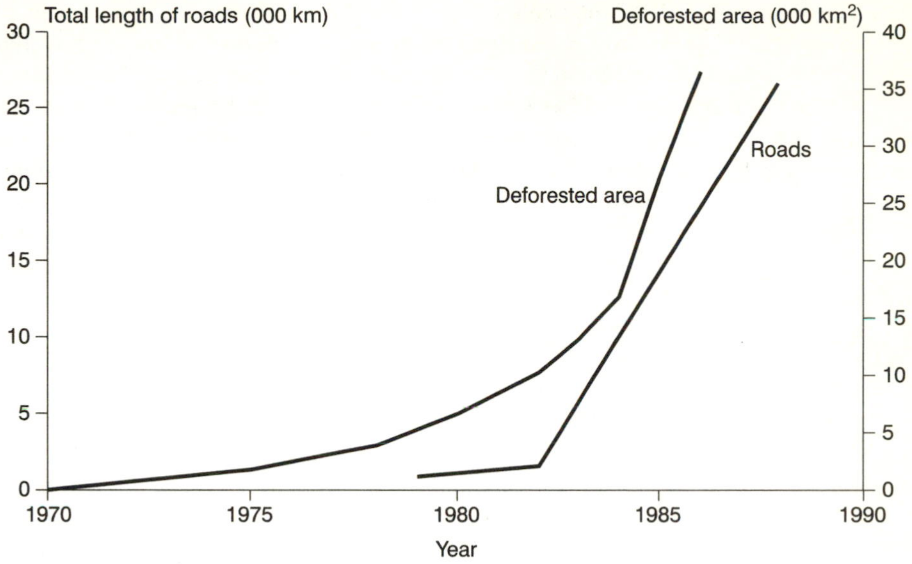

Source: Southworth et al, after Frohn et al

Figure 1.3 *Road development and deforestation, Rondonia, Brazil, 1968–88*

simply emulating a process of deforestation and conversion of land to agriculture, which the Northern countries have carried nearly to completion and which has contributed to their economic advancement.[20] Virtually all of Europe's virgin forests have disappeared over many centuries, cleared for agriculture and/or to fuel the Industrial Revolution, replaced by a few species in intensive and unsightly plantations. In the continental United States (US), the same process began in the 19th century, and less than 5 per cent of primary forest is now intact. For example, 96 per cent of virgin redwoods have been logged, most in the past 50 years. In Canada, logging is a major industry and source of income, employment and 'stumpage' royalties to government. At current rates of harvesting, the last stands of Canadian old-growth temperate rainforest will disappear in 15 years, well before the last of the Amazonian rainforest vanishes.[21]

Second, the loss of forests is largely attributable to the failures of markets and governments in the industrial world to place adequate value on the goods and ecological services they provide.[22] Whether or not the near-total destruction of virgin forest in Europe and North America and its replacement with plantation forest is sustainable behaviour is open to debate. However, clearly a voracious appetite for wood products in the industrialized countries, increased by market signals that do not reflect environmental costs and values, is a main cause of world deforestation. Furthermore, the industrialized countries themselves are not only importing timber, but arranging, funding and profiting from deforestation. In countries such as Russia, Malaysia, Indonesia, Guyana and Honduras, major logging and plantation forest concessions have been sold to Japanese and American logging and paper firms.

Desertification and soil degradation

Desertification is more controversial in terms of its possible connection to man-made change. There is dispute as to whether normal cyclical drought causes land degradation or whether drought itself is caused by reduced vegetation due to mismanagement, such as overgrazing or fuel wood collection, to the point of becoming self-perpetuating. For example, Calder has argued that remote sensing shows the idea of Sahelian desertification south of the Sahara to be a 'far-fetched' assertion that can be explained by the region's normal but highly variable rates of rainfall; and there has been sharp criticism of the 'received wisdom' among international agencies that the Sahel has been subject to creeping desertification and that up to 10 million hectares of cropland is lost each year to soil erosion and desertification.[23]

Mannion recognizes the uncertainty in the debate over the Sahel, but says that there is a significant problem in regions which are adjacent to many of the world's hot arid zones, including the rain-fed croplands, irrigated lands and rangelands in China, Southern Africa, Pakistan, Australia, Argentina, North America and in a number of the former Soviet republics. Most available evidence, he argues, 'points to human activity as the more important catalyst' and he cites 170,000 square kilometres of man-made desertification in China since 1920.[24] Conway's assessment of the competing claims is that, for all the power of the argument against a simplistic notion of widespread 'advances of the deserts' in developing countries, 'in many parts of the world soil degradation is a reality and some of the most severely affected regions of the developing world ... are precisely those where many of the rural poor and chronically malnourished now live'.[25]

Salt intrusion and soil degradation

Salt intrusion or salinization is a process of land degradation associated with poor irrigation design, caused by the leaching of salts out of the soil in irrigated fields or with rising water tables and high evaporation rates that together bring toxic salts to the surface soil. In extreme cases the land has to be abandoned. Some 40 per cent of the world's food production is on irrigated land – about 260 million hectares – and some 10–15 per cent is estimated to be degraded by salinization and waterlogging. For example, in Syria more than half of the country's irrigated land is reported to be affected; in Egypt and India the figure may be around 30 per cent. Salinization of surface waters and soils is a significant problem wherever farming is at risk of drought and overextraction of fresh water, and some estimates suggest that it removes some 1.5 million hectares each year from production.[26]

A catastrophic case of salt intrusion and land degradation through ill-conceived irrigation design is associated with cotton production in Central Asia and the shrinking of the Aral Sea, once the world's fourth largest inland freshwater sea. Until about 1960, when irrigation began, the Aral Sea contained about 10 billion tons of salt. But as the rivers that feed the sea were tapped for irrigation, the water inflow fell below the evaporation rate and the sea began to shrink. It has now lost over 60 per cent of its water and 40 per cent of its surface area, and its coastline has retreated as much as 48 kilometres. A windblown salt/sand mix is being deposited on the surrounding farmland, villages and towns at the rate of about half a ton per hectare per year.[27] The increased salt content in the air and water has sharply reduced the amount of available drinking water in the region and wiped out the once-thriving Aral fishing industry. This water already contains large amounts of pesticides and fertilizer residues which have given rise to a major increase in birth defects and other forms of ill health, especially respiratory diseases.[28] The general effect of salinization is that:

> *Once living villages and ecosystems are dying as the Aral continues to disappear. Because of the rapid growth in the amount of salt in the sea itself, crops are being ruined ... and livestock are starving without grass to feed on, in addition to the effects ... on the local people's health.*[29]

A BBC television report in 1999 on the Aral disaster concluded that a decade of international declarations of concern, reports by Western experts and the build-up of evidence that poor irrigation practices were destroying the sea and the regional economy as well as people's health had produced little progress. The mayor of one of the former fishing ports of the sea, now reduced to a sandy town miles from the shoreline, made the grim joke that if every 'Western expert' who had visited the disaster area had brought a bucket of water instead of writing a report, the Aral Sea might be on the way to being restored. As it is, the Aral Sea remains one of the most shocking illustrations of the former Soviet Union's official disregard for the environment and for public health, and of the scale of the eco-disasters that can be visited on local and regional environments by the unrestrained exploitation of resources.

Conversion of wetlands and valleys

Wetlands are intensely important as habitats of waterfowl, fish and other species, as filters for pollutants and as buffers for floodwaters. Their loss to urban sprawl or tourist development is another factor in land degradation and the exposure of croplands and settlements to the risk of flood, salinization and pollution. The loss of wetlands can be seen as largely the result of 'intersectoral policy inconsistency', leading to the systemic failures of markets and economic regulators to recognise the value of the ecological services that the areas perform.[30] All too often, wetlands have been regarded as areas for conversion to other uses – which may be of dubious long-term value compared with the functions performed by the original ecosystems.

Wetlands are one of the most intensively and damagingly converted ecosystem types in the world. Estimates of wetland areas lost are: Europe, up to two-thirds; US, over 50 per cent; Asia, over 25 per cent; and large areas of mangrove swamp and coastal wetland, important for flood protection and fisheries as well as other services, have been lost in countries such as the Philippines, Thailand and Indonesia; half of the original area of the Florida Everglades has been lost; and the rich biodiversity of wetlands is at risk in many areas.[31]

Hydroelectric projects are a controversial source of energy and potentially cause damage to land conversion associated with industrial growth. In the past 50 years, the amount of water behind large dams has increased some 25-fold to roughly 13 per cent of the total run-off of rivers to the ocean. Pearce suggests this is 'a substantial interruption to the planet's hydrological cycle'.[32] In 1950 there were some 5000 large dams in the world; by the early 1980s the figure was some 36,000 – more than half of which are in China – and many had displaced large numbers of people and destroyed many valley habitats.[33] Many environmentalists and engineers suggest that large dams are a case of technology from the North inappropriately exported via multilateral and bilateral aid and loans to developing countries. The problems include:

- the accumulation of silt, often at 10 to 20 times the predicted rate;
- short reservoir lifespan for this reason;
- the threat of catastrophe in earthquake zones;

- the flooding of scarce fertile land, forcing resettlement of tens of thousands of people: some 21 million people in India have been dislocated by dam-building in the last 40 years; and
- the alteration of natural flood cycles, which can have dramatic downstream effects.[34]

In Colombia, the capacity of the Anchicaya Reservoir was reduced by siltation from 5 million to 1 million cubic metres in just 12 years. The Aswan Dam on the Nile resulted in the annual loss of 100 million tons of sediment for fertilizer, now replaced by chemicals; erosion of the Mediterranean coastline by 2 kilometres in places; and destruction of Egypt's Mediterranean fishery.[35]

Many other large dams are proposed or in construction: there is hardly a large river system left on the planet which is without its grand scheme. Among the most significant projects is for the largest dam in the world in China at the Three Gorges on the Yangtze River. The project, denounced by non-governmental organizations (NGOs) worldwide and opposed by many within China despite government suppression of protests, will displace well over 1 million people and flood hundreds of villages and large tracts of farmland and wildlife habitats. Nor is the era of major dam and hydro projects over in the West: in Quebec the James Bay project will flood a vast area of wild land and deprive the Cree Indian tribe of significant territory.[36]

Urbanization

While world population has increased fivefold in the past 200 years, the number of people living in urban areas has increased five times more. Within a few years, half the world's population will be living in cities, and during the 21st century a more uniform level of urbanization will spread around the globe, tending toward the 75 per cent levels of urbanization that are prevalent in industrialized countries. This implies a virtual reversal of the current ratio of urban to rural population in many developing countries.[37] Because of their sheer scale and complexity, the problems of managing big cities and urban regions will be increasingly severe in the 21st century. In cities, people tend to consume more resources per capita and to produce more wastes than their counterparts in rural areas. Cities as different as Lagos and Toronto are now engaged in a desperate search for somewhere to dump the daily outpouring of garbage.

It is in the developing world that the urbanization of the 21st century will occur. At the turn of the century, the growth rates of the great industrial cities of Europe and the US in 1875–1900 are matched or exceeded in the mega-cities in the developing countries (Table 1.4). The proportion of the population in cities in Latin America rose from 41 per cent in 1950 to 73 per cent by 1995; and in Africa over the period since 1975 from 25 per cent to 35 per cent; by 2015 nearly half the population of Africa and Asia will be urban.[38] The movement from the countryside that this implies constitutes one of the great mass-migrations in world history.

In India, for example, rural poverty and caste are forcing many people, especially the unskilled and the landless, to seek employment in the larger cities. Lack of successful land reform, the extremes of rural poverty, the hope and often the reality of better chances for work and income in the city, and improved transport, encourage this movement. Bombay grew by 2.3 million people to 10 million in the decade between 1971 and 1981, with Delhi and Calcutta experiencing similar growth rates. Nearly half of Bombay's population live in what are officially categorized as slums, in

Table 1.4 *The rate and scale of population growth in selected industrial cities, 1875–1900, and developing cities, 1975–2000*

City	*Annual population growth (per cent)*	*Population added (millions)*
Industrial cities (1875–1900)		
Chicago	6.0	1.3
New York	3.3	2.3
Tokyo	2.6	0.7
London	1.7	2.2
Paris	1.6	1.1
Developing Cities (1975–2000)		
Lagos	5.8	10.2
Bombay	4.0	11.2
São Paolo	2.3	7.7
Mexico City	1.9	6.9
Shanghai	0.9	2.7

Source: Industrial cities from Tertius Chandler, *Four Thousand Years of Urban Growth: An Historical Census*, Lewiston, NY, Edwin Mellen Press, 1987; developing cities from United Nations, *World Urbanization Prospects: The 1996 Revision*, New York, 1998, cited in Worldwatch Institute, *State of the World 1999*, Washington, DC, 1999 (www.worldwatch.org)

dwellings made of tin, bits of wood or old sacks, often adjoining a main road or railway track. About 1 million of Bombay's residents live on the streets. The strains on human services and physical infrastructure are severe, and air and water pollution, waste-disposal problems and health problems are endemic. Bombay's population at the turn of the century is some 18 million, comparable to Mexico City and São Paulo among the mega-cities of the South.

The United Nations (UN) Habitat II Conference in Istanbul in 1996 addressed the key issues arising from the growth of cities in the industrializing world. The picture is not unremittingly bleak: the mega-cities are often the site of remarkable adaptations and ingenuity in making high-density urban living tolerable for even the poorest citizens. Cities are mines for materials, allowing for the development of many waste recyclers and traders, and urban agriculture has risen as population pressures grow. Cities can contribute to sustainable development by virtue of their concentration of people and services, making efficiency gains in energy and materials use in cities particularly valuable and feasible because of the scale of their consumption. But the lesson of urban development in much of the OECD world is that unsustainable trends are hard to turn around: the tendency of cities to sprawl as affluence rises and suburbs grow, the concentration of air pollution and chronic congestion, and the growth of waste. Finding innovative and transferable innovations in urban resource management will be crucial to environmental quality and public health in the new century.[39]

Industrialization: the globalized manufacturing economy

Urbanization invariably sustains industrial developments that generate economic growth and provide much-needed employment, but also contribute to air and water pollution and ill health. The unchecked pollution and damage to public health experienced in the original wave of industrialization in Western Europe have been repeated in every nation embarking on the path to industrialism. At the extreme are environmental catastrophes such as Bhopal, responsible for the death of more than 4000 people; and the environmental devastation centred on heavy industrial complexes throughout the ex-Communist states of Eastern Europe and especially in the former Soviet Union. But much of the current process of industrialization is the result of inward foreign investment or the growth of small and medium enterprises, over which it is difficult to exert pollution control. Taiwan, for example, has more than 80,000 small factories responsible for its rapid economic growth and equally dramatic pollution.

Bangkok provides an example of the costs and benefits of rapid industrialization. In 1989 alone, Japan invested US$1.2 billion in Thailand, almost all of it flowing into the Bangkok region. Thirty thousand Japanese managers, representing nearly a thousand Japanese companies, provide around a third of a million industrial jobs and fuel a growth rate of 10 per cent per year. Hundreds more factories opened in the 1990s and the great bulk of Thailand's gross industrial output is located in the capital region.

In addition to phenomenal economic growth, which opens up new markets for OECD country exports, the environmental costs of industrialism are also obvious. Lignite-burning power stations and vehicles in an almost continuous traffic jam emit clouds of pollutants which include almost a ton of lead a day. Five hundred new cars per day, almost all of which are Japanese cars assembled locally, come on to the streets of Bangkok, accompanied by some 700 motorbikes, leading to immensely time-consuming and polluting commuter journeys. There are millions of tons of liquid toxic wastes generated each year which are dumped, mostly untreated, into the water-courses. The Chao Phraya River, which receives millions of cubic metres of untreated waste daily, is virtually dead after it leaves Bangkok, just as the rivers of the big industrial centres of the developed world were grossly polluted in the earlier decades of the century.[40]

Now that Bangkok is 'full', industrial estates are built in outlying areas, including a US$356 million national petrochemical complex and a US$1.5 billion heavy industry and port complex. However, Bangkok's chronic congestion and rising labour costs are causing many Japanese investors to look to Kuala Lumpur as a location for industrial plant investment. Given the almost unlimited supply of Japanese investment funds, the cycle of industrialization represented here is likely to continue throughout most of the major cities of Asia.

The combined processes of urbanization and industrialization worldwide are a major cause of urban sprawl, air pollution, water contamination from human and industrial wastes, and of the overuse of water resources. Many of the world's rivers have turned into open sewers. In Eastern Europe and Russia, Communist rule was responsible for calamitous levels of pollution and threats to public health from unchecked industrial development. In Poland, 95 per cent of rivers were unfit for human consumption when the country finally overthrew Communist rule, and 50 per cent were so polluted with waste chemicals that they were unfit for industrial use. And while the collapse of much old industry since the opening to the market in Eastern Europe and Russia, the rise of democracy, new investment and Western aid have all helped to reduce gross pollution in many parts of the former Soviet empire, there has been a failure by West and East alike to make the environment a priority in reindustrialization and new market development. In Brazil, where two-thirds of the population lives in nine cities, less than 10 per cent of sewage is treated. In much of the developing world of the South, urban growth has led to severe problems of waste management and water quality. Some 220 million of the urban poor lack access to clean drinking water and some 420 million do not have access to basic latrines.[41] However, such problems are hardly confined to developing countries: despite progress in reducing pollution since the 1960s, North America's Great Lakes suffer from a legacy of toxic pollutants such as polychlorinated biphenyl (PCB), which have been associated with learning disabilities and possibly infertility in the region. Similar toxicity levels can be found in the North Sea and the Mediterranean.

Similar problems of urban management are found across Asia, Africa and the Americas, in cities such as Mexico City (18 million people by the year 2000), São Paulo (17.7 million) and Shanghai (14 million). In Mexico City, for example, the cloud of pollution which hangs over the city comprises millions of tons of ozone, carbon monoxide, sulphur dioxide, heavy particles and faecal dust from shanty towns built on dry lake beds. In Asia, rapid urbanization, industrialization and the growth of motor traffic endanger the health of millions.

These problems of poverty, poor infrastructure and environmental degradation are compounded by a trend to cut public expenditure and by a lack of skilled administrators in local government, who are often lured either into central government or the private sector by higher financial rewards. And while global environmental issues such as the greenhouse effect dominate Western debate, the immediate threat to many city-dwellers is local: the lack of clean water, basic services and effective pollution control.[42]

Intensification of land use due to population growth

A trend that is related to urbanization is population growth in rural areas up to urban densities. On the Indonesian island of Java, for example, the population has grown from 5 to 95 million this century, with density of settlement reaching some 1000 people per square kilometre by the year 2000. Densities are also growing rapidly on the other main Indonesian islands, aided by the government-sponsored migration of the Javanese, nearly three million of whom have moved to Sumatra alone. The result is intense competition for land use between industry, human settlements and agriculture, and for water and the remaining timber resources. Mannion comments:

> *What remains unclear is whether this redistribution of the Indonesian people has actually reduced the environmental problems associated with high populations where deforestation and soil erosion are acute. Or does it mean that the problems of environmental degradation are being magnified and transferred into hitherto uncompromised regions? Once again, the interplay between politics and environment is apparent.*[43]

For Asia generally, population projections make it clear that existing urban areas cannot accommodate the overall population increases. Population growth combines with the shift of people towards urban areas to create intensively settled regions around the major cities. McGee calls these *desakotas* ('village-towns' in Indonesian), in which population densities are near urban levels.[44] These regions are characterized by:

- large populations engaged in small-scale cultivation, mainly rice, but with an increasing proportion of employment in manufacturing (such as beverage, cigarette and textile production) or small-scale trading;

- a fluid and highly mobile population dependent on cheap transport, such as two-stroke motorcycles, buses and trucks, with an intense movement of people and goods; and
- an intense mixture of land use with agriculture, cottage industry, industrial estates, suburban development and other uses existing side by side.

This new form of Asian urbanization, McGee argues, challenges the Western paradigm of urban transition, based on the historical experience of Western Europe and North America in the 19th and 20th centuries. However, it also parallels the emergence worldwide of a new form of regional urbanization based on dispersed urban functions linked by the intensive use of road transport. It may be that the desakota is an Asian version of this phenomenon.

The city of the future: a crisis of automobility

In spite of their wealth and resources, major 'city-regions' in the West, such as New York, Tokyo and London, with populations between 10 and 28 million, require tremendous ingenuity and resources to deal with traffic congestion, public transport, water extraction, air pollution and waste disposal. The more these regions sprawl, the more intractable the problems become. Yet a common feature of urbanization in the industrialized world in the late 20th century has been the radical decentralization of employment, housing, retailing and leisure pursuits to what has hitherto been agricultural land, well away from the city centre. In many of these cities of the future the traditional city centre loses its unifying function altogether.

The new urban pattern is most obvious in the sprawling 'mega-counties' and suburban 'edge cities' of the US, like the Los Angeles–San Diego metropolis or the 7000 square miles of urban sprawl in the Baltimore–Washington Metropolitan Area. In these regions, the structure of employment and retailing location has changed dramatically: in just five years from 1982 to 1987 the proportion of office space in suburbs in the US increased from 42 to 58 per cent.[45] The location of retailing has shifted even more decisively to the suburbs: city centre retail sales are commonly less than 10 per cent of the regional total.

This decentralized lifestyle results in tremendous increases in vehicle trip generation and tens of thousands of trips per day to and from a typical shopping mall of around 1 million square feet. In the US, suburban roads and houses replace over 1 million hectares of farmland annually, further decentralizing urban areas and reinforcing car-borne commuting and shopping patterns and making public transport, cycling and walking less viable for trips of all kinds.[46] In effect, the economy and the lifestyle of these regions are entirely dependent on the private automobile.

Although America is in the vanguard of the trend towards car-dependent suburban sprawl, fuelled by both decentralization and economic growth, the 1980s witnessed its emergence on other continents, such as in the south-east of England, in the Tokyo–Osaka belt, and around booming cities like Bombay, Kuala Lumpur and Mexico City. Similar growth can be expected whenever income levels rise sufficiently. A key element in the crisis of automobility is the complete failure of policy-makers to reflect environmental and social costs in the price paid for road transport by consumers, and the consequent absence of any market pressures to restrain traffic growth and the land use patterns that promote car-dependence.[47]

In the decentralized urban region, there are fundamental alterations in the nature of the traffic problems: congestion spreads in space, with the worst problems no longer on radial routes leading to the city centre but far from the urban core on circumferential highways, along suburban roads, and even in rural countryside. Endemic congestion pervades the entire regional highway network. Congestion now also spreads in time. In some regions the rush hour lasts 14 hours a day, and leisure and shopping trips extend it through the weekend.[48] In America, the combination of sprawl and traffic has reduced much of suburbia to a place of strips and malls and interchanges and vast parking lots; of signs and overhead wires and dying trees in concrete pots; of toothless main streets and decaying empty areas at the centre of our cities, and equally bleak half-empty areas at their periphery.[49]

The world growth in car ownership will continue, and the problems of the West will spread to Asia and Eastern Europe as economies modernize. There is likely to be a near doubling of the number of vehicles in the world by 2020, producing a global fleet of a billion vehicles. Worldwide motor vehicle sales are forecast to increase steeply in Asia, Latin America and Eastern Europe, dashing hopes that the industrializing countries might 'leapfrog' the damaging car-intensive developments seen in the OECD world; Asian markets are growing especially fast and the Chinese government is planning for a massive growth in the country's car fleet. The car is a symbol of affluence worldwide and, despite the side-effects of gross pollution, congestion, urban sprawl and accidents, humanity is apparently addicted to automobility.[50]

Air pollution

The world vehicle fleet is already the largest single source of global air pollution, and it accounts for 20–25 per cent of greenhouse gas emissions. Road traffic is the fastest growing source of carbon dioxide emissions. The contribution of road transport to environmental problems is huge: vehicle emissions are implicated in damage to public health, contributing to respiratory diseases as well as wider environmental hazards – cars are said to cause some US$93 billion worth of damage to health and environmental quality each year in the US.[51] The cumulative effect of these problems has given rise to the notion of a 'crisis' of automobility; the potential growth in vehicle numbers compounds the sense of impending global crisis.[52]

Industry also makes an enormous contribution to air pollution. Although the West has made much progress in reducing smogs and cutting lead emissions from vehicles, low-level ozone pollution from vehicle emissions, sulphur emissions and nitrogen oxides and dust and soot particulates persist as problems in the developed world and have become a massive problem for the urban environments of the developing world and the former Soviet Union; gross air pollution associated with the North's earlier phases of industrialization is being replicated in China, India, Thailand and other developing countries. The result of industrial expansion is not only waste gases from power stations and factories, but also thousands of new trace gases whose impacts are little understood. Some effects are localized, some contribute to wide-ranging effects such as acid rain and atmospheric change. Other problems of local and regional air pollution are well documented.[53] A more recent realization concerns the global impact of air pollution and fossil fuel consumption, and in particular the contribution of transport emissions to the potential for global warming, which is described below.

Global climate change

No problem more dramatically illustrates the scale of our industrial interaction with the biosphere than the possibility of global climate change. The basic situation is that:

> *The atmosphere has been exploited by all without reference to the possibility of ultimate degradation, or to the access rights for the different parties. It has been treated as a free and infinite resource, and humanity is now faced with the realization that it is neither, and indeed that a portion of the reservoir has been 'used up'.*[54]

The main concerns are depletion of the stratospheric ozone layer and the enhanced greenhouse effect. The depletion of the ozone layer results from the effect of a group of pollutants called chlorofluorocarbons (CFCs) in the atmosphere. The chlorine released depletes the ozone in the upper atmosphere which filters out cancer-causing ultraviolet radiation. These chemicals are used in aerosol propellants, refrigerants and in the production of electronic components and certain plastics.

The main fears over the human impact on the atmosphere relate to the potential threat of man-made 'enhanced warming' of the earth's surface and lower atmosphere due to increased levels of carbon dioxide and other atmospheric gases. Acting like the glass in a greenhouse, these gases trap heat inside the atmosphere: the 'greenhouse effect' is essential for the survival of life, but there is a growing scientific and industry consensus that human activities are forcing further warming and that this could result in sea level rise, more extremes of weather, localized collapses of ecosystems and widespread risks to food production, water supplies and public health. The science of global warming is still contested, but the uncertainties are being reduced: the correlation between human greenhouse gas production and the rise in average temperatures worldwide since the 1980s is widely seen as a significant one and the reason to take precautionary action against climate disruption.[55]

Most of the gases produced by human activity arise from industrial processes, energy consumption and transport, and the remaining sources are divided between

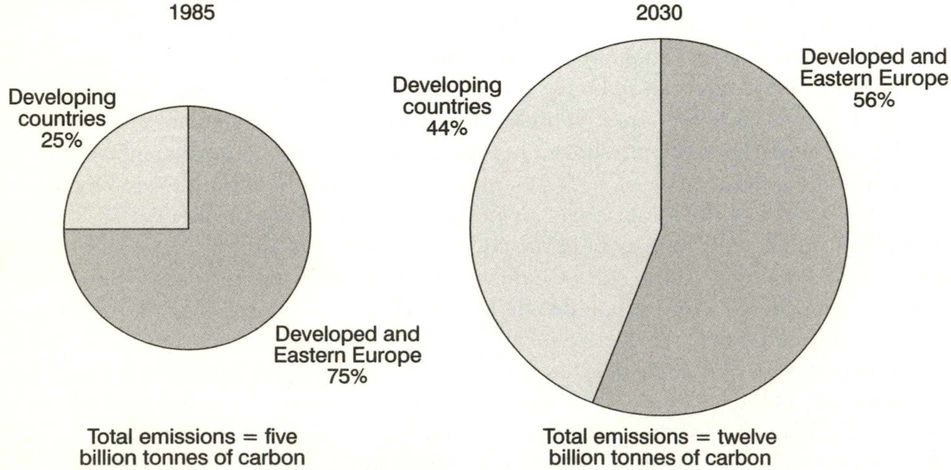

Figure 1.4 *Distribution of carbon dioxide emissions between developed and developing countries in 1985 and 2030*

Table 1.5 *Carbon dioxide emissions by region*

Tonnes per person per year, 1995 data	
Africa	1.06
Middle East and Central Asia	4.89
Asia/Pacific	2.31
Latin America/Caribbean	2.58
North America	19.34
Western Europe	8.58
Central and Eastern Europe	9.25
OECD average	10.97
Non-OECD average	2.40

Source: WWF/NEF, *The Living Planet Report*, WWF, Gland, 1998

carbon dioxide produced by wood burning and methane from a variety of agricultural sources. The production of greenhouse gases is mainly a function of industrialization and consumption; atmospheric carbon dioxide is increasing by just under half of 1 per cent per year. Carbon dioxide emissions globally have risen steadily in the 1990s and fossil fuel use has risen. The OECD world, with North America dominant as a greenhouse gas emitter, vastly outweighs the developing world in its current and historic contribution to the global warming threat; although the greatest growth in future will occur in China, India and other developing countries as they industrialize further. Figure 1.4 and Table 1.5 show the enormous disparity in emissions between the developed and developing worlds in terms of their contributions to CO_2 emissions and of CO_2 tonnes per person per year.

The modelling of climate change and scenarios for global warming impacts is a very inexact science still: the scenarios range from moderate warming and slight sea-level rise, to the catastrophe of large rises in sea level and even the 'runaway' greenhouse effect from the operation of positive feedbacks effects between atmosphere, oceans and ecosystems. The regional effects on the world's climate are also still highly uncertain, but there is general agreement among climate researchers that global mean temperature will rise by 1–2°C by 2030, with the main effects in polar regions where changes of as much as 7–10°C are possible. There would be a shift of temperate conditions towards the poles, greater climatic instability with more storms and droughts, and a rise in mean sea level from a combination of thermal expansion and melting ice. Tickell comments on the significance of these changes:

> *Change is at present taking place at a rate of some ten times faster than the average over the last 10,000 years, and at a rate many times faster than that since the last ice age. Indeed the rate of change could be so fast that it could cause disruption to ecosystems comparable to those which caused major extinctions of species in the past.*[56]

The effect of globalization

The man-made greenhouse effect is a worldwide phenomenon, bound up with the globalization of industrial systems. Socioeconomic interactions, and the production and distribution of environmental risks, are now problematic on a global scale. In terms of climate change, for example, globalization effects are apparent in at least three respects.[57] First, greenhouse gases, wherever released, disperse rapidly into the global inventory of gases. This is, in effect, systemic global pollution. Second, the impact of this over time may be a change in the global circulation of air and water and a change in temperature differential between tropical and polar regions. We thus face cumulative global impacts.

Third, no individual country, with the arguable exceptions of the United Kingdom (UK) and US, will find it economical to reduce greenhouse gas emissions unilaterally. A realistic effort will have to involve an international regulatory regime, covering the larger fraction of world energy consumption, and lasting at least 50 years. Unprecedentedly, policies and implementation must therefore be global. Such solutions require the participation of nearly all the world's governments, and major shifts in the consumption patterns of the industrialized world in particular, which is responsible for by far the largest proportion of global carbon dioxide emissions. The Rio Summit of 1992 and the hard-won Kyoto deal in 1997 represent a start, and while the inevitable shortcomings in the agreements compared to the potential scale of the problem are all too apparent, the fact that the world community has reached any consensus so soon after the identification of the threat is remarkable.

But the real test of the international community's commitment to tackling the ecological impacts of globalized industrialism will come when we face the need for tougher binding targets for carbon dioxide cuts and the creation and policing of systems for trading emissions, creating carbon sinks and re-engineering energy production and consumption systems. The constraints on achieving such an international long-term consensus and effective implementation of carbon dioxide reduction strategies are identified by Grubb:

> *Reaching such an agreement will be extraordinarily difficult. An agreement that bites would be quite unlike any previous environmental agreement. It would have major implications for some of the world's largest industries, and for land use policies in the developing world. It could affect international trade flows, and alter patterns of economic development.*[58]

The main difficulties in negotiating any agreement to reduce the greenhouse effect are:

1 Control will have profound and costly political and economic implications – necessary measures will appear to consumers as 'sacrifices' (for example, less car use) and will therefore be unpalatable for politicians to champion.
2 Countries vary greatly in past and current contribution.
3 The impacts of global warming, such as sea-level rise and the costs of control will vary greatly between countries.
4 Many countries at very different stages of economic development would need to be involved in negotiating an agreement.
5 There are long time lags involved in the implementation of any programme to modify carbon emissions.[59]

Points 2 to 4 involve basic questions about international equity and the nature of sustainable development. For example, can development be less sustainable – that is, more polluting – in one region, and more so in another to redress historical imbalance?

There are other global pollutants, such as industrial PCBs which have spread among the seas worldwide and have been introduced even into the bodies of the Innuit (Eskimo) peoples in the Canadian Arctic. There are also other global effects arising from the capacity for access to all corners of the earth. For example, international tourist arrivals increased 15-fold between 1950 and 1990: tourism is now the world's largest civilian industry and of great importance to the economic development of many lower income countries.

The sheer volume of the movement of people, goods and information across borders and continents has created a qualitatively new situation of global interaction which we are only beginning to understand. Because of advances in biophysical remote sensing, for example, we can begin to track the physical effects of global interactions. But we are far from understanding the social, political and cultural implications of this valuable information; there are layers and layers of human systems represented which are as yet invisible to us. The complex process of interaction between poverty in the developing countries, environmental destruction and global change is a profound challenge to natural and social science, and the collection and interpretation of the data we need to understand our predicament has barely begun.

We know that the planet is now girdled by supranational economic and political systems, and that the extent of the problems we can observe requires some supranational system of stewardship for the planet. But how can we exercise this responsibility? The stakes are high: we will achieve either a more balanced world or one stricken with environmental disasters and gross disparity between the rich and the poor. Lourdes Arizpe analyses the challenge:

> *The way in which it will go will depend, partly, on how quickly and accurately science is able to cope with the challenge of thinking and analysing phenomena from a global perspective. The social sciences face a fundamental challenge in studying global change. As has been pointed out, the 'sociosphere' cannot be seen with the eye when a photograph of the planet is taken from outer space. For this and other reasons, the impression is sometimes given that the changing textures of the geosphere and biosphere are merely natural phenomena when, to a large extent, they are subject to a human-driven process, one deeply involved with the human use of the resources of the planet.*[60]

Conclusion

We have not intended a comprehensive survey of the world's environmental problems; there are many others we might have mentioned. We have not considered, for example, the possibility of serious water shortages – half of the world's population may suffer from water shortages in the coming decades.[61] We have not discussed problems of the management of industrial toxic waste or nuclear waste, or the pollution of the seas, which receive 7 million tons of ship-borne waste a year. Longer range threats to the survival of the mega-cities are also looming because of the extreme vulnerability of the great coastal and estuarine cities to sea-level rises and storms induced by global warming. There is also the rise of environmental disasters and refugee movement: the Red Cross reported in 1999 that in the previous year environmental refugees displaced by drought, floods, hurricanes, deforestation and soil degradation outnumbered, for the first time, people fleeing from war.[62] Many were fleeing from the impact of the El Niño climate cycle – a pattern of drought, flood and storms that may be exacerbated by global warming.

A number of general points can be made. One is that all of the issues catalogued above are very complex problems. Direct cause and effect are often far from obvious and there is bound to be some disagreement among scientists. Yet the severity of the problems suggests that doing nothing while waiting for definitive scientific judgement (which may never come) is not an option. Also, the degree to which the problems exist is not universally agreed because they involve value judgements. How much rainforest can we afford to lose, and how much of this natural capital could or should be replaced by reforestation in the United States or Europe or Australia? How much right do the citizens of a deforested, wealthy industrial country, like Britain, have to challenge the resource use policies of a still heavily forested, poorer country like Brazil or Malaysia?

Finally, a number of key issues are clear:

1 The resource systems of the planet are now bound up with social systems through our exploitation and management of them, and social, economic and political factors will play a highly significant role in resolving the complex environmental issues stemming from this fact. Many problems of ecological degradation arise from shortcomings of institutions, and in particular from failures in integrating environmental factors into decision-making. This is reflected in market failures to treat resource values adequately, and in the fragmentation of policy-making on the environment and its interactions with economic systems.[63] Many problems are also simultaneously both the cause and effect of poverty and inequalities in international and national economic orders.[64]

2 The very complexity of the problems suggests that understanding and resolving them must depend on a very wide range of human knowledge and skills, extending over the scientific, economic, political and philosophical fields. In other words, teamwork is essential. Prediction of the effects of human interventions will be difficult and the continuous monitoring of vulnerable ecosystems is crucial.

3 The lack of apparent agreement on the existence and severity of these problems, and on the responsibility for, and means of, resolving them among many peoples and nations suggests that the development of conceptions of common interest require negotiation, mediation and consensus-building as the only viable methodologies.

4 Finally, globalization does not imply that the only viable solutions are global ones. On the contrary, all global problems have local implications and therefore offer scope for local action. The magnitude of the problems, and the need to involve local people in their resolution, suggest that coordinated efforts must take place on a number of levels of human endeavour: international, national, fluvial, regional, citywide, in the neighbourhood and in the home. No level of effort is likely to be more effective or superior, all efforts must be sustained and linked, and solutions will involve both centralized and decentralized action.

The next chapter turns to the concept of sustainable development, and the implications of global industrialism and recent changes in the world's political and economic systems.

2

Sustainable Development and Political Change

> *The power and reach of the market system have been truly remarkable and have often been underestimated in the past. But a reliance on the market system often does not produce better results, when results are judged in terms of human lives and freedoms and not in terms of commodity productions only. The role of public action can be very important not only for equity but for efficiency in securing human freedoms and dignity. This applies not only to the Third World but to the richer economies.*
>
> Amartya Sen[1]

The environmental challenges facing humankind clearly transcend the capacities of science and technology to provide technical solutions. They have many ramifications for politics and other fields, including culture, philosophy and religion. Any programme to tackle such metaproblems will therefore require many kinds of expertise.

As noted in the Preface, appropriate responses fall into three broad categories:

1. Strategic and philosophical reflection: on the future course of industrialism as a form of social organization for the fulfilment of human needs; the extent to which 'market-friendly' policies can result in sustainable development; whether high economic growth, no-growth or some middle option is the more viable in environmental and social terms; the need for greater equity on a world scale and for self-determination and the empowerment of local communities in the face of the globalization of the industrial economy.
2. The development of organizational and regulatory capacity for managing sustainable development, at scales from the global to the local. This is not only about the implementation of policies for promoting sustainable development, but about encouraging debates about our visions of the future and how to realize them, and the pursuit of new knowledge and skills for both human development and environmental management.
3. Research and development to generate new knowledge and appropriate technologies, especially in sustainable energy, agriculture, transport and low or even zero emissions and low-energy manufacturing.

The three types of response each contribute to the successful realization of the others. This book focuses on the second type of response, with particular emphasis on non-hierarchical action networks for building skills in environmental management. We will set out a management approach which, we will argue, is more responsive to the nature and complexity of the problems outlined in the first chapter, and which can help us to overcome many of the constraints on good environmental management which arise from our existing forms of top-down policy-making and industrial development. Within the term environmental management, we include urban and regional planning and rural development.

The emerging global problems affect the most local level, and every environmental challenge is part of a nested hierarchy of local, fluvial, regional and international problems and opportunities. Appropriate responses to global problems will include local initiatives, following the well-established dictum, 'Think globally, act locally'. But equally important is the need to act simultaneously at all levels, in a mutally reinforcing manner, but no amount of local action can be effective if it is undermined by regional trends or national policies. The action network approach to environmental management that we propose facilitates international learning and local action in a continuous reinforcing cycle.

Environmental issues are not separate from management issues and methods: the two are fundamentally intertwined. Many of the constraints on good management arise because of the nature of the issues themselves, and any efficient and effective response must address those issues. We argue that environmental management is a social and political process, not a technical exercise, and therefore no one should be involved in management at any scale without some grounding in these issues.

Action-Network Approach

The proposed approach to environmental problems is one in which the process of discussion and debate gradually broadens and deepens into practical action on the issues of sustainable development. In short, we know what the process might look like, but where it will lead in any given context is the business of the participants. The process underpinning the action-networking approach seeks to promote:

- active participation in conditions of equality, based on teamwork;
- a process of mutual, non-hierarchical learning-by-doing or action learning, intended to develop new perceptions, new skills, and confidence;
- horizontal integration between sectors of human interest such as agriculture, health, transport, housing, etc, and vertical integration between policy-making groups, including big business, and community levels;
- temporal integration – that is, between short-term action and long-term vision; and
- collective self-development and self-management.

Are Some Countries 'Developed' Already?

The approach set out here also implies that habitual distinctions between so-called developed and developing (or less developed) countries are not only meaningless in terms of sustainability, but paternalistic and destructive of the idea of mutuality. We therefore substitute the terms 'lower income' and 'higher income' countries for 'developing' and 'developed' in the rest of the book. In so doing, we agree with Rahman that this is no mere semantic distinction, but that the mistaken perceptions encouraged by the terminology have contributed to a 'most fundamental loss' for lower income countries, which is 'obstruction of the evolution of indigenous alternatives for societal self-expression and authentic progress'.[2]

Having dispensed with the notion that countries and their citizens who are fortunate enough to be wealthy are somehow more developed, we adopt a definition of development which covers all countries on earth with equal applicability:

> *Development is a process by which the members of a society increase their personal and institutional capacities to mobilize and manage resources to produce sustainable and justly distributed improvements in quality of life consistent with their own aspirations.*[3]

This is a good definition of the general purpose of environmental management. It is important to note that, while the higher income, industrialized countries may have more experience of formal environmental policy and management, they contribute disproportionately to the environmental crisis and face a challenge equal to, if not greater than, that of the lower income countries. Below we cite some arguments for the idea that sustainable development, as far as it exists, occurs mainly in lower income countries. Finally, as will be seen from the case studies later in the book, the action network model is equally relevant in high-income regions such as California as it is in the townships and countryside of Ghana.

Growth or No Growth?

There are complex debates in progress about the meaning of the term sustainable development. Originally proposed in the World Conservation Strategy in 1980,[4] the term gained widespread currency as a result of its promotion by the World Commission on Environment and Development, better known as the Brundtland Commission. Their definition of sustainability is 'development that meets the needs of the present without compromising the ability of future generations to meet their own needs'.[5]

Since the term came into common currency, the proponents of sustainable development have fallen into two broad groups, with many variants on the basic position. One advocates continuing economic growth, made much more environmentally sensitive, in order to raise living standards globally and break the links between poverty and environmental degradation. The other calls for radical changes in economic organization, producing much lower rates of growth as we know it, or even zero or negative growth. The World Commission was firmly in the first camp, equating sustainable development with 'more rapid economic growth in both industrial and developing countries' which 'will help developing countries mitigate the strains on the rural environment, raise productivity, and consumption standards, and allow nations to move beyond dependence on one or two primary products for their export earnings'. The World Commission anticipated a five- to tenfold increase in world industrial output at some point in the 21st century.[6] Mathews summarizes this position: 'Global economic output must continue to grow rapidly, if only to meet basic human needs, to say nothing of beginning to lift billions out of poverty'.[7]

It should be emphasized, therefore, that the 'sustainable growth with redistribution' side in this debate is not looking to increased industrial production for the sake of profits alone; nor does it propose 'business as usual'. Rather, what is at issue is how to increase wealth in an environmentally sound way in order to make major redistributions of income – for example, from North to South – and thereby alleviate poverty and improve quality of life worldwide. The Commission argued that high rates of ecologically responsible economic growth are essential both to reduce poverty in the low income world and for environmental improvements to be affordable worldwide.

Many others, however, believe that the sustained economic growth represented by present levels of industrial activity is the root cause of the global problematique. Growth as we have known it, in this view, has led to dangerous stresses on the environment resulting in a process of degradation and pollution which threatens the living conditions of generations to come. The 'no or low growth' school argues that the only viable option is to curtail economic growth, change lifestyles to reduce consumption of damaging industrial products and fossil fuel energy in the North, and redistribute resources more fairly on a global basis. The Canadian ecologist Rees sees sustainable development as:

> *an opportunity for humanity to correct an historical error and develop a gentler, more balanced and stable relationship with the natural world. This view also raises moral considerations such as the need in a limited world for more equitable sharing of the world's resources.*[8]

The questions of how much economic growth is sustainable, and what kinds of growth can be sustained, are complex, especially given the reasonable aspirations of lower income countries to higher levels of economic growth and the obvious material benefits which come with it. The record of economic growth in generating environmental degradation suggests that at the least what is required are sophisticated skills in growth management. Chapter 12 gives an example of a process designed to foster such skills and policy ideas. It is clear that the low/no growth approach can only be a very long-term strategy, politically inconceivable under any other circumstances; yet 'business as usual' is not an option, as recognized by the sustainable growth camp. The gap between the schools of thought is not always as large as it seems in terms of recognition of key environmental constraints on economic activity. Both camps would agree that one critical aspect of any sustainable path seems to be the adaptation of our activities to the carrying capacity of the planet.

Sustainable development and carrying capacity

Carrying capacity concerns the number of people who, sharing a given territory, can be supported at any time on a sustainable basis, taking into account known resources, as well as sociocultural factors.[9] This suggests two principles of sustainable development. One is that renewable resource harvest rates (including that of soil quality) should equal regeneration rates to give sustained yield. The other is that waste emission rates should not exceed the natural assimilative capacity of the ecosystem. Regenerative and assimilative capacities are treated here as 'natural capital', and failure to maintain these represents unsustainable capital consumption. Carrying capacity can thus be defined as the maximum rate of resource consumption and waste that can be sustained indefinitely in a region without impairing ecological productivity and integrity.[10]

Difficult issues arise in relating this to economic activity in the market. One is that the market as we now know it has no means of determining the optimum scale of economic activity from an ecological point of view and runs the risk therefore of exceeding carrying capacities as a matter of course. For example, people will continue to purchase and use more and more automobiles over the next two decades, even though many argue that current levels of traffic congestion and air pollution, including global climate change, from cars have already reached crisis levels. This apparent folly arises as people commonly ignore the ecological limits to growth because no economic signals are given to indicate that they are being approached or exceeded.[11]

Arguments for new forms of economic 'signalling' – such as road pricing or environmental taxes – in order to discourage unsustainable consumption and promote new patterns of behaviour have been refined considerably in recent years.[12] There is no doubt that there is scope for using market-based instruments to promote sustainable development and combat global problems such as climate change and loss of biodiversity.[13] The use of market mechanisms combined with the corrections of institutional failures can be shown to contribute to wildlife preservation and maintenance of crucial but vulnerable and hitherto undervalued ecosystems.[14]

Advocacy of such measures tends to be associated with the view that ecological sustainability and modified forms of economic growth are compatible. Allocating monetary values to environmental assets is often rejected by environmentalists as an unacceptably instrumental approach to nature. However, advocates of market-oriented environmental economics rightly note that some form of explicit or implicit valuation is necessary to make any decisions on protecting or exploiting ecosystems or species.[15] Assigning monetary values has the potential to help correct many failures of markets and regulators in valuing ecosystems. It can be seen at least as a useful tool in the long-range task of greening the industrial economies we have to deal with.

However, implementing new forms of economic valuation to be effective in the immediate future is immensely difficult. In particular, appropriate valuation calls for much-improved information on ecosystems and human interactions with them. Sustainable development requires an immense store of scientific knowledge about stresses on ecosystems and limits to carrying capacity. Our understanding of the 'services' provided by ecosystems and the critical stresses on them is subject to radical uncertainties. These arise from: the massive complexity of the interactions; the problems of data gathering; reliance on modelling due to the impossibility of experimentation in many cases; and the fact that the 'object of study' is dynamically changing the world over as ecosystems are affected by industrialization and population growth. Given these constraints and the kinds of difficult value judgements involved in such topics as deforestation, the development of clear, efficacious and timely economic signals is problematic.

Another difficulty is the inadequacy of Gross National Product (GNP) or Gross Domestic Product (GDP) as the general index of national well-being and measure of economic growth. There are many limitations to the GNP/GDP measures and here we just touch on a limitation that is particularly relevant to environmental considerations. This is that when GDP (or GNP) shows an increase, economic growth is said to have taken place.[16] But production often has an unrecorded environmental cost. If a forest is logged for its timber, the money value of the timber is included in GDP but nothing is subtracted to reflect the loss of the forest. Much economic growth is the result of commodifying nature and turning it into goods for sale, but GDP does not record the resultant decline in environmental wealth. Similarly, if industry or agriculture pollutes a water supply and people buy bottled water instead, as is happening in many countries, GDP goes up because bottled water costs far more than tap water. Once again GDP goes up as the quality of life declines.

There is also a social dimension to this problem, which is that GDP only takes account of economic activity in the formal marketplace, which is basically defined as that activity recorded quantitatively within given statistical systems. Resources not covered by the market are ignored: trees that maintain the integrity of a watershed are valued only in terms of timber, for example. GDP also does not accord any value to human activity in the informal economy, which is often the work of the poor, nor to what is called the caring or the 'love' economy – for example, women caring for children or elderly relatives. Recent calculations suggest the value of domestic production in the US, Britain and France to be about 40 per cent of GDP.[17] All this essential activity is invisible in conventional assessments. Finally, there is a 'time problem', in that accounting conventions discount future values, although the future value of scarce natural resources, like a rainforest, may be far higher than now and certainly no less.[18]

To address these issues, environmental economists are now looking at ways in which natural capital can be included in an overall indicator of national wealth, which could also include social measures such as infant mortality, male and female literacy and life expectancy. A variation of this is the argument that, for the majority of the world's population, biomass production is the basis of survival, the main source of income and the protector of the environment. Agarwal and Narain, for example, suggest that 'Gross Natural Product' would be a far more accurate indicator of welfare than the cash-based Gross National Product.[19]

A further limitation of markets in relation to carrying capacity is that in the past era of 'empty world' economics – that is, with apparently unlimited natural resources – it was assumed that man-made capital (a house) was an appropriate substitute for natural capital (a forest), and that development was limited by a lack of man-made capital. But many would argue that we have now irrevocably entered the era of 'full world' economics in which natural capital is limited and in which what Pearce terms 'critical capital' environmental assets (such as the ozone layer) cannot be substituted at all.[20] Sustainable development, on this argument, requires that the overall stock of existing natural capital should remain more or less intact, with critical resources maintained in working order for future generations.

This raises the question of the sustainable use of non-renewable resources. One important line of current thinking is that any investment in the exploitation of non-renewables should be paired with a compensating investment in a renewable substitute (a 'shadow project'). For example, in the case of coal extraction, paired tree planting can serve as a sink for the carbon dioxide which results from burning the coal and as an alternative renewable source of energy for the future. The general principle is clear, but much debate is required about the shadow projects to be carried out as compensations and about the accounting conventions to be used.[21]

Another concern is the risk that relatively minor adjustments – for instance in environmental taxation or other market-based measures – are not sufficient because we may be very close to key thresholds in our abuse of carrying capacity. For example, Rees argues that while human society depends on many ecological resources and functions for survival, carrying capacity is ultimately determined by the single vital resource or function in least supply.[22] On a global scale, climate change may be an

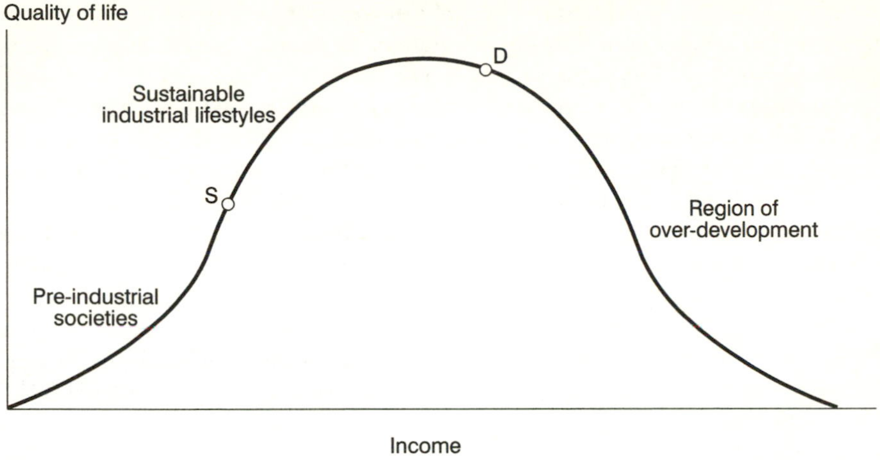

Source: Professor M Thring (unpublished)

Figure 2.1 *Income and quality of life*

example; on a regional level, the environmental disaster of the shrinkage of the Aral Sea may be another.

Finally, following from these points, Daly argues that there is a fundamental misunderstanding about the word 'growth', which is generally taken to be synonymous with an increase in wealth.[23] Thus it is argued that we must have growth because only if we become wealthier will we be able to afford the cost of environmental protection. Daly questions whether economic growth, at the current margin, is really making us wealthier. Rather, as economic growth pushes us beyond the optimal scale relative to the biosphere, it makes us poorer in fact.

Thring calls this situation 'societal over-engineering' and explains it in a simple graph (Figure 2.1) where the upward curve describes a sustainable but non-industrial lifestyle – for example, of hunter-gatherers in the Brazilian rainforest.[24] The area at the top of the curve, between points S and D, describes a sustainable, industrial lifestyle where the advantages of modern science, education and medicine generate the maximum quality of life in a sound environment. The downward slope represents an unsustainable lifestyle, in which the quality of life is decreasing in spite of rising incomes. Unfortunately it is never unambiguously clear when we have arrived at D and are therefore passing out of the zone SD into the realm of over-development.

The location of point D is the nub of political debate about sustainable development. Societies may pass well beyond point D before they become painfully aware of the environmental and social consequences of overconsumption, which is itself addictive. For example, Georgescu-Roegen argues that humankind is now addicted to all the technological devices which enhance our physical powers and provide us with increased comfort.[25] It is this addiction which drives our endless pursuit of natural resources and takes us out of zone SD. For the lower income countries around the world, including Eastern Europe, the question is whether they can 'leap-frog' over the unsustainable excess consumerism of the rich countries and design their emerging societies within zone SD while they still have the chance. Their scope for action offers both a risk and an opportunity. Chapter 14 describes an African energy network which intends to assist its member countries to do just that.

Daly describes the conditions which hold in zone SD as those of the steady-state economy, which keeps within limits of population, throughput of industrial goods and inequality.[26] The steady-state economy is ecological in orientation; physical growth is economic only as long as the marginal benefits of growth exceed the marginal costs. Daly gives an analogy: a library with a constant stock of books which is limited, say, by storage space or maintenance budget. For every new book acquired, an old one must be recycled and no book would be replaced unless the new one was qualitatively better. The quality of the library would improve although the quantity of the books would remain constant. He suggests that 'a steady-state economy, far from being static, is a strategy for forcing qualitative improvement and sustainability'.

The idea of the steady-state economy, Daly notes, is not new. He cites John Stuart Mill's chapter 'On the Stationary State' in *Principles of Political Economy*. He also notes that for most of the history of mankind, near steady-state conditions held. Only in the past two centuries in the West has growth become the norm.

The steady-state economy is an attractive concept. Other authors have taken it up – for example, Alexander, who prefers the term 'steady-flow' for its dynamic implications:

> *Steady-flow means movement and process. Steady-flow is like a dependable river or stream. Flowing merrily along, many interesting things happen, sometimes in unexpected and exciting ways. The size of the stream flow, the quantitative aspects change little. Quantitative limitations on the use of the earth's resources allow the regenerative capacity of Gaia to remain constant or increase.*[27]

There are huge problems in adjusting market mechanisms and political values to such notions of sustainable development and carrying capacity, and we have reviewed just a few. The implication of Daly's 'full world economics' is that all resources, including clean air, are now under threat from continuing, unsustainable industrialism. Political mediation is the only alternative to war over these scarce resources or to authoritarian imposition of sustainable activity. It is plain that a shift towards sustainable development within democratic systems will demand changes in behaviour that in turn will demand intense political debate and trade-offs in attempts to forge consensus.

Above all else, therefore, sustainable development, however defined through economic concepts, will be the result of a process of mediation among environmental, economic and social goals. This will include political choices over methods of valuing the environment: the use of new economic valuation techniques cannot be divorced from ethical and political considerations concerning environmental protection, human development and the exploitation of resources.

It is in this essentially political process that improvements in human resource capacity and new organizational concepts can make a major contribution to the realization of sustainable development. We offer a revised, working definition of the process underpinning sustainable development:

> *A continuing process of mediation among social, economic and environmental needs which results in positive socioeconomic change that does not undermine the ecological and social systems upon which communities and society are dependent. Its successful implementation requires*

> *integrated policy, planning, and social learning processes; its political viability depends on the full support of the people it affects through their governments, their social institutions, and their private activities.*[28]

In the light of this, we suggest that the 'process' of sustainable development must precede the product. We cannot yet establish what sustainability amounts to scientifically and economically; but we have an idea of what unsustainable development paths look like and we can identify general directions towards improving policy-making to avoid them. We can also experiment with new forms of policy-making to promote more sustainable development.

Once the truly political nature of the sustainable development process is understood, there is great potential to build a consensus around specific problems, and to broaden that to encompass diverse approaches to sustainable development – for example, in watershed management. In later chapters we will suggest ways in which mediation can become an important tool for environmental management and give some examples. Here, having introduced the notion that environmental management is a political process, we look at some of the main socioeconomic trends in the world which are relevant to a more innovative approach to environmental management.

World Trends and the Politics of Environmental Management

There are three recent major world trends which sharpen the need for understanding the politics of environmental management. These are: the spread of industrialization or its by-products into every last nook and cranny of the planet; the failure of socialism and the reaffirmation of capitalism as the dominant economic system of the world; and the rapid spread of Westernised consumerist culture to almost all the peoples of the globe.

The momentum of industrialism

Global economic output has quadrupled since 1950. The current high-income countries account for only 16 per cent of the world's population and 24 per cent of its land area. But their market economies account for about 72 per cent of the world's GDP, 78 per cent of all road vehicles and 50 per cent of world energy use. They generate 76 per cent of world trade and 55 per cent of the world's carbon emissions. The newly industrialized Asian countries (NICs) are queueing up to join this élite group.

Chapter 1 documented many of the effects of industrialism and the relentless commodification of natural and even human resources for economic gain. This is the culmination of the 250 years of industrial production which began at the Iron Bridge in England and which was spread worldwide by colonialism. The scientific–technological–industrial revolution initiated a movement which now threatens to escape our control. The amazing fact about this dynamic process is that we now seem within striking distance of its logical conclusion – Daly's full world economics – in which we have colonized, by resource exploitation or pollution, every last bit of the planet:

> *We must understand that we already live in a largely, and increasingly, and irreversibly, artificial world. 'Nature' and the 'natural world' (in the sense of an environment [id] uninfluenced by human activity) scarcely exist anywhere.*[29]

The implications are described by Anderson:

> *Even though the air is thick with talk of paradigm shifts and predictions of new global post-industrial civilization, we seem unable – or afraid – to grasp the truth of how the world has changed, or what it means to govern. Evolution no longer follows the Darwinian rules. That vision is as obsolete as its first cousin, Newton's clockwork cosmos. Today the driving force in evolution is human intelligence. The world has changed; and the human species, which has wrought the change, is now being required to change in response to the conditions we have created. The change calls for a massive reappraisal of basic ideas We are talking about a transition in the evolution of the planet itself.*[30]

The situation is made yet more complex by the unequal distribution of the existing benefits of industrialization. For example, the richest fifth of the world's population account for around 80 per cent of global GNP and 81 per cent of world trade; the poorest fifth accounted for 1.4 per cent of world GNP, and their incomes are at least 60 times less than those of the richest fifth.[31] Around 80 per cent of total global pollution is the responsibility of the one-fifth of global population in the industrialized countries owing to their dramatically higher consumption of the planet's resources. The difference is stark: Germany uses 7 times more energy per capita than Egypt, 14 times more aluminium than Argentina and 130 times more steel than the Philippines. And yet Germany's per capita consumption rates are generally still less than those of the US. The average North American, for example, uses as much energy per capita as 525 Ethiopians, suggesting the grossly disproportionate burden on the planet's ecology.

Although this inequality is glaring and morally unjustifiable, it would be a mistake to impute evil intent to the overconsumers. The lure of consumerism is powerful and many people in lower income countries would like nothing better than to emulate lifestyles common in the advanced industrial economies. Commodification and consumption of industrial products are part of a 'modernization' process in which most of humankind would willingly participate. At the family level, acquisition of consumer goods is an extension of the drive to satisfy basic needs. At the village level, incipient commodification is often the first step towards integration with national and world economies and money-based exchanges. For example, Vandergeest documents how peasants in the rice and palm-sugar growing area of the Satingpra peninsula in southern Thailand initiate commodification in order to circumvent traditional relations of domination and control by an old élite – in other words, to modernize their situation.[32]

However, continued global industrialization is untenable in its current form. For example, if the lower income countries were to have the same standard of living as the industrialized countries, total global industrial output would need to rise by more than 130 times, resulting in unimaginable resource depletion and pollution. Even if we just look at the proportion of the world's population, mainly in Asia, who are likely to achieve higher income status in the next 30 years, and even if we project a continuing

Table 2.1 *Life expectancy and GDP per capita*

Country	*Life expectancy at birth*	*GDP per capita (1993 US$)*
Japan	79.6	20,680
Sweden	78.3	17,900
Greece	77.7	8950
Spain	77.7	13,660
The Netherlands	77.5	17,340
Costa Rica	76.4	5680
USA	76.1	24,680
Barbados	75.7	10,570
Cuba	75.4	3000
Portugal	74.7	10,720
Belize	73.7	4610
Georgia	72.9	1750
Sri Lanka	72.0	540

Source: UNDP, *Human Development Report 1996*

downward trend in energy use per unit of GDP, their industrial achievements could increase carbon dioxide emissions fivefold using current energy sources.[33] This is in addition to the constant rise of carbon dioxide from current sources. Despite the recent downturn, there will be enough purchasing power in the Asian markets alone to double the number of cars in the world, from the current 500 million, in this 30-year period. Almost all of these cars would be produced as well as consumed in Asia, as auto production and assembly spreads beyond current centres in Japan, Korea, Malaysia, India and Thailand. In Thailand alone, one Japanese company already assembles a car every three minutes for domestic consumption.

Clearly there is no going back on industrial production and the promise of the better life it offers to the citizens of lower income countries. But the ecological limits to industrial growth as we have known it are in view, and we therefore need a new model of sustainable 'eco-industrialism' which is less energy- and resource-intensive than the traditional industrial system.

There may be a clue in areas of the world with sustainable resource use and low levels of non-renewable energy use, but also with a high quality of life, as measured by infant mortality, literacy and life expectancy. Carley and Spapens, for example, compare GDP per capita and life expectancy at birth in different countries (Table 2.1).[34]

The difference in quality of life compared to economic achievement, and thus resource consumption, is paralleled by other indicators. Sen attributes the difference to well-coordinated government policies in health, education and social security. This idea that there can be a substantial difference between economic and human development is explored at length in the UN Development Programme's Human Development Reports, which since 1990 have presented an index of quality of life as an alternative and corrective to conventional macroeconomic indicators.

In another example, Kerala State in southern India has been proposed as a model of sustainable development by Alexander and others.[35] In Kerala, a per capita GNP in 1986 of US$182, compared with $17,480 in the United States, indicates a very low throughput of industrial products and generation of pollution. And yet Kerala, for historical and political reasons, has a very low birth rate, low infant mortality, a life expectancy of 70 years, an adult literacy rate of 78 per cent, compared with 43 per cent for India as a whole, and a female literacy rate of 66 per cent, compared with 25 per cent for India as a whole. To find similar indices of quality of life, one needs to look to European countries such as Spain and Portugal, with ten times the industrial throughput and pollution. Alexander concludes his analysis by suggesting that Americans become eco-tourists in Kerala to learn something of the true nature of sustainable development.

The collapse of Communism and the market revolution

A second trend affecting environmental management in a profound way is the spectacular collapse of the communist states in Eastern Europe and elsewhere in the early 1990s, and the wholesale abandonment of Marxist–Leninist forms of economic and political organization on a worldwide basis. As a result, old ideas about economic policy and the role of the state are being challenged and cast aside.

The demise of Marxist–Leninist socialism, richly deserved and commendable in itself, has given rise to much dangerous self-congratulation in the West about 'a victory for capitalism'. The danger is that the urgent need to re-examine the direction of industrial capitalism and the implications for environmental quality of excessive private consumption will be deferred or made more difficult. Putting aside this risk for the moment, it is worth considering the failure of the Communist experiment as a major historical event in the late 20th century and on a par of significance with the rise of environmental metaproblems.

The failure of Communism is twofold: the moral failure of the one-party state based on totalitarian oppression and social control, and the practical failure of the centralized command form of economic management. In the Eastern European countries and the former Soviet Union, therefore, the challenge has been to make the shift from a command to a market economy linked into the world economy, and to shift from the one-party state to pluralism, without continuing the destabilization of civil society through crime and gross income disparity which characterizes the transition in the late 1990s. These interrelated processes constitute economic and political liberalization. The restructuring process or 'market revolution' involves liberalizing prices, freeing trade, selling state companies, dismantling monopolies and establishing a fully convertible currency.

The market revolution has not been confined to Eastern Europe and the former Soviet Union. Governments in countries as diverse as Brazil, Mexico, Bolivia, Venezuela, Jamaica, Malaysia, Zimbabwe and Ghana have converted from socialist to market economic policies, introducing, albeit at different rates, the now familiar package of assaults on the centralized economy: the establishment of a workable domestic price system, increases in exports to cover debt repayments and imports, opening the domestic economy to international competition, elimination of distortions in the foreign exchange market, public spending cuts, tax reforms, and privatizations. These reforms are often spurred by the insistence of the International Monetary Fund on such 'structural adjustments' as a precondition for loans. In the 1990s, for example, Zimbabwe tempered years of largely unworkable import and export controls with a new trade liberalization programme received warmly by its somewhat beleaguered private sector.

Clearly the latter part of the 20th century brought a new consensus worldwide that market forces will play the dominant role in the creation of the world's wealth. The consolidation of liberal capitalism and the rise of environmental meta-problems has proved a convenient conjunction, for it exposed the commonality of environmental problems in East and West under markedly different, but nonetheless industrial, systems.

But there is real danger for the environment in a headlong rush to embrace capitalism.[36] The recent ruinous demise of many Communist regimes may have demonstrated the superior adaptability and efficiency of liberal capitalism by comparison with collectivist economies. However, while Marxist analyses of the socioeconomic 'contradictions' that would bring down capitalism have proved to be flawed, the capitalist economies have yet to overcome the emerging ecological contradictions which threaten them.

For the lower income countries, neither their own long-term economic and environmental viability, nor the need to reduce global warming, can allow for unrestrained economic growth via industrialization on the traditional Western model. Yet there will be every tendency to pursue this path to development. For example, in China, since 1984, economic modernization has meant that independent rural industry has grown at a rate of 37 per cent per year, four times that of state industries. This has put a severe strain on energy supplies and scarce raw materials, and 8.5 million hectares of farmland are lost to new construction every year.

The need to devise an alternative, sustainable industrial path is also pressing because industrialization and urbanization are transforming lower income societies and turning many of their inhabitants into wage-dependent consumers of manufactured goods.[37] Today's poor countries are growing richer at a far faster rate than today's industrialized countries did at a similar stage of development. Britain and the US, for example, required 60 and 50 years respectively to double real incomes per head at the early stages of industrialization. Recently South Korea and China have required only 11 and 10 years to accomplish the same. Given these rates of growth, by about 2025 the total number of consumers with industrial consumption habits similar to those of the developed world could be five times that of today.[38]

Here we can return to the danger that the recent failure of Communism will obscure the growing need for forms of community and collective action at local and international levels – allowing individual efforts to be subservient to a common cause or larger entity – such as state or even international controls to maintain the world's environmental quality. It is this characteristic tension in capitalism between individualistic, entrepreneurial action and the need for communal mechanisms that should shape political debate for the foreseeable future. This debate shapes the context for attempts at environmental management for sustainable development.

It is worth elaborating on this point. The secularization of society since the Industrial Revolution – that is, the marginalization of religion – has been accompanied by the recasting of spiritual debate and arguments over values into competition between political ideologies of Left and Right. The essential political conflict in industrialized societies has been over the attempt to achieve the material benefits of modernization while maintaining or building forms of community. The dynamics of industrialization, as noted by commentators early in the industrial era, tend to corrode traditional forms of community.

So capitalist development poses problems for conservatives and liberals who wish to secure a role for 'traditional values' as well as to promote business-led prosperity. It also challenges social democrats, socialists and others of the Left who may wish to undermine tradition but need to replace it with forms of community in order to combat the atomizing and fragmenting forces of industrialism. Both sides now face huge problems: for the Right, the seemingly unstoppable fragmentation of the old forms of community such as the family; and for the Left, the failure of social democracy and communism to build forms of community that are more potent than tribalism and nationalism, as is evident in Eastern Europe and the former republics of the Soviet Union in the aftermath of Communist rule.

The end of history: a flawed thesis

An obvious danger lies in allowing the failure of Communism to be taken as a vindication of capitalism as it exists. At the extreme of this tendency was the 'end of history' thesis advanced by Fukuyama in the heady days of the fall of Soviet Communism in the early 1990s. The parameters of the debate are instructive, given the global spread of consumerism but also dissatisfaction with it. Fukuyama argued:

> *What we may be witnessing is the end of mankind's ideological evolution and the emergence of Western Liberal democracy (Capitalism) as the final form of human government. This phenomenon extends beyond high politics and can be seen also in the spread of consumerist Western culture in such diverse contexts as the color televisions now found throughout China and the rock music enjoyed in Prague, Rangoon and Tehran [id]. We might summarize the content of the universal homogeneous state as liberal democracy in the political sphere combined with easy access to VCRs and stereos in the economic.*[39]

This view conflates capitalism (an economic system) with consumerism (a value system) and with liberal democracy (a political ideology), and then assumes the righteousness and inevitability of the whole package. This is by now a common misconception which makes it more difficult to think intelligently about environmental issues and how to implement change in the capitalist system. State, economy and human values are separate, although none exists by itself and each influences the others. On the one hand, it is true that so-called 'socialist' states have been undemocratic and repressive. But on the other, it is equally true, as Heilbroner points out, that capitalism has no inherent dependence on, or affinity with, political freedom[40] – or with environmental quality, we might add. Later we consider why economic and political liberalism should not be confused.

Fukuyama himself recognized the vacuity of the materialist future he forecast, but appears to see no alternative.[41] Critics have attacked the thesis with passion. For example, Jonathan Sacks, the Chief Rabbi of Britain, responded in a BBC Reith Lecture:

> *Fukuyama's analysis takes us deep into irony. Because such a brave new world suggests a massive impoverishment of what we are as human beings, its accuracy as a prediction is matched only by its narrowness as a prescription. The human being as consumer neither is, nor can be, all that we are, and a social system built on that premise will fail [id]. Modernity is the transition from fate to choice. At the same time it*

dissolves the commitments and loyalties that once lay behind our choices. Technical reason has made us masters of matching means to ends. But it has left us inarticulate as to why we should choose one end rather than another.[42]

Fukuyama's identification of economic liberalism with liberal democracy has also been attacked:

Mr Fukuyama writes from an American perspective, which takes the success of economic liberalism for granted as a natural concomitant of liberal democracy. Yet economic liberalism poses a serious threat to greater democracy; the free market gives increasing power not to the ordinary worker or trader but to the big and essentially unaccountable corporations that are allowed to grow unchecked.[43]

Fukuyama is right, however, that the demise of Communism, global trends to economic integration and improved communication mean that hitherto collectivist economies have opened up to the West. This is partly because, as the former Soviet Union withdrew support from the economies of its former clients among the lower income countries, they were forced to open up to Western capital and to allow greater economic flexibility. Following from this is external and internal pressure for multi-party democracy and for increased consumption. The resultant lessening of state control and the burgeoning private sector (both multinational and backyard industries), raise significant challenges to environmental monitoring and control. Again there is no guarantee that the resultant development will be any more sustainable than the previous collectivist industrial effort.

The culture of consumerism

Another risk of postulating the end of ideology is that it obscures the fact that the demise of Communism is less a victory for capitalism per se than the culmination of decades of ruinous misrule in the countries concerned and a demand for access to the rapidly spreading culture of consumerism. Rabbi Sacks summarizes the situation for Russian Communism in its last days:

In the end, the colour television had proved a more seductive prospect than The Communist Manifesto. *Politics had moved beyond ideology. As Eduard Shevardnadze, the Soviet foreign minister, put it, 'the struggle between two opposing systems had been superseded by the desire to build up wealth at an accelerated rate'. Dialectical materialism was over; mail order materialism had taken its place. Eastern Europe had discovered the discreet charm of the bourgeoisie...*[44]

Consumerism exerts a powerful hold, nowhere more so than in the United States and, like the industrial system itself, it is spreading worldwide to become one of the most powerful ideologies of the 21st century. Yet it is entirely possible that consumerism is an inferior and grossly inappropriate value system for a world facing mounting environmental crisis. Already there have been some rebellions against consumerism – for example, in anti-materialist, anti-Western Islamic revolutions. In the West itself, many environmentalists are questioning excessive materialism. For example, Leiss argues that:

> *In a lifestyle that is dependent upon an endlessly rising level of consumption of material goods, individuals are led to misinterpret the nature of their needs and to misunderstand the relationship between their needs and the ways in which they may be satisfied.*[45]

These concerns are generally 'post-materialist' in so far as they tend to arise after wants and needs are well met, or where consumption is already at a level which many people feel is excessive. And at present, only a tiny and electorally insignificant minority of Westerners are questioning the consumerist ideology from within through 'downshifting' or attempting to limit their consumption of goods and services while maintaining their quality of life.

The problem for the world's environment is that only a small minority of the world's population is in any position to adopt such a post-materialistic perspective and only a very small minority of these choose to do so. Conversely, the billions not yet anywhere near the materialistic standards of the developed world feel, with justification, that they have every right to fulfil their material needs and desires through industrialism, just as the rich world has done.

Among these people, 70 per cent will be concentrated in just eight countries: China, India, Indonesia, Brazil, Pakistan, Bangladesh, Nigeria and Mexico. The Chinese and Indians together are around 2.3 billion people. The approach to sustainable development of these eight countries will be a major factor in the world environment. But the developed world can hardly have expectations unless they themselves are prepared to make radical changes in their own lifestyles.

The spread of Western-style consumerism across the globe is serving to erode core values in many traditional cultures, and great cultural traditions, such as those of China, India and Africa, are now facing fundamental changes because of the criss-crossing encounters of individuals, institutions, societies and cultures on an unknown scale.[46] Although new possibilities for synthesis and co-operation are opening up, this trend may also result in a severe loss of cultural diversity just at the point when we are questioning the dominant paradigm. The Swedish sociologist Egero summarizes the situation:

> *The post-industrial countries are facing the challenge of an ultimately necessary transition to ecologically sustainable economies. Today, however, when history is said to have come to an end, there is not even a theory to guide our way to a realization of such a transition. A similar uncertainty concerns the way forward for many poor countries in the South. I believe I am justified in interpreting the crisis in these countries as in no small part a 'cultural crisis', a result of West-supported development strategies aimed to 'bypass history' and carry the country in a swift change to a modern industrial society.*[47]

Environment and Political Culture

A basic assumption of this book is that environmental issues are quintessentially political, for they involve trade-offs between different, sometimes mutually exclusive, options in society and choices which extend over long time scales with far-reaching consequences. These trade-offs – for example between more, cheaper goods and environmental quality – cannot be addressed within the market economy alone: they involve more than monetary values and are bound up with competing ethical and political viewpoints. The trade-off process invariably involves some level of social organization which can mediate among competing interests and objectives. This often involves the state, with the lead of its government, but may also increasingly involve other major social formations which bring interests together – for example, the United Nations at the international level; and, as described later, networks of organizations at lower levels from the public, private and community sectors. Finally, because of the long lead time for major industrial or infrastructural investments, like highways or dams, and the need to anticipate environmental impacts, it is not enough to mediate; states must also plan for the future. In the modern capitalist economy, however, many forms of planning by the state are contentious.

It is worth considering why the market economy does what it does so much better than the command economy. First, the profit-oriented objectives of the private firm are clear, simple and unhindered by conflicting claims. This means that the cost of inputs can be related to outputs in a direct manner that is impossible in government and that incentives can be linked to the achievement of certain outputs – say, for example, market share. Second, the use of information and reaction are the key to success: the private firm responds to new information (feedback) in the society (the marketplace) with a rapidity that is impossible in government and engages in self-correction. The penalty for not self-correcting is failure – customers will vote with their feet, which they cannot do in a command economy except by resorting to the black market. Increased complexity in the world economy, and increased information and choice, reinforce the advantage of the market which, although far from perfect, has this critical feature of self-correction. In short, the successful firm in the market is adaptive and responsive. Successful environmental management emulates these traits.

Given the efficiency of the market economy in delivering goods, but also the absolute need for mediation at the interface of humankind and nature, one major challenge to sustainable development is to understand the history and alternatives for the relationship of the state to the private sector, and of both to the voluntary (NGO) sector. In particular, given the basic tension between the need for communal action to maintain our environment and the need to preserve and enhance individual freedom and the opportunity for initiative, we must begin to establish an understanding of the relationship of what we call political culture to market operation. Bell calls this question of state–society relationships 'of the public interest and the private appetite the salient problem for the polity in the coming decades'.[48]

The first step is to understand that modern capitalist societies work on two levels (Figure 2.2). The first is the level of the market economy – that is, the level of the individual and the firm. At this level, in economic terms, market arrangements are the best approach to the realization of goals and objectives for the reasons given above. Activities at this level are important to material well-being. They also tend to be efficient and basically irrepressible: it usually requires the full power of the state to

LEVEL	FOCUS	OBJECTIVES	CHANGE AGENTS	BEST APPROACH
• Level of *political culture*: The international community, the nation state, the region, the municipality	• Political relationships • Ethical systems • Longer-term, strategic, holistic and cumulative aspects of human existence • The broader externalities of market arrangements • Meta-organization	• Societal effectiveness in terms of quality of life for this and future generations	• Cultural consensus • The state • Other important social or voluntary organizations • Political leaders	• Dialogue • Cooperation • Reference to ethical frameworks • Pluralism
• Level of the market economy: The firm and the economic individual	• Economic structures • Market operation • Market enhancement • Individual and family well-being	• Economic efficiency for material well-being in this generation • Individual freedom	• The economic entrepreneur • Global and other corporations	• Competition in a market economy

Figure 2.2 *Two levels of social organization*

repress market transactions, which spring up as black markets when forbidden. However, the market is not a political or moral philosophy, but only a mechanism of economic transaction and one which is not likely to generate sustainable development. This is for the many reasons described earlier, but also because market transactions must be profit-maximizing or utilitarian, or they are nonsensical.

Market operations are necessary, therefore, but not sufficient for a sustainable, healthy society, environmentally or socially. As Sen puts it, 'the market mechanism is an essentially incomplete specification of a social arrangement' which can be adjusted by political will to work in different ways.[49] A second, higher order of human activity is necessary. This can be termed the level of political culture, which can derive and attain higher order social goals, define and address environmental problems, and promote human development. Some of these higher order goals (state supported research and development or vocational training, for example) can be important in attaining efficiency at the level of the market; others promote quality of life in areas where social benefits cannot be quantified and economic efficiency is not paramount. Higher order goals cannot be derived from considerations of economic efficiency alone.

In this conception, politics is not about the enforcement of commands or the exchange of political favours, but rather 'a process by which citizens come to see the world and themselves in a different way'.[50] A society operating in this manner would be 'like a classroom, a debating chamber, a Quaker meeting or a Jewish Yeshiva'. Only in such a mode can the members of society redefine their common purposes so that the public realm denied by individualism can be recreated and sustained.[51]

The development of such a political culture can be nurtured by the state but need not be a function solely of the state. Now that command economies have lost credibility and welfare state bureaucracies have been too often revealed as inefficient, the idea that 'civil society' should be the primary arena of political activities has become a major theme of debate, especially now that old ideologies in the industrial world are fading. In many societies, political culture reflects a measure of societal consensus which can be traced to long-standing traditions and organizations quite apart from the state. Religion, the tribe, the trade union, the educational system, the voluntary association – these can all be agents for the development of consensus. This is, of course, no guarantee that consensus is socially progressive – for example, societies may be consensually racist – or environmentally sustainable. This suggests that the process by which consensually held values and social goals are derived must have reference to moral considerations.

For environmental management, we need to understand the role of consensus, which is a sharing of views and values by a broad constituency within a society. In participating in any public policy debate, an objective should be to assist the development of a sufficient degree of consensus for action. At best, consensus reflects a transcendent societal view which goes beyond the individualism of the market but is complementary to it, reflecting a marriage between market economics and social responsibility. This involves trade-offs between individual freedoms in the marketplace and the quality of public life – for example, in a recognition that taxation to fund public services can raise the quality of life for the whole community and that a low rate of contribution by the well-off towards public goods will in the long run diminish their welfare as well as that of the less affluent.

It is also important to note that we use the term 'political culture' here rather than talk about the state or government per se, because the mediation process between economy and biophysical environment is far more complicated than the bipolar state–market distinction suggests. Clearly the state has an important and increasing role in maintaining environmental quality. But the state's direct role should not be dominant: in order for policy to be based on the fullest possible understanding of the tasks and problems in hand, the activity of the state should be complemented by that of other structures and organizations contributing to the maintenance of environmental quality.

Action networks and state action

State action can be complemented by other organizations in civil society that are able to take on a role in mediation between the demands of human development and the protection of natural environments, and to foster the necessary drive towards consensus on sustainable development. This idea takes us to the heart of the action network approach. These networks can include voluntary organizations or NGOs, citizens' groups, representatives of the education system, firms and business groups, trade unions, the church or any combination of groups working together.

In the ideal networking concept, government, business and community organizations of many kinds become equal players in a broad partnership. This kind of coalition can either buttress the weak state apparatus, as is the situation in many lower income countries, or it can temper the power of the state or of business where that is a problem. This notion that civil society can play an important role in environmental management is also in tune with calls for more attention to local and regional autonomy, particularly in the light of the globalization of economic activity and consumer culture, and the resultant erosion of cultural diversity and identity at the local level.

In this regard, Bell makes the crucial point that many of our problems – especially the environmental ones – are often either too small or too big for the nation state to handle adequately.[52] Thus local/regional groupings and international structures come to the fore and, indeed, are mutually reinforcing. Following chapters describe a concept of mutually reinforcing 'nested networks' which can realize these ideas.

Conclusion

Despite widespread use of the term, there is little in the way of consensus on what sustainable development will look like as a product: whether it is reconcilable with continuing, albeit modified forms of economic growth, or whether ultimately it demands a 'steady state' economy. It is clear, however, that the process of making development sustainable is about more than devising new economic tools and methods of valuing the environment, urgent and important though this is. The sustainable development path in industrial and industrializing countries will be a political, not just a technical, process. It can be seen as a continuing process of mediation and trade-offs between different goals and aspirations; it cannot be divorced from the wider issues of political culture, values and social tensions.

We have argued that the demise of Communism, the emergence of the worldwide trend towards market economies and Western consumer culture, the lessening of control by the state and the possibility of rapid economic growth in some of the world's lower income countries, pose major challenges to the realization of sustainable development. In particular there is a tension between the entrepreneurial individualism of capitalism and the need for societies to develop a sophisticated political culture which can derive and implement higher order social goals, like sustainable development. New skills for developing social consensus around issues of sustainable development could play an increasingly important role in environmental management.

In the following chapters we will explain how the development of 'environmental constituencies' around specific issues or tasks can be broadened into action on sustainable development. The action-network approach, described in Chapters 8–14, is emerging as a methodology for accomplishing this. Chapters 3 and 4 consider in more detail the question of values and political culture in relation to environmental management.

Part II

The Western View of Humankind and Nature

Introduction

The two chapters in this section explore the historical background to the relationship between humankind and nature in Western society. The understanding of this relationship was transformed by philosophers of the 16th to 19th centuries, reacting against a broad view of nature which held sway for centuries. This enormous philosophical programme helped to give rise to, and was nurtured by, the Reformation and the Renaissance. It was at the core of the Enlightenment, which provided the foundation for liberal political values in the West.

This creative period of intellectual, political and scientific activity has shaped structures and beliefs in Western society and in the modern state. Further, the broad value system it developed, which at the beginning of the 20th century was mainly confined to the West, is spreading rapidly, as states as diverse as Malaysia and Mexico aspire to, or achieve, industrialized status. Now, not only is the capitalist basis for economic life accepted worldwide, but Western liberal political procedures and values are spreading into Eastern Europe and the former Soviet Union and to hitherto quasi-socialist states such as Ghana, Tanzania, Zambia and Zimbabwe. The acceptance of Western political values and institutional structures increasingly has become a condition of aid to lower income countries.

The Industrial Revolution and subsequent dramatic population and economic growth gave rise to many of the serious environmental problems described in Chapter 1. But the opportunity for their development, the fertile ground of beliefs and values, can be traced further back to the philosophy of the Enlightenment. European philosophy created a powerful secular world, with religion progressively shifted to the margins of society, and in which debate over values increasingly took the form of competition between secular political ideologies of Left and Right.

As part of this revolution in thought, Newtonian science saw the rational human observer as separate from nature, which enabled nature to be studied in a detached, analytic fashion. This approach has generated a vast amount of scientific knowledge, but it has also marginalized a spiritual, emotional or holistic perception of the relationship of humankind to nature, as had been common in earlier civilizations. Nature now became a realm of impersonal objects to be studied, then 'conquered' or exploited by man. This world view separated facts from values. The need to analyse nature in a systematic fashion also gave rise to the compartmentalization of knowledge in academic disciplines.

In the sphere of production, both the capitalist, and later Marxist, industrial systems, while bringing many unprecedented material benefits, encouraged the packaging of nature into discrete commodities to be bought and sold. The Newtonian view of nature, as separate and inert, helped to validate this process. Much of industrial growth over the past 200 years has consisted of this commodification of nature and life's experiences into new products for the marketplace and into numbers for entry on corporate balance sheets. To compound the problem, the pollution generated by the industrial process has been put back into the natural environment. In economists' terms, the costs of these pollutants, either for nature or future generations, have been 'externalized' – that is, not included in the prices charged for the products. Neither the producer–polluter nor the consumer has paid.

Finally, out of the scientific, technological, philosophical and commercial innovations of the Enlightenment arose the modern secular state which institutionalized a separation between the economics of business – the 'private' sector – and the realm of joint social organization – the public or state sector. In liberal capitalism, fundamental importance has come to be attached to individual freedom in private or civil life. This private society is considered to be the area of life where individuals develop the strength of their creative forces in order to promote knowledge, wealth and progress. Conversely, it smacks of a now discredited socialism to insist that a collective or public interest exists outside the marketplace, and that either the state or 'civil society' (voluntary organizations, the press, interest lobbies, etc) have an important role in maintaining or enlarging that public interest, often at the expense of individual freedoms. Yet environmental quality is just such a public interest, and it is hard to conceive of a political system maximizing individual economic freedom and also resulting in a sustainable environment.

Now the rise of environmental problems, and concern about the ultimate communal good – the atmosphere itself – highlights the debate between the *laissez-faire* approach and one favouring government intervention in private life for environmental maintenance. As we shall see, the debate has run for at least 300 years, with no sign of a resolution.

There are two basic questions involved:

1 Is the provision of a high level of environmental quality compatible with maximizing individual freedom?
2 What balance between public or state action and private activity will maximize quality of life and what trade-offs are involved?

Chapter 3 takes up the issue of the influence of the scientific worldview on management of the environment. Chapter 4 looks at the evolution of political thought in the West on the question of the relationship of the individual to the state and society, and the implications for environmental management.

Finally, it may seem odd to some readers that we have reached back to sources that are centuries old to understand the modern world and prospects for the 21st century. The reason we believe that this is helpful is that our present ways of thinking are 'short-termist' and culture-bound. We need to see how the original reasoning and insights of thinkers have given rise to larger doctrines, been reinforced in the process and explicitly shape how we think and act today – and how we are likely to think and act in the 21st century, unless we consciously do otherwise.

3

Science and Technology and the Natural World

Natural science as a form of thought exists and has always existed in a context of history, and depends on historical thought for its existance. From this I venture to infer that no one can understand natural science unless he understands history and that no one can answer the question of what nature is unless he knows what history is.

R G Collingwood[1]

The important questions are not whether we respect capacities in some absolute sense or agree always to trade off conflicting objectives. Rather, we should be asking which characteristics of the environment merit protection for present and future people or for their own sake, and what is appropriate to put into (or keep out of) the balance... Resolving these questions cannot be reduced to an exercise in technical rationality ... nor can it be left to markets, which systematically undervalue environmental resources. Science helps, but cannot tell us how we wish to live. So we reach the conclusion that planning for sustainable development requires rigorous, intersubjective judgement.

Susan Owens[2]

The environmental movement has an ambivalent relationship with science. On the one hand, scientific research has alerted the world to many serious environmental problems, such as global climate change, the threat to the ozone layer, and the degradation of water supplies. Objective testing and reasoning about environmental problems from a scientific perspective debunks modern myths and provides sound information about the severity of those problems, and their trends, and allows participants in the debate to speak with some authority.

For example, scientists from Britain's Nature Conservancy Council (NCC) were able to establish that organochlorine insecticides used by farmers were accumulating in the food chain and were a threat to health. This was not a question of opinion, but of authoritative scientific fact. Speaking about attempts to persuade the agrochemicals industry to assist in changing these farming practices, the former Director-General of the NCC states '... had not the scientific base of ecology and conservation been already so sound, the successful agreement with the industry could not have been concluded'.[3] Government, NGOs and environmental pressure groups all rely on scientific authority and method to a great extent.

Turning to the field of environmental management, we find that some of the world's most innovative thinkers, policy advisers, managers and administrators are scientists by training, and often eminent in their fields. They are a tremendous human resource to address environmental problems, in part because of their perceptive analysis of areas of life that are invisible to the non-scientist.

On the other hand, and in spite of the obvious contribution of science to our understanding of the environment, many people are also deeply concerned about the role that science and technology have played in bringing about environmental problems:

> *After all, scientists invented the CFCs which are threatening the ozone layer. Technological advance allowed humans to develop nuclear power, which in turn has brought us persistent environmental problems. It was scientists who developed the pesticides which in the past three decades have contaminated our food and our wildlife. Some environmentalists see scientists as active collaborators in our society's ecological destructiveness.*[4]

Part of the reason for this ambivalent view of science is that in the last 50 years in the West we have allowed the authority attributed to science to become exaggerated. This should not necessarily be laid at the door of scientists. Rather it arises from the obvious contribution of science to industrial advancement through technology, which has steadily improved standards of living over time. This has fostered a strong belief in the value of continuous scientific advance and supported what has been called 'a fixation with technology'.[5]

Another difficulty is that in overestimating the authority of science, we have become blind to the inherent limitations of the scientific method, particularly when dealing with complex humankind–nature interactions. Many scientists would agree. Factors which affect the accuracy and validity of any scientific conclusion are the size of the sample in relation to the whole population and the representativeness of the sample. Biologists, for example, if they are studying whole plants or animals and the simpler cells of which they are composed, can seldom study those units in large numbers.[6] The range of difficulties increases as we move into the realm of humankind–nature interaction which requires joint natural and social scientific research to begin to untangle a myriad web of influences. Here sufficient sample sizes are often impossible, and intervening and dynamic variables of culture and social organization make scientific assessment more of an art than the kind of science we have traditionally relied on. It is worth noting here that ecology, as a science, is a departure from the traditional model. It concerns itself with complex networks of organisms and habitats and with dynamic relationships – for example, feedback loops and 'chaotic' indeterminacy in the behaviour of physical and biological systems – rather than with mechanistic cause-and-effect chains.

Increasingly there are calls for such interdisciplinary analysis – for example, in tackling global climate change – but such approaches are also relevant for almost any environmental problem. Take, for example, the problem of water pollution in the Weija Reservoir in Ghana. Once scientists working at the Institute of Aquatic Biology in Accra understood the scientific aspects of the problem, they used the action-network approach, through the IDEA programme described in Chapter 11, to build a team to analyse its broader dimensions. They found that the underlying causes of pollution in the watershed arise from rapid urbanization; intensification of agriculture, including monoculture, deeper ploughing and inputs of fertilizers and pesticides; fuelwood collection along the length of the river; and logging activities in the upper reaches.

Problems are compounded as modernization erodes the traditional, sustainable methods of river management which have evolved within the tribal framework.

Frontier Science and the Human–Ecosystem Interaction

This kind of complex environmental management situation precludes straightforward, cause-and-effect scientific analysis of the problems and also precludes simple solutions. Science has an important contribution to make, but complementary kinds of expertise are required to analyse a problem correctly, including the knowledge of local people, such as fishermen and farmers.

In fact, all 'frontier' science, whether astrophysics or ecology, must depend on elements of judgement and interpretive skill. This accounts for the common situation where opposing scientific opinions are brought into play to substantiate both sides of an argument. In well-established fields there may be little or no controversy. However, there are many 'frontier' areas in human–ecosystem interactions, which is why ecology, nutrition, and so on are marked by deep disagreements among experts. These are to be expected, but they can subvert public confidence in the image fostered of 'science' as a clear-cut, logical path to the cause-and-effect understanding of events. Myriad influences can only be understood through intensive data gathering – which is often very hard – and lengthy analysis. Replication of conditions – for example, toxic spills or nuclear accidents – may be impossible. The links between, say, health, food and the wider environment are inherently complex; and the 'object' of study is a moving target, always changing as new technologies are introduced, and these interact with other variables to produce new forms of risk.

The debate over the 900-foot high Tehri Dam in the Himalayan mountains of Uttar Pradesh provides a good example of expert disagreement. The project is intended to provide power to the industrial cities of north-east India. Scientists, environmentalists and local people are furiously debating the location of the dam, the soil stability, the effects of weather on run-off, the effects of the reservoir on the weather, the seismology and geology of the region, the effect of the dam on seismic activity, and the likely rate of siltation in the reservoir. The soundness of the research upon which the engineering is based is being questioned.[7]

These scientific arguments are part of the larger debate over whether the dam needs to be built at all – that is, will it contribute to development, and if so, to whose development: the local people who will be displaced or the urban residents and industry who will make use of the power provided? If development benefits are likely, the next question is: will they outweigh the social and environmental costs, and by whose criteria is a decision to be made? Some scientists question whether the impondment of the reservoir itself will not trigger geological instability sufficient to cause damage to the dam and widespread flooding and death downstream. Good hard science is only one factor in the complex mediation processes over such a project, and in such a tense political atmosphere is it any wonder that scientific authority is invoked on both sides of the debate?

Such examples also serve to raise more fundamental issues about the role of science and technology in modern development, particularly about:

- the uncertainty of control in industrial societies; and
- the assumption in the Western view that it is appropriate for mankind to 'dominate' nature.

Uncertainty of Control in Industrial Societies

Our inability to anticipate negative environmental and social impacts and to control our apparently sophisticated technology raises questions that extend to many areas of life. The continued risk of nuclear holocaust is an extreme example. In the field of nuclear energy, the nature of the technology itself magnifies the effect of human error in accidents such as those at Chernobyl or Three Mile Island.[8] At Chernobyl a fire in the reactor sent graphite rods exploding through the cement roof. A cloud containing more than 200 types of radionucleides spread across the Ukraine and Byelorussia, and the effects of radioactive fall-out were found in sheep as far away as England and Wales. The legacy of radioactivity remains in the Welsh hills.

The implementation of new technology often takes place in such a subtle and incremental fashion that we are unable to understand its cumulative effects. This is the case in any assessment of the environmental repercussions of innovation and diffusion of technologies in such fields as agrochemicals, toxic wastes, nuclear power and the massive commitments to fossil fuel consumption by power stations, industry and the world's 500 million motor vehicles.

To understand the influence of established scientific worldviews on the environment it is helpful to consider the processes of scientific and technological development, as well as its products, paying particular attention to the interaction of technical, socio-political and cultural factors. To get at these more basic concerns about the assumptions of Western science, it is helpful to distinguish what has been called the 'orthodox representation' of environmental issues from what has been called an 'alternative environmental agenda'. Grove-White describes the orthodox view:

> *On this representation, the problems of the environment are seen as a set of objectively existing physical problems, discovered in nature, through the methods of natural sciences – a group of physical problems arising from specific human interventions in natural systems. In all these cases we can detect important assumptions about human behaviour. These are dominated by the assumptions of rational choice theory – by the view of the human subject as rationalist–individualist calculator. The paradigm of human behaviour is economistic. Human beings, whether individuals or nation states, overwhelmingly seek to maximise their utilities. In political language, they pursue their interests.*[9]

There is nothing inevitable about this conception of humanity. Rather it is an historical and cultural artefact, derived from a positivistic view of scientific knowledge and the assumption that a detached, objective observation of nature is unproblematic. But there is an alternative view which questions some of the fundamental assumptions of Western societies:

> *In industrial societies we have become more and more locked into a range of deep structural commitments – industrial, infrastructural, technological. These mean that, socially, more and more, we are running to stand still. Our social systems are ever more perilously interdependent and enclosed, because of the encompassing and increasingly complex nature of technologies... Most of these structural commitments are propelled by technological change, which is almost always producer-led. Most of the choices on these matters have been made blind, in the absence of any significant assessment of potential wider social consequences.*[10]

In this view, rational choice and objective assessment of physical problems are severely limited by the structures of industrial modernity and by the effects of successive technological innovations. The spread of the car is a good example: almost unwittingly and within the space of about 65 years, industrialized countries have reorganized their societies around the car. The result is that we now face a crisis of congestion, pollution and car-dependence. In the United States this is said to have 'eliminated town and country simultaneously, replaced by a vast suburban wasteland'.[11] In Britain, the dangers of road traffic mean that most British children are no longer allowed out of the house without an adult escort: in the two decades between 1970 and 1990, the proportion of British seven- and eight-year-olds allowed to walk to school unaccompanied has fallen dramatically from 80 per cent to just 9 per cent.[12] Nor is there any likelihood of abatement, short of a radical change in the use of vehicles and the planning of transport systems worldwide, as the number of vehicles in the world is predicted to treble by 2030. This trend is unsustainable and a clear case of technology out of control, with choices about its exploitation made blind.

The Western View of Nature

The Western view of the world, in which nature is 'out there', separate from man, and in which human progress involves increasing domination over the natural world, has its origins in the revolution of thought from the Renaissance and Reformation which also gave rise to liberal capitalism. But this in turn was part of the larger redefinition of humankind and its relation to the world, which had its culmination in the Enlightenment. One aspect of this rethinking of the human condition and potential was a wholesale change in the means of knowing the world, based on the development of scientific method.

With the work of Copernicus, whose model of the solar system displaced the earth from the centre of the universe, humankind was for the first time able to formulate 'laws' which appeared to hold good in the furthest reaches of the heavens, and this transferred to scientists new powers of knowledge that was previously reserved for scholars of the Church. The Renaissance view of nature is also based, according to Collingwood, on the emerging human experience of designing and constructing machines:

> *by the sixteenth century the Industrial Revolution was well on the way. The printing press and the windmill, the lever, the pump, and the pulley, the clock and the wheelbarrow, and a host of machines were established*

> *features of daily life. Everyone understood the nature of a machine, and the experience of making and using such things has become part of the general consciousness of European man. It was an easy step to the proposition: as a clockmaker or a millwright is to a clock or a mill, so is God to Nature.*[13]

It is at this time that modern science begins to diverge from philosophy and theology. Galileo writes of the language of the 'vast book' of Philosophy: 'It is written in mathematical language, and the letters are triangles, circles and other geometrical figures, without which means it is humanly impossible to comprehend a single word'.[14] The implication is that the truth of nature consists in mathematical facts; what is real is that which is measurable and quantitative.

Francis Bacon took the proposition one step further. Knowledge acquired by scientific analysis could be put to work to give the human race mastery over nature:

> *From this perspective, knowledge is regarded not as an end but as a means, expressed and applied in technology, by which humans assume power over the material world. A high premium is thus attached to the growth of knowledge because it is on this that the enhancement of human powers through the development of technology depends.*[15]

The Scientific Revolution, which presaged the Enlightenment and the Industrial Revolution, was most dramatically marked by the work of Newton, who developed both a world model and the scientific method upon which modern natural science is based:[16]

> *Newtonian physics, the crowning achievement of the seventeenth century, provided a consistent mathematical theory of the world that remained the solid foundation of scientific thought well into the twentieth century.*[17]

In the Newtonian conception, reality is likened to a continuously operating machine composed of isolated parts, which relate mechanistically together to make the whole.[18] By the use of the scientific method these relationships can be discovered, understood and ultimately manipulated for man's purposes. At the core of the scientific method is the principle of analysis, in which the scientist, emotionally detached and neutral, through making empirical observations of the selected parts of nature, seeks to uncover causal connections between them, within a framework of universally applicable theories.[19] Priority is thus given to the parts, studied in distinct disciplines, over the whole.

The Newtonian legacy

Modern science is associated, then, with a view of nature as something separate and value-free; and Enlightenment ideas about science and progress encouraged the notion that nature should be dominated by humanity in the name of material and social progress. It is important to note, however, that such conceptions also found support in the Judeo–Christian tradition which preached the dominion of man over nature. In the words of Genesis: 'replenish the earth and subdue it: and have dominion over the fish of the sea and over the fowl of the air and over every living thing that moveth upon the earth'. And, of course, pre-Enlightenment societies in Europe, and many elsewhere, were marked by many unsustainable practices and often a lack of ethical restraint in dealing with nature: their key constraint was the level of technology to which they had access.

It would thus be quite wrong to see the rise of Western science and industrialism as a radical break with a pre-Enlightenment world in which mankind and nature invariably existed in sustainable harmony. However, it is clear that industrialization and the rise of modern scientific research provided both the means and an ideology of progress with which Western societies could exploit nature as never before.

As a result of the intellectual revolution of the Enlightenment, Western science and scientific method assumed an ascendancy over all the other forms of knowledge in industrial societies; so much so, that knowledge which is labelled 'unscientific' is taken to be wrong. Scientific method provided the technology by which European industrial man set out to conquer both nature and the peoples of the earth in the 18th and 19th centuries. Moreover, the unequivocal attachment to economic growth in industrial society depends on the continual advances in scientific knowledge, which is the basic prerequisite for the development of the technology upon which industrial society depends for the 'subjugation' of nature.

What are the implications of the legacy of Newtonian scientific method over our ways of thinking? There are two problems: the fragmentation of knowledge and the effects of interaction. Under the Newtonian model, because each of the parts of the great machine was in some fixed relationship, small fragments of reality could profitably be studied in detail; all such studies, it was assumed, could gradually build up a picture of the universe. But the more this mode of analysis became adopted, the more the perspective on the bigger picture was lost, until the point arrived when fragmentary analysis became the objective and holism was increasingly viewed with suspicion as unscientific. The physicist David Bohm calls this 'the habit of fragmentary thought'.[20]

The problem is compounded by disciplinary reductionism in which highly specialized disciplines in the natural and social sciences, isolated from each other, have sought 'to explain the whole through the construction of theories specific to their respective perspectives'. Jones calls this the searchlight effect, in which an intense beam of light gives detailed knowledge of a part of reality, leaving the rest obscure.[21]

This syndrome of knowledge fragmentation, or reductionism, has today become:

> *the principal handicap in knowing and solving the global problems that confront mankind. More than that, numerous pressing problems for the evolution of civilisation, which cover several different and specialised areas, cannot be understood and explained.*[22]

Such an emphasis of the parts of the system at the expense of the whole is not only typical of the natural and social sciences, however, but has become a general characteristic of Western culture. Specialization, division of labour, individualism – all are expressions of the modernization process.[23]

Another problem has to do with the nature of causality in the highly interactive humankind–nature relationship, and a fundamental limitation of the scientific method. Causal explanation in the natural sciences rests on the basic assumption that an event to be explained can be isolated or insulated from the effects of its surroundings. In other words, we must be able to demonstrate that *A* is directly affected by *B*, and not by *C*, *D* or *E*; that acid rain causes certain effects and that certain industrial processes have caused acid rain. But when science works with complex metaproblems there is no way of observing cause and effect, where every action causes multiple interactive effects. There is no way of bounding the problem in a rigorous fashion because the number of actors and independent actions creating what are called 'intervening' variables is indeterminate.

This indeterminacy defines what we call a 'turbulent' environment – turbulent because the interactive effects are inherently unpredictable. This is the uncertainty of control discussed earlier. Rather than scientific prediction, the best that can be hoped for might be called 'realistic expectation', and our expectations must be tempered by our knowledge of the reality of the turbulent environment. Instead of prediction, the intellectual and emotional basis on which we appraise our increasingly uncertain future must rest on wisdom derived from understanding the implications of past actions – wisdom being the very fusion of knowledge and ethical values, which overemphasis on the scientific method has done much to separate. We return to the concept of the turbulent environment in Chapter 8.

In relation to the resolution of complex environmental problems, our existing capacity for generating new wisdom is poor and our chosen socioeconomic and cultural system conditions us against so doing. Unfortunately, too, our commonplace vision of progress in terms of ever-increasing production and consumption may also condition us against the backward reflection that is necessary to understand our environmental predicament. Worse still, excessive consumption is itself a form of conditioning – it is an addiction from which withdrawal becomes increasingly difficult.

In summary, the evolution of detached scientific method, by providing a justification for the utilitarian commodification of nature, presents us with four problems:

1. Our knowledge of the world has become fragmented by the compartmentalization of experience, making it difficult to understand complex socioenvironmental interactions. One response has been to develop more 'holistic' approaches, although there is much debate about what this means.
2. Conventional scientific method is predicated on the functional separation of humankind from nature: this colours our perceptions and may lead to overemphasis on technical solutions to solve human problems.
3. Scientific method has been extended to the study of humankind itself in the social sciences through positivism, but this has been largely unfruitful. The response most relevant to environmental management has been participative action research, described in later chapters.
4. Western science has encouraged us to detach knowledge from values. This has reinforced a utilitarian approach to life. But wisdom is the conjunction of knowledge with ethics – we have not increased our wisdom therefore at the rate of our material progress or the destruction of nature. One response has been to rekindle the discussion about the moral dimension of the humankind–nature relationship in the environmental debate. This is part of a broader movement in advanced industrial democracies to shift political debate to a moral ground which the sociologist Anthony Giddens calls 'life politics'.[24] This is a realm of debate in which the classic political issues of industrialism – class conflict, workers' rights and condi-

tions, and the extension of civil liberties – lose their centrality and issues relating to the quality of life and the trade-offs between individualism and communal values become crucial.

The Study of Humankind in Relation to Nature

Before going on to say how these new responses contribute to innovative approaches to environmental management, it is helpful to look at the social sciences, which have developed in parallel with the natural sciences, often apeing the scientific method, albeit not very successfully. These are important because, as the complexity of environmental problems becomes obvious, so does the need for multidisciplinary approaches that combine the natural and social sciences.

The fusion of Enlightenment thinking in political philosophy, examined in Chapter 4, with the scientific worldview, gave rise to a literature concerned with methodological issues in the study of social life. These issues continue to engage social scientists to this day. Having established a powerful rationale for the mastery of nature, Western philosophers looked for some similar means of analysing man himself. In particular this was stimulated by the prospect of finding in social processes the analogues of Newton's laws of physical processes.

Thomas Hobbes, for example, set out in *Leviathan* to build a 'civil science' made up of clear principles and closely reasoned deductions based on postulates derived from observations about human nature.[25] Based on the idea that all knowledge was derived from sensory perception, he set out to study first the nature of the individual human being and then to apply the principles of human nature to economic and political problems, guided by the belief that there were laws governing human society similar to those governing the physical universe.

The scientific approach to social knowledge also impressed the 19th century utilitarians Jeremy Bentham and John Stuart Mill. They argued that the concepts of social contracts and natural rights, put forward by John Locke and others, were misleading, and that it was more productive to use observation to uncover the basic, definable elements of actual human behaviour and to use this information for rational decision-making.

Two profound developments of the early industrial period served to reinforce this social scientific approach. First, the French Revolution demonstrated that fundamental and age-old institutions, hitherto invested with a degree of permanence and inevitability, could be transformed or overthrown. This meant that new societal structures were possible and encouraged the view that their nature could be derived from rational, scientific analysis – logical, empirical and quantified.[26] Second, large-scale production associated with the industrial era was based on the use of rational calculation of the potential demographic and spatial spread of markets for new goods.

The fundamental propositions of the rationalist tradition stemming from the Enlightenment are:

1 that human nature is essentially the same at all times and places;
2 that universal human goals, true ends and effective means, are discoverable in principle; and

3 that methods akin to Newtonian science may be discovered and applied in morals, politics, economics and human behaviour toward the elimination of social ills.[27]

The relevance of the social sciences

Other philosophers, particularly Comte, worked to fuse the notion of rationalism with the methodology of the natural sciences and to extend this to the fledgling social sciences. In *Cours de Philosophie Positive*, Comte argued that the true philosophic spirit would henceforth explore reality with a certainty and precision that was previously unknown in intellectual life. In Comte's scheme of positive philosophy (positivism), the natural and social sciences taken together formed a hierarchy of decreasing generality and increasing complexity, beginning with mathematics, then physics, chemistry and biology, and then moving into sociology, the science of human conduct. As with natural phenomena, it was argued that social phenomena are subject to general laws which will become apparent through scientific study. Benton suggests the search for such general laws is at the heart of the rationalist conception of both natural and social life, and: 'the implication is clear: an extension of scientific thought to social phenomena will generate systematic knowledge of society to which all must assent'.[28] The underpinnings of positivistic philosophy are described by Giddens:

> *reality consists of sense impressions; an aversion to metaphysics, the latter being condemned as sophistry or illusion; the representation of philosophy as a method of analysis, clearly separable from, yet at the same time parasitic upon, the findings of science; the duality of fact and value – the thesis that empirical knowledge is logically discrepant from the pursuit of moral aims and the implementation of ethical standards; and the notion of the unity of science: the idea that the natural and social sciences share a common logical and perhaps even methodological foundation.*[29]

The notion of a positivistic social science gained currency, particularly in America after the Second World War, based on the success of the 'science' of economics in the Keynesian post-war reconstruction. Other disciplines, such as sociology and psychology, attempted to emulate economics and emerge as sciences. The attraction of the positivist approach lay in its apparent advantages in assisting social engineering, just as such manipulation was possible in the natural world.

Quantitative social science took hold. An emphasis on quantification is closely allied to the overall positivist approach in which an assumption of rationality is fundamental to any explanation or prediction of human behaviour. In this approach large samples of people, whom social scientists have empirically observed and wish to generalize about, must be assumed to be acting rationally. The only other alternative is that observations are of random behaviour and no explanation or prediction is possible. Equally, rationality must be assumed if social scientists are to substantiate statistically what are, at first instance, abstractions or generalizations.

There are two areas of concern here. First, abstractions will be simplified pictures of a complex reality and no quantitative models can encapsulate the multidimensionality of human existence. Reductive attempts at modelling invariably lead to criticism:

> *Empirical methods such as simulation, optimisation, and multivariate statistical modelling all represent very considerable abstractions from the normal reality most of us would agree upon. Our discontinuous, nonlinear, stochastic, uncertain, and ill-defined world is stretched, shortened, trimmed, compressed, and moulded until it fits into the procrustean bed of the analytical methods at hand.*[30]

Problems of quantitative modelling have been discussed at length and are familiar to most social scientists.[31] The main objection is not that tools such as statistical modelling are not useful, but that they can be misused or overvalued in that their simplification of reality is conveniently taken for reality itself. Although such tools can be important when they contribute additional dimensions to an understanding of complex social problems, they are not surrogates for reality, nor can they be comprehensive, and so they are not in themselves a very useful guide to action. But they are often taken to be sufficient for action – for example, in the use of cost-benefit analysis in assessing development projects, like the large dams traditionally funded by the World Bank. Finally, quantitative techniques are often predicated on simplistic methodological assumptions – for example, the choice of a discount rate in cost-benefit analysis – which often cannot withstand either methodological or political scrutiny and which themselves represent value judgements.

A second concern arises when social science or rationalist decision techniques are purported to be politically neutral or value-free. But all such techniques are value-laden in themselves in that they may reflect the priorities of some dominant social group and exclude consideration of the values of groups that are less powerful but often highly affected.

Quantitative analysis can also undervalue social, environmental, spiritual and other intangible dimensions of political problems – many dimensions are not amenable to quantification. In particular, a focus on 'dollars and cents', as discussed with regard to GDP, means that we tend to ignore other dimensions of life which do not fit into these equations. There is also a more profound concern that decision processes, many apparently value-free, are invariably rooted in ideological assumptions and can represent a form of technocratic domination which precludes ethical considerations and opposing views in the fundamental decisions affecting societies.

The result of the development of positivistic social science and rationalism as a mode of decision-making was that:

> *the whole problem of values remained unsolved, especially so far as its practical manifestation in policy formation was concerned, no secure links were forged between philosophy, particularly moral and political, and sociology. This was disastrous.*[32]

Emerging Perceptions of Humankind and Nature

Although the legacy of the Newtonian view is strong in everyday life, there are a number of emerging paradigms: in science itself and in two perspectives which might be called 'local traditionalist' and 'holistic'.

Developments in physics beyond the Newtonian model

In science, the Newtonian conception has been drastically revised since the mid-19th century. Since the 1920s advances in the field of subatomic physics known as quantum theory have provided the main basis for progress beyond the Newtonian model of the world as a mechanism. Developments in quantum theory are resulting in a fundamental rethink of not only the Newtonian world model with its notions of linear causality, but also of the epistemological presuppositions upon which all previous scientific thought has been based:

> *Unless modern quantum theory is in error, the world simply does not exist in a definite state without our observing it. Before matter can peep forth, even as a pebble or a snowflake, it has to be observed by a consciousness. Something must sustain it in and above the void of non-being. That something, it seems, is the mind.*[33]

The result may be a constant interaction between mind and matter, and a definition of reality conditioned by the observer. In short, the world 'out there' is not wholly independent of our observation, which in turn affects that world. According to many physicists the idea of material reality without consciousness is impossible. The concept begins to emerge of reality as a field of interacting networks of complex systems at many levels of organization.

Care is needed here. Quantum theory can lend support to all kinds of views and there is no definitive interpretation of the field. There is obviously much still to be uncovered; however, it is true that any interpretation of quantum theory undermines the old Newtonian conception of the cosmos. The fundamental uncertainty affecting the observation of the subatomic world limits us to prediction of the probabilities of events.

Elsewhere in the new fields of scientific research there is a growing interest in the behaviour of complex dynamic systems, whether inorganic or biological, which defy traditional reductionist analysis. Insights into the 'chaotic' properties of complex systems such as the atmosphere, and even of apparently simple, predictable ones such as a pendulum or an orbiting body, suggest that there are inherent limits to the predictability of events on the large scale just as there are on the quantum level.[34] This indicates that some convergence may be in prospect between interpretations and research interests in 'mainstream' science and the 'holistic' approaches to natural philosophy outlined below.[35]

The relevance of local knowledge

A second emerging paradigm is quite different. This perspective argues the case for local knowledge: a mode of understanding in which science is not dominated by Western assumptions and methods and is relevant to the local culture. For example, priests play an important role in maintaining water quality in Ghana – a cultural form of sustainable development evolved over many centuries. There are many such examples of indigenous knowledge which is often eroded by Western science and modernization: traditional agricultural irrigation in Rajasthan or Bali; sustainable rainforestry in Brazil and Borneo; hunter-gatherer lifestyles in the Canadian Arctic, the Australian outback or the Kalahari Desert. This represents a vast repository of knowledge of sustainable development that has been refined over millennia and is now under desperate threat from insensitive modernization.

However, it is important to note that a 'local' emphasis may not always be wholly conducive to development. For example, Pakistan has attempted to develop Islamic science and economics. Inayatullah notes an advantage in local enablement and self-esteem, but warns that this emphasis may also lead to situations where old power structures, such as those of the mullahs and the landlords, are renewed:

> *Here, while science has been placed in an alternative cultural site, it has lost its openness to critique and debate – an openness necessary for any creative development. While freed from modernity, this indigenization of knowledge perspective has become frozen in historical-ideational religious traditions.*[36]

This limitation indicates the need for local knowledge and Western approaches to be integrated – used selectively where appropriate and with both open to modification in the light of experience. A simplistic rejection of Western science is as flawed as a simplistic imposition of the Western approach.

The human ecological perspective

A third emerging paradigm is the holistic or human ecological one. The term 'holistic' was coined by Jan Smuts in 1926 in his book *Holism and Evolution* as meaning 'the whole is greater than the sum of the parts', but also embracing a hierarchy of explanation, the lowest rung of which is Newtonian mechanism. This view has re-emerged as what has been termed the new holistic paradigm. In the writings of Fritjof Capra, for example, science, religion and values are reconciled through a reinterpretation of modern physics. The aim is:

> *not towards a local science but a new universal science that is not reductionist, but holistic, with truth simultaneously having many levels and at the same time grounded in a consciousness that exists ontologically prior to the intellectual mind.*[37]

The holistic paradigm is characterized by: 'an emphasis on totality, the replacement of the observer by the participant, thinking in terms of processes, an affinity with systems theory, and by ecologism as distinct from anthropocentrism'.[38] There are three important aspects here for environmental management.

First, holism takes exception to the Newtonian view that the dynamics of complex systems can be understood by aggregating knowledge about the components of the system. This does not deny the importance of directed scientific research, but suggests that a higher level of integration is necessary that can bring quantitative scientific knowledge together with qualitative sociocultural knowledge and ethical values.

The point is clear with respect to the modelling of global environmental change and the contribution of science to remedial or adaptive policies. Climate modelling is constrained by limits not only on computing power but also on our comprehension of the chaotic nature of atmospheric processes and their interactions with other complex systems such as ocean currents. The uncertainties in the science underlying the modelling and the charged political context of research into, for example, global warming,[39] have led to the description of the analysis of global environmental change as 'second order science', distinct from the 'consensual' science of better understood research with no direct impacts on human life.[40] Second order science cannot be insulated from political issues and values concerning our relationship with the natural environment.

Second, the notion that the scientist can be a detached observer is rejected along with the notion of a wholly objective universe. Rather, participants define their reality interactively with nature and each other. Third, holism looks at human society and nature as an integrated system or network which is non-hierarchical – all elements are linked together but there is neither top nor bottom, centre or periphery. A characteristic of the network is an intricate linkage of cause, effect and feedback.

The holistic approach recognizes the inescapability of integrating an ethical dimension into the science of global environmental change. There is not the space here to discuss environmental ethics in any detail, but a simplified categorization of viewpoints is possible:[41]

A Technocentric: resource-exploitative, growth-oriented.
B Managerial: resource-conservationist, oriented to sustainable growth.
C Communalist: resource-preservationist, oriented to limited or zero growth.
D Bioethicist or deep ecological: extreme preservationist, anti-growth.

The technocentric view (*A*) tends to take a wholly instrumental approach to nature. It is resolutely anthropocentric and places faith in the capacity of technology to harness nature and substitute man-made capital for natural resources where required. As noted in Chapter 1, this approach tends to ignore the implications of our ignorance of the dynamics and potential for collapse of ecosystems that are stressed by overexploitation or pollution. It also neglects the value that many find intrinsic in wildlife and landscapes.

At the opposite extreme is the bioethicist view (*D*), in which moral rights are conferred on other species and humans are required to respect intrinsic value in all nature and live in harmony with it. This broad approach is highly unlikely ever to appeal to enough people to form the basis for a realizable economic programme. It also provides little or no guidance on deciding between human development and nature preservation in cases where human and non-human interests – in theory equal – are in conflict.[42]

Neither of these positions is compatible with sustainable development as we have defined it: seeking to enhance diverse forms of human development while maintaining the natural capital stock for future generations.[43] The technocentric position risks unsustainable disruption of ecosystems; and the bioethicist view is politically unacceptable and impracticable in the face of the industrialization of the planet and the aspirations of most of the world to better quality of life and chances for human development.

The intermediate positions *B* and *C* are those associated with human 'stewardship' of nature, with differing emphases on the extent to which development should be constrained and modified by environmental considerations. Our perspective here combines elements of both the 'managerial' and 'communalist' approaches, recognizing the need for sustainable growth to improve human development and environmental protection in the poor world, and the need for radical policy change and movement towards steady-state or steady-flow economic development in many aspects of the industrial world's consumption and production patterns.

What must be stressed is that implicit or explicit adherence to a general set of values concerning our impact on the natural environment is inescapable. We cannot develop our understanding of global environmental change and sustainable development paths without reference to guiding values; and disputes over the meaning of sustainable development are essentially about the values that underpin the decision-making processes we use in assessing our impacts on the environment.

Conclusion

Probably the greatest failing of positivistic philosophy and science has been the attempt to separate fact from value, by the argument that the basis of scientific knowledge can always be separated from ethical considerations. This gave rise to the mistaken notion that science could be in all circumstances value-free, or neutral and objective. What is now clear is that scientific and technological development for industrialization hitherto focused mainly on one goal – growth – and on the means of achieving it, can no longer be divorced wholly from social goals or ethical and ecological considerations.

As to the broader debate over the role of rationality in public policy, the assumption that behaviour is rational or irrational is a false dichotomy. It is better to realize that behaviour in an uncertain world will often be based on 'situational' reasoning, and that to be rational means to attempt to be efficacious and judicious in a context of uncertainty, vested interest and inevitable ignorance of the overall long-term impact of decisions.

4

Political Ideas and Sustainable Development

If we see liberty only as a set of legal rights, then what was once a common good, a shared tool for progress, becomes an increasingly bitter zero-sum game.

Geoff Mulgan[1]

It is in their role as citizens, not consumers, that individual people will create a sustainable economy ... it is through collective political choices that sustainability will be achieved.

Michael Jacobs[2]

The Western post-Enlightenment view of humankind is founded on a wholly new perception of the relation of individuals to society. In medieval and many non-Western social systems, the individual is considered a minute part of a greater fixed system. In the liberal society of the West, human beings are often imagined to be self-sufficient cells, from which society is constructed.[3] In this conception, people need not accept the social order as given, but may refashion it to suit their needs. The crucial issue for political philosophy then becomes the nature of the relationship between the self-sufficient individual and the larger social organization.

Political debate relates directly to the framework of ordered relationships which enable us to live together and satisfy our communal wants and needs.[4] Political philosophy, in addressing the problems and prospects of social organization, is both explanatory and normative – that is, it asks how a political society does or could work, and passes judgement on whether it works well or badly. The history of political philosophy provides some key insights into constraints on resolving the environmental crisis, particularly the tension between legitimate desires for individual freedom and the need for social control, often by the state, to realize the 'common good'.

By the 16th century, political writers began to elaborate a distinction between public and private interests, and the domain of the 'contract' between citizens and the state, which is to provide the basis for modern political theory. From the 17th to 19th centuries, the philosophy of liberalism emerged, nurtured by the creative thinking of many of the same Enlightenment philosophers who developed the Western scientific method. Utilitarian liberalism became the philosophy of capitalism, with science and technology providing the means for the commodification of nature and industrialism on a world scale. At the same time, emerging notions of liberal democracy gave rise to ideas of individual freedom outside the confines of Church and state.

The thrust of much political thought and action towards freedom and individuality was paralleled by moves towards more rationalized organization and constraints on individualism to meet communal needs, such as public order and the security of the state, and later, problems of poverty and environmental degradation. The vexing question of the trade-off between individual freedom and government authority has been a central point of concern in the Western political tradition. A resolution has yet to be worked out of this fundamental tension between reasonable desires for freedom and the need to restrain this freedom in the interests of the common good.

Democracy and Sustainable Development

It is unlikely that this tension between freedom and control is resolvable in the sense that a once-and-for-all balance can be derived based on philosophic or economic criteria for any country. Rather, following from conclusions in the last chapter, we argue that the appropriate balance is situational and derived from debate or democratic mediation.

We believe that this is a fundamental aspect of sustainable development. However, we use the word 'democratic' in the sense of an equality of power among environmental stakeholders and in people taking control of their own environments, and thus 'owning' both problem and solution, rather than from any notion of imposing Western institutional structures, many of which have never worked in formerly colonized countries. This commitment to dialogue also rules out simplistic ideological viewpoints from right or left and, of course, the authoritarianism that has been so prevalent and damaging in many non-Western countries. Rather the requirement is for intelligent debate, fully aware of the intellectual reasoning and tensions which underpin the Western democratic ideas being exported worldwide. Whether non-Western leaders agree that such ideas are appropriate or not is for themselves and their people to decide. But analysis of the origins of the debate is surely useful.

A related problem is that sustainable development, reflecting a concern for the future even to unborn generations, must imply comprehensive planning for that future. Many of our problems arise from a failure to plan. Such planning at the societal level could only be initiated or undertaken by an agency with a societal overview, and however sophisticated participatory structures of civil society may become, it is difficult to imagine the state not playing a crucial role. But strategic planning by the state is tarnished by the collapse of Communism in the East and the problems of the overloaded welfare states in the West, and the unreliability of most long-term planning processes.

The imperative of sustainable development suggests some new role in planning for the state, but one substantially different from past experiences of state planning. In later chapters we will argue that this new role for the state is to provide strategic guidance and to create the conditions to unlock innovation in the private and community sectors, often by devolving responsibility within a broader framework which encourages information flow about societal options. People often use the term 'enabling state', and we apply that to the concept of sustainable development.

In this chapter we look at the gradual emergence of the concept of the liberal, democratic state, developed through the philosophies of Hobbes, Locke, Bentham, Mill and others. Although we have argued that the state, acting alone, cannot guarantee environmental quality, the state is first and foremost the provider, or guarantor, of public goods, by direct provision or by regulation, which is a form of coercive social control. Consideration of the tension between individual freedoms and the social control required for sustainable development can profitably begin with a brief history of changing views of the role of the state.

The Individual and the State

The two most influential concepts in the development of the theory of the state have been the idea of the state as a structure of power, which is clearly distinguishable from civil society in general; and the endemic problem of reconciling the authority of the state to intervene in society by law with the liberty of the individual. Most modern democratic theory:

> *... has constantly sought to justify the sovereign power of the state while at the same time justifying limits upon that power. The history of this attempt since Machiavelli and Hobbes is the history of arguments to balance might and right, power and law, duties and rights. On the one hand, the state must have a monopoly of coercive power in order to provide a secure basis upon which trade, commerce and family life can prosper. On the other hand, by granting the state a regulatory and coercive capability, liberal political theorists were aware that they had accepted a force which could (and frequently did) deprive citizens of political and social freedoms.*[5]

Questions of whether the state has the right to impose constraints on the freedom of individuals in pursuit of a common good are thus always on the agenda of societies which subscribe to Western notions of democracy. Unfortunately, this is not a question that allows a clear-cut answer, except in relation to extreme cases. At one extreme, if all relationships and all expectations end up being governed by the state, the result is totalitarianism. Conversely, sustainable development is probably impossible under conditions of excessive individualism. Extreme state control is thoroughly discredited; the excesses of individualism represent a more subtle danger.

Can individualism be excessive?

An analysis by Lane of individualism in the United States is instructive, for the US in many ways epitomizes the successful liberal democratic state.[6] It is the most privatized, market-oriented major economic power, with the highest proportion of the ownership of the means of production in private hands.[7] Its approach to capitalism and its culture are massively powerful influences on the rest of the world through global media such as film and television.

In his examination of the nature of individualism in the US, Lane makes a distinction between two types of individualism: utilitarian individualism – that is, maximization of economic self-interest, and expressive individualism – that is, self-actualization in feeling, intuition and experience. He identifies the source of a serious problem in American society as excessive and aggressive utilitarian individualism, which results in a fundamental decline of a sense of community, a degradation of the quality of public life and public space, and a retardation of opportunities for expressive individualism to be realized. This problem – that is, the fear that competitive individuals would preclude achievement of the public good – is in his view the 'most important unresolved problem in American history'.

The problem of excessive individualism in American society was also identified by de Tocqueville 150 years earlier in *Democracy in America*. The rise of neo-conservatism and 'yuppyism' in the 1980s served to sharpen a concern over this problem, as does the continued reluctance of the US Government to make binding commitments to reduce its contribution to greenhouse gas emissions, in spite of having by far the highest per capita consumption of fossil fuel energy in the world. In America 'the self has become the main form of reality' with the result that:

> *... the yearning for community, while real and strong, is being overwhelmed by the self-seeking of individualism and self-interest that is exacerbated by the current political and economic emphasis on privatization ... as a result the last 20 years have seen a pronounced trend toward the dismantling of public administration and an overt rejection of the idea of the public interest.*[8]

This strong, but ultimately debilitating, strain of American individualism, Lane argues, 'flows directly out of the political theories of John Locke' and is enshrined in the Constitution of the United States. The framing of this Constitution may be viewed:

> *... as an exercise in compromise and expediency marked by young, ambitious men setting out to create a vigorous, large commercial empire. Notions of freedom, equality of opportunity, and the sanctity of property all contribute to the model of American economic man, contending for gain and individual aggrandizement, and defining the public interest in terms of a system that maximizes opportunity for self-interest.*[9]

The catalogue of environmental ills presented in Chapter 1 indicates the ecological consequences of industrial policies in which expressive individualism is constrained, whether by utilitarian individualism or by what might be called utilitarian collectivism. The extreme cases of these latter approaches to politics in modern societies are, respectively, the US and the Communist states. The ruin of Communism has been caused by ecological as well as economic and ideological disaster: Communism is now a proven case of unsustainable industrial development. However, as we noted in Chapter 2, there is a serious risk that many will see the failure of Communist models for industrial society as evidence of the desirability of the utilitarian individualist model of liberal capitalism. While American-style capitalism has proved itself more efficient by far, it also runs grave ecological risks through favouring minimal restraint on individual choices in the market.

In order to increase understanding of the problems for environmental management posed by this style of economic development and political thinking, it is useful to look back at the origins of present ideas about the relationship between state and individual. Key themes in Western political thought on this issue are:

- the idea of the secular state, divorced from other institutions such as the Church, in the writings of Machiavelli;

- the need for the state to regulate individual behaviour and the possibility for what Thomas Hobbes calls the 'achievements of civilization' to arise out of this control;
- the importance of individual freedom, and the right to refashion the state to serve new ends, based on the voluntary consent of the governed, from John Locke;
- a distinction between the individual, acting in self-interest, and the citizen who sees his interests served by the pursuit of the common good – that is, the civilizing effect of civil society, from Jean Jacques Rousseau;
- the importance of the use of information by private entrepreneurs, which is the 'guiding hand' of capitalism as first perceived by Adam Smith;
- the use of the utilitarian principle as the sole ethical element in social and economic policy, as expounded by Jeremy Bentham;
- the important perception that liberal democratic capitalism needs to be continuously reformed on an incremental basis, as argued by John Stuart Mill;
- the neo-conservative arguments of Friedrich Hayek and others, which restate the key ideas of classic liberalism; and
- a critique of those arguments based on the need for sustainable development.

These themes are elaborated below.

The emergence of the secular state

The long drawn-out transformation of the feudal order in Europe gave rise to the development of secular politics and modern sciences as autonomous bodies of doctrine and research, no longer dominated by either religious beliefs and church power or the norms of traditional hierarchies. The first important exponent of secular politics was Machiavelli, writing in the early 16th century. The emergence of the concept of the state in Western political philosophy can be traced back to Machiavelli's *il stato* in his study of political management, *The Prince*.

Machiavelli's stress on the importance of the stability of the secular state is a recurring theme and still of major interest in political science. It arose from his concern to escape the conditions of uncertainty which characterized the feudal period in Italy. Machiavelli was also the first political philosopher to argue *raison d'etat* as an explanation and defence of political action, in which the common good ceased to be linked to God, but became associated instead with the interests of the state. Only after Machiavelli did the concept of the state become a central object of political philosophy. It is important to note here also that, in escaping from the confines of Church dogma, Machiavelli downgraded notions of morality in state affairs: the self-interest of the state becomes the sole criterion for decision-making.

Conceptions of state control

In the century after Machiavelli, England was also confronted by instability and civil strife, both religious, between Roman Catholics and the new Protestants, and between the landed aristocracy and a rising middle class. The result was civil war. This situation drove Hobbes, in *Leviathan*, to examine the failure of sovereign authority in England. The war, in his view, represented a regression to the natural condition of man outside of the bounds of civil society.[10]

In Hobbes' writing can be found an emphasis on a secular, stable state, a Leviathan, governed by a sovereign power as inevitably better than the anarchic condition of natural, individualistic man. The actions of individuals created the state, and subsequent law and justice were created by the sovereign who secured the state and who was implicitly obeyed by the individual members. The motive of this, as Hobbes put it, '... is the foresight of their own preservation, and of a more contented life thereby, that is to say, of getting out of the miserable condition of war, which is necessarily consequent to the natural passions of men'.

The state, in Hobbes' view, made possible the achievements of civilization, and was constituted by social contract which, once entered into voluntarily by individuals, becomes a compulsory association wherein:

> *Every man should say to every man, 'I authorise and give up my right to govern myself to this man, or this assembly of men, on this condition, that you give up thy right to him' and this done, the multitude so united in one person is called a Commonwealth.*[11]

Here Hobbes recognizes and institutionalizes the state's right to regulate individual behaviour for the general good. In this way a political power is created in the form of a strong secular state, pre-eminent in political and social life, and absolutely necessary because of the deleterious, self-seeking nature of individuals' behaviour and patterns of interaction.[12] Civilization is impossible without this regulation and the option to do away with it is not available once the contract is made.

In Hobbes' work we find the first conception of the state as the willing amalgamation of the interest of individuals. It may be ruled subsequently in a top-down manner, but it arises from the consent of the governed. Hobbes also provides a rationale for state intervention from a conception of a greater good to be had from regulation of individual behaviour. Hobbes' views, in other words, both substantiate environmental control by government and the pursuit, by state action, of what he called 'the achievements of civilization', one of which now would certainly have to be sustainable development.

Voluntary consent

John Locke's reaction to the English Civil War was different. In *Second Treatise*, a reply to Hobbes, he stressed the role of consent as the basis of all political power in the form of a voluntary, rather than a compulsory, contract between governor and governed. In Locke's view, men are free, equal and rational in nature and need not submit to any arbitrary or absolute power. The instability of England was due to the exercise of arbitrary power by the monarchy, which engendered a natural rebellious reaction. The rulers of England, the embodiment of the state, had damaged their contractual relationship with the governed by taxing without consent, by creating armies and by limiting the religious liberties of the citizenry.[13] Man had natural rights, including life, liberty and property, and these could not be abrogated by the state. A state of nature, which was a state of liberty rather than Hobbes' state of licence, was preferable to bad government, and good government was created by a social contract to assist peaceful living and to protect property.

In Locke's work, government is seen as a contract based on the consent of the governed, to be dissolved or altered when it no longer served its purpose of safeguarding the right to life, liberty and property. This state was not only temporary but limited, and had to be prevented from suppressing natural rights by constitutional limits on the extent of its authority. Government was by consent, and consent could be revoked by individuals and the government thereby changed. In Locke's view the creation of government is a burden that individuals have to bear to secure their ends. While the state exists to safeguard the rights and liberties of citizens, it must generally be restricted in scope and constrained in practice to ensure individual freedom.[14]

Locke's views on the danger of arbitrary or absolute power of the state were reinforced by his view, set out in the *Essay Concerning Human Understanding*, that the acquisition of human knowledge was constrained by the inherent limitations in our ability to perceive reality. In the face of our limited knowledge, tolerance and a degree of scepticism about the ability of the state to govern were called for.

In Hobbes and Locke we find two important themes in modern thinking on the state: conservatism in its original conception and the beginning of liberalism. In Lockean ideas, which retain considerable influence today, we find the origins of liberal thought which was taken to America and which emphasized the right to liberty and the right to revolt against arbitrary authority. Here are the intellectual roots of the revolutions to come in France and America, in support of the varieties of secular liberalism and against conservatism in the form of monarchy. With Locke we see the origin of the main philosophical arguments for the liberal democratic state, not based on any beliefs about the intrinsic nature of the state, but because of a modern conception of a man's rights.

This raises a basic question about the idea of sustainable development: can private rights, inviolable by the state, include environmentally damaging actions or actions with environmentally damaging by-products? The former presents us with little difficulty, but the latter case encompasses many areas of human action that may need to be brought under government control in future. For example, many people the world over consider the use of a car as the sine qua non of a modern lifestyle. In the US, one worker in seven owes his or her job to the car industry. In many lower income countries, the car is held to be a symbol of modernity, so much so that alternative, cleaner but 'old-fashioned' forms of transport are abandoned or outlawed – for example, bicycles from main roads in Shanghai, bicycle rickshaws from the centre of New Delhi and Jakarta, or donkey carts in Cairo. But given the energy consumption and environmental and social damage caused by the car, how do we balance conflicting rights? What does it mean to say that rights are inviolable? And who decides? A polluting majority or an environmentally conscious minority? Such issues must increasingly come to the fore as we move towards environmental control policies which are intended to have a more than marginal effect.

The idea of self-government

The already evolving tension between the idea of a common good promoted by the state versus the need for individual freedom from state control was approached from a new direction by the French philosopher Jean Jacques Rousseau. He provides a counterpoint to the evolving notions of Lockean liberal democracy by contrasting the natural man, who is whole but concerned solely with himself, with the citizen, who understands his good to be identical to the common good.

In his book *Emile*, Rousseau attempts to reconcile man's selfish nature with the demands of civil society. He emphasizes that the passion of selfishness is changed by the very experience of living in a stable society. Man is not virtuous in a state of nature; virtue only comes about in a society based on law and the unselfish virtues can increase with time. In *The Social Contract*, Rousseau argues that such civic virtue is ensured by the development of what he calls a 'civil religion' inculcated by the sovereign. The dogma of Rousseau's civil religion includes tolerance, sanctity of the social contract and respect for the law. We can think of Rousseau's civil religion as an appropriate value system, nurtured by government.

However, Rousseau was unhappy with the existing ideas of social contract and he therefore proposed a more utopian arrangement: a system of self-government in a direct democracy in which all citizens would be actively involved in the process of government rather than simply voting periodically for a representative to take decisions. Here the idea of self-government is posited as an end in itself and a political order is proposed in which the affairs of the state are integrated into the affairs of ordinary citizens.[15] There are many proposals in current environmentalist writing for such 'direct democracy'.

The legitimate authority of the state in Rousseau's conception is based on 'the common good embodied in the general will', which takes precedence over individual will. The general will cannot be developed by a divisive, selfish, class-structured society, but only by a one-class society of working proprietors, and such a society was to be achieved by government action:

> *It is therefore one of the most important functions of government to prevent extreme inequality of fortunes; not by taking away wealth, but by depriving all men of the right to accumulate it; not by building hospitals for the poor, but by securing citizens from becoming poor.*[16]

Rousseau also begins to consider the difference between simple majority rule and the desirability of working towards consensus on difficult issues. He argues that two rules are applicable:

> *One, that the more important and serious the deliberations, the closer the winning opinion should be to unanimity. The other, that the more speed the business at hand requires, the smaller the prescribed difference in the division of opinion should be. In deliberations that must be finished on the spot, a majority of a single vote should suffice.*[17]

In Rousseau we find the origins of important ideas in modern political thinking, particularly in the areas of participation and equality. Rousseau has been claimed as an antecedent by many utopian thinkers for his emphasis on direct citizen participation. This foreshadows an important theme in modern thinking on community development and planning – namely, the focus on the value of 'bottom-up' efforts by citizens to take control of their own lives. It is not surprising, therefore, to find aspects of Rousseau's philosophy in many contemporary Western ideologies, for he went well beyond the visible manifestations of the state to consider psychological and moral aspects of human endeavour and organization. For example, the idea of a civil religion that encourages an unselfish civic virtue which can increase over time is close in many ways to the idea of an evolving, less materialistic value system which can encourage an ecological ethic in our time. Rousseau sees a role here for the state in inculcating such civic virtue, just as many environmentalists may argue that the state has a role, through education, to promote a more sustainable society.

Liberalism: the philosophy of capitalism

Adam Smith was the economic philosopher of the emerging liberalism of the 18th century and his theory of entrepreneurial decision-making set out in *The Wealth of Nations* (1776) is at the heart of classical economics. Smith's main argument was that the free, decentralized action of economic agents in a system of competition and private property brings individual advantage and a common good, which is defined as the aggregation of individual wealth. The result of these thousands of decisions is not chaos but an underlying, orderly process – the 'invisible hand' of capitalism – and maximum efficiency in the allocation of societal resources.

At the time, Smith's economics were radical, in so far as they proposed limitations on sovereign power in deference to market operations, with the benefits accruing to the emerging bourgeoisie rather than solely to the mercantilist class. Smith emphasized the importance of the production of wealth and the abolition of special privilege. Beyond this, the hidden hand of *laissez-faire* economics would bring maximum utility to the most people and national wealth in the aggregation of individual wealth. In *The Wealth of Nations*, Smith compiled examples of government mismanagement under the mercantilist system, and then argued that markets alone could assemble and convey essential information about scarcity and value, and therefore must be left alone to allocate resources.[18]

The essential problem of liberalism, as Smith saw it, was to develop a political system that would produce governments that would nurture a free market society and protect citizens from the natural tendency of the self-same government to exert social control. Freedom in both political and economic spheres was essential. In the economic sphere, all must be free to engage in business, and those who benefit themselves are taken to benefit the nation as a whole. The government was not to interfere in the workings of this natural economic system. But Smith also spelled out a positive, if strictly limited, role for governments which included the protection of the rights of private property.

In summary, the essential ideas of liberalism are that:

- all economic phenomena are connected and interdependent;
- free competition is what makes production and exchange most advantageous for everyone;
- economic freedom is the condition of prosperity and growth; and
- intervention by the state generally produces effects opposite to those it intends to pursue.

Smith's invisible hand would probably have continued to work well had the economic conditions of the 18th century continued to hold. But the burgeoning Industrial Revolution had three effects which substantially altered the ability of the market to allocate resources effectively: the emergence of a growing industrial proletariat; accelerating scientific and technological development, which continually increased the dominance of humankind over nature; and growing functional interdependence between private and public sectors.[19] The growth of the urban proletariat instigated a necessary shift from the limited variety of liberalism known in the 18th century to the kind of liberal democracy which exists in the West today. This is discussed immediately below, while the other two effects of the Industrial Revolution are discussed in the conclusion of the chapter.

Utilitarianism and the rise of liberal democracy

The evolution from liberalism to liberal democracy initiates an important theme in Western political ideas. This democratizing of liberalism began with the rise of utilitarian philosophy in the early 19th century, and particularly in the work of Jeremy Bentham (1748–1832). Bentham's conception of the functions of utilitarian government were even more limited than Smith's, not extending beyond the maintenance of security and property and the promotion of a free market economy in which utilitarian principles could promote the greatest good for the most people.

The significance of Bentham's utilitarian philosophy lay in his rejection of a moral dimension in the social calculus of capitalist, industrial society. Utilitarianism, in arguing that the good of all could only be achieved by self-regarding individualism and the pursuit of wealth, removed the need for lingering doubt about the consequences of exploitation. The utilitarian framework provided a moral exemption from consideration of the negative effects of industrialism by asserting that whatever served the individual served society.

Although the obviously harmful social and environmental consequences of industrialism quickly tempered utilitarian thought in the late 19th century in Western countries, it returned in the 1980s in the guise of 'yuppyism', by which the unbridled pursuit of wealth and ostentatious consumption were sanctioned by neo-liberal politics in much of the West.

Socially responsible capitalism

The issue of how to deal with environmental and social problems within the confines of liberal capitalism was addressed by the Victorian philosopher–economist John Stuart Mill. With his idea of a reformist, socially responsible, yet essentially liberal, capitalism, Mill provided a rationale for the modern state of a type which governs in most Western countries. It is this tradition, of incremental adjustment and reform within liberal capitalism, which is the emerging model the world over.

Unlike the 19th-century Utopians or the Marxists, utilitarians such as Bentham had no vision of a future society because, for them, liberal, 19th-century capitalism was the correct model of society. All that was required was democratic government with periodic elections, a free market and minimal state interference beyond ensuring the security of property. But two facts about life in the mid-19th century demanded new thinking. One was that the working class was acquiring new political power and might therefore be dangerous to property-holders. The other was that the environmental and social conditions of the working class were so self-evidently bad that some liberals felt that the situation was morally unjustifiable and that action must be taken.

Mill saw the liberal democratic state as a means to improve mankind (without having to change the nature of the state) and that democratic politics could be a mechanism of moral development.[20] Mill felt that the income inequality of capitalism was unjustifiable, but that the fault lay, not with capitalism itself, but in its lingering feudal origins. Mill and others therefore inspired a series of incremental social reforms which had the effect of greatly reducing class conflict in Britain and other industrial countries.[21] At this time the Western state assumed its first overtly environmental role in social legislation and in public health. As a result, real incomes, along with housing and environmental conditions, improved dramatically in the late 19th century. Mill's enduring legacy is not in his economic analysis, but in his advocacy of reforming liberal democracy within the capitalist system. As we will see in Chapter 6, Mill also put forward powerful arguments for the decentralization of decision-making in the modern state.

The 20th-century state: a condition of conflict

Mill's liberal vision was extended and challenged by social democratic and socialist ideas on the control of market forces. Proponents of a strong regulatory role for the state argued that the evils of society are due primarily to the unregulated working of the institutions of private property and that unjustifiable inequalities of wealth and opportunity should be removed, and industry organized to promote social ends, by nationalization where necessary.[22] This conception of the state usually resulted in a commitment to guarantee a minimum standard of living for the poor, a Keynesian macroeconomic role for the state in fiscal policy and a considerable measure of state intervention in industry. Social democracy provided a constructive and useful outlet for radical social ideas and advanced social reforms, without commitment to a revolutionary party or to a dogmatic ideology.[23]

Liberal capitalism was thus transformed in the 20th century in many Western countries into welfare capitalism, in which government is expected to secure employment, to stabilize income and to provide social housing and medical benefits for those at the margins of the capitalist system. Following Mill, the role of participation in democracy, particularly concern about the nature of pluralism, became a focus of political philosophy. Centralized, professional administration may be inescapable in the modern state owing to the complexity of the administrative task, and the power of the bureaucracy is best countered by strong political institutions such as Parliament and the party system. In the absence of these representative political institutions or in socialist states, the bureaucracy would elevate itself into a unitary state bureaucracy and replace pluralist public and private bureaucracies, and the checks and balances, of the liberal state.

More recent thinking on pluralism is characterized by the view that power is distributed among a range of competing interest groups and that these groups attempt to influence political decisions by exacting whatever leverage they may have over the working of the system in a continuing process of bargaining. In this way the democratic nature of the liberal state is ensured by the working of this pluralist system of conflict and negotiation over values.

In Chapter 8 we argue:

1 that new networks involving civil society not only counter the power of the state, but can contribute substantially to the goals of environmental management; and
2 that the typical situation of conflict over social objectives in the democratic state can be 'managed' in a positive manner to contribute to sustainable development.

However, the parallel institutionalization of pluralist and competitive civic life, which is presupposed in Western democracy, may be more difficult beyond the West as the idea of beneficial conflict is not readily translated to many non-Western cultures. The religions of East Asia, for example, are imbued with a more holistic conception of human society in which harmony and solidarity are set above competition.[24]

Modern neo-conservatism

In the West, the post-war consensus on the usefulness of state intervention lasted in the US through Kennedy and Johnson's Great Society programme in the late 1960s, and in a slightly more entrenched fashion in Canada, New Zealand, Australia and Europe to the 1970s and early 1980s. The consensus, based as it was on expanding economies, low inflation and full employment, was broken by the post-1973 oil crisis and recession. By the late 1970s there was growing discord and confusion about the appropriate role of the state and its relation to economic well-being.

The economic and political developments of the 1970s and 1980s provided an opportunity for neo-conservative theorists to mount this 'market friendly' critique of the state which continues to be influential through the 1990s:

> *Social welfare derives from individual satisfaction. Most individuals, most of the time, understand their own preferences and how to choose in their own interest. The state should allow individuals to advance their own welfare according to their own lights rather than enforcing on them some vision of the good life.*[25]

This argument is a restatement of the views of Smith and Bentham. There are many variations on the neo-conservative position. However, Hayek has probably had the most longstanding influence on thinking about the state's role in the management of national economies and the working of government. Since the publication of *The Road to Serfdom* in 1944, Hayek was a foe of 'planning' in its various guises and is therefore worthy of some attention.[26]

Hayek's arguments restate the Smithian proposition that the impossibility of adequate information for planning in an uncertain world provides a central argument for the market against the state. In *The Road to Serfdom* he argues that planners working for the state, however well intentioned, are bound to lessen total welfare in society. This is because the socioeconomic world is marked by extreme complexity and planners can never hope to understand it in its totality. When they try to form policy options based on what must be incomplete information and lack of relevant facts, the result will be costly economically, freedom will be limited, and overall welfare will decline. Conversely, the market, made up as it is of numerous small decision-makers, does not pretend to have complete knowledge and because it need only be concerned with market-specific information, it can engage in self-correction. The predisposition towards the overburdening of government in the welfare state underlines the benefits of the minimal state, in which individuals are the best judge of their own welfare.

However, in Hayek's argument, tendencies towards anarchy also must be resisted by a framework for law and order that defends property rights. So the state cannot be extinguished: liberty and economic freedom require the state as 'nightwatchman' to guarantee the ability to enjoy property and to exercise consumer choice. Although property rights must be protected by law, the minimal principle of state interference extends to taxation (except for law and order, and defence of the sovereign state), which is the primary instrument for redistribution of income or wealth. Minimalness – that is, liberty – is incompatible in this conception with income redistribution.

In particular, a target for neo-conservative criticism was provided by the many obvious problems associated with an interventionist state after the recession of the mid-1970s. These included the growing cost of welfare provision and a concern that this cost is a drag on economic growth, which is usually accorded the highest priority in domestic affairs of the state. Another problem, given the tendency for interventionist states to centralize services and to redistribute income between socioeconomic groups and between regions, was that large administrative bureaucracies had been created. These, so the argument goes, lack market discipline and accountability and are therefore inefficient. A related argument is that the administrative system of the welfare state simply does not work very well because of turbulence in national and world economic systems. In other words, government is unable to predict the unforeseen changes and unintended consequences of policy intervention on individuals, families or institutions. Government, with unresponsive bureaucracies, lacks the market's quick feedback mechanisms and responses and wastes funds in pursuing its aims.

In general the neo-conservative view of the conjecture of politics and economics represents a fusion of libertarian value judgements and an analysis of the market as an instrument of policy. The market is taken to be the best means for attaining libertarian, individualistic or utilitarian objectives, and the role of the state in society is severely curtailed.

Whatever the merits of past forms of state intervention, what is important for our purposes is that there has been a substantial change in attitude towards the state. This neo-conservative ideology is unsympathetic to traditional notions of state planning that appear to infringe on economic liberty and an expanded role for the state is no longer viewed as an objective in any country. Unfortunately, just when sustainable development clearly requires sophisticated intersectoral planning, the baby of planning is being thrown out with the bathwater of state control of the economy. In Chapter 8 we demonstrate why the needs of a consensus-building approach to sustainable development suggest neither a minimal nor a maximal role for the state, but an *enabling* role.

Sustainable development and social relations

Since the time of Adam Smith, the liberal and recent neo-conservative arguments remained remarkably consistent and rather simplistic: the market provides a socially optimal allocation of resources and therefore maximizes social benefit. While this is a powerful argument at what we have called in Chapter 2 the social level of the market, there are aspects of modern industrial societies that undermine this dogma. One is the accelerating scientific and technical development that has enabled humankind to dominate nature and which has broadened the scope of the human manipulation of natural resources. This presents two problems.

First, the market-is-optimal situation only held when population and pressure on resources were much smaller. The social costs involved in the private use of collective unpriced resources, such as air, water, the highways etc, were much less when their unused portions were substantial relative to those used in production, but they constitute an inherently rising proportion of conventionally measured GDP as they cease to be 'free' goods.[27] Pricing is then called for to regulate their use, but such pricing will not spring up naturally under *laissez-faire* systems.

Second, the increasing domination of nature by humankind has opened up an increasing range of feasible options in any given situation, which means more and more decisions are likely to be controversial or, in other words, political. The very success of the capitalist system, working at the level of the market, reinforces the need for a higher order body to mediate among feasible options. This has invariably reinforced the role of the state and widened the range of political argument.[28]

Another effect of industrialism is increasing specialization in social functions. This has a double effect. It creates a higher degree of efficiency in pursuing objectives, but also increases the degree of interdependence among individuals and organizations. This means that the likelihood and range of unanticipated disturbances also increases. The binary model of regulating social regulations by individual contracts is no longer complex enough for the degree of social interdependence in the system.

In Chapter 8, drawing on the literature of organization theory, we will define the situation created by interdependencies as 'turbulence' and we will define the characteristics of the turbulent environment. The appropriate response to turbulence, we will argue, is interactive and flexible management by participatory networks. Here, for the purposes of this chapter, the interaction is between the state and the society, and what is important is neither the state alone, nor individuals alone or in groups (civil society), but the productive relations between them – that is, the quality of the overall society itself.

What are some of the characteristics of a high quality society? One is a sense of society as more than either a collection of individuals or an impersonal structure:

> *Society is an instrument for transacting business, an insensitive bureaucratic beast that frustrates our quest for meaning. But ultimately it must be viewed as a mode of man's spiritual being. The social contract by which we are bound is cooperative by its very nature; it is only an acknowledgement of our belonging to a larger scheme of things called the cosmos.*[29]

A second factor is the need for some new relationship between state and society in the economic sphere, neither centralized planning nor *laissez-faire*. This approach recognizes the importance of the market for microeconomic decisions, but also the necessity of government intervention to assist in the process of deriving goals and objectives for a sustainable society, and for controlling externalities by incentive or regulation. It would not deny the necessity for societies to act as a whole through their political processes to realize aspirations beyond the capabilities of market economics.

A third factor is the need for what Bell calls 'a return to civil society', defined as 'a return to a manageable scale of social life, particularly where the national economy has become embedded in an international frame and the national polity has lost some of its independence'.[30] This emphasizes NGOs and voluntary associations working at the community and regional levels to balance the increasing centralization of power in the international economy, and the draining of initiative and control away from localities. A counterbalancing force is required, not only to fulfil reasonable ideals of democratic participation, but as the only course open for the realization of sustainable development. What is required are genuine, workable mechanisms for 'thinking globally and acting locally'.

In addition to generating local, knowledgeable and committed action, civil society plays at least two important roles. The first is that participation can nurture civic spirit, which is defined as 'the presence and authority of a moral conscientiousness, which binds a man to his contractual and other obligations, without needing to be underwritten by a torrid network of ritually reinforced social links'.[31] The self-regulating actions of civil society, buttressed by civic spirit, can reduce the need for state action in environmental management without lessening the quality of the society.

It is also the case that democratic procedures, combined with knowledge about environmental issues provided by uncensored and conscientious media, are well suited to the task of monitoring and controlling high-risk, complex technologies. Democratic procedures invite dispute, create dissatisfactions and stir citizens to anger. Democratic procedures, with public service media, are:

> *essential correctives to the wishful (Hayekian) belief in the decentralized anonymity of the market as a superior self-correcting mechanism in a world of complex pressures and interconnections. They are also important correctives to the mistaken trust in the therapeutic powers of unbridled technical expertise.*[32]

Conclusion

This chapter began by looking at a classic and long-standing dichotomy in Western politics between individual freedom and the idea of social control by the state for the common good. However, this bipolar perspective is too simplistic to account for complex relationships in an industrialized, Westernized world. Re-emerging notions of civil society, not simply defined as non-governmental bodies, but a more potent interaction of individuals, government, NGOs and business, offer a clue to new directions for the state and other organizations involved in sustainable development. Before moving on in the new direction, we need to understand more about the complex economic world that has developed in the post-war period and its environmental dimension. This is the subject of Part III.

Part III

Global Integration and Local Democracy

Introduction

This section turns to the present organization of world business and finance, the emerging global culture of industrial consumption and consumerism, and the implications of these for sustainable development.

Chapter 5 examines the main elements of the international economic system as it has developed since 1945 and its environmental dimension. The post-war years have seen an unprecedented growth in production and world trade, the growing integration of economies and the development of a culture of consumerism in the West. The process of 'globalization' is now taking industrialism, in a 'top-down' process, to all corners of the world, and Western consumption patterns are being emulated in the developing world and the ex-Communist countries wherever possible.

Despite the material success of the capitalist industrial model, however, the global economic order has severe impacts on the environment: the great inequalities between the high- and low-income countries, as exemplified in the Third World debt crisis, contribute massively to environmental degradation. The culture of consumerism in the West also degrades the environment and we consider how it may be reaching social as well as ecological limits to growth. Chapter 5 examines the problems of the integration of environmental management and sustainable development in the key policy areas of the global economy: the trade framework, development aid, developing countries' debt, technology transfer and the role of the transnational corporations.

In Chapter 6, these 'top-down' global economic arrangements and trends to international integration are contrasted with growing demands for 'bottom-up' local participation, both to fulfil democratic aspirations and for effectiveness in policy and implementation. This endemic tension between the powerful trend toward specialization and integration which characterizes the modern industrial system, and aspirations for the local control of social, economic and environmental forces, is likely to be increasingly relevant to concerns about sustainable development. Chapter 6 examines the main forces behind the demand for centralization and international integration on the one hand and that for decentralization on the other. In many cases, the very nature of environmental problems requires action on a local or regional basis, albeit within national and international contexts. Unfortunately, the trend to centralization is powerful and it is difficult to turn to the real world for examples of genuine political decentralization in pursuit of sustainable development at the scale of the region, often the appropriate level for carrying out environmental management tasks. The chapter analyses a 'new decentralist' approach to regional control for sustainable development and the powerful obstacles to its realization.

5

The Global Economy: Interdependence, Inequality and the Environment

I meant no harm. I most truly did not.
But I had to grow bigger. So bigger I got.
I biggered my factory. I biggered my roads.
I biggered my wagons. I biggered the loads.
Of the Thneeds I shipped out. I was shipping them forth.
To the South! To the East! To the West! To the North!
I went right on biggering ... selling more Thneeds.
And I biggered my money, which everyone needs.

Dr Seuss[1]

Capitalism has shocked its critics before with its ability to adapt to, and even thrive under, challenging new conditions. It may be that tomorrow holds wave after wave of green technological breakthroughs, a planetary New Deal, a revolution of values, massive ecological restorations, enlightened and effective forms of global government... We do not know. What we do know, or should, is that none of this will happen by itself.

Tom Athanasiou[2]

I've seen the best minds of my generation destroyed by capitalism / no longer starving, hysterical, naked, / but portly, Prozac-fed, Armani-clad, / dragging themselves through neon shopping malls at / dawn looking for a cashflow fix... WHO know in their hearts of this hellshock, yes, these / best minds of my generation, who control and mould the / global brainbox and cannot bear to recognise the most / obvious connections between what they do / and don't do / and the destiny of this toxic orb.

Richard Neville[3]

The fall of the Berlin Wall and the collapse of Communism did not simply spread democracy and transform international relations. This transformation also removed the last great barrier to the global spread of capitalism, which had already made significant inroads in the developing world and parts of the Soviet bloc during the 1980s. The final decade of the century saw a disorienting, spectacular acceleration in economic change and technical innovation, both promising new tools for sustainable development and threatening the ecological and social foundations of many states. This chapter considers features of the global industrial economy that contribute to environmental degradation and social turmoil, and those that can play a key role in overcoming them. In particular we examine the trend described as 'globalization' or 'integration' in the international economic system. This encompasses a number of the developments of the post-1945 period that have accelerated and intensified in recent years: the global spread of industrial production; the development of intricate linkages between national economies through the growth in trade and developments in communications and transport; and the global reach, through mass media, of images of Western consumer culture.

Integration has so far largely been a feature of the development of the 'higher income' countries (defined as those with membership of the OECD), whose interdependence through trade, technology transfer and communications has increased steadily. Massive inequalities in the world economy persist between the higher and lower income countries, and there are huge divergences between and within the lower income countries themselves. It seems that neither the spread of the industrial system as we have known it in the OECD countries, nor the structural inequalities between rich and poor in the international economy, can be reconciled with sustainable development. Thus it is important to examine the global economic order and consider the changes in its design and direction that will be needed to realize sustainable development.

Towards the Global Industrial Economy

The nature of 'globalization'

It is by now a commonplace to note that national economies are becoming more interdependent and that there has been a 'globalization' of markets and of industrial production. The process is far from new: we are in the midst of an intensification of trends originating in the Western colonization of much of the globe and in the Industrial Revolution, whereby more and more countries have been brought into trading networks as producers and consumers of goods on an industrial scale.[4] The global spread of industrial systems means that there is no prospect for any nation state of 'insulating' itself from changes in the economic climate, from major pollution flows and from the policies of international actors such as the transnational corporations (TNCs). As TNCs develop, there is an increasing flow of managerial and specialist personnel across frontiers; as more and more countries industrialize, so international pollution flows increase; and the development of computerized communications networks has created global flows of information and capital that ignore frontiers, making it virtually impossible for developing countries to resist pressures to follow Western development paths.

Globalization is a multistranded phenomenon: it encompasses cultural and political trends as well as economic processes which together form a dynamic complex of issues which pose major challenges for policy-makers everywhere:

- A reduction, to varying degrees, in the capacity and will of national governments to influence TNCs.
- Faster innovation and transfers of technology, ideas and products by companies via international networks of supply chains, the Internet and investment links.
- An increase in the *potential* ability of more 'mobile' corporations to exert pressure on states to grant tax concessions and other concessions over regulation, by threat-

ening to move investment elsewhere and by breaking ties of loyalty to their 'home' states.
- The global reach and influence of television, advertising and media companies, made easier and more powerful by new communications and information technologies.
- The extension of neo-liberal policy on free trade via the World Trade Organization (WTO), supported by the 'structural adjustment' strategies imposed on indebted developing countries by the International Monetary Fund (IMF) and the World Bank, leading to a convergence on short-term economic policies which fail to take full account of longer term social and environmental costs.
- The spread of Western industrial production and consumption to much of the developing world, with real gains in living standards for many millions in countries such as India and China, but long-term pressures on the environment, local cultures and welfare systems.
- The exacerbation of deep inequalities between affluent nations and the poorest ones, and within many countries – rich, developing and very poor alike. In 1999, UN Development Programme research shows that the 225 richest people in the world had a combined wealth of over $1 trillion dollars, equivalent to the wealth of nearly half the world's poorest people. This grotesque imbalance in the distribution of wealth and power creates huge strains on social cohesion in many parts of the world, rich and poor.
- The end – for the time being – of Cold War confrontation and the consequent rise of civil conflicts and local confrontations between states which call for strengthened systems for conflict prevention and peace-keeping.
- The global spread of new technologies with potentially massive impacts for good and ill on the environment and economy – for example, technologies for genetic modification of crops.

Perhaps most significantly, the spread of industrial production and consumption across the globe has boosted the policy-making power and influence of the transnational corporations and of international institutions. Some TNCs now outweigh whole states in terms of GDP and policy leverage: they constitute 'virtual nations', as the environmentalist Tom Burke has argued, which do not operate within a system of global law as nation-states do.[5] The institutions of global governance discussed below – the UN, the WTO, the IMF, the World Bank, and so on – have gained in responsibilities and influence, but lack the resources, democratic legitimation and framework of powers to match up to the realities of globalization. There is no global competition policy and no global environment agency to humanize the emerging global capitalist order. So far, we have relied on the voluntary commitments of the multinationals, the scrutiny and protests of NGOs, the policy frameworks of governments and the behind-closed-doors decisions of international agencies to develop a global economy that is compatible with democracy, social justice and environmental sustainability. As the UK's Secretary of State for International Development, Clare Short, has said:

> *The major issues of poverty, human rights and democracy will be shaped by the international institutions that we put in place. No nation state can control these forces. In order to manage globalisation equitably, we need to strengthen and shape the UN, the World Bank, the IMF, the World Trade*

> *Organization and other international institutions. There are massive distributive decisions to be made, but they will be controlled by how we shape our multilateral institutions, not by how we behave as individual nations… Global integration and interdependence are a reality… The challenge of our age is to manage this interdependence in a way that is equitable and environmentally sustainable, that maximises the benefits of interdependence and minimises its costs.*[6]

Globalization of industrialism is the dominant issue of contemporary politics and economics. It is bound up with problems of democratic accountability at the international level, of social cohesion and deep inequalities, and of developing strong international policy frameworks to regulate multinationals and improve the quality of our international agencies. Below we consider its key elements in more detail.

The last two decades of the 20th century saw a spectacular increase in international economic activity – and of turbulence in the globalizing economy. Much of this was a result of the liberalization of economic policy regimes in the West and of the spread of neo-liberal prescriptions for economic management around the developing world, processes that were begun in the 1980s. According to the Worldwatch Institute, gross world output of goods and services amounted to some US$20 trillion in 1990, up by $4.5 trillion from 1980; and international trade in products grew by 4 per cent a year on average in the 1980s. The Institute claims that 'growth in global economic output during the eighties was greater than that during the several thousand years from the beginning of civilization until 1950'.[7]

During the 1990s, the process went further but also began to generate turbulence and localized crises in economic management arising from the scale of financial flows and interdependence between economies which have accompanied the rise in trade and investment. Gross world product expanded from US$31.6 trillion in 1990 to over US$39 trillion in 1998, with global growth of over 4 per cent in 1997;[8] but growth rates were very uneven, with deep inequalities between the OECD world and the poorest developing countries, and extreme growth spurts in the most dynamic of the newly industrializing states contrasting with dramatic declines in industrial activity in Russia and other parts of the ex-Communist bloc. The decade saw new heights of trading and stock market values in the US, but also deep recession in the early 1990s in countries such as the UK, and the 1997 'contagion' crisis, as financial collapses in South East Asia created economic shock waves which were transmitted rapidly around the world trading system, eventually contributing to a massive financial crisis in Russia. By the end of the 1990s, no one could be in any doubt that globalization of capitalism was the dominant fact of political and economic life, and that as well as generating great wealth and innovation it was capable of destabilizing economies and wrecking ecosystems across the world.

The process of globalization is far from complete. The great expansion in world trade in the 1980s and 1990s was largely an increase in trade within the industrialized world, and hundreds of millions of people still live on the margin of the international industrial system. The advance of international trade and the growth of industrial competition for the West from developing countries – notably the so-called 'Asian Tiger' economies of East Asia – has so far had relatively few effects on employment structures in the advanced industrial economies, except in mature mass-manufacturing markets. The Western lifestyles made possible by industrial development are available to only a minority of the world's population. Moreover, the evolution of the economic system has outstripped that of international political cooperation and regulation, a fact that will surely dominate the politics of globalization in the early decades of the 21st century.

None the less, it is true that the industrialization of the lower income countries is proceeding apace; and that for nation states and individuals alike it is becoming impossible to 'opt out' of the global process of industrialization – modernity is a near-universal condition.

Actors in the global economy

The growing integration of the international economy has been assisted, promoted and challenged by numerous international institutions and structures. The main actors are described briefly below.

The International Monetary Fund (IMF)

The IMF, along with the World Bank and GATT (now the WTO – see below), was created in the aftermath of World War II as a result of the wartime allies' conference at Bretton Woods in 1944 on the post-war restructuring of the international economic system. The IMF is an agency endowed by subscriptions from member countries. The IMF has become a lender to member states and through this role it has become increasingly involved in efforts to restructure the economies of lower income countries. It still faces a critical task in helping the ex-Communist states of Eastern Europe and the former Soviet Union, and the new entrants to the global trading network in Africa, Latin America and parts of Asia, to adjust to a market-based system.

The World Bank

Originally the International Bank for Reconstruction and Development (IBRD), the World Bank was established to finance post-war reconstruction in Europe. This role was diminished by the implementation of the Marshall Plan and the Bank's focus shifted to Third World development. The Bank is a major lender to lower income countries. Much of its activity concerns rescheduling the crippling debt burdens built up by developing countries: by 1997 the external debt of all the developing countries was US$2.2 trillion, with US$269 billion paid in debt service in 1997, up from US$191 billion in 1990.[9] The roles of the World Bank and the IMF have become increasingly blurred in recent years: the agencies cooperate closely and hold a joint annual conference. Both have begun to modify their policies in the face of criticism from environmentalists and social justice campaigners, as we discuss later.

The World Trade Organization (WTO) – successor to the General Agreement on Tariffs and Trade (GATT)

The World Trade Organization (WTO) is the third element of the post-war international economic order. It is an inter-governmental forum for periodic rounds of negotiation aimed at reducing barriers to free international trade. The latest round was begun in 1986 in Uruguay and did not conclude as scheduled in late 1990 as a result of disagreements on agricultural subsidies. The Uruguay Round concluded in 1994 and established the WTO as a policing and dispute resolution agency. The WTO process has proceeded with further negotiation on dismantling national restraints on trade in services and on foreign direct investment (FDI). The WTO increasingly became a target for environmentalist and social justice campaign groups worldwide after the end of the Uruguay Round: its attempt to begin negotiations for a new round of liberalization talks at Seattle in December 1999 ended in violence and confusion as demonstrators disrupted the conference and poor preparation and deep-seated disagreements between the US, the European Union (EU) and the NICs stymied progress.

Transnational corporations (TNCs)
Also known as multinationals, the TNCs are a massively powerful force in the globalization of industrial production and consumption, and in the growth of world trade and manufacturing. They are also a key source of technological innovation. TNCs now account for at least 20 per cent of global production and over two-thirds of international trade. TNCs are discussed in more detail later.

International trading blocs
In the 1980s, as competition mounted between companies in the advanced industrial countries, and as competition increased in manufacturing sectors from newly industrializing countries (NICs), there was a move towards the development of regional trading blocs in the North. The aim is to provide larger markets for producers in member countries, to promote economies of scale and to stimulate growth. The most developed of these blocs is the European Union, which is completing its 'single market' for goods and services free of national trade barriers. The EU forms a 'common economic space' with the countries of the European Free Trade Association, establishing a free trade zone of some 400 million people, the world's largest. In 1992 the US, Canada and Mexico concluded a free trade agreement, establishing the basis for what could develop into a trade zone covering the Americas. The rapid growth of the Asian NICs has encouraged speculation that a Far Eastern bloc could emerge, led by Japan. Fears have been expressed that the development of blocs may promote protectionism and further disadvantage lower income countries in the world economic system.

Non-governmental organizations (NGOs)
The NGOs – covering charities, independent aid agencies, environmental activist bodies, Church organizations, trade unions and other bodies from 'civil society' beyond government and business – justify their inclusion as major actors in the global economy by virtue of their developing capacity to act in a coordinated fashion across sectors and across frontiers. NGOs have grown explosively in recent decades: by 1996 over 20,000 were active in three or more countries (up from under 1000 in 1956); and more than a million NGOs are said to be active in India alone.[10] NGOs in the environmental field have begun to form alliances not only with some enlightened corporations but also with social justice and anti-war NGOs, most notably in the campaign for debt relief, Jubilee 2000 (as discussed later). In the 1990s, campaigns initiated and led by NGOs began to have significant effects on global economic governance. NGOs were instrumental in sinking the planned Multilateral Agreement on Investment (MAI), as discussed later. They launched successful campaigns against planned activities by Shell and Monsanto, among other TNCs, and the campaign against Monsanto effectively led to the end of the company's independent existence and to a global debate on genetically modified foods. They played a major part in undermining the ill-prepared

WTO talks in Seattle in 1999. They also mounted a sustained critique of the World Bank, the IMF and the WTO, undeniably influencing the terms of debate and strategic thinking in those bodies. By the end of the 1990s, NGOs were becoming a sought-after partner for TNCs and governments in conferring the stamp of social and environmental legitimacy on their policies and products, by virtue of the high levels of public trust commanded by NGOs compared to corporations and governments. At the same time, their very success was drawing attention to their lack of accountability and transparency, and scrutiny of NGOs' performance seems bound to increase as their influence grows.

Trends in the international economy

The developing role of the actors described above has been crucial in recent years in the main structural trends in the international economy. The spread of industrial development throughout the world means that broad secular trends observed in the evolution of the advanced industrial countries begin to emerge also in some lower income countries as they industrialize. These include a diminishing contribution to GDP of agriculture as the importance of manufacturing grows, and the rising share in GDP and total employment of the service sector, as manufacturing industry matures and income levels rise among the population.[11]

There is increasing competition for the advanced industrial economies in agricultural products and mature manufacturing sectors from a number of newly industrializing countries. This demands a shift in the higher income economies towards areas in which they can achieve comparative advantage, such as high technology manufacturing, technology-based services and other high value-added activities. In turn, the NICs of the 'first generation', such as Taiwan and South Korea, already face growing competition in low-tech manufacturing as more countries build up their manufacturing capacity. Increasing competition generates pressure for protectionist policies to safeguard jobs and key companies as countries attempt to restructure sectors in which they have lost comparative advantage.

National economies become increasingly interdependent through trade between and within corporations. In the period 1960–80 international trade grew faster than output, with the result that imports rose as a proportion of GDP in the advanced industrial countries. Thus far, integration through trade has been largely confined to the industrialized world: two-thirds of world trade is accounted for by TNCs and much of this is taken up by trade within these corporations' operating divisions. However, the NICs will enter progressively more fully into the world of the advanced industrial economies, and already the more advanced of the NICs are fully exposed to the globalizing culture of consumer brands and advertising. Private investment flows from North to South grew from US$5 billion in 1970 to over US$100 billion in 1992. And by 1997 net private capital flow into Latin America and the Caribbean region alone was worth nearly US$120 billion.[12]

The development of a massive international currency market following the end of the post-war system of fixed exchange rates has brought further integration of the higher income countries' economies and investing institutions. The flow of savings today is global in scale, and intermediaries handling savings for investors use computer systems that switch funds from place to place in an instant. Transactions in foreign exchange by the end of the 1990s amounted to some US$1.5 trillion a day.[13]

The new world of international capital flowing through computer systems and telecommunications networks is the most striking example of global economic integration. The interdependence it produces was demonstrated by the near-simultaneous crash of securities markets around the world on 19 October 1987, and by the 1997–98 'contagion' as the effects of financial crises in East Asia rippled around the world and damaged investment and growth prospects in Latin America and Russia. This 'virtual' system is to all intents decoupled from the 'real' economy of material goods and production which it both finances and destabilizes: foreign exchange markets now turn over some 60 times the value of world trade. As Held et al remark, compared to the scale of trading just a few years ago, '… this is not just a staggering increase; it is a different type of activity altogether'.[14]

The diffusion of technology and advances in transport technology and telecommunications have played a fundamental role in spreading industrial development and in increasing the pace of industrialization. The World Bank has underlined the impact of technological advance on the time taken for economic growth to double per capita output for various countries. The time needed to achieve this has progressively fallen: from 60 years in Britain after 1780, to 34 for Japan after 1885, to 20 years in Turkey after 1957, to only 10 years in China after 1977.[15]

Rapid growth has, however, not been experienced by all lower income countries and there has been a notable fragmentation of the developing countries in the last 20 years. Countries once lumped together under the heading of 'Third World' states have diverged radically in income levels, growth rates and industrial structures, and accordingly have very different current prospects for development in the 1990s. Growth in GDP per head, for instance, has varied enormously among regions over the past 40 years and continues to do so. Growth rates per capita in the 1990s varied hugely: 3 per cent or more on average in China, Argentina, India and Indonesia, contrasting with real falls in GDP per head in Russia and much of the old Soviet bloc, and throughout Africa, especially in sub-Saharan states plagued by civil war, AIDS and corruption.[16]

These indicators conceal great regional variations over time, as shown by World Bank figures. In Asia, GDP growth in the NICs from 1965 to 1989 far outstripped that in countries such as India. In Latin America, there were large gaps between the performance of Brazil and poor countries such as Bolivia. In much of sub-Saharan Africa real incomes per head actually *declined* in the last quarter of the 20th century.[17]

Such big disparities indicate a shift in economic fortunes among a number of NICs in the direction of the advanced industrial economies in terms of growth rates, income levels and industrial capacity, and on the other hand the prospect of many lower income countries making minimal progress at the periphery of the international economy. The massive population growth that is certain in many lower income countries will effectively wipe out gains in export performance and output. In 1989 the number of people living without enough food and shelter – the absolute poor – was some 1.2 billion – one-fifth of the world's population; despite the rapid economic growth in the mid- and late-1990s in many NICs, and notably in parts of China and India, this total was barely changed by the end of the century. So the proportion of the absolute poor has fallen slightly as NICs have developed, but the number living on less than a dollar a day is over 1.3 billion.[18]

What do these trends in the international economy mean? Are the gross inequalities between the rich and poor countries likely to be overcome? For some analysts of the world economic system, the disparities between developed 'core' economies and the diverse low income countries of the global economic 'periphery' reflect deep structural relations that are crucial to capitalism as a world system. On this analysis, there are profound forces in the operation of the core economies that will maintain unequal development to the advantage of Western capital.[19]

An alternative view, increasingly popular through the 1980s and 1990s among international economic agencies and Western governments, is that uneven patterns of development are not inevitable. Rather they reflect the results of different approaches to economic policy. On this analysis, it is possible for low income countries to break out of the poverty trap if they adopt proven 'market-friendly' policies. According to the World Bank, studies of the recent history of economic development suggest that success or failure is largely a result of developing countries' own policy choices, although the Bank stresses the need for the high-income countries to help by lifting trade restrictions and providing financial support. As noted earlier, the market-friendly approach involves minimal state intervention in markets, clear systems for market regulation, free trade, careful fiscal and monetary policy to contain inflation, concentration of public spending on education, health and the environment, and cuts in military budgets. Throughout the 1990s, this consensus has promoted a major development in the world economy towards a widespread adoption of market-friendly policies. This trend is considered in the next section.

The ascendancy of capitalism in the 1990s

The movement in the international economy towards a liberal market version of capitalism began in the mid-1970s in the West. By the start of the 1990s there was a rush among former Communist countries to embrace the liberal capitalist model of industrial development. In reality, there is not yet so much a complete embrace of liberal capitalism, much less democracy, by developing and ex-Communist countries, as a general disenchantment with collectivist models of industrial development and a move to copy policies that have brought material prosperity to the West. And in the wake of the 1997–98 turbulence in global markets which traumatized the economies of Russia and Indonesia among other countries, there has been a discernible rise in anti-Western and anti-market sentiment, most notably in Russia. None the less, capitalist models of development now have vast attraction for millions of people in the ex-Communist countries and the South. What are the factors behind this new ascendancy for liberal capitalism, which is so far reinforcing the trend towards global integration?

First, market-based approaches have been seen to deliver the goods, literally, to millions of people, despite the inequalities of income and opportunity that persist in the West. The trend towards more *laissez-faire* economic policies in the West which got underway in the late 1970s was associated with the massive boom of the mid- and late-1980s. Western governments engaged in deregulation of industrial sectors; focused on controlling inflation regardless of the consequences for unemployment; privatized state-owned industries, and promoted free enterprise. The approach was most radical in the US and the UK, but variations on the strategy have been pursued throughout the industrialized world. The industrial and financial interdependence of the higher income countries meant that avowedly socialist and social democratic governments were obliged to adopt many free-market policies and to swim with the tide. By the late 1990s, little remained of Western socialism; in 1997, for instance, a Labour Government was elected in the UK which had adopted free-market principles and preached the need for flexible labour and a straitened welfare state in the face of globalization.

Second, there was a steady process of disillusionment in the Communist world and in many lower income countries with collectivist economic policies. This was fuelled by observation of Western growth since the oil shocks of the 1970s, which had a severe effect on many Communist countries as well as on low income oil-importing countries, and by rising awareness of the inability of Communist economies to compete technologically with the West. Already by the mid-1980s, some Communist countries (such as Hungary and China) and many lower income countries with large state-run industrial sectors, had joined in the move towards deregulation and privatization.

Third, this tendency was promoted by the activity of the World Bank and the IMF in the wake of the 'debt crisis' that erupted in 1982 (see below). As the two agencies were called upon to assist more lower income countries with debt repayment crises, they linked the provision of loans to conditions about structural adjustment in the economies in question. This meant that financial support and advice was linked to the implementation of programmes for market-friendly structural reform in the economy.

Fourth, the collapse of Communist regimes in Eastern Europe and the Soviet Union in 1989–91 effectively eliminated Communism as a model for industrial development. This economic failure, and the environmental calamities associated with it, have been so great that there has been a dramatic reaction in the post-Communist states in favour of a rapid transition to a market economy.[20] The mood in the former Communist world of the early 1990s was often 'ultra-capitalist'. The new spirit of enthusiasm for the market was summed up by the former Soviet Republic of Kyrgyzstan's invitation to Western companies in October 1991 to invest in what was promised to be an 'El Dorado' for entrepreneurs.[21] The slow, chaotic and crime-ridden transition to market economics and democracy in the ex-Soviet bloc outside central Europe has dampened such enthusiasm and has led to disenchantment with the simplistic free-market nostrums of Western advisers, but no alternative has emerged to capture mass support.[22]

The general shift towards free market economic policies conceals some wide variations in policy, and even more in the extent to which liberal democracy accompanies liberal economics. There remain also important areas in which the market is not allowed to reign supreme. The NICs have pursued a strategy with strong elements of state intervention and selective protectionism in order to build up capacity in key sectors; and the agricultural sector has continued to be heavily subsidized in the West, especially in the European Community. As discussed below, there remain many barriers to free trade between nation states, and in particular between the higher and lower income countries. There is, moreover, no guarantee that the liberalization of the ex-Communist world in Eastern Europe, Russia and the Asian ex-Soviet states – the most striking case of conversion to market principles – will finally meet with general success over the next decade after so much sacrifice and disorientation for the average citizen. The political turmoil, lack of law-abiding institutions and civic spirit, environmental degradation and infrastructural backwardness of many of the countries in question are likely to deter much hoped-for foreign investment. In the absence of long-term aid and technical support on a large scale from the West, which failed to offer strategic programmes for a sustainable transition in the 1990s, it is unlikely that private investors will move in on the scale required to achieve the progress hoped for in living standards.

The policy urged by the World Bank, the IMF and Western governments for the ex-Communist countries and for the liberalizing states of Latin America, Asia and Africa has been and remains one of the rapid deregulation of prices, privatization of state enterprises and trade liberalization. The strategy is similar to the structural adjustment austerity programmes urged upon debt-ridden lower income countries in the 1980s.

However, two key issues arise. First, the lower income countries of the developing world and the ex-Communist countries have very different industrial structures and political backgrounds, and there is in any case no consensus about the efficacy of the World Bank/IMF structural adjustment programmes over the last decade. Second, as there is no precedent for the momentous transition from Communism to capitalism, there is no solid evidence to indicate that a full-blooded adoption of liberal market economics will produce greater industrial success, increased living standards and improved environmental quality in the short to medium term. On the contrary, there seems to be a strong possibility that undue austerity and prolonged transition pains will produce immense social strains that could lead to authoritarian rule again, this time of a nationalist–populist kind.[23] The institutions and mental habits developed under communism have been hard to change in many countries, and disillusionment and disorder have set in to varying degrees across the ex-USSR, with some areas undergoing economic, political and social breakdown – as in the former Yugoslavia and parts of the Caucasus.

For all the pains of the transition towards liberal capitalism, however, it is likely that ex-Communist and developing world governments will want to persist with the move to the market and join the NICs in their pursuit of Western levels of prosperity. While the outcome of the market-friendly revolutions is much in doubt, there is a possibility that some of the countries in question will achieve greatly increased levels of economic growth and per capita income, and aspire to approach Western living standards. Ironically, the drive for economic growth and hunger for Western styles of consumption in the NICs and the ex-Communist world are developing precisely at the point at which consumerism in the West is beginning to appear socially self-defeating and ecologically unsustainable. This is the subject of the next section.

The Limits to Consumption

Given the wretched condition of the 20 per cent of the world's population classified as absolutely poor, and the inadequate standards of health, sanitation, education and housing endured by hundreds of millions of others, no one can deny the aspirations of the developing world and ex-Communist countries to higher living standards. But critical questions are gradually making their way on to Western political agendas:

1 Can the rest of the world attain Western levels of affluence without causing fundamental ecological degradation and global warming through increased energy use and the exhaustion of resources? If not, what paths to higher living standards are sustainable?
2 How much consumption is *enough* in the industrialized world?

The issues are intertwined. The industrialized nations, increasingly aware of the threats of global warming and the loss of biodiversity, and the threat of mass migrations from poor countries to the rich world, cannot deny other countries the right to improve their living standards. On the other hand, it is evident that the planet could not sustain the globalization of the American consumer lifestyle as we now know it. Even a moderate rise in living standards for the mass of the world's population would seem to imply radical changes in the production and consumption habits of the world's most voracious consumers – namely, the citizens and corporations of the West – and Western acceptance of a steady state in energy consumption. The acceptance of limits to consumption would be a fundamental turning point in the evolution of industrial societies; for decades, politics has been geared to the assumptions that economic growth is a prime aim of government policy and that individuals must be able to look forward to steady improvements in living standards. The question 'How much consumption is enough?' has not been asked. However, the problems of global environmental change have begun to put it on the agenda, and there is a growing awareness in the industrial world of the social and ecological limits to consumption.

The culture of consumerism

While the benefits of increased availability of good food, labour-saving devices and home comforts are obvious, there has been a persistent current of criticism and unease in the West about the cultural consequences of growth in consumption. The target of this criticism (also levelled by many in the ex-Communist world and in the lower income countries) is the rise of a culture of 'consumerism'. This is a term much used but rarely defined. It might be summed up as a cluster of attitudes and habits that associate success, happiness, status and self-esteem primarily with the acquisition of a steadily rising income and access to high quality goods and services. It is brutally expressed in the message of a Californian car bumper sticker: 'The guy with the most toys when he dies wins.'[24]

Laments about acquisitiveness are hardly new: the US environmentalist Alan Durning cites examples of criticisms of 'consumerism' from the 1st century BC onwards.[25] He argues, however, that the acquisitiveness of modern Western societies is of a special kind. First, it involves consumption on an unprecedentedly colossal scale by a minority of the world's population. Second, it is promoted by forces specific to modernity which have become more powerful with each phase of industrial development in the West and now reach out to affect the entire world.

The consumer boom of the post-war period

The post-war decades have seen an explosive growth in the consumption of raw materials by industry and of goods and services by individual citizens. The trend has been propelled by advances in technology and productivity, rising per capita incomes and the falling real cost of many goods and services. The statistics of GDP growth and increases in world trade cited above translate into phenomenal changes in personal and corporate consumption over the last five decades: huge increases in car ownership and mobility, consumption of plastics and other synthetic materials, and the establishment of refrigerators, telephones, televisions, video recorders and microwave ovens as basic items of normal lifestyles.

The scale of Western consumption is made all the more astonishing when compared to levels elsewhere. The 1.25 billion people in the advanced industrial countries consume vastly more, on all key indicators, than the 3.4 billion who are adequately fed and clothed and the 1.3 billion who live in absolute poverty. The 5 per cent of the world's population in the US consume around one-third of the world's resources. The high income countries, home to 20 per cent of the earth's population, account for 60 per cent of world energy use.[26]

The forces behind the culture of consumerism

The scale of current Western consumption is thus of a different order from anything known in pre-industrial times and the earlier periods of modernity. What drives the development, other than technical change, population growth and rising income? Durning identifies 'distinctively modern features' that contribute to over-consumption and consumerist attitudes in the West:[27]

1 The influence of competitive social pressures in industrial societies, in which money becomes a dominant indicator of success, status and self-worth as modernization increasingly marginalizes traditional cultural forces, such as religious belief, that could provide a strong countervailing influence.
2 The expansion of the world of commodities into the household and the sphere of 'local self-reliance' during the industrial era: goods and services provided at home or locally have been replaced increasingly by goods and services provided by the industrial market.
3 Governments have encouraged patterns of land use leading to the 'need' for the increased consumption of cars and fuel; failed to require producers to reflect environmental costs in the prices charged to consumers; and devised national economic policies on the assumption that 'more is better'.
4 The ever increasing volume and sophistication of advertising has turned shopping into a leisure pursuit.

The globalization of advertising

The forces of advertising have been present since the early phases of industrialism. They now have a global reach, principally through the spread of communications networks that bring advertising to billions of people, including a growing number in the ex-Communist and lower income countries. The 1980s and 1990s saw a qualitative shift in the impact of advertising and in its promotion of a link between well-being, status and consumption. The resources devoted to advertising worldwide increased enormously in the 1980s, in the NICs as well as in the advanced industrial countries, reaching US$237 billion in 1988. Growth continued in the 1990s, with US$413 billion being spent on advertising in 1998 – over 1 per cent of global output.[28] Economic growth in the NICs has provided large new markets for consumer goods and for advertising. The iconography of the mass consumption culture – logos, brand names and packaging of global products such as Coca-Cola and Nike shoes – is recognized throughout the developing world, just as it is embedded in the daily life of the rich countries.

The spread of market-friendly governments means that previous restrictions on popular access to advertising outside the West are falling away rapidly. The vast majority of the new audience for Western advertising is in no position to afford the goods and services paraded in advertisements and television shows, but naturally appetites are aroused, just as ours have been for decades. Keen popular awareness of the material well-being of the West was undoubtedly a major factor in the collapse of the Communist regimes of Eastern Europe, alongside profound disillusion with the political and economic systems.

The 1980s also saw a large increase in the reach and capacity of global telecommunications networks – for example, through satellite broadcasting. In the 1990s this was taken further, and complemented in spectacular fashion by the rise of the Internet, the fastest growing communication medium in history. The Internet has grown by some 50 per cent per year since 1995 and by 1999 some 1 in 40 people in the world had access to the Net.[29] The pattern of access to the Internet and to telecommunications is still heavily skewed: the US dominates Internet use, while rural areas in the developing world, especially in Africa, are largely deprived of basic telecommunications. But the explosive growth of the Net and the falling real cost of communications suggest that wireless systems and other technologies that are not dependent on costly cable infrastructures will help poorer countries to improve access for their people in the new century.

The progressive globalization of television and the Internet means that the imagery of Western affluence is available to hundreds of millions of people in the former Communist world and in the lower income countries. It is also available through the development of global travel. Migrant workers from low-income countries see for themselves the standards of living enjoyed in the West; and in the developing world, as tourism reaches ever more countries and ever more remote regions, Western affluence is advertised in the form of tourists and the facilities built to cater for them.

The limits to consumerism

The weight of transnational corporations is backed by the pervasiveness of advertising, the global reach of images, familiar products and sales messages, the incessant association of new and better goods with well-being and the difficulty of opting out of modernity in any meaningful way.

The globalization of the industrial system is producing a gradual erosion of local cultural distinctiveness in production and consumption, and a spread in desire in low-income countries for the products most associated with Western affluence – cars, televisions, jeans, trainers, fast food, the products with 'designer' brand names.

But while the factors behind consumerism may appear almost irresistible, there is a growing awareness in the advanced industrial countries that further development of many aspects of the culture of consumption will prove to be unsustainable. We are increasingly aware of limits to growth, though not in the sense of the physical exhaustion of many key resources, as feared by the Club of Rome in 1972.[30] These limits are social and ecological, relating to environmental degradation and the ultimately self-defeating nature of key forms of consumption.

Research and everyday experience indicate that there is little correlation between high levels of consumption and personal happiness.[31] The achievement of high levels of income and consumption often comes to seem 'hollow', and the erosion of religious belief in industrial societies means that for many this feeling can develop into a sense of personal meaninglessness.[32] In Western societies, the superabundance of consumer choices and information media threaten the individual with information 'overload': many people in the West would admit to feeling confused and oppressed by what the American novelist Don DeLillo calls the 'blur and glut' of consumer culture, the disorienting sense of 'too much everything'.[33]

We can go beyond the intimations of sensory overload and spiritual emptiness that crowd modern novels and cultural critiques. The idea that there is something fundamentally self-defeating in modern consumption patterns was given more rigorous economic expression by the late Fred Hirsch in his seminal analysis of the social limits to growth.[34] Hirsch noted the widespread dissatisfaction that accompanies the pursuit of affluence and related it to the inevitable degradation in quality of the key goods in industrial societies. Certain goods that confer status and special well-being – what Hirsch terms 'positional goods' – are only of value and can only bring satisfaction if they remain relatively scarce. As they become widely available, their quality diminishes and the satisfactions they offer are sharply reduced. Since positional goods are precisely those to which many citizens most aspire, this is a crucial limitation on the development of consumerism. As Hirsch puts it, 'The life depicted in the glossy magazines clearly is attractive to many of us. The snag is that much of it is unavailable to very many of us at once, and its diffusion may then change its own content and characteristics'.[35] The process can be illustrated by reference to two of the goods most desired in industrial society: cars and holidays.

The car is a potent symbol of consumer culture. However, ownership of a car in itself is not usually the prime source of satisfaction. The benefits of car driving depend upon access to road space and the free and rapid progress to one's destination. But as more and more people acquire cars, so the benefits of access to road space diminish, and disbenefits, such as congestion, pollution, frustration and noise begin to mount up. In Hirsch's terms, the positional good of free access to the road is diminished in quality as car ownership rises. Moreover, the process of rising car ownership itself promotes the acquisition of more cars, if only because there is diminishing demand for, and thus less provision of, public transport: those without a car are forced to become drivers. In this sense, the competition for positional goods becomes a self-defeating process, with ever-decreasing quality of experience of the goods for all concerned. The process is tempered by advances in car facilities which make the experience of chronic congestion perhaps less unpleasant than that of overcrowding on public transit systems; but the general point is clear.

Access to cars allows access to beautiful places, and the rise in incomes in the West has led to a huge increase in tourism at home and abroad. Holidays and access to desirable places are also positional goods, and their value to the consumer is diminished once they become widely available. Exotic locations fill up with Western tourists, and native cultures become more and more like the ones back home. 'Unspoilt' landscapes attract more and more visitors whose presence requires the construction of more roads, car parks and other facilities, thus rapidly 'spoiling' the scenery and atmosphere; spectacular views are gradually blocked by the numbers of people wanting to take pictures of them. The syndrome is increasingly familiar: the devaluation and destruction by tourism of the very thing which the tourist comes to see.

The awareness of social limits to the satisfactions that positional goods can bring is accompanied by the realization that there are also key ecological constraints on certain forms of consumption. As noted earlier, the worldwide fleet of cars is forecast to grow spectacularly on present trends, with increased ownership in the lower income countries and ex-Communist states as well as in the West.[36] The spread of market-oriented economies is likely to accentuate the trend, in the absence of radical policy changes, since reliance on private transport, and the development of land use patterns that promote it at the expense of public transport systems, have been distinctive features of capitalist societies.[37] Yet, as noted in Chapter 1, a massive increase in car use worldwide will exacerbate the problem of global warming and air pollution; no technical advances in engine design and emission controls will help us to avoid this outcome at the global level. The threat of pervasive urban gridlock, already well on the way in major cities, is a real one, and by the late 1990s transport policy-makers were beginning to address the complex issues of demand management and redirecting transport use towards public transit and cycling, walking and tele-substitution of journeys by new information technology applications.

Similarly, there is an ecological dimension to the growth in tourism, which shows few signs of abating in the West and which is likely to become increasingly popular in the NICs as incomes rise. There is relentless pressure on the human ecology of tourist destinations: on local cultures, buildings and settlements. And there is parallel pressure on natural ecosystems, even in the remotest corners of the earth: the Everest base camp area is littered with the refuse of trekkers and climbers, and cruise ships now tour the Antarctic coast. The numbers of people and jobs, and the sums, involved in tourist travel are unprecedented:

> *... as the travel industry goes global, developed and underdeveloped countries alike are embracing it as never before as an important facet of the economy... 625 million tourists visited a foreign country [in 1998]. Receipts, excluding air fares, rose 2 per cent to $445 billion... Over the next decade the industry will generate 5.5 million new jobs worldwide and will account for almost 12 per cent of global gross domestic product. Currently about 68 million jobs depend on the industry.*[38]

Consumption and Sustainability

We are still at an early stage in our understanding of social and ecological limits to growth in consumption. It is evident, however, that indefinite increases in certain forms of consumption are incompatible with sustainable development. How this awareness can be translated into practical measures in environmental management and economic policy is much less clear. It will require above all measures that reflect the full cost of environmental damage in prices paid by corporate and individual consumers, and no doubt policies for rationing access to roads and vulnerable tourist attractions. However, major political problems arise in considering the limits to economic growth and consumption. These relate to equity within the Western industrial countries, and between them and the rest of the world.

First, the experience of near-continuous economic growth over decades has accustomed politicians and electors in the West to expect future increases in incomes, production and consumption. Despite growing, though still limited, awareness of the social and ecological constraints on indefinite expansion, the idea of limits to consumption is unfamiliar in Western politics and to Western consumers. Raising the question, 'How much is enough?' inevitably leads to the consideration of equity and distribution of income and opportunity. If there is to be rationing of road space and access to fragile tourist destinations, how can it be made fair? Will the rich be unaffected, while the less well-off lose out? Issues of equity and distribution are diminished in political potency and are less threatening when most groups in society can feel that their standards of living are increasing, but they come to the fore in any discussion of a 'steady state' in key areas of consumption.

Second, there is the relationship between high- and low-income countries in a world in which ecological limits to growth as we have known it are in sight. Many lower income countries have been following a broadly Western model of industrialization as a proven route to progress and prosperity. In recapitulating many of the phases of development experienced by the industrialized countries they have also repeated many environmental mistakes, frequently with the enthusiastic cooperation of Western corporations and governments, and are often impatient of Western criticism of environmentally destructive policies. If the industrializing countries are to avoid the unsustainable evolution of production and consumption patterns, the high-income world must set a positive example of sustainable development and provide the financial and technical support which is necessary to raise living standards in the South and protect the environment effectively.

Much the same applies in the case of the ex-Communist states of Eastern Europe and the former USSR, where the end of the old regimes and the rush towards the market-oriented modernization of manufacturing and commerce has been accompanied by an impatient popular desire to achieve Western standards of living, a desire frustrated outside Central Europe by economic and political turbulence and the lack of legal and technical frameworks for development on the Western model. In this case the countries in question are poised on the threshold of new industrial development. If they simply follow the 'traditional' Western model of modernization and are encouraged to do so, a huge opportunity for environmentally sound modernization will have been missed and major new pressures on local ecosystems will emerge. The experience of the ex-Communist countries in the 1990s has shown that economic restructuring has dominated policy agendas, with environmental sustainability pushed down the list of priorities except where aid is available from the West or pressure has been applied by the European Union for more efforts in environmental management.[39]

Any move towards sustainable development demands policy change in four key areas of the international economic system, such that environmental management becomes an integral part of economic decision-making and relationships between the high- and low-income countries become more equitable. In all four areas, referred to as 'pillars of neo-colonialism' in a speech in 1991 by the Indian politician Manekha Gandhi, the inequitable relations between rich and poor countries have contributed massively to unsustainable environmental change:

1 the terms of trade between high- and low-income countries;
2 debt and development aid;
3 technology transfer; and
4 the role of transnational corporations.

These four areas are discussed in the remainder of this chapter.

The Terms of International Trade

The enormous expansion of international trade has been a fundamental element in the globalization of industrialism and in the spreading influence of capitalism. The key institution in this field has been the General Agreement on Tariffs and Trade (GATT), succeeded by the World Trade Organization (WTO), whose rules cover some 90 per cent of world trade in goods and which by 1999 included 135 countries. The latest phase (the 'Uruguay Round') of GATT negotiations on removing trade barriers began in 1986 and was due to finish in late 1990, but was stalled by disagreements over cutting subsidies to agriculture. The Uruguay Round, concluded in 1994, not only established the WTO and a much-expanded realm for free trade, but also saw the rise of concern that the impacts of GATT agreements on the environment were largely being ignored by the organization. These concerns reached a peak in the run-up to the WTO's abortive Seattle conference in December 1999, when environmental and social campaigners disrupted the talks and forced acknowledgement from President Bill Clinton that their views needed to be better aired and integrated into future negotiations in the WTO system. The planned 'Millennium Round' of the WTO will have to reflect environmental and social concerns to a far greater extent than previous negotiations have done, and in the wake of the Seattle fiasco there is growing consensus that the WTO is in need of fundamental reform.

Tensions in trade policy

Negotiations over the terms of international trade highlight numerous tensions not only between the high- and low-income countries but also within the industrialized world. These concern the legitimacy of protectionist policies and the extent to which free trade is desirable and politically feasible in relation to particular sectors and countries. The main area of conflict in trade policy among high income countries is agriculture. There is major disagreement between the United States (backed by other industrial countries and also by developing countries in the so-called 'Cairns Group') on the one hand, and the European Union on the other. The US seeks drastic cuts in farm subsidies within the EU, which spends over 40 per cent of its budget on its Common Agricultural Policy (CAP), which provides subsidies to farmers and has helped to generate enormous surpluses of dairy products, beef, grain and wine. Surpluses have been 'dumped' at low cost on developing world markets to the detriment of local producers, and low-income countries' access to European food markets has been restricted through tariff systems designed to protect European farmers. Progress in reforming the CAP to give incentive for more organic farming, less intensive crop management and greater protection for habitats and wildlife has been painfully slow despite the huge cost and evident inefficiencies and perverse consequences of the policy.

The alliance between high- and low-income countries pressing for cuts in farm subsidies within the European Union and Japan is a rare instance of North–South agreement in trade policy. Usually the lines of conflict are clearly drawn up between the high- and low-income countries. There is strong pressure from each side on the other for the removal of tariff barriers and other measures designed to protect domestic agriculture and industry. Lower income countries demand access to Western markets in which they face tariff barriers. Such tariffs are set in politically sensitive areas such as agricultural sectors in which some poorer countries would have an advantage if free trade was in force. And many developing countries regard Western pressures for greater environmental and social protection as a smokescreen for the further protection of Northern commercial interests and the imposition of costs on the South which it is in no position to bear.

Distortions of international trade result from non-tariff barriers as well as from tariffs, and the former do not yet come under the control of the WTO. The GATT's and the WTO's progress in reducing tariffs in recent years has been balanced by increased protectionism in other forms. This is a result of growing competition and reflects the increased vulnerability of domestic producers in all sectors. The developing world has been especially disadvantaged by these changes:

> *By 1986, 21 per cent of exports from developing countries to the OECD were covered by so-called hard-core nontariff barriers: quotas, voluntary export restraints, the Multifibre Arrangement [which limits textile imports by developed countries from developing ones] and other highly restrictive measures. This number does not even include other restrictions such as price restraints or health and safety regulations. Since the mid-1980s, industrial countries have done almost nothing to roll back the accumulated protection.*[40]

> *Where are the countries of the southern hemisphere in all this [preparation for the Seattle conference]? ... Many of them have no ambassador to the WTO, and complain that they have made concessions without getting anything in return – especially in the field of textiles and clothing. Their priority is to see the commitments given to them in the Uruguay Round enacted.*[41]

Critics of the stance of the industrial countries argue that they are guilty of applying double standards in trade policy. Protectionism in lower income countries is opposed and the virtues of market-friendly policies are loudly proclaimed, yet selective trade barriers are maintained against developing countries' exports, at major cost to them. The World Bank notes that the value to developing countries of exports that have been forgone owing to the industrial countries' trade barriers is comparable to the total value of development aid. It is also argued that selective protection has played a key role in the development of the industrial economies and has been crucial to the success of the NICs in building up manufacturing expertise. In the light of this, critics of the Western position argue that the lower income countries should be allowed a higher degree of protection until their needs are better met in the international system.[42] However, even though the end of the Uruguay Round in 1994 saw agreement on phasing out textiles protection in the OECD world and on reductions in Western agricultural subsidies, these commitments are being met only slowly and are offset by the impact on the poorest countries of debt burdens, international economic turbulence, political instability, corruption and the low level of investment they receive from the North.

The disputes that marked the GATT Uruguay Round also highlighted the contribution of inequitable trade policies and inappropriate free trade measures to unsustainable development. We discuss below two key areas in which the international terms of trade have played a part in ecological degradation: the lower income countries' reliance on commodities in an unfair trading system; and the failure to integrate environmental issues into the policy-making of the WTO.

Commodity prices and lower income countries

A major problem in trade policy for many of the lower income countries is their reliance on exports of basic agricultural and mineral commodities in order to earn foreign exchange. This is particularly marked among countries in sub-Saharan Africa and the poorer Asian states. The critical factor in dependence on particular commodities is the extreme vulnerability of the economy when commodity prices fall.[43] For lower income countries without indigenous fuel reserves, the years since the mid-1970s have seen the worst of all worlds: falls in non-fuel commodity prices and, in the 1970s, large rises in oil prices. Declines in non-fuel commodity prices are related to three key developments:

1. Recessions in importing countries and consequent decline in demand.
2. Sectoral restructuring in the industrialized world, leading to a shift away from heavy manufacturing towards light industry and services, and the reduction of demand for raw materials in manufacturing. New technological developments have allowed a reduction in the use of materials through miniaturization and the substitution of synthetic materials for natural ones.
3. Increased output of commodities by lower income countries in an attempt to boost earnings, with resultant gluts and depression in prices.

Dependence on commodities in a world economy in which demand is falling or static has led to a general economic and environmental decline in the affected lower income countries. Falling earnings from commodity exports led to a drop in living standards and pressure to maximize production in order to try to keep up earnings. In many cases food production and peasant agriculture have been neglected in the interests of maximizing cash crop exports, and poor countries have had to import food on a large scale.[44] As economic pressure mounts, the cropping of agricultural commodities and extraction of raw materials may be increased beyond sustainable levels, thus undermining economic and environmental security.

Countries in this situation find it extremely hard to afford domestic investment or to attract Western investment in order to diversify agriculture and industry and reduce dependence on commodity exports. Attempts at diversification are also made more difficult by trade barriers in export markets and by pressure from the West to remove domestic restrictions on trade. Finally, dependence is worsened for countries with large foreign debt burdens, since a major proportion of export earnings is not invested at home but instead disappears to creditors in the West to service the debt.

There are two further dimensions to commodity dependence that serve to reinforce the vulnerable position of lower income countries in terms of trade and environmental security. First, the inappropriateness of much agricultural commodity production, given the needs of the mass of the population. This relates to the emphasis in many low-income countries on earning foreign exchange – largely to service debt – from the export of cash crops at the expense of local food production.

Second, the pricing of commodities has also played a part: as we have seen, non-fuel primary commodities have declined in price in recent years, putting low-income producers at an extreme disadvantage. Commodity pricing, in most cases, has not been subject to international commodity agreements that compensate low-income countries by promoting price stabilization and assisting them to diversify. To achieve this, the industrialized countries would need to agree to commodity prices that reflected the full environmental costs of production, and would also need to provide technical and financial support and reduce trade barriers to exports from the developing world in order to assist diversification.[45] The pricing issue also relates to other 'commodities' in the low-income world, such as tropical forests and tourist attractions, resources that have not been priced in such a way as to reflect their full environmental value. In areas such as the timber trade, lower income countries receive a return for the tropical forests' resources that fails to reflect the full environmental value and encourages overexploitation.

Yet economic studies which integrate environmental valuation suggest that low-income countries have been losing out by degrading ecosystems in pursuit of cash cropping, and that the West ought to pay far more for forest products, ecological services provided by Southern habitats and the conservation of biodiversity. And it has been argued that the underuse of fossil fuels by developing countries compared to the smaller populations of the rich world means that the poorest countries are owed vast sums by the former for the disproportionate damage caused by Northern consumption patterns. The NGO Christian Aid calculates that the developed world's bill on its carbon dioxide 'account' is three times greater than the debt owed by developing countries – US$612 billion compared with US$200 billion.[46]

International trade and environmental management: the need for integration

The problem of inappropriate commodity pricing raises a wider issue – that of the failure of the key agencies in the international economic system to develop policies on the terms of trade that take environmental quality into account. This lack of integration of environmental considerations in international trade policy emerged as a major issue for the first time during the Uruguay Round of GATT talks.[47] While the World Bank and the IMF had been for years on the receiving end of criticism from environmentalists over debt and aid policies, international trade was relatively neglected by the campaigning NGOs. It became clear in 1990 to many environmentalists that the GATT negotiations were proceeding with virtually no consideration of the effects of trade liberalization measures on the global environment:

> *... environmentalists have had no opportunity to learn of, assess and respond to present trade initiatives. Trade negotiations proceed, and agreements are concluded without even the most perfunctory consideration of the enormous environmental consequences that flow from them.*[48]

The complaint was unheeded by the WTO; by the time of the Seattle conference of 1999 exactly the same critiques of the process and the body's lack of environmental and social policy integration were being mounted by NGOs, politicians and policy analysts, as well as by a rag-tag army of individual protesters in the streets of Seattle. The WTO had, it was widely argued – as was eventually acknowledged by political leaders after the conference collapsed – failed to learn from the criticisms levelled at it and stood in need of radical reform.[49]

Governments and agencies such as the World Bank made numerous declarations in the 1980s in support of sustainable development, yet the nations involved in the GATT talks in the Uruguay Round were making decisions that could undermine any progress towards sustainability in the global economic system. The key problem is the potential conflict between the liberalization of trade and the need for the regulation of exports and imports in order to conserve natural resources and safeguard ecosystems. The thrust of the Uruguay Round was to remove restrictions placed by countries on activities such as logging within their borders and the export of rainforest products, and the rejection by GATT of import bans on products deemed to be environmentally unsound. In a landmark ruling in 1991, the GATT overruled an American ban on imports of Mexican tuna fish (claimed to be fished in a way that killed dolphins in unsustainable numbers) on the grounds that the restriction violated free trade. Critics of the GATT, and like those of the present WTO, argued that a blanket rejection, in the name of free trade, of such restrictions will simply lead to the unsustainable cropping of resources.

International free trade agreements are also regarded with suspicion by environmentalists on the grounds that they promote 'harmonization' of national standards by reducing to the lowest common denominator, rather than seeking a general increase in quality thresholds. The Uruguay Round's agenda included proposals from the US for the global harmonization of food safety standards, including controls on pesticide use, which have led critics to argue that environmental and social standards in individual countries would be seriously diluted, benefiting only TNCs in general and US exporters in particular.

Similar arguments were made – successfully – by NGOs and developing countries against the proposed Multilateral Agreement on Investment (MAI) which was put forward by the OECD as a framework for governing and facilitating TNC investment worldwide. The MAI was widely seen as a mechanism for giving rights of establishment to TNCs at the expense of governments, and without corresponding responsibilities for promoting and respecting social and environmental standards. It also excluded the developing countries from negotiation, although these would have been especially affected by the MAI's proposals on lifting restrictions on foreign investment across the board. Negotiations on the MAI, whose formal negotiation was launched virtually in secret in 1995, were abandoned by the OECD after a determined and well-coordinated campaign by NGOs and other civil society bodies which led to a weakening of Western governmental support throughout 1997 and 1998. It became plain that the proposed agreement was politically untenable and incompatible with international agreements on social protection and environmental sustainability. Moreover, in the wake of the Uruguay Round controversies, the secretive process by which the MAI was designed drew still more attention to the lack of transparency and accountability in the international economic agencies.[50]

Trading bloc regimes have also been criticized on similar grounds for producing 'downward harmonization', weakening social and environmental regulations in the pursuit of an open market: for example, the US–Canada free trade agreement obliged Canada to weaken its regulations on pesticides and resource development;[51] and there has been persistent tension in the European Union between the development of the European integrated market and the requirement in the EU treaties of the 1990s for a high level of environmental protection to be a fundamental goal of the Union.[52]

The problem of the balance between trade liberalization and restrictions based on the need for sustainability is immensely complex. It is clear that, as was argued by the proponents of free trade under the GATT, restrictions on trade could be set up on environmental grounds as a convenient excuse for protectionism by industrial countries against one another and against lower income countries. Thus there is a need for sensitive rulings in the WTO regime that do justice to environmental concerns, maximize free trade where possible and ensure that lower income countries are fairly treated.

The debate within the GATT and WTO frameworks has always revolved around the polar concepts of 'free trade' and 'protectionism', and has ignored questions of environmental sustainability. It has also failed to achieve deep cuts in state subsidies – in the West as much as in the developing world – to polluting industries. In theory, free trade should assist sustainable development by attacking harmful subsidies; in practice, these have been largely unchecked as the WTO regime has concentrated on ensuring free flows of finance and goods. The WTO has failed to take into account the international agreements we already have on environmental and social protection, and has failed to bring sustainability into its judgements on what counts as a breach of its rules. In the wake of Seattle and the collapse of the MAI, the debate should now focus on the conflict between sustainable and fair trade on the one hand, and unsustainable and inequitable trade on the other; and then on ensuring free trade within a regime which underpins high environmental and social standards and makes these available to the poorer countries.

For this to happen, there will have to be a fundamental reorientation of the WTO system to allow the integration of environmental and social policy considerations. In 1990 Stephen Shrybman proposed an amendment to the GATT agreement that would make explicit 'the priority of environmental protection and resource conservation' in any conflict with free trade, with the onus on the free trader to prove that environmental restrictions are unreasonable and not imposed in good faith.[53] It is highly likely that some such reform to the WTO framework will be essential if the negotiations in the new century are to avoid the kinds of protests that helped to wreck the Seattle talks in December 1999.

The lack of integration of environmental management in the GATT/WTO regime is underlined by the fact that GATT's working group on trade and the environment never met in the two decades after its establishment in 1971. However, following the mounting protests from NGOs and some Western governments over the failure to consider environmental issues in the Uruguay Round, the GATT decided in October 1991 to activate the working party in order to investigate the conflicts between trade policy and sustainable development. This was the GATT's first step in the process of policy integration, on which the other international actors in the global economy (such as the World Bank) had already embarked, largely as a result of pressure from environmental NGOs. But the process has been even slower than in the Bank and the IMF, and at Seattle in 1999 it was evident that many lessons from the critique of the Uruguay Round had still to be learned.

Development and Dependency: Problems of Debt and Aid

The popular perception of low-income countries in the West is dominated by images of hunger, appeals for aid and grim statistics on the monumental debts owed to Western banks and governments. The 1980s saw crises of indebtedness in the developing world and wide recognition of the adverse environmental, economic and social effects of the aid policies pursued by Western governments and the World Bank. The 1990s saw, in parallel with the mounting critiques of the WTO regime and the proposed MAI, a large-scale campaign to reduce and write off debt owed by the poorest countries. By the end of the decade NGOs, the governments of developing countries and Church campaigners had succeeded in persuading some Western governments to take radical action. That this issue presents a key test of governmental attitudes towards sustainability and the interdependence of states in a globalized economy is not in doubt. The problems of debt and aid are linked and point to deeper issues of environmental management and the need for the integration of environmental policy with development aid strategies.

Scale and origins of the debt crisis

The level of external debt accumulated by developing countries and by former communist states is huge: almost US$2.2 trillion in 1997, almost double the figure for 1980. Over half was owed to commercial creditors, nearly one-third to governments and 17 per cent to international agencies such as the IMF and the various arms of the World Bank. Debt service payments by developing countries in 1997 totalled US$269 billion and account for large slices of public funds: in Kenya, debt service in the late 1990s took some 25 per cent of state spending, compared with just 2.7 per cent on health.[54] The numbers involved in the debts of developing countries are colossal, yet the total of over US$2 trillion is small compared to the total value of world output – over $38 trillion in 1997 – or the annual turnover of the 200 biggest transnational corporations. And the debt owed by the 'highly indebted poor countries' (HIPCs) at the bottom of the international pile to the US is said to amount to the cost of two B-2 bombers or the accounting errors in one year of the Pentagon's budget.[55]

In short, the problem of debt is by no means that it is so large that it threatens the stability of the global economy: the 1980s crisis was effectively over for the Western banks by the end of the decade, as they made large provisions against potential losses and reduced their exposure by selling debt on secondary markets. The problem is that the scale of debt is large enough for individual developing countries to suffer massive deprivation and underinvestment in public services and vital infrastructure as they attempt to service their debts. For example, by 1997 the debtor countries of sub-Saharan Africa were indebted to the tune of over 70 per cent of the region's entire annual income – a burden of debt which grew in the 1990s while more affluent regions such as Latin America saw a relative improvement in the ratio of debt to GDP.[56]

The crisis which finally led to the reforms of the late 1990s began in 1982 with Mexico's threat to default on its repayments, triggering panic among Western banks and governments and drawing attention to the mounting debt burden on low-income countries. How did this burden become so crushing? The origins of the debt crisis can be traced to the oil price shock of 1974. The massive rise in oil prices placed a severe strain on the economies of low-income countries that needed to import oil, and also generated vast reserves of currency for the oil producers which had to be 'recycled' by the international financial system. Much of the money was lent to lower income countries to help them to cope with the oil shock, and much was borrowed by oil exporters such as Mexico on the assumption that oil prices would stay high and that export earnings and investment returns would enable easy repayment.

The lending and spending spree of the 1970s came to an abrupt end for several reasons. First, there was a second large oil price rise in 1979, putting yet more pressure on oil importing countries. Second, recession in the West spurred the sharp decline in commodity prices discussed above, leading to falls in export income for many low-income countries. Third, interest rates in the West rose rapidly in the early 1980s as a result of US economic policies: tax cuts and increased military spending by the Reagan administration led to a budget deficit which was financed by raising interest rates to draw in foreign investment. Capital flowed into the US and interest rates elsewhere rose in response, massively increasing the interest bill to be paid by the indebted low-income countries at the same time as they faced a crisis of falling export earnings.

The crisis was not only precipitated by this grim conjunction of events. Short-sighted and reckless lending policies on the part of Western bankers played a key part. Vast sums never reached the people and projects most in need, but went into the pockets of corrupt officials and politicians in dictatorial regimes, or were squandered on costly and inappropriate projects. Fortunes have been taken out of low income countries in the form of capital flight – the movement of funds into safe deposits in the West by rich individuals and companies, and sometimes by corrupt officials. Corruption and grossly unproductive investments have thus reduced the value of loans to low-income countries and contributed to their difficulties in servicing their debts.[57]

Defaults on external debt have been avoided and the international financial system has succeeded in confining the debt crisis to the debtor countries. But while creditors in the West have bought themselves time to make provisions against defaults and to grant reductions in debt to selected countries, the burden of repayment has barely been lightened for the low-income debtors. The 1980s saw the net flow of wealth from rich to poor countries come to an end:

> *Developing nations paid $77 billion in interest on their debts [in 1989] and repaid $85 billion worth of principal. Since 1983, the traditional flow of capital from North to South has been reversed: the poor countries pay more to the rich than they receive in return, a net hemorrhage that now stands at more than $50 billion a year.*[58]

The growth of the debt burden has imposed heavy costs on the natural environments of the low-income countries. The desperate need for foreign exchange with which to service debt has been a factor in the overexploitation of land and the destruction of forests in order to boost cash crop earnings. The misuse of loans on corrupt dealings, military expenditure and 'prestige' projects with no productive returns have involved gigantic opportunity costs in terms of sustainable development and environmental protection. And the diversion of resources towards debt repayment has meant that there is little or no capital for environmentally and socially sustainable development projects.

Debt management has involved an increase in the dependence of low-income countries on Western governments, TNCs and international agencies such as the World

Bank and the IMF. The process of rescheduling debt, allowing selective write-offs and providing additional loans to tide countries over has largely been carried out by the IMF and the World Bank. The management of debt relief has been based to a large extent on setting strict conditions on debtor countries' economic policies in the hope that these will lead to improved performance and renewed credit-worthiness. The conditions set have typically involved the provision of new loans and other assistance in return for the implementation of 'structural adjustment programmes' (SAPs) worked out by the international agencies. SAPs tend to involve a strategy to privatize state-owned businesses; to promote export sectors to gain revenue; to cut state subsidies to sectors such as agriculture; and to control inflation.

SAPs have been intensely controversial.[59] Their implementation has generally involved cuts in social expenditure that have reduced the living standards of the poor; they have led to governments selling off assets to Western investors in order to reduce debts and swap equity for debt; and, while some governments (especially in Latin America) have achieved great improvements in economic performance and social stability after persevering with SAPs and other reforms, it is not clear that the SAPs' economic goals have always been realized, through the poor design of programmes and inadequate controls on privatization and market development. Their environmental impact can also be damaging: privatization of state assets may simply mean that companies and land are sold off cheaply to TNCs which then develop the assets with little or no regard for the environment.

The 1990s saw the implementation of SAPs on a massive scale in developing countries as part of debt reform programmes and as part of the hoped-for 'transition' of ex-Soviet bloc societies from Communist dictatorship to liberal market-based democracies. The IMF, the World Bank and Western creditors insisted on rigorous economic reform programmes as the price for further aid, debt rescheduling or new lending. The SAP-based 'shock therapy' of privatization and market deregulation has had some successes, albeit purchased at a high social cost, as in Poland and the Czech Republic; but it ended the 1990s largely discredited as a result of the disastrous failures of the approach in Russia, where over-hasty deregulation combined with corruption, outmoded infrastructure and weak democratic structures to produce an economy that was dominated by organized crime and appalling poverty.

SAPs have been widely seen in the South and by Western social campaigners as a means of turning developing countries into amenable players in the globalizing system of free trade and TNC-dominated investment.[60] There is no question that SAPs have had this effect in many cases. But the failings and misuse of SAPs should not blind us to the extreme miseries inflicted by many governments in developing countries on their own peoples, through economic failures as much as political injustice. The lesson of the SAP experience is not that structural reform is always and everywhere an example of malign Western imperialism, nor that it always hurts the poor and helps the rich. Programmes of 'structural adjustment' of some kind are inevitable in societies and economies undergoing upheavals as they attempt to come to terms with industrial globalization or with the end of dictatorial regimes, or with both at the same time. Many developing countries and ex-Communist states have suffered immensely not only through the mistakes and over-rigid market prescriptions of the IMF and the World Bank but also, and in many cases far more so, from corruption, warfare, lawlessness and the exploitation of the poor by their rich compatriots. The SAP experience has been a flawed one above all because economic policy prescriptions were imposed in an inflexible way by Western policy-makers who believed they possessed a fundamental strategy for healthy development – which happened to involve short-term pain for long-term gain. The economic template of the SAPs was overlaid on a great variety of local conditions with inadequate understanding of the governance issues, of the social and environmental implications of SAP measures, and of the local political dynamics and the capacity of local economies and citizens to absorb change and seize new opportunities.

The lesson is not that we do not need SAPs, but that structural change hurts and needs careful political management, building consensus and understanding and treating citizens as partners in design and implementation – using the kinds of action-network techniques described in Parts III and IV. Where democratic processes exist, SAPs can be introduced in such a careful and sensitive manner; where they do not, the risk is that SAPs designed with poor attention to the issues of governance make bad situations worse. The balance of the SAP experience of the last two decades of the 20th century is that the programmes have in many cases made life worse for the poor, while having little impact on the overall rates of economic growth; however, SAPs have often been a catalyst for changes which in the long run help the poor in countries where the government has been corrupt, violent and oppressive. SAPs which are sustainable will have to have been designed to be more helpful to the poor and managed within a wider strategic framework of policy for social and environmental sustainability.[61]

The redesign of SAPs is a key issue for the new century as Western governments and agencies attempt to move away from the debt policies of the 1970s and 1980s. Debt relief and forgiveness, as we will see later, could be the catalyst for a new approach to the SAPs, 'good governance' and conditions on aid.

Development aid and lower income countries

Compared to the huge sums owed by debtor countries in the developing countries and ex-Communist world and to the capital flows in the international trading system, development aid is a relatively minor item. Debt service costs in the 1990s far outweighed the value of aid. As noted above, in the 1980s there was a net flow of resources from low-income to high-income countries: aid money was effectively sent straight back in the form of interest payments. Although this state of affairs came to an end in the 1990s, with investment, loans and aid to developing countries creating a net transfer of wealth from North to South, the debt burden – and the costs imposed by corruption, war and military spending – remained high enough to keep the poorest countries in a dismal condition. In 1995, despite the overall net flow of funds to the South, developing countries still paid three times more in debt interest than they received through international aid programmes.

The sums involved in aid are large and represent an important source of capital for the poorest nations. But aid funds have declined since the early 1990s, both absolutely and as a proportion of GDP in the industrialized countries. In 1992, on average some 0.35 per cent of the GDP of the industrialized world was spent on aid; by 1997 it reached an historical low point of 0.22 per cent. The total sum also fell, from just under US$60 billion in 1992 to under US$48 billion in 1997. This represents not only a decline in real terms during a decade of great prosperity in the richest countries, but also a complete failure by Western donors to live up to the aspirations agreed at the 1992 Rio Earth Summit, which called for US$125 billion in annual aid transfers to fund the development of poorer countries on socially and environmentally sustainable lines. The US, despite its immense wealth and its major contribution to global problems such as greenhouse gas emissions, actually saw its aid spending fall as a proportion of GDP to a mere 0.10 per cent in 1995. Only four OECD countries – Denmark, The Netherlands, Norway, Sweden – managed by 1997 to meet the Rio target of aid spending as 0.7 per cent of GDP.

This trend, which undermines the ambitions set out at Rio and the UN aspiration for the numbers of people in poverty in the South to be halved by 2015, seems to be related to a number of factors: the end of the Cold War and the link between military alliance and aid; the rise in domestic demands on budgets, in particular the demand for spending on welfare, health, poverty and unemployment in the North; the decreasing need for aid to fast-growing Southern states; and a mood of scepticism about the value of aid to countries – especially in Africa – which seemed mired in corruption and civil conflict. Thus the 20th century closed with a mood of 'aid fatigue' among the rich countries despite the evident needs of the poorest countries for more ambitious assistance to put them on the path of sustainable development and stability.[62]

Much of the financial and technical assistance referred to as 'aid' comes in the form of soft loans from North to South, and thus actually amounts to a mild addition to recipient countries' debt. Moreover, aid is linked in other ways to the great structural inequalities between high- and low-income countries, and within low-income countries. First, much Western aid money is provided with the intention not only of helping the recipient but also of assisting domestic producers and boosting economic performance at home. Aid projects supply machinery and services from 'donor' countries, and assist in developing jobs at home and export markets overseas.

Second, the aid business has been distorted throughout the post-war period by the Cold War and the linkage of development aid to what the superpowers and their allies regarded as their security interests. Vast sums have been spent on military aid to allies and clients. In many cases this resulted in enormous waste, as funds flowed to dictatorships that misused them in pursuit of disastrous economic policies and through corruption: the Mobutu regime in Zaire provides a particularly grim example.[63]

Third, aid has often failed to help the poor in recipient countries and has played its part in promoting unsustainable development at the expense of the environment. This outcome stems from the combination of the two distortions noted above. Tied aid that benefits business in donor countries is unlikely to produce results that benefit, say, the rural poor in recipient countries. The kinds of projects that will result in the purchase of Western goods and services on a large scale tend to be big engineering ventures such as dam-building or high technology agricultural projects involving imports of Western pesticides and fertilizer. Such projects have generally not involved either rigorous environmental impact assessment or consideration of their effect on the living standards of poor people.

Debt and aid: towards sustainable policy

The problems posed by debt and development aid are thus intertwined, and stem from a major failure of policy integration. The style and direction of lending and aid have often encouraged the inappropriate use of resources. Industrial countries and multilateral agencies have not integrated environmental policy sufficiently into their aid and debt policies, despite acknowledgement of the need and in spite of the personal commitment of several leading actors, such as the head of the World Bank, James Wolfensohn. However, there are grounds for hope that the new ideas emerging will lead to more environmentally and socially sensitive and sustainable programmes for aid and debt relief.

First, persistent criticism from NGOs and from lower income countries has had its effect on the multilateral agencies and on Western governments. The World Bank has taken steps to improve its expertise in environmental policy, strengthen environmental impact assessment for development projects funded by the Bank, provide support to countries devising National Environment Action Plans, and commit itself to the reduction of poverty in a way that is compatible with sustainable development. Western governments now feel obliged to speak of sustainability as a key policy aim of their aid to low-income countries. Throughout the 1990s, the rhetoric and the annual reports of the IMF, the World Bank and UN agencies increasingly reflected the critique made by NGOs of traditional debt and aid policies, and acknowledged the need for more environmental and social policy integration into development policy, and for more transparency in the decision-making processes surrounding the development strategies of the global agencies.[64]

Second, the end of the Cold War has transformed the aid scene just as it has changed the international security system. The former Communist countries have largely withdrawn from bilateral commitments as domestic troubles have mounted; and Western states in turn have finally felt able to put pressure on dictatorial governments once tolerated in the name of strategic interests. Western governments and the multilateral agencies began in the early 1990s to link the provision of development finance to observance not only of market-friendly economic policies but also policies that were favourable to democratic politics. At the 1991 IMF/World Bank conference both agencies called for massive cuts in global arms spending as a key part of the redirection of aid and of lower income countries' public expenditure towards education, primary health care, family planning, improved nutrition and environmental protection. Since then the World Bank has slowly begun to respond to the environmentalist and social justice agendas of NGOs and developing countries, and its annual World Development Reports in the 1990s stressed the association between democracy, good governance and capacity for sustained and sustainable economic progress.[65]

Third, under the influence of NGOs and the experience of aid policy setbacks, the multilateral agencies have shown signs, in the post-Cold War world, of wishing to see equally dramatic changes in the policies of the rich countries as in the politics and economies of the low-income ones. The 1991 IMF/World Bank conference saw attacks by the directors of both bodies on the military spending of the industrialized countries and on the failure of the West to agree on a strategy of debt relief for the poorest debtor nations. The then head of the World Bank's Strategic Planning Division raised the possibility that sustainable development may involve the acceptance of forms of 'conditionality' on the industrialized world:

> *The task now is to rethink the function and structure of international institutions to make them responsive to the new demands imposed by the emerging, fractured global order. For example, in the same way that multilateral institutions impose economic policy conditions on developing countries in exchange for access to financial resources, is there any way a*

> *supranational institution could impose conditions on the developed countries on issues such as energy use, resource depletion and preservation of the environment? Can we devise alternative organizational and institutional arrangements capable of transcending the autonomy and sovereignty of industrialized nations and impose, if necessary, some of the changes that all of us agree are essential for human survival and a more equitable world order?*[66]

This sums up well the key questions now at the heart of development thinking for the new century. There has been a gradual convergence of ideas among NGOs, governments and international agencies over the course of the 1990s, and we can see the beginnings of a consensus on the nature of development aid, debt policy and sustainable development. The fundamental elements of this emerging consensus are as follows:

- Development policies have paid far too little attention to the issues of governance – the capacity of developing and ex-Communist countries to design and implement reform programmes which will stabilize their economies and put them on a sustainable development path, and to foster efficient, accountable and democratic institutions.
- Policies on lending and aid have failed to integrate social and environmental factors into the design and implementation of programmes.
- The OECD countries need to invest in the long-term sustainability of the South in their own ultimate self-interest, and to increase funding for environmentally and socially sustainable technologies and other investments in the developing world.
- The most heavily indebted poor countries will never be in a position to repay their debt and need to have the burden lifted in order to stand a chance of sustainable development.
- Poverty and social exclusion must be tackled along with the problems of ecological degradation since poverty and demands for better living standards often fuel the unsustainable exploitation of local environments.
- Improving education and work prospects, especially for women, is vital to the success of long-term programmes for population control and stabilization.
- Extreme inequalities in wealth and power are associated with unsustainable development and more equitable societies tend to have better economic performance.

So much of the critique of the international economic agencies over two decades has begun to be absorbed and taken seriously. In addition, the international agencies have learned fundamental lessons from their failures over the 1980s and 1990s. The World Bank drew these lessons from the global financial crisis of 1997–98:[67]

- Sound macroeconomic conditions are not enough to sustain equitable growth: the economic criteria used by the Bank and the IMF to judge the acceptability of governments' strategies are too narrow to give guidance in a turbulent, globalizing system.
- Institutions matter: the crisis underlined the contribution of poor regulation, the lack of democracy and accountability and financial transparency to economic instability and loss of confidence among investors.

- Social development, inclusion and safety-nets are vital: the crisis hit the poor hardest and emphasized the need for mechanisms to protect the most vulnerable from the shocks to which the emerging global economic system is prone.
- Only through partnering can development successes be scaled up: the interdependence of social, environmental and economic problems and solutions demands that new programmes be designed through partnerships between 'donors and other stakeholders'.

The most striking illustration of the gradual success of NGOs and other campaigners for sustainable development in influencing policy-makers has been the coordinated global campaign for debt relief for the poorest developing countries. The heavily indebted poor countries (HIPCs) suffered severely in the closing decades of the 20th century from the debt burden, which exacerbated the ills inflicted by civil wars, ethnic conflicts, natural disasters, global economic turmoil and corruption. The Jubilee 2000 campaign – an alliance of NGOs, churches and other religious bodies, politicians and individual citizens spanning the globe – was instrumental in raising public awareness of the plight of the HIPCs, countries with no prospect of repaying their debt and suffering intensely from the burden imposed by servicing debt. The campaign, calling for debt forgiveness at the Millennium (conditional on HIPCs directing the saved funds to social and environmental investment), was a spectacular illustration of a global 'action network' (see Chapters 13 and 14) linking sectors throughout civil society. Like the campaign against the MAI discussed above and like many environmental campaigns against TNCs, the movement made effective use of the Internet and other new telecommunications technology to coordinate action and information across frontiers.[68]

In large part because of the pressure of the Jubilee 2000 campaign, OECD governments began to make concessions on debt relief policy. At the summit of world leaders in Cologne in 1999, the G7 group of leading industrial nations agreed to seek ways to cancel US$100 billion of debt owed by HIPCs. This programme would bring together the IMF, the World Bank, NGOs and governments in a common strategy for converting debt service payments into investment in the HIPCs to assist the poor.

Although by the end of 1999 much of the detail of the financing mechanisms for this scale of debt forgiveness remained unclear, much progress had been made in reducing the qualification period for poor countries seeking debt reduction and in announcements by individual countries about contributions to a new trust fund for debt relief. In late 1999 Gordon Brown, the UK Chancellor of the Exchequer, responded to the Jubilee 2000 campaign directly, announcing 100 per cent cancellation of bilateral debt owed by the poorest countries:

> *This debt relief will only achieve its real goal as part of a programme for poverty relief and economic development. This year has seen a major and decisive shift in international policy towards poverty. For the first time, the development of anti-poverty and economic policy will go hand in hand. For the first time, civil society in the poorest countries will engage in their own poverty strategies. And both the IMF and the World Bank will show how together macroeconomic, structural reform and anti-poverty programmes can bring less poverty and more growth.*[69]

The condition for UK debt cancellation, intended to set a precedent, was the direction of all the money saved in debt servicing to poverty reduction and to investment in education, health care and other social programmes.

Much remains to be done before we see profound structural changes in the relationship between North and South. The debt relief programme announced at the Cologne summit does not lift the full burden from HIPCs, and it is hard to design and implement mechanisms to guarantee the targeting of saved funds into investment in anti-poverty schemes and other programmes to pursue sustainable development. But the outlines of a new 21st century partnership or 'bargain' between North and South can be glimpsed in the debt relief breakthroughs of 1999. Elements of a global compact that builds on these to promote sustainable development could be as follows:[70]

- The acceptance by developing countries of conditional debt forgiveness which would transfer all saved funds into programmes for poverty elimination, public health, primary education, disease control and prevention (especially AIDS, TB and malaria).
- The acceptance by developing countries of international audits of the spending of debt savings, conducted by independent partnerships of international agencies and NGOs with local NGOs, researchers and policy-makers.
- The acceptance by the OECD countries of the need to draw up a new MAI reflecting social and environmental sustainability issues and to reform the processes and rules of the WTO to produce a fair and sustainable free trade regime and to eliminate perverse subsidies which damage the environment and job creation.
- Acceptance by the G7 states and by the international economic agencies of the need for greater inclusion of developing countries in preparations for international summits on globalization, and for the inclusion of partnerships of NGOs, business and other groups from civil society in designing and evaluating new treaties, strategies and programmes for sustainable development.
- Support by OECD governments and trade blocs for fair trade and sustainable consumption partnerships established between NGOs, Western businesses, industry associations and farmers and other small-scale traders in developing countries.
- The promotion of new aid programmes funded by rich countries via the World Health Organization, UNDP and UN Environment Programme, for which developing countries would be eligible if they demonstrated the achievement of specified cuts in military spending and policies to protect key ecosystems and species, combat corruption and promote democracy.
- These new funds would be greatly increased budgets for: boosting Southern access to vaccines and improving public health infrastructure; investment by developing countries in renewable energy technology and other sustainable technologies; adjustment to climate change in the South; access to biotechnology research and development to improve local food production.
- New funds would be justified as compensation from North to South for the costs of climate change intensified by the fossil fuel consumption of the rich countries, and as payment for the ecological services provided by Southern ecosystems.
- New funds could be raised from new forms of global tax, to be collected via national governments in the North initially; these taxes could include levies on the carbon content of energy consumption, on international currency transactions or on Internet traffic.

Altering structural adjustment conditions on debt relief and aid in order to promote environmental protection, cut military spending, reward democratic reform and improve the lot of the poor will be formidably hard but would provide a powerful impetus towards sustainable development. Such a reorientation of aid policy, however, will need to be part of a general recasting of Western approaches to the low-income world. What is needed is not traditional aid or loans but a partnership, funded by the OECD world and above all by the US and EU, to invest in what the Harvard economist Jeffrey Sachs calls 'global public goods'[71] – sustainable environments, public health, knowledge and education, stable food and water supplies, reduction in conflicts and a rise in political stability. The key point is that fundamental reform must apply to the rich world as well as to developing countries if sustainable development is to be approached. There needs to be a structural adjustment on the part of the rich world, especially in relation to the terms of international trade and to two further components of the emerging global economic order: technology transfer and the regulation of transnational corporations. We turn to these below.

Technology Transfer

The process of industrialization is all about the transfer (sale or donation) of technology. Technology in this sense does not just mean finished products and process equipment, but includes know-how, in the form of expert personnel, information services, training programmes, manuals, and so on. The key issues in technology transfer in the emerging global industrial system concern:

- the access of low-income countries to technologies, knowledge and to the information technology networks in the West;
- appropriateness of technologies; and
- integration of technology transfer with policies for environmental protection.

The access of low-income nations to new technology is constrained by many aspects of the inequitable economic order described above. Although a number of newly industrializing countries have become important exporters of some technologies – for instance, South Korea in consumer electronics – they have done so by adopting more or less mature technologies developed already in the West; and the poorer low-income countries remain constrained by their weak position in the international trading system. Their ability to import new technologies is limited by their economic weakness, as is their capacity to build up a home-grown technological base, which is a very costly way of lessening their dependence on the imports of technology. In this situation, a major role is played by direct foreign investment and technology licensing by transnational corporations. However, the debt crises of the 1980s and 1990s, the instability of many low-income countries, and the attractiveness of the increasingly integrated markets of Western Europe and North America have reduced direct foreign investment by TNCs in lower income countries. This investment is becoming more concentrated in the industrializing countries with good growth prospects.

The policy for improving the access of low-income countries to technology cannot be based therefore mainly on the decisions of corporations on investment and licensing, but must also involve aid flows from the World Bank and other official agencies.

This raises the question of the appropriateness of technology transfer through these various mechanisms.

Inappropriate and appropriate technology

The degree of appropriateness attached to any given technology depends on answers to the following basic questions:

- how far a given technology serves a country's development needs in an environmentally sound fashion;
- how far it represents a productive use of resources;
- whether its use is likely to lead to sustainable wealth creation; and
- how far it can be maintained by local people rather than by overseas experts.

It is easy to see that much technology transfer from the high- to low-income countries in the form of aid and technical assistance has been wholly inappropriate in these terms. The 'mega-projects', such as massive dams and highways favoured by donors, financial agencies and the élites of many low-income countries, have soaked up resources that could have been used on more productive and sustainable schemes. Often closely related to this are deep-rooted corruption and organized crime, both in rich and poor countries. In the wake of the Cold War, both seem to have spread and become significant obstacles to achieving sustainable development, above all in the poorer countries. The most glaring example of inappropriate transfer is the diffusion of weaponry, on which low-income countries spent some US$38 billion a year in the late 1980s, mainly on imports from the industrial world. While spending fell after the end of the Cold War, conflicts in and between developing countries still soaked up disproportionate sums, while spending levels in the US and other rich states remained high. In 1995, impoverished countries such as Sudan and Angola, along with financially unstable and socially riven states like Pakistan and Russia, spent 5 per cent or more of GDP on military budgets, a higher proportion than the US.

With the end of the Cold War and the growing pressure in the multilateral agencies to make development aid conditional on 'good government' as well as on structural adjustment in the economy, there is some cause to hope that the transfer of military technologies will be curbed. But inappropriate civil technology is also deadly for the environment and for the well-being of people. The modernization of the South has seen a repetition of many of the features of industrial development in the West and the ex-Communist countries that are now costing billions of dollars in environmental repair work: the gross pollution of air, soil and water by heavy industry, the profligate use of energy, the dumping of toxic wastes and the obsession with the motor car. This is because the mature technologies that generate these problems have been the cheapest and easiest to import or develop on licence from the West, and have been identified with 'progress'. Licensing agreements for new technologies are harder to conclude and command higher royalties, and the skills to exploit them are scarcer. Thus the low-income countries are often in a poor position to 'leapfrog' stages of modernization and go directly for state-of-the-art technologies that are cleaner and less energy intensive.

This issue is especially relevant, of course, to the global environmental threats that have been recognized in recent years: global warming and stratospheric ozone depletion. In the light of these threats, key mature technologies massively diffused in the industrial world and readily available to the low-income countries are 'inappropriate' with a vengeance: the internal combustion engine, CFCs, coal-fired power stations, and so on. Appropriate technology capable of providing a partial solution to these problems is only now being developed and diffused in the West – for example, energy-efficient lighting and heating systems and energy-generation plant. Much of the new technology in these areas cannot be afforded by the low-income countries, including the ex-Communist industrial states.

The issue of inappropriate technological development also relates to the neglect of indigenous skills and local knowledge, which count as technologies in their own right. In the newly industrializing countries there is generally a view among governing élites that local skills and expertise are somehow primitive and thus need to be discarded in favour of Western products and processes. This 'top-down' view has been encouraged for years, of course, by Western commercial interests. The downgrading of local techniques in resource management and agriculture often means that potential sources of wealth are lost and replaced with inappropriate imported technologies that are costly to develop and maintain. In agriculture, the introduction of 'off-the-shelf' Western technologies into Africa at the expense of local people's farming knowledge is now widely regarded as a prime example of inappropriate technology transfer.

While there is evidently a role for advanced Western technology in improving agriculture in low-income countries, it must be as a complement to long-established and sustainable local knowledge, not as a wholesale replacement for it. Appropriate energy technology for rural areas in low-income countries often will best be developed as an 'intermediate' hybrid of Western or domestically produced equipment and local fuel inputs, designed with the participation of local people. For example, the Harayana sustainable energy project in India involves the development of biogas generators, gasifiers and solar water-heaters to make a village self-sufficient in renewable energy.

Unfair technology transfer from South to North

The debate over technology transfer tends to be based on the assumption that the transfer is all in one direction – from the high-income North to the low-income South. In fact, massive transfers of technology have been going on for years from the developing world to the industrial countries in the form of genetic resources. Southern seeds for crop plants represent a technology of fundamental value to low- and high-income countries alike, for which the low-income countries have had no means of charging. Seed varieties have been collected for decades by Western scientists and companies, and have been developed intensively in the industrial world with no 'royalty payments' going to the farmers who originally bred them in the low-income countries. The advent of new biotechnologies in the rich world and the ability of TNCs to exploit Southern bioresources by patenting bioengineered varieties of them to establish a grip on the supply of seed to farmers, have made this an explosive issue for rich–poor world relations.[72] As Jeffrey Sachs has put it,

> *... just as knowledge is becoming the undisputed centrepiece of global prosperity (and lack of it, the core of human impoverishment), the global regime on intellectual property rights requires a new look. The United States prevailed upon the world to toughen patent codes and cut down on intellectual piracy. But now transnational corporations and rich-country*

> *institutions are patenting everything from the human genome to rainforest diversity. The poor will be ripped off unless some sense and equity are introduced into this runaway process.*[73]

This inequitable relationship must change, since the industrial countries are now aware that their seed banks are inadequate to the task of conserving varieties and that genetic resources are being eroded at an accelerating rate in the South as forests and other crucial ecosystems are destroyed. There is growing pressure on the high-income countries to establish international funds for the payment of developing countries for the conservation of genetic resources and ecological 'services' – for example, as performed by the rainforests – and for the patenting of traditional local knowledge, including plant varieties. Such developments would lead to large transfers of money and sustainable technology to the low-income countries.

Sustainable technology transfer

There is no single 'package' of appropriate technology that can be devised to suit the needs of all countries, but the key elements of a portfolio of appropriate technologies can be identified. These concern energy efficiency, minimal waste generation, maximum resource efficiency and, above all, the 'soft' technologies for sustainable development such as technology assessment, environmental impact assessment, and training and research systems that involve local people in the analysis of problems and in devising solutions.

This last point is crucial: technology transfer should not be seen as a purely commercial and technical operation, but as a social transaction demanding attention to local circumstances and appropriate local management. The 'soft' technologies that are vital to effective technology transfer include new approaches to environmental management explored in Chapters 7–9 and in the case studies that follow. In essence this means that the transfer of technology must be integrated with policies in other areas that are designed to promote sustainable development. While this task demands the involvement of intergovernmental agencies, national governments and other public agencies, and the transfer of resources on a large scale through official mechanisms to the low-income countries, it must also bring in the private sector. This leads us finally to consider the role of the transnational corporations (TNCs) in technology transfer and the development of sustainable industrial systems.

Transnational Corporations

TNCs are corporate networks with production facilities and subsidiary companies in more than one country. Some 81 per cent have headquarters in OECD countries and are a key force in the internationalization of industrial production and of Western consumer tastes. There are over 53,000 TNCs with some 450,000 foreign subsidiary companies; their power reaches far into supply chains of smaller producers throughout the world; and the scale and power of some TNCs have been greatly increased by mergers and acquisitions which increased significantly in number and value in the 1990s.[74] The TNCs have been for many years the object of vehement criticism from the South and from Western NGOs as 'neo-colonialists', playing a key role in the degradation of the environment and exploitation of working people in low-income countries. The view of TNCs as leviathans trampling the earth is encouraged by contemplation of their weight in the global economy:

- The TNCs dominate international trade, accounting for 70 per cent of it, and in particular they control almost all world trade in many primary commodities such as tea, coffee, copper, forest products and bauxite.
- They dominate direct foreign investment.
- Some have turnovers that exceed the GDP of small low-income nations.
- They are a key source of technology transfer for the industrializing countries.
- They are responsible for most of the world's technological innovation, including the development of environmental protection technologies.

By any standard, then, the TNCs constitute a critically important element of the global economy, yet their global reach is not matched by international regulation. The environmental impacts of the TNCs are controlled by the regulations of the various countries playing host to them and by whatever policies for self-regulation they devise on environmental protection. The microeconomic linkages forged by TNCs and their host country customers and suppliers amount in some cases to the cartelization of markets, but there is no international anti-trust law to regulate TNCs' competition. The international political and institutional capacity to deal with the consequences of globalization at the level of the corporation is almost wholly lacking.

The TNCs have an immense impact on the global environment and, in the absence of global regulations on their behaviour, it becomes crucial to know how they respond to international guidelines and national environmental law, and how they develop internal standards for environmental protection. On this point, recent research reveals a patchy response by TNCs, but also considerable potential for the positive development of corporate strategies. A survey in 1991 by the United Nations Centre on Transnational Corporations of over 200 TNCs with annual sales of over US$200 billion indicated that their environmental policies were influenced most strongly by home country legislation and very little by international guidelines and global ecological problems.[75] The majority had no integrated environmental policy. The environmental challenges that were best understood were those on which Western countries had developed the most extensive legislation, such as air and water pollution. Those lowest on the agenda were the issues associated with the low-income countries – loss of biodiversity, soil erosion and explosive population growth.

The main message from this research was that environmental policy in the largest TNCs is as yet unintegrated: the performance may go beyond legal requirements in any particular country, but there is a long way to go before TNCs develop proactive strategies that raise environmental standards on a company-wide basis, and take global and Southern environmental problems as seriously as they have begun to take those of most concern in their domestic bases. Yet the research showed that there were some grounds for optimism on this score:

- Respondents to the UN survey said they wanted more international standard setting.
- The TNCs are conscious of public opinion in the West in relation to industrial accidents with severe ecological consequences and thus are keen to promote a 'greener' image.

- Perhaps most significantly, there was a reported trend towards centralized standard setting within the TNC, whereby the parent company lays down environmental quality standards and targets for the entire operation. This development could offer opportunities to environmental lobby groups and international agencies to collaborate with TNCs in policy development and ensuring the consistent implementation of corporate strategy in different countries.

Since this research was undertaken, many TNCs have accepted that they need to integrate sustainable development thinking into their core business operations and strategic planning, to push for better international policy-making and standard setting, to communicate better with their 'stakeholders', including consumers and NGOs, and to cooperate with NGOs rather than to fight them. The lessons have been hard for many corporations: consider the turmoil unleashed within Shell by its public relations disasters in conflicts with Greenpeace and other NGOs in the mid-1990s, and by Monsanto after it failed to understand the rising public and NGO opposition to its approach to genetically modified food technologies. Increasingly, TNCs such as Shell, Rio Tinto, BP and IBM are developing policies and techniques for reporting publicly on their environmental and social performance and goals, and for measuring the environmental and social impacts of their products and processes. And more TNCs have begun to seek collaborative relationships with NGOs in setting standards for sustainable production and harvesting, as in the Marine Stewardship Council and Forest Stewardship Council established by the WWF with business partners such as Unilever to certify sustainable fishing and forestry practices among member organizations.

Such voluntary initiatives and business NGO partnerships will proliferate as TNCs come to see them as vital sources of public trust, social legitimacy and ultimately of new competitive potential.[76] But most TNCs remain largely untouched by the pressures from the emerging global networks of NGOs and consumer lobby groups. There is a growing acknowledgement of the need for more systematic regulation of the new global marketplace in which TNCs flourish. The TNCs need to be regulated within an international regime on competition, investment, trade rules, and environmental and social standards that requires them to observe policies that are compatible with sustainable development and fair trade. This kind of international economic framework is a distant goal and will take complex and lengthy negotiation, but it is at the top of the agenda for 21st-century global governance.

Meanwhile, it is crucial that TNCs are encouraged to live up to the rhetoric of high-profile international business groupings in favour of sustainable development, to adopt and diffuse new environmental technologies, and to adopt sustainable policies on a voluntary basis across countries.[77] For this to happen we need to continue to go beyond confrontation between TNCs, developing country governments and environmental NGOs. While campaigning and tough criticism must go on, there must also be a recognition that the TNCs are a fundamental element in the global economy and will remain so. Their dominant position in international trade, research and development and technology transfer means that their cooperation in the creation of a sustainable global economy is critical. The scope for more proactive policies within the TNCs and the tapping of TNCs' expertise and wealth in the development of sustainable policies is such that international agencies and environmental lobbies should look hard for ways of collaborating with the TNCs as well as confronting and constraining them. The 'soft technology' for this may well exist in the form of the action-centred networks discussed in Parts IV and V.

Conclusion

In this chapter we have considered the key features of the emerging global industrial economy. This consists of an intricate and interconnected system of networks that must be reformed on many levels if the process of sustainable development is to be realized. The global economy is characterized by dynamic but grossly uneven development, reflecting the outcome of colonial history and the scientific and technological ascendancy of the West; by Western domination of international trade and technology transfer; by the massive financial and technological power of the TNCs; by the dependence of many low-income countries on the TNCs and Western governments because of indebtedness, inappropriate aid, and the ruinous economic, social and military policies of many Southern and ex-Communist élites; and by the export to the low-income countries not only of welcome aspirations to democracy and improved living standards, but also of the profoundly mixed blessings of Western tastes in consumption, Western modes of industrial production, liberal market economic policies and the pollution problems of affluence.

The key issue is how far the existing elements of the global industrial system can integrate environmental consciousness into their operations and thereby adapt to a sustainable development path. The overriding environmental failure of the economic order has been its lack of integration of ecological concerns into 'mainstream' policy-making. However, there are numerous signs of hope. The IMF and the World Bank have begun to make important changes in policy to promote sustainable development. There is a greater understanding of the social and ecological consequences of debt and aid, and the beginnings of a constructive strategy for eliminating the worst of the debt burden of the poorest countries. But more work is crucial to build mechanisms for promoting the integration of environmental management and anti-poverty policy into the core activities of the WTO, the IMF, the World Bank and the TNCs, as well as of national and regional governments throughout the world. In this context the analysis of organizational constraints and the proposals for organizational innovation and 'action networking' across sectoral and institutional frontiers, which are developed in Chapter 7 and the following chapters, are of great relevance. Before turning to these, however, we examine further political constraints within which new approaches to sustainable development must be devised.

6

Top–Down or Bottom–Up? The Dilemma of Development

Social mobilization at local levels needs to be backed by mobilization around policy issues that require national and even international resolution. A global capitalism requires a global approach to the environmental question.

John Friedmann[1]

People already have the knowledge; what they must have are the rights over their local environments. This is the big problem in the world today. The vast majority of people have become passive observers, and a few people are taking decisions for everyone else. That is the prime reason why the environment is being destroyed.

Anil Agarwal and Sunita Narain[2]

It is a central contention of this book that good environmental management is not a technical exercise separate from everyday economic and political life or something tacked on after the fact of development, but that it can only come about when environmental values are embedded within economic and political systems. For this to occur it is first necessary to understand something of those systems and the basic tensions that affect them. In modern political systems, particularly democratic ones, an enduring tension exists between top-down forces and bottom-up aspirations.

This tension, essentially involving the forces of centralization and decentralization, is of concern in environmental management for two reasons. First, at a general level, it provides much of the political context for unfolding debates about the meaning of sustainable development in many countries. The range of tensions is growing as the world economy integrates but also as more and more ethnic or nationalist groups aspire to self-government. At the extreme, as in the recent civil war in the former Yugoslavia, society and the environment are ruined, and nothing sustainable can hope to be created except in the long term. But in many non-violent circumstances, tension is also endemic which can be negative, as with the gradual erosion of the basis for federalism in Canada, or generally positive, as with the forging of the European Union, but also strengthened regionalism within nation states in the Union, such as Catalan autonomy or the advent of the Scottish Parliament. In these cases the tension between centralization and decentralization is fundamental to the dynamic of the political system.

Second, and more specifically, is the meaning of self-management whereby people define their own problems and take control of their own environments. This is fundamental to the network approach espoused here, but it begs the questions of scale and participation. Who decides how sustainable development is defined for what unit of territory: the neighbourhood, the town, the region, the province, the nation state or larger, and who participates in its implementation? In many cases sustainable development has no hope of realization where the problem is defined at the wrong scale, either too grandly or in too limited a way, or where relevant stakeholders are excluded from participation. There are no ready answers, but a grounding in the arguments is needed if we are to try to tackle some of these basic questions.

Centralization and Decentralization

It is in the interplay between two criteria for good government put forward by John Stuart Mill, democratic participation and efficiency, that fascinating issues arise concerning the relative advantages and disadvantages of top-down versus bottom-up action and control for sustainable development. In *Liberty*, Mill argues for local self-government from a conception of the absolute priority of individual liberty, which he understands as the absence of restraint in relation to the self-regarding actions of individuals, groups and local political authorities. Just as the individual has a right to liberty in personal matters, there is a similar '... liberty in any number of individuals to regulate by mutual agreement such things as regard them jointly, and regard no persons but themselves'.[3] Here local self-government provides an important institutional buffer against the abuse of power by greater society.

The other great value of local control argued by Mill is efficiency in the management and delivery of local services by virtue of responsiveness to local need. He states '... it is but a small portion of the public business of a country which can be well done or safely attempted by the central authorities'.[4] Local officials could be held accountable and this ensured a measure of efficiency in meeting local needs.

Chapter 5 documented the integration of the world economy which increasingly impinges on all aspects of life and which is experienced by individuals and communities largely as a 'top-down' transformation of social and physical environments. In this chapter we see how action by government to support economic development and to buttress its own power also tends to be centralizing, but also how there are increasing demands for democratic participation and decentralization of control.

Trends to centralization within national boundaries are associated with:

- the rise of the modern state;
- increasing control by central governments of policy funding and the redistribution of resources on a territorial basis;
- cultural homogenization; and
- extension of administrative control through professions and bureaucracies.

Trends to decentralization are often the result of:

- political responses to ideological regionalism or ethnic nationalism;
- measures for the promotion of regional economic development;
- measures to mobilize local resources and generate commitment;
- functional responses to government overload, bureaucratic unresponsiveness or the continual failure of centralized policy initiatives.

At a deeper level, decentralizing tendencies may also be a reaction against the socio-economic forces in modern life that produce homogeneity, the concentration of power and the centralization of functions. They may reflect the deep-seated impulse in 'post-traditional' societies for political participation, emancipation, and the realization of democratic values.[5] Both centralizing and decentralizing forces operate simultaneously in modern societies, which creates a dilemma for environmental management.

The tension between centralization and decentralization is more complex than it may first appear. At a basic level it represents the difference, say, between top-down approaches such as that of the World Bank, the IMF or national governments the world over, compared with very local, usually NGO-led, environmental initiatives. Examples of the latter range from the expanding network of Groundwork Trusts in Britain and Europe, described later, to the many thousands of village projects in lower income countries, such as the Kibwezi Women's Project in Kenya which promotes small-scale, sustainable business initiatives such as brickmaking and honey production. Much of the debate is polarized by these two divergent approaches, centralized or community-based.

In reality the tension is more pervasive. It permeates our lives and our concerns for development, whether in higher or lower income countries. It is a basic problem of the modern state in which demands for democratic participation and the devolution of decision-making may clash with demands for economic efficiency and decisive policy-making at national or international levels. For example:

- In relation to the European Union, some member states are concerned that the EU is over-centralizing decision-making on environmental policy and impact assessment procedures, and rapidly encroaching on the sovereignty of the state. For others, however, the centralization of many aspects of policy in Brussels has come not a moment too soon for the purposes of environmental protection, which they feel receives no more than lip service from national government.
- This type of issue will be replicated on a world scale over questions such as ozone depletion and global warming. Unless there is a great increase in willingness to enter into binding agreements, it may not be long before countries will need to be pressured into giving up large areas of environmental policy to supranational agencies.
- At the national level there is growing concern about how best to organize the state for the purposes of pollution control and sustainable development. For example, in Nigeria the Federal Environmental Protection Agency (FEPA) has had to wrestle with the challenge of how to organize environmental policy, monitoring and scientific testing in the 30 Nigerian states, taking into account the very limited resources available for administration and the many political and cultural constraints. Their solution is to devolve as many functions as possible to the states while retaining a necessary degree of policy and control within the federal government. For many countries, Britain and Canada included, the reorganization of government functions can be an important aspect of exerting environmental control.
- At the local level, there are many examples where local NGO-managed projects are successful in countries as diverse as Britain and Kenya, but there are also many other well-intentioned local projects that are undone by the effects of international economic integration. Urban renewal efforts may be undone by the effects

of decisions taken by multinational corporations headquartered in other countries. This lack of real control is a classic problem of local development.

There is, of course, no one right answer to the dilemma of how to balance top-down and bottom-up forces, either by reference to the criteria of democratic participation or efficiency. Both forces must be harnessed to the needs of sustainable development, in a flexible and balanced approach that is sensitive to local circumstances.

There is also a broader issue at stake. This is the endemic tension between the powerful trend toward specialization and integration which characterizes the modern industrial state, and aspirations for the integration of social, economic and environmental forces on a regional or local basis for the purposes of sustainable development. In many cases the very nature of environmental problems requires action on such a territorial basis, but within national and international contexts.

Unfortunately the trend to centralization is powerful and it is difficult to turn to the real world for examples of genuine decentralization in the pursuit of sustainable development, at least at the scale of the region, which is often the appropriate level for carrying out environmental management tasks. In the next section we analyse an intelligent proposal by some 'new decentralists' for regional control for sustainable development, along with the powerful obstacles to its realization. We examine below the main forces behind the demand for centralization and international integration on the one hand, and that for decentralization on the other.

Top-down: the trend to centralization and international integration

First and foremost, government has to service the economic system as the ultimate source of the material resources upon which its political survival depends. Government must also monitor, control and organize its utilization of these economic resources.[6] Clearly, central governments have an overriding interest in retaining responsibility for economic policy and demand management.

After the First World War, and especially during the Great Depression, central governments in the West started to build up their monopoly of economic intervention and planning. This position was consolidated during the Second World War, and after the war most states assumed responsibility for economic stability through Keynesian management of the economy. This trend to greater government control coincided with the concentration of economic power in the hands of oligopolistic, multinational corporations. The state of any national economy thus became both a national and a supranational issue. Most national governments see it as in their interests to manage the economy on behalf of oligopolistic corporations, often by providing the infrastructure upon which industrial production depends, access to natural resources, financial and tax incentives and export credit guarantees, in addition to supportive monetary, fiscal and trade policies.

Market-friendly conservative governments have recently sought to decrease government expenditure as a proportion of GDP and to subject more aspects of society to market mechanisms, following the doctrines of economists such as Hayek and Milton Friedman. However, most central governments, whatever their professed *laissez-faire* stance, are unlikely to diminish their hold over economic management without a struggle. Paradoxically, the rhetoric of the 'freedom of the market' is often used at the same time as policies on public spending drastically restrict the power of local government agencies. In Britain, for example, more than a decade of attempts to impose a supposedly minimalist, *laissez-faire* state has only served to reinforce centralist trends. As Rhodes notes, Thatcherism '... provided the clearest assertion yet of the centre's belief in its right to govern'.[7] Jenkins puts it more dramatically:

> *In order to liberate the individual from the State it has had to wield the power of the State in order to devolve economic choice upon the sovereign consumer, his democratic possibilities have been narrowed.*[8]

Following from this, Eversley makes the point that so long as major decisions on economic management rest with central governments, these decisions will predetermine all lesser decisions related to regional economic development and environmental management, and thus pre-empt much of the decision-making power in the regions and localities.[9] In Canada, for example, central government decisions on the timing and location of oil and gas exploration and production, and the provision of generous grants and tax incentives to multinational energy corporations, seldom have anything to do with local needs and may run counter to them. This illustrates that local considerations often get short shrift when national issues are at stake.

Other centralizing forces

The centralizing tendencies in the modern state based on the imperatives of economic management are complemented by other factors. These include population growth, the drift from the country to the city as agriculture becomes more mechanized, and the increased mobility of city dwellers responding to changing labour market conditions. In the West, and to an ever greater extent in the rest of the modernizing world, these factors contribute to a decline in the individual's orientation around a place and a rise in orientation around functional groups, such as professional colleagues. Centralization is also reinforced by professionalization and the growth of bureaucracies. Professional knowledge and the allegiances of bureaucrats to central government often transcend local allegiances and patterns of life and lead to their erosion.

A related factor is cultural homogenization, brought about by improved transportation and the development of communication networks, especially radio and television. Sharpe notes, for example, that where an emergent national media system carries advertising, centralization and 'metropolitanism' are enhanced by the promotion of worldwide mass consumption.[10] The penetration of American consumer culture to every corner of the globe via satellite television is a case in point. Smith argues that such developments are '... a powerful socially homogenizing force that undermines parochial sentiment and interest in the uniqueness of regional cultures'.[11] Modern politics reflect the tension between such forces, and the attempts of cultural movements and organizations to preserve local culture and language as, for example, the struggle of native groups in Canada and New Zealand to preserve their cultural identities.

In every case, financial control is the acid test of the balance of power between the central and the local. The potential for conflict is clear:

> *On the one hand, it is impossible to have meaningful local political autonomy without corresponding financial resources. On the other hand, many*

> *advocates of an energetic economic policy claim that central steering of subnational expenditure policies is inevitable.*[12]

It is probable that constitutional, or ad hoc, devolution of power is virtually meaningless without corresponding transfers of control over financial resources.

Finally, the advent of the modern state has raised expectations for territorial justice within the nation, and central governments are usually the only level of administration able to reallocate resources between subnational units, based on need. This process serves to concentrate power at the centre, and indeed constitutes one of the major ethical arguments in favour of central power. As Bogdanor notes: '... territorial justice is a fundamental aspiration in most modern democracies, and it can easily serve to reconcentrate powers at the centre'.[13] The same holds true for many aspects of environmental, transport and land-use planning – for example, in watershed systems which cut across administrative boundaries and demand centralized arbitration and control.

Trends to decentralization

Despite the centralizing trends noted above, the modern world is marked also by countervailing pressures on the centralized nation state and supranational bodies. There is general agreement that decentralization should involve a genuine transfer of power – that is, the transfer of legislative, judicial or administrative authority. Decentralization thus usually requires the creation of local political or administrative institutions. The notion of decentralization covers a wide range of concepts. For example:

> *It can be defined as the transfer of responsibility for planning, management and the raising and allocation of resources from the central government and its agencies to field units of central government ministries or agencies, subordinate units or levels of government, semi-autonomous public authorities or corporations, area-wide regional or functional authorities, or non-governmental private or voluntary organizations.*[14]

Within this conception of decentralization, based on a number of country studies, Rondinelli and Nellis suggest four sub-categories:[15]

1. Devolution is the creation or strengthening, financially or legally, of subnational units of government, whose activities are substantially outside the direct control of central government.
2. Deconcentration is the handing over of some administrative authority or responsibility to lower levels within central government ministries and agencies – a shifting of workload from centrally located officials to staff or offices located outside the centre.
3. Delegation involves the transfer of managerial responsibility for specially defined functions to organizations outside the regular bureaucratic structure.
4. Through privatization or the creation of arms-length agencies, governments divest themselves of responsibility for functions either by transferring them to voluntary organizations or by allowing them to be performed by private enterprises.

Political or ethnic nationalism

There are many reasons for decentralization. One is the increasing desire for political representation at the regional level. Outside the classic pre-1945 federations (Australia, Canada, Switzerland and the US), political regionalism is a recent phenomenon, based on convictions that decentralization is essential in a true democracy, and that regional (or local) underdevelopment runs counter to notions of territorial justice. In many countries, political regionalism is a reaction against dictatorial regimes that are associated with a high degree of bureaucratic centralization and lack of local autonomy.

The political form of decentralization is generally shaped within a federation or a regionalized administrative system. The initial impetus may be a political crisis, decolonization and/or liberation, and subsequent political bargaining. In any case, whenever subnational units of government have been established, central government generally recognizes that it cannot function solely on the basis of national minorities. Instead, two 'political logics come into play ... one, the classic democratic logic of one man – one vote, the other the logic of cooperation between entities differently constituted'.[16] The recognition of the two logics is institutionalized by either an organization designed to facilitate central–regional (or local) bargaining, or through the representation of provincial units at the centre to secure the resolution of territorial conflict. However, the creation of a subnational level of government sets up a new locus of power:

> *Elected provincial assemblies will claim they are best able to represent public opinion in the areas of their jurisdiction, and their electorates may support this claim. The assemblies will enjoy a degree of legitimacy arising from popular election, and those who have elected them are likely to resent intervention by the centre, whatever formal powers central government enjoys. Even if constitutional theory dictates that ultimate legislative power remains with central government, the political facts may well indicate that power has been nearly irrevocably transferred.*[17]

Another force towards political decentralization is regional or ethnic nationalism, when groups with a common culture demand a greater degree of self-government and an enhanced share of national resources. To share a culture means to share a language or a religion or a history, and often the notion of cultural and especially language and/or religious heritage is seen as a fundamental democratic freedom which cannot be denied by the state. Such nationalism is often a reaction against over-centralization in the modern state. In highly centralized and bureaucratic India for example, separatism in Punjab and Assam threatens the integrity of the state. Many commentators attribute this to the abuse of central power by New Delhi, particularly in the economic sphere.[18]

The experience of the ex-Communist states in the aftermath of the 1989–91 period of revolution illustrates this reaction well. The weakening of central authority led to an explosion of demands for increased ethnic and regional autonomy within federal systems (the former USSR, Czechoslovakia, Yugoslavia) or for outright independence. Authoritarian over-centralization in the Communist years produced a dynamic trend towards ethnic nationalism once the dictatorships fell, often leading to a degree of political and economic disintegration that threatened to be ultimately destructive of local culture and economic prospects – as in the violent break-up of the former Yugoslavia and the intermittent wars in the ex-Soviet Asian republics. During such radical and rapid disintegration, environmental considerations are likely to be laid to one side and it may be many years before any progress is possible.

In its most radical form, then, outright separation is demanded by radical action – for example, by the Tamils in Sri Lanka. The problems of separatism in the Punjab (and Kashmir and Assam) have been laid at the door of over-centralization:

> *Yet a closer look at India's problems suggests that most of them have been aggravated precisely by the abuse of central power. The energies of a naturally entrepreneurial and hard-working people have been stultified. A monstrous bureaucracy has been created. Controls breed evasion and corruption, and corruption breeds violence.*[19]

The list of more modest, non-violent forms could go on and on. The Polish journalist Ryszard Kapuscinski, considering the fervent calls by near-starving refugees in an Ethiopian camp for independence for a region of Somalia rather than bread, muses:

> *I thought about that powerful, dominating force: the need to feel at home, to be independent, to lock oneself within the four walls of one's own national, religious, racial or cultural home. It seems that in so far as the twentieth century was one of ideology, the next might become the century of nationalism.*[20]

In some cases, interest in cultural heritage can diminish during a process of the integration of regional economies and traditional cultures into the global economic system. A common result of that integration for cultural minorities and indigenous peoples is alienation from both tradition and from the modern lifestyle of consumerism. In Canada, for example, suicide, divorce and alcoholism rates among native people rose alarmingly following the 'opening up' and modernization of Canada's north in the 1950s and 1960s. Such problems for native people continue in Canada and the United States to this day, but also out of this alienation arises renewed interest in the former traditional, usually sustainable, way of life. The act of asserting cultural independence can contribute to renewed self-respect within ethnic minorities, increased demands for self-government, and perhaps to some creative fusion of tradition and modernity. In Canada, the dramatic decision to carve a huge new territory called Nunavut out of the Northwest Territories in 1999, to be controlled by the mainly aboriginal residents, creates the opportunity to tackle the physical, moral and political aspects of these issues in a direct and exciting manner.

The demands for more suitable forms of representation arising out of political or ethnic nationalism can take many forms, from neighbourhood committees to regional parliaments. Agarwal and Nairan report on the recent development of village-level control in Rajasthan, authorized under the state's Gramden Act of 1971.[21] This act, inspired by early Gandhian leaders, allows a village assembly, the *gram sabha*, made up of all adults, to manage the resources within the village boundary and to judge, prosecute and penalize those who violate a self-imposed environment and land-use plan. Given this degree of self-control – which is highly unusual within India's extensive bureaucratic structure – Rajasthani villages are devising the effective means of sustainable management of their own environment. This is not for the purpose of increasing GNP in monetary terms, but to increase the 'gross natural product' upon which villagers' well-being depends.[22]

At another level, regional parliaments have recently been created in Spain to defuse Basque and Catalan separatism. The functions of such parliaments – for example, in taxation, spending or environmental control – then become an open question which increasingly needs to include discussion of the potential for sustainable development.

Finally, cultural nationalism is of interest to our purposes for at least two reasons. The first is that cultural diversity is as important to sustainable development as biodiversity, and for much the same reasons. The erosion of traditional knowledge and skills in the face of relentless modernization is a grave loss to the repertoire of environmental management, whether in the case of the skills of Amerindians in Guyana, Innuits in the Canadian Arctic, or peasant farmers in Indonesia or India. These skills invariably represent knowledge that has been evolved and refined over many generations and, once lost, are unlikely ever to be retrieved within the context of modern science and industrialism. Moreover, innovative thinking on management is moving in the direction of fine-grained, localized responses to the seemingly overwhelming range and complexity of the problems that face us. The erosion, and even extinction, of cultures and their knowledge reduces the range of possible responses we might make to the global *problematique*. Even in a strictly functional sense, this is a profound mistake.

Second, and again from an instrumental point of view, once a cultural group organizes politically, the common symbolic system makes for efficient collective action because organizational costs are relatively low.[23] Political entrepreneurs often exploit this organizational advantage to make collective claims for resources and control. There is no particular reason why environmental activists could not do likewise. A common culture can circumvent the need for a lengthy process of searching for common meaning and definition of the nature of sustainable development. We are not claiming, of course, that this will necessarily happen, but only that cultural nationalism may provide an opportunity for defining and implementing local forms of sustainable development.

Functional decentralization

Another spur to decentralization is the remoteness of central government from its regions and its clients, which can result in poor communication, deficient design and implementation of programmes, and squandered resources from information overload, bureaucratic ineptitude, 'buckpassing' and political patronage. A whole literature on service decentralization and implementation has arisen. Peeters, for example, argues that decentralization may be the solution to overcoming government overload, which he argues is a common characteristic of the modern state.[24] Decentralists argue that assessment of needs and the delivery of services can be made more efficient and effective by localizing the administrative structure. Closely linked to this is the demand for more responsiveness and access through participation – for example, to counteract bureaucratic dominance and to ensure citizens' involvement in such areas as education or environmental planning as much as in the political act of voting.

Core, Periphery and Regional Self-Development

After ideology and ethnicity, impetus for decentralization also comes from the need to mobilize resources for self-development. This can be a direct reaction against the integration of regional economies into the international economic system, a process which can debilitate sustainable local economies. This process, by which peripheral, often agricultural, regions become the ultimate victims of apparent national economic progress, is not new, but is part and parcel of the trend in industrial societies to functional integration of economies at the expense of spatial integration. For example, Weaver describes the process in 19th-century England:

> *Both the small scale territorial community and the biological family were alienated from the production process, and people in ever-increasing numbers were pushed off the land to become urban factory workers. This freed the countryside as well for organization along factory lines. The metropolis boomed, becoming itself an extended factory – surrounded by the squalour of working class housing. The countryside was first reduced to a position of political and economic subservience, and then, in much of the industrial West, it was all but obliterated as a social environment.*[25]

There are many modern parallels, not only in lower income countries, such as Africa which has had to shift to the chemically intensive monocultural farming of export crops, but also in the continuing dramatic changes in the rural economies of countries such as Britain and the United States, where communities have been profoundly changed by a shift to high technology factory farming. In the 1970s, some of the older industrial regions themselves – the 'rustbelts' – became part of the economic periphery as a result of deindustrialization and the rise of the service/office sector economy in new centres of economic growth.

This powerful conception of uneven spatial development as a basic element in capitalism is captured in the terminology of 'core–periphery' analysis which holds that dominant regions are the locus of decision-making, and exploit and discriminate against less developed regions for their own gain. Residents of those disadvantaged regions thus become alienated from the national state. Although not without its limitations, this core–periphery metaphor is a helpful heuristic device for thinking about colonialism, the rise of the modern state and regional social movements in terms of power, managerial control and the dimensions of democratic action.[26] Some regions in the higher income countries are part of the periphery, and whole countries, such as many poor African states, are also part of the world's periphery.

Attempts to avoid or overcome peripheralization at the level of the region have given rise to various attempts at regional development planning. Although the Scottish ecologist Patrick Geddes can be credited with an early conception of the viability of the region as a level of ecological understanding and action, regional planning per se is often traced to the early activities in the 1930s of the Tennessee Valley Authority in the United States, which harnessed hydroelectric power as a lever for improving the fortunes of one of America's poorest regions.

Although planning at the level of the region is probably critical to sustainable development, regional planning need not necessarily involve genuine decentralization of power. All its institutional trappings, regional development departments or agencies, development grants, controls over industrial location and the like, can serve to centralize power in the national government. This is because regional development policy invariably institutes new financial and administrative instruments which are controlled ultimately by central politicians and bureaucrats. It is for this reason that regional planning is sometimes disparagingly referred to as 'technocratic regionalism' by its more radical critics, such as the 'new decentralists' or ecoregionalists. It is instructive to look at their proposals for what they consider to be the genuine regional decentralization of power.

The new decentralists' proposals

This group of environmental planner–philosophers addresses the issues of the regional decentralization of power in relation to sustainable development. Hebbert suggests that the terms for this debate have been set by the emergence of a strong decentralist school whose leading exponent is John Friedmann.[27] He sees development planning, including for the United States, as a field with technical, moral and utopian dimensions:

> *The first dimension answers to the question of how we can best achieve the ends we seek. The second answers to the question of how we shall live with one another. It is fundamentally a question of social and environmental ethics. And the third addresses the long-term future and our vision of what life for all of us might be like. It is what inspires us beyond the mundane affairs of politics. Utopian visions enshrine our hopes.*[28]

The new decentralism questions the very organization and goals of the world development process as we know it, and the likelihood that it could ever possibly lead to sustainable development. Friedmann argues that function has superseded territory as the mode of the economic organization in the world. This has resulted in a global development crisis in which ways of thinking and modes of action are based on false assumptions about the inevitability of the functional integration of the world economy.

Such integration is based on abstract, rational and large-scale economic behaviour, as opposed to small-scale, local or regional patterns of integration. The latter take place in real, territorially delimited places, while the former takes place in increasingly abstract, functional space, bridged by high technology communication and involving large-scale, impersonal human interactions. Functional integration in production, transport and technology is epitomized by vertically integrated multinational corporations and international banking activities. In many cases the power of functionally organized institutions is supranational. The assumption made by proponents of functional integration as a development path is that smaller scale communities (localities, regions or even nation states) can only develop through interaction with more 'highly developed' communities or countries, and then only by accepting the larger unit's definition of development. This is part and parcel of the paternalistic view of the 'underdeveloped' world by the 'developed' world, which is discussed in Chapter 2. Whether we accept this view or not, we must accept that, in current conditions, it is backed up by the sheer financial power and economic control of international capital.

The situation of Guyana in South America provides a stark example of the process of functional integration. Burdened by a debt of US$1.7 billion for a dwindling population of less than a million, Guyana has launched an IMF-sponsored Economic Recovery Programme which involves a massive sell-off of the natural resources of its near-pristine rainforest. First in line was an Anglo-Dutch company which purchased logging rights to 1.1 million acres of rainforest. This was followed by the purchase of 4 million acres by Korean and Malaysian companies, the latter said to be partly responsible for the dramatic deforestation of Sarawak.[29] Canadian, Australian and Brazilian mining companies are purchasing mineral rights, and Brazilian businessmen have paid for a US$30 million road which bisects Guyana south to north and will open up 140,000 square kilometres of rainforest to development.

Although the Guyanese have every right to determine their own path to development, it is an open question whether such events as these are compatible with long-term, sustainable development benefiting the Guyanese people, including the Amerindians who already live a sustainable lifestyle. Chapter 11 reports an effort by the environment agency for Guyana to establish a policy framework which is strong enough to deal with such issues.

The dramatic costs of functional integration in general are summarized by Friedmann as the apparent gains in production at the cost of the devastation of nature, the ruthless destruction of traditional ways of life, the exploitation of labour, inequality between rich and poor, and gross regional disparity.[30] Friedmann argues that, even where the usual kinds of development planning are attempted, they invariably fail because they leave untouched the effective balance of power between core and periphery political communities.

The solution suggested is decentralized regional integration based on territorial units with the highest possible degree of economic sovereignty. Friedmann's proposal is underpinned by his earlier, influential theory of societal planning, called 'transactive' to denote that knowledge is joined to action through personal transactions, and that theory itself is transformed by effective learning.[31] This 'learning society' is to be organized through decentralized control of the means of production and distribution, and the development of a cellular socioeconomic organization that maximizes personal interaction and dialogue and promotes the capacity for independent action by communities.

Friedmann has applied his concepts of societal learning to problems of regional development, particularly thinking about South America, where he had worked. In *Territory and Function* he explores the dichotomy between functional and territorial integration of the regional economy as a prelude to arguing for an economically decentralized, territorial basis for sustainable development, which he calls agropolitan development.[32] The objective is 'an argument from political theory' and a 'fuller rationale for a decentered system of societal guidance' based on 'a dramatic devolution of power'. Here societal guidance is defined as a process of decision-making involving both state and private sector at the level of territorially organized social formations.

The fundamental, radical argument of the decentralists is that growth should be based on the mobilization of resources in an integrated way within a defined region and not on criteria dictated by international market forces. This principle of territorial integration refers to 'those ties of history and sentiment that bind the members of a geographically-bounded community to one another'. Territorial communities are informed by 'deep attachment to their territorial base'. The ties between people in these communities are created by face-to-face relationships. The boundaries of territories are those of natural political communities which are defined as 'political parties, social movements, and other groups of citizens mobilised for a political purpose, to the extent that they are independent of the state'. Here, political community is explicitly defined as a territorial form of organization that exists to the extent that it is free from state interference and manipulation by capital.

The basic objective of the decentralist approach is the development of a region's resources and human skills for the benefit of the residents of that region. Policies are geared towards meeting basic needs, social development, labour-intensive activities and appropriate, intermediate technology. In this way development would be sustained by the territorial hinterland and its population, rather than by an uncontrolled 'trickle-down' of resources from national and international agencies. Considerable decentralized power would rest with regional government to carry out economic and social development policies and to counter the destabilizing effects of functionally integrated institutions. Such powers, Friedmann argues, would need to include strategic and selective protectionism, import substitution and a regional focus for transportation and communications.

Where functional integration is the dominant mode of development, Friedmann argues that planning is implemented 'from above' by the state and meant to further the state's interests in maintaining its own legitimacy and serving the interests of capital. Where territorial integration is the dominant mode, planning is developed 'from below'. Friedmann feels that a move away from functional organization will be precipitated by crisis and breakdown in the world economy and subsequent reconstruction along territorial lines. He finds evidence that this has begun in the ethnic nationalist movements: the Basques, the Corsicans, the Scottish nationalists, the Québecois and others. These are taken as evidence of the emergence of a post-statist economy where the role of the nation state is on the wane in favour of territorially based planning and governing organizations.

Radical decentralism: reasonable and utopian?

This new decentralist vision has many attractive features. Many proposals for sustainable development embody features of this conception, and they seem both reasonable and utopian. It is instructive to consider why apparently reasonable proposals can also be utopian, and to examine the problems of implementation that confront them.

First, an obvious constraint is that the approach would be difficult to implement in regions or countries which have a high degree of dependence on exports for income and imports for development – for example, those with small internal markets or dependent on primary commodities such as copper, bauxite, coffee, etc. Also, transport systems in most countries are physically oriented towards core areas or major cities and this reinforces the centre at the expense of the periphery.

Second, while the peripheries of many countries are irrelevant to the needs of international economic actors and are therefore grossly underdeveloped, there is no evidence that the situation can be redressed without action by the self-same central governments which connive in part (sometimes unwittingly) to exploit the peripheral regions. Indeed, curtailing the ability of central governments to exercise national economic and industrial policy may reduce the overall economic growth of the country, which may or may not be acceptable to the various regions. Also the protectionist measures that Friedmann proposes would run counter to any structural adjustment measures, such as those described in the previous chapter, and could shore up unsustainable policies.

Third, any real increase in regional financial control diminishes the ability of central governments to shift resources or redistribute income. Indeed, central redistribution is usually necessary to pursue a measure of social justice, which, it can be argued, should be a fundamental goal for the modern state. Inefficiencies in the use of resources may result from the lack of central direction, and opportunities will be limited to redistribute income from rich to poor regions. In Canada, for example, the degree of devolution of control over natural resources puts the province of Alberta at an advantage over the poorer Maritime provinces in terms of royalties paid into the provincial treasuries whenever the price of a barrel of oil is high. In the Canadian system, these royalties are not redistributed by central government, although other opportunities for redistribution exist.

More recently, Friedmann recognizes that redistribution cannot be radically decentralized, but he questions which central state agency has the power to intervene effectively in the distribution of income:

> *Is it the municipality? Its financial resources are extremely limited. Is it the state (as in the state of California)? Is it the federal government? But when it comes to acting locally, the federal government is like a bulldozer. Perhaps my question is misguided and the search for an appropriate central state is less important than a search for a new politics of redistribution, implying political mobilization at all levels, from urban neighbourhood to the national (and even international) arena.*[33]

Fourth, there is a problem with the territorial approach in so far as private corporate power may be more controllable by the nation state and international agencies than by localities. Certainly there is evidence that, despite the immense power of the multinational corporation, the international state system also has the potential to have a powerful effect on the character of domestic events. Friedmann also recognizes this criticism of his proposals, as the quote at the beginning of the chapter shows. Friedmann's observation points to the need for what we will define later as 'nested networks' for environmental action, which link levels of policy and action from the local to the international.

Fifth, it does not necessarily follow that regional political independence will foster a locally generated economic transformation. Even if it did, there is no further guarantee that the principal beneficiaries of decentralization would not be established local élites. Although Friedmann argues that the state is always 'aligned with the dominant class in society and will use its powers to safeguard the basic interests of this class', he fails to explain how the same situation would not be replicated when power is devolved from the nation state to what must clearly be a territorial, state-like entity, whether it is called a province, a municipality or even a political community within particular boundaries. This ignores the likelihood that existing inequitable top-down power relations will be replicated in the regional bodies.

Finally, for better or worse, events have so far refuted the regionalist ideal, first of Geddes and Lewis Mumford, and now of Friedmann. Their ideas are powerful and attractive, but the organized region has yet to prove a more potent force than the great functional mobilization of the late 20th century around nation states and supranational entities. This is not, however, to denigrate their ideas, but only to suggest that reasonable debate about their possibility must reflect on the potent forces of centralization weighed against the regionalist ideal. As with many utopian visions, there is a great gap between 'here' and 'there', and little in the way of guidance as to how even to begin the journey. This is not to say that, however difficult, it is not a journey worth attempting. Part V gives examples of more modest regional frameworks for sustainable development which draw on the network approach to environmental management.

Conclusion

Understanding the economic and political relations between centres and peripheries, territorially or functionally, is fundamental to understanding the wider context for environmental management. Management agencies stand in some relation to large-scale forces and most are in constant tension between the demands made on them for environmental policy and action, and the institutional arrangements governing their ability to act.

While the relative degree of centralization among levels of government is often dictated by judicial arrangements and/or legislation, there is often scope for altering these. On the one side, decentralization can provide choice, differentiation, and local knowledge and responsiveness in meeting needs. Decentralization of urban government to neighbourhood office has been a common theme in the last decade – for example, in Brussels, Rotterdam, Paris and Toronto. However, arguments for the centralization of some functions may be compelling as well, because territorial justice, income redistribution or the need for large-scale environmental management – for example, to deal with acid rain – may depend on the existence of an agency with a national overview which is able to act as a national or international arbitrator. In other cases, functions like land use or transport planning are most effectively undertaken by regional and national authorities. In Toronto, the decentralization of some functions of local government to the neighbourhood level is paralleled by the shifting of other functions, such as transport, to regional government and to the abandonment of the mid, city level of government. This recognizes that the growing environmental problems associated with transport can be dealt with only at the level of the region and in the context of national transport policy.

At the beginning of this chapter, we claimed that the answer to the decentralization dilemma is that there is no one right answer. The appropriate degree of decentralization in any situation is that point where major areas of both functional responsibility and political participation are maximized. This hypothetical equilibrium is described by the ungainly but now common term 'subsidiarity', a principle of decentralization first put forward by Kohr in 1957.[34] The subsidiarity principle states that tasks should be undertaken at the lowest level in society by which it can be managed effectively, and that higher levels should support lower ones to ensure that they have sufficient means to undertake the required tasks. Ungainly or not in terminology, this is a reasonable approach.

From this it follows that functional responsibility for the stabilization and promotion or control of economic activity, and ultimate responsibility for sustainable development and national and international pollution control, will reside with central governments. Central governments also have enabling functions, including strategic monitoring, structuring power relationships, the provision of incentives and influencing organizational culture. Conversely, the provision and maintenance of many public goods and services, including the local environment itself, should be managed locally, especially where the costs and benefits are borne locally.

However, not all activities are neatly compartmentalized and there are often cases where benefits are national or regional but environmental costs are borne locally. Hydroelectric projects are a classic example, but there are many others. Here there are bound to be disagreements over the appropriate level of government for adjudication and planning. As Mawhood notes, 'there is no such thing as a deductive theory of political decentralization, working downwards from first principles to logical prescription'.[35] Rather, the only basis for resolving such a fundamental issue is a continuing process of negotiation and mediation among competing jurisdictions within the conventions of a democratic political framework.

This being the case, it is not surprising that the tension between top-down and bottom-up development is endemic in modern society. In many cases the quality of the relationships between central and subnational levels of society are critical to the successful design and implementation of environmental policies. However, the decentralization debate can also become confused where decentralization itself is assumed to be the function of a central authority. In reality, of course, non-centralized and voluntary organizations and NGOs may be quite independent of the state and may well act for many local interests.

Problems of integrating levels of activity in environmental management are common to all but the simplest city states, and even the explicit constitutional arrangements in federated states have not saved them from addressing these issues. What remains underappreciated is that all socioeconomic systems are products of compromises and adjustments between centralizing and decentralizing forces, and endemic tension is built into such arrangements because of the undecidable nature of these arguments. The essence of this contradiction, therefore, is that there are no perfect systems in which different tiers of government, and local and national organizations, relate as autonomous and independent entities.

Any notion that the contradiction is somehow resolvable in the longer term is entirely at odds with the fact that regionalism or federalism is an 'open-ended' contract, in which the balance of power shifts along with economic and social conditions. Continuing constructive debate over organizational arrangements is not therefore the exception but the rule in the modern state. As Bogdanor notes:

> *There will, inevitably, be conflict and tension between different layers. The task of creative statesmanship must be not only to ensure that such conflict does not threaten the very basis of the state; but also to turn conflict into creative channels so that federal or regionalist states can achieve their aims of diffusing power and ensuring for the territorial groups in the state effective representation. How this is to be achieved is a task for the politician and not for the jurist.*[36]

This point is echoed by Frenkel: 'Interdependence is a result of the complexity of modern life. It cannot be spirited away by some clever constitutional formula'.[37] The case is reinforced by the fact that, except at the highest level of generality, there is no unitary public interest. Even the meaning and method of sustainable development will be vigorously and continually debated. Proposals that assume such unity of interests over the definition of sustainable development will never be implemented, attractive though they may be.

This is both the task and the context of environmental management: problem analysis and communicative action in what we will define in more detail as a turbulent environment, described in part by simultaneous and conflicting trends towards economic centralization and political decentralization. These forces are important factors shaping the context of environmental management and will invariably result in shifting organizational arrangements of the state.

An increasingly important aspect of these fluid organizational arrangements will be the action-centred networks recommended later in this book. These will form to accomplish particular tasks and evolve or disappear when those tasks are completed, or when the requirements themselves change. In terms of management style, the fluidity of the situation will be less threatening, and even exciting, to managers who understand that political, organizational and professional interactions in the management process often contribute more to social betterment than products or plans themselves.

It is also important to note that decentralization within networks will have administrative and political aspects, and while these are sometimes overlapping, they are neither the same, nor substitutes for one another. They are, however, complementary. In Chapter 8 we look at the rationale for operational decentralization. In Chapter 9, we will consider how this form of decentralization relates to the more difficult political decentralization discussed above, and how mediation can be applied within the context of environmental management.

Part IV

Innovative Management for Sustainable Development

Introduction

The rapid evolution of environmental problems, and greater public awareness and concern, bring pressure on governments to unify policies and develop more credible environmental management systems. The main obstacles to this are political and organizational.

Some governments do little or nothing because of fear of internal conflict, or because political resources are fragmented or ideological divisions intense. Even in stable countries, governments regularly pursue contradictory policies, attempting to clean the environment while allowing or even subsidizing behaviour which does the opposite. Politicians lack the will or a motivation that is strong enough to force them to undertake the difficult mediation among conflicting economic, social and environmental goals that diverge substantially from the status quo – for example, to control traffic growth. Generating political momentum for new ideas is a major task and one to which environmental managers contribute, within organizational and bureaucratic constraints. Campaigning NGOs make a particularly marked contribution to setting the agenda for political debate on the environment.

A main organizational constraint on management for sustainability is the idea of 'limits to governance'. For example, Peter Self noted:

> *There is increased expectation of public administration, and indeed of political systems generally, in the post-1945 world. These expectations have led to a big increase in the formal tasks and responsibilities of government, but of course it does not follow that these tasks have been adequately implemented. Clearly they have not.*[1]

Apart from the tension between centralizing and decentralizing forces, there are two other potent limits to governance. One is the dynamic nature of the modern world system which gives rise to endemic uncertainty. Organizational analysts call this 'turbulence', a concept examined in Chapter 8. The other limiting factor is 'fragmentation', in policy and institutional terms, in our societies which remain largely compartmentalized. That fragmentation exists is no surprise: previous chapters have set out why this common condition is likely to worsen before it gets better. These conditions mean that management systems that depend on rigid, deterministic control are likely to fail. But it is the scarcity of political will and skills to overcome these conditions that is the critical issue:

> *A widely recognised 'managerial gap' exists between the demand for and supply of indigenous management talent at nearly all levels, and this gap constitutes a major, if not the major, constraint in achieving economic (and) social development.*[2]

One fruitful response compartmentalization is multiagency action networks which attempt to understand uncertainty and develop strategies to manage it. As the notion of self-sufficient organizations gives way to more complex networks, organizational and managerial skills in joint working become critical to environmental management and sustainable development, often as important as the substantive nature of any issue. The development of localized management skills, entrepreneurial abilities and modes of partnership is therefore a critical but largely unaddressed aspect of environmental management. At present, Western (and Westernized) societies are weak in such competence, even though their higher level of interdependence means that most traditional bureaucratic approaches to management are of limited value.

A key constraint in human resource terms, then, is insufficient skills in newer 'integrating' styles of management. This is true for both higher and lower income countries because where higher income countries gain in sophistication of training, they often lose in terms of long-term, entrenched compartmentalization in bureaucracies. Fortunately one does not need to go back to university to learn the new management skills: 'on-the-job' is often a good place to begin. At least three preliminary steps are necessary.

First, to think about and understand the main constraints on more integrated management approaches. These can be thought of as 'soft' organizational problems that are additional obstacles to the resolution of any 'hard' environmental problem. They are often a spanner in the works of good management, even where excellent science and adequate funding are available. Improvements in environmental management come about from an understanding of the true nature of constraints on integration and from investment in human resources specifically to address those. The constraints then become part of the agenda for action for resolving any environmental problem. Chapter 7 begins this process of analysis, but it is not exhaustive; every environmental manager could add to the list from his or her own experience. In any event, a list of generic constraints is only useful in so far as it encourages us to analyse our own situation.

Second, having understood a range of constraints on integration, it is necessary to understand the potential of the modern management organization to deal with turbulence. This means developing innovation to manage successfully in a rapidly changing environment and structuring organizational arrangements in a manner that is appropriate to the nature of the problems themselves. The action network, engaged in consensus-building and 'organizational learning', is an appropriate response, making the connection between our understanding of the constraints and what should be an evolving plan for action. Chapter 8 looks at the ecology of management organizations, drawing on recent thinking from organizational analysis.

Finally, it is necessary to take positive steps. Chapter 9 suggests basic principles and methods for action networking. Following that, Part V goes on to illustrate, in a number of cases, how the basic principles of the network approach work in a variety of settings around the world.

7

Constraints on Integrated Management

Many failures in development are not failures of production or technology. Instead, they are institutional failures. An alternative view of development accepts the sustainability imperative and places the institutional dimension in the forefront.

David Gow and Elliot Morss[1]

There are any number of generic constraints on the development of successful, integrated environmental management. A main feature of the action-network approach is the systematic identification of such constraints so that each becomes part of the focus of the environmental management task, and resources are devoted to understanding and overcoming them. This chapter looks at the constraints on integration suggested by the recent literature of environmental management, development and public administration, and by field experience.

The Complexity of Environmental Problems

Serious environmental problems are invariably part of socio-biophysical systems characterized by both complexity – that is, many relevant factors in an unclear relationship and a high level of interaction, which means that the relationship is constantly changing. In such a system, organizations interact dynamically with the natural environment.

Complexity now extends to every level of analysis. For example, the Club of Rome argues that the world's economic, social, financial and cultural systems are highly interdependent, with the result that the earth is 'a stressed system'.[2] Interdependency is compounded by the uncertain nature of political and economic change at all levels from the international to the local. Complexity compounded by uncertainty is a central challenge of the world problematique.

Complexity equally bedevils regional efforts at environmental control and planning. The water pollution problems in the Weija Reservoir in Ghana, mentioned briefly in Chapter 3, are a good example of this kind of complexity (Figure 7.1). These problems are reported in more detail in Chapter 11. Although a small river by African standards, the Densu's function as a water supply for more than two million inhabitants of Accra and the packed river basin communities, as well as for drainage and irrigation, have caused it to be described as Ghana's most important river.[3] The main causes of pollution in this watershed arise from:

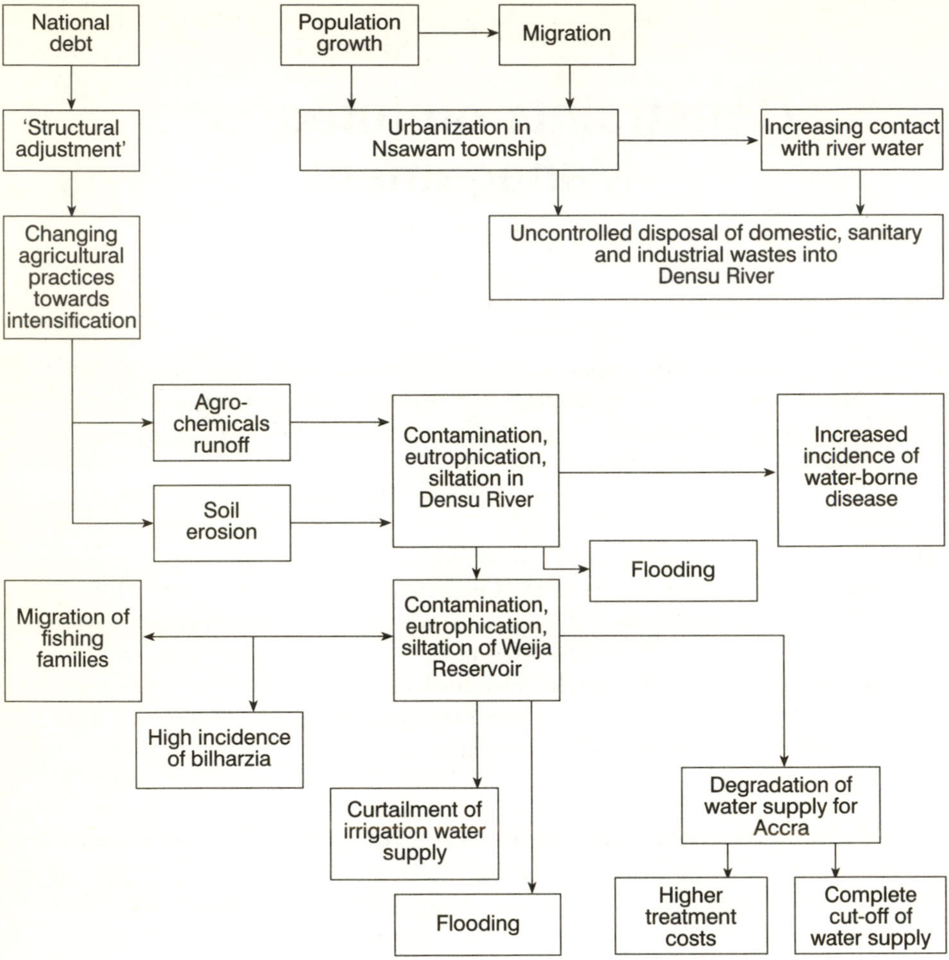

Figure 7.1 *Densu River and Weija Reservoir watershed management problem*

- rapid urbanization, stemming from migration from rural areas, and resulting in the direct, uncontrolled discharge of household and industrial wastes and sewage;
- the intensification of agriculture, stemming in part from structural adjustment, including deeper ploughing and the usual inputs of fertilizers and pesticides, resulting in the reduction of natural vegetation, soil degradation, the heavy run-off of silt, eutrophication and pollution;
- the legal and illegal logging activities in the upper reaches of the river basin, and fuelwood gathering and charcoal burning along the length of the river.

The problems are compounded because modernization in Ghana is resulting in the erosion of traditional, sustainable methods of river management. In this example, many thousands of producers (businesses and larger industries, small industries, small farmers, and so on) contribute unwittingly to either water pollution or siltation, which results in widespread flooding during the rainy season and drying out during the dry season. The environmental management system that might respond to these problems is nearly as complex as the problem itself: 11 agencies in central and local government have been identified by the project team as having substantial control over activities in the Densu basin, in addition to the complex mosaic of tribal controls. The river basin itself stretches over eight district administrations, each of which has an interest. But road connections between the lower and upper reaches of the river are poor or non-existent, and this hinders communication and recognition of the integrated nature of the watershed ecosystem.

This kind of complex environmental management problem is not unusual: equal environmental and organizational complexity might be found in virtually any river basin in the world with both urban and agricultural uses. This kind of complexity precludes straightforward cause-and-effect analysis of the problems, and also precludes simple solutions implemented by any agency acting alone. In dealing with this kind of 'turbulence', static, formal management approaches by one or two agencies are less useful than a network approach which gradually builds up a partnership of relevant stakeholders. Just as one agency is unlikely to resolve such a problem, so also is one government acting alone. Thus the team of stakeholders will often involve government in partnership with private and voluntary sectors.

The management approach will also need to stress continual feedback and adjustment in policy and action to suit the emerging needs of the many stakeholders. This 'adaptive' management often requires:

- the development of an emerging consensus among all vested interests as to the real dimensions and boundaries of the problem, and often a shift in professional orientation and organizational culture towards more holistic problem definition;
- a partnership approach to implementation among all the relevant agencies; and
- the development of new skills and responses as dictated by the changing nature of the problem, and the need to mediate among the differing objectives of various agencies.

Chapter 11 documents how an action-network approach in Ghana helped to develop a sophisticated understanding of problem complexity in the Densu Basin, and gradually shifted an initial concern over water pollution to a commitment to a programme of sustainable development.

Failure of the Command and Control Management Style

A primary requisite for public sector management and development is a competent bureaucratic system, and administrative reform is a near universal goal of contemporary societies. However, the record of achievement is poor. J Reisat, for example, remarks that '... the dilemma of administrative reform in these (lower income) countries lies in the mediocrity of results'.[4] This is not surprising as many countries acquiring independence in the post-war period will have had little or no experience in the operation of the Western-style bureaucracies bequeathed to them.

However, higher income status confers no special advantage, and administrative reform is equally difficult to implement in Western bureaucracies. Since the 1930s, unheeded administrative recommendations of various American presidential commissions have far exceeded the number adopted.[5] Numerous reviewers document the continual post-war failure to implement radical reform in the British Civil Service until the 1980s, despite '... endless royal commissions and other investigative bodies which have produced endless reports and proposed numerous reforms'.[6]

The advent of more complex problems in the modern state has only served to compound the problem. A recent article entitled 'The Organization of the '90s' in the business management journal *The McKinsey Quarterly* notes that, in the private sector, rigid, hierarchical 'command and control' (C&C) organizations are now 'competitively disadvantaged' due to slow response, lack of creativity and initiative, and excessive cost.[7] The same is true in the public sector. Such traditional C&C bureaucracies may be characteristically well suited to dealing with planned change, but not with the rapid 'unplanned' change which is typical of environmental problems, in which knowledge about the problem develops only when the problem is already serious, evolves rapidly, and for which any solution must involve overlapping public, private and voluntary sector initiatives. In this case:

> *...successfully developing a high performing organization requires that senior managers overcome commonly-held misconceptions and lead a change process that blends top-down with bottom-up initiatives.*

With this in mind, many analysts are now proposing alternative, looser, task-oriented management structures. These have been called by many names, such as 'small scale administrative cadres',[8] 'multi-disciplinary project teams',[9] 'interorganizational approaches to natural resource management'[10] and 'parallel structures to bureaucracies'.[11]

For example, Haas argues that an important consideration in institutional design is the rapidity with which institutions recognize and respond to new environmental threats, which result in unplanned change.[12] Knowles and Saxberg propose that unplanned change requires the development of informal organizations and temporary groups, to work in parallel with existing bureaucracies.[13] Zand suggests that managers of bureaucracies sponsor 'collateral organizations' – interdisciplinary task forces with members from several departments to identify and solve problems not amenable to solution by formal systems.[14]

An important aspect of the action network methodology is such an informal, task-oriented group, whose membership is free to grow or contract. This type of informal organization:

> *... must be differentiated from the formal structure and relationships in dealing with change. The networks of interactions in the informal organization can reward, discipline and punish their members. They can and do absorb and accommodate changes which management cannot anticipate in the design of policies, systems, tasks and procedures. The informal organization represents a dynamic aspect of the formal organization. Though managers have regarded these networks with suspicion, many have recognized them as flexible adjuncts to all levels of the formal work organization.*[15]

As the case studies will show, the informal organization, which may be part of a wider network, is also an excellent organizational vehicle for moving from specific environmental management tasks to broader tasks of sustainable development. This is for two reasons:

1. The informal organization can expand or contract its membership to draw on the necessary political, bureaucratic or technical skills required to address the specific problem or task identified; and
2. The informal, task-oriented organization is characterized by learning-by-doing and can therefore 'grow into' more sophisticated tasks.

The potential to move beyond environmental control issues to long-range development planning is also suggested by the development literature. For example, here is Sagasti's proposal for an 'unconventional' evolving institutional framework for national development planning:

> *The institutional design required for a new approach to development planning is that of an evolving network that should be flexible, open and capable of restructuring itself over time. The planning units that compose the network would not conform to a hierarchical organization and each would relate to the structure of political authority and power in a variety of ways that are also likely to change over time.*[16]

Sagasti proposes some of the elements of such a network: a social intelligence unit, a planning unit, temporary issue-oriented task forces, coordination committees to link planning units with all types of non-governmental organizations, social science research centres and an international support network. The methodology put forward in Chapter 9 offers one option for developing such a planning framework.

Unwitting Failures of Policy Integration

These failures often have their deep roots in the organization of the natural and social sciences into compartmentalized disciplines, discussed in Chapter 3. One result tends to be the inadequate definition of environmental problems based on single discipline perceptions and solutions: 'an agricultural problem', 'an economics problem', 'a transport problem', and so on. It is not that discipline-based science is not essential to the process of understanding, but that another, higher order of analysis is also necessary. This is to enable critical recognition of the inevitable limitations of our perceptions, and to integrate scientific knowledge with the many sources of social, economic, cultural and intuitive knowledge that is relevant to complex issues.

This failure of perception is compounded by the compartmentalization of government and international support agencies into poorly communicating departments or sectors pursuing divergent and often competing objectives. It is common that government departments do not interrelate policy or action; indeed, there is seldom a reward for doing so. The result is an unwitting failure of horizontal integration (Figure 7.2). For example, a consequence of the introduction of high-energy agriculture in India has been increased food production, but this has also increased income disparity because of a failure to implement land reform.[17]

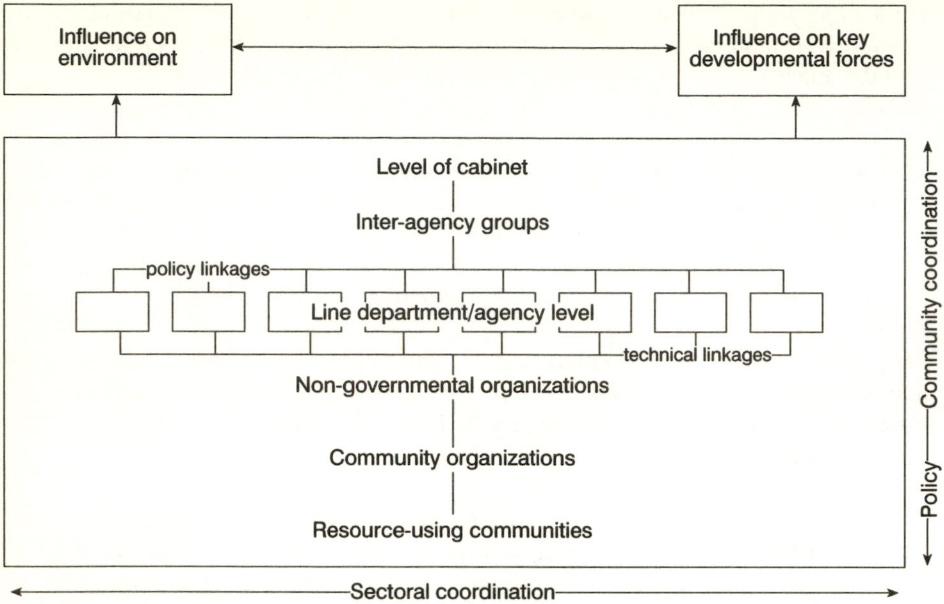

Figure 7.2 *Interorganizational linkages which contribute to policy integration*

The Administrative Trap

A failure of integration often results in what has been aptly called the 'administrative trap' by Baker (Figure 7.3). This describes the common mismatch between the nature of environmental problems and the sectoral problem-solving structures in government which disaggregate ecological problems, recognize and treat symptoms as the problem itself, and generally remain inadequate to the task. Baker describes how the current administrative trap in lower income countries was inherited lock, stock and barrel from their colonial predecessors:

> *The administrative structures of the LDCs were generally inherited intact from former colonial powers, and are typically organised vertically into sectoral, or functional, ministries and departments (Agriculture, Education, Health, etc). This works reasonably well until the system encounters a problem of a very broad and highly integrated nature – such as desertification. Then it tackles the parts which are identifiable to each ministry and then each ministry tackles the symptom as a problem in, and of, itself.*

Government departments caught in the trap single-mindedly tackle complex ecological problems by way of their vertically integrated, single sector systems (farmer; Extension Service; Ministry of Agriculture; UN Food and Agriculture Organization). This results in consistent, expensive failure to resolve problems which, by their very nature, require multisectoral responses.

For lower income countries, a persistent case is the failure of 'donor coordination'. This is reported to be the Achilles heel of development assistance:

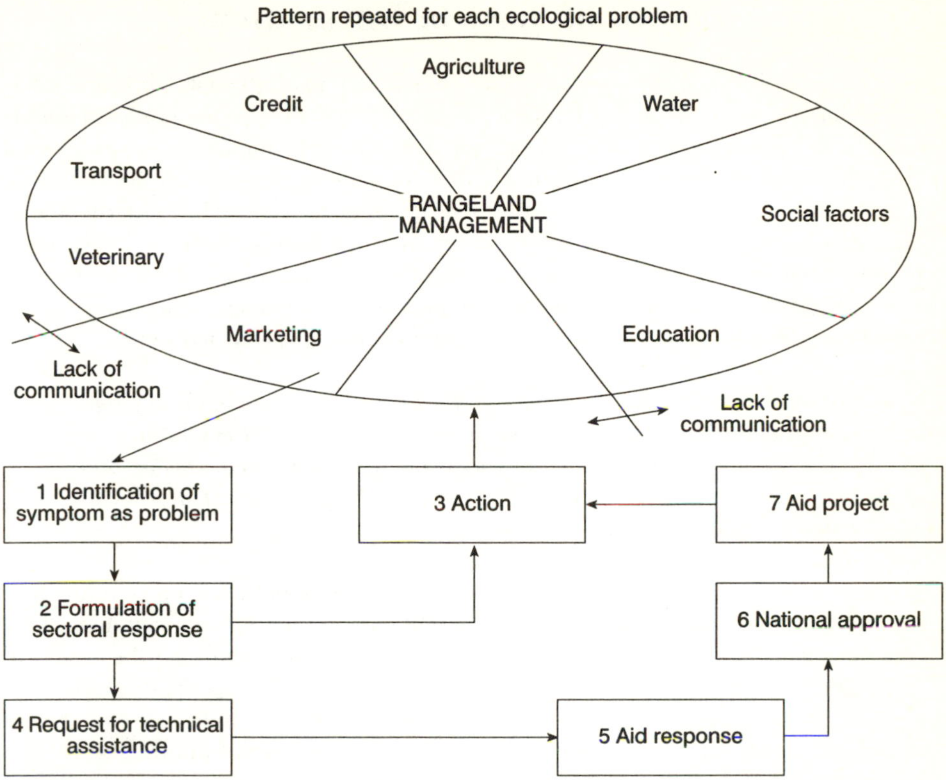

Source: Baker[18]

Figure 7.3 *The administrative trap: a sectoral approach to ecological problems*

> *Countries with a weak institutional base, exposed to multiple donors' institutional development efforts – sometimes contradictory – and presenting conflicting guidance, face a potential nightmare.*[19]

Coordination among donors is unlikely owing to differences in long-term goals, and even to short-term, local objectives, sometimes owing to a sense of competition. Whittington and Calhoun argue that donors who regularly and rhetorically call for coordination simply do not mean it, and that it is one more exercise in what has been called the ritual of planned development.[20] They argue that at the heart of the problem is a patronizing attitude of donors based on a mistaken belief in their own bureaucratic efficiency and in the inefficiency of the host country's bureaucracy.

Failures of horizontal integration bedevil every environmental management and sustainable development task. Virtually the first step, therefore, in any action programme must be to invite representatives of a range of relevant government departments and agencies to join some kind of an advisory group to address the specific, visible environmental problem identified. This provides an organizational base from which to begin a process of horizontal integration. The issue is taken up again in Chapter 9.

Failure of Vertical Integration

Poor vertical integration is the result of the common failure of understanding and information flows between the policy levels of government and small-scale production units or individual resource users who may generate substantial, cumulative environmental impacts. A real challenge of sustainable development is to maintain the economic contribution of small producers, while also keeping to acceptable environmental standards. But the sheer number of producers and their independence of government control systems challenges traditional approaches to management. Often the motivations and constraints under which such small producers operate are little understood at the policymaking levels of government. For example, Montgomery notes that:

> *Millions of small-scale household-level actors produce most of the environmental degradation in the [lower income] countries. But environmental policy planners are almost entirely unaware of details about whether and how current practices that are encouraged by government destroy or conserve natural resources.*[21]

This ignorance results in policies which appear reasonable but often prove difficult or impossible to implement. Failures of vertical integration can be compounded by the large economic and cultural gap between the policy-making level and the reality of life at farm or village level, a reality which is often characterized by the drive for basic survival. The fine distinctions of policy and law are not applicable and government control structures are weak or non-existent. A gulf between the public and private sectors, indicated by different organizational cultures and different objectives, can also heighten this constraint.

An important aspect of the network approach is that environmental action teams attempt to overcome compartmentalization by initiating action only on specific, highly visible environmental tasks, and by attempting to develop new levels of both horizontal and vertical integration around those tasks. Such tasks are usually environmental problems about which there is considerable agreement that 'something must be done', such as obvious and damaging water pollution. The specificity of the task gives a measure of credibility to the effort of integration, while confining the initial effort to the stated task can disarm potential critics who may be threatened by the idea of a parallel organization to the traditional bureaucracy. Network-based advisory groups can become a kind of a low-key, non-threatening task force with a specific environmental objective.

Lack of Reward in Bureaucracies

A related constraint, which reinforces others, is the lack of a reward in bureaucracies for goal-oriented, intersectoral approaches. At the most basic level, in lower income countries, there is often simply not enough money available to pay an adequate wage to Civil Servants. For example, one Nigerian NGO is blunt about the difficulties of environmental enforcement: 'Most of the enforcers are pretty poor and are more interested in making extra money in order to make ends meet, rather than do what they are paid to do.'[22]

But the reward problem is hardly confined to lower income countries. In many countries, an enthusiasm for an inter-sectoral approach can jeopardize a career, and within most governments there is little impetus to liaise with departments competing for influence and limited resources. Brandl, considering public administration in the United States, comments:

> *... the sorry condition of the public policy domain lies in the fact that the great bulk of the government's policies are implemented through bureaucracies – that is, through organisations in which workers are managed by being subject to directives, but rarely rewarded, penalised or inspired.*[23]

Although hardly a panacea, the network approach, which includes a system of regular, interdisciplinary peer reviews, can provide a measure of systematic support or non-pecuniary reward, and is therefore a useful adjunct to the bureaucratic structure.

Over-Reliance on Institutional Reform

Although institutional reform is often part of a high-quality management approach, there is a common tendency to assume that if only the 'right' institutional arrangements can be brought into being, adequate environmental management will result. This is not only fallacious, but risks diverting attention away from the need to meet environmental challenges by attention to the broad range of national needs in terms of legislation, human resources and finance, as well as institutional structure.

Of particular concern in many countries is the question of whether an environmental agency or a ministry will deliver the best results. There is, of course, no correct answer. Baker thinks that this is a red herring which can perpetuate the administrative trap for a host of reasons:[24]

- An environmental ministry is like every other ministry, and probably less powerful than the main financial and industrial ministries, unless it has some powerful statutory authority which gives it power over others. Creating a new ministry does not change the weakness of existing horizontal linkages.
- Much of the environmental legislation will already belong to other ministries such as Health, Agriculture, Industry, Mining and Resources and others, and there is no clear reason why any new ministry should have any control over this legislation.
- The creation of a new ministry or agency can divert attention away from real needs, such as for intersectoral planning.
- The potentially conflicting roles of an environment ministry – as policy-maker, policeman, coordinator or project inspector – may not be resolved productively.

Probably most important, the usual absence of any clearly stated national policy regarding the relationship between environment and economic development invariably marginalizes environmental concerns. This leaves the ministry unable to affect major structural decisions, while fighting a rearguard action against damaging developments with inadequate weapons.

Failure to Learn From Experience

Within the traditional bureaucracy there is often little motivation to learn from past experience and even less to admit, analyse and learn from past mistakes. Raking over past failures is generally considered poor form and seldom brings any career benefit. But accepting the need for such learning is essential for the type of adaptive environmental management argued here, for it provides the rationale for active monitoring to generate feedback for making the necessary incremental adjustments to policy and implementation.

What we will describe in detail in the next chapter as action learning leading to innovation can assist this process. The rationale is set out by Hulme:

> *If project evaluation is to contribute effectively to the process of 'learning from experience' then a new focus is required. It will be necessary to move on from the cosy ground of formal structures, techniques and procedures to the more ambiguous and less clearly defined task of analysing learning processes within and between agencies involved in development initiatives.* It will recognise that the lessons of experience are not neutral data, but a strategic resource *[author's emphasis]*.[25]

Failure to Confront the Management Process

There is a variation of the previous constraint which is that most politicians and bureaucrats involved in public decision-making and management have little interest in improving the processes of decision-making and, indeed, little interest in considering the process at all. For example, Baker summarizes the concerns of delegates at big international environment conferences:

> *The delegates, representing administrations, made fairly sure that their national position papers presented their actions in the best possible light, rarely looking at the public management system per se. There was rarely, if ever, any explicit discussion of policy and management issues for the public sector, and certainly no criticism of existing policy.*[26]

There are obvious reasons for this. There are few votes in reviews of management and administration, progress takes time and politicians seldom look past the next election. Bureaucrats have little motivation to upset the status quo. There is a larger issue also, which is that there is seldom any public pressure for reform, unless the 'organizational culture' of the society itself values forward-thinking, strategic planning.

Contextual Constraints

These constraints arise from the specific nature of national political systems, and from religious, tribal and other cultural factors. Such factors are part of a grey area of environmental management. For example, the influence of corruption must be addressed, if only obliquely and diplomatically. Once again, a Nigerian team is forthcoming on the problems of environmental enforcement in the face of what it calls 'bigmanism': 'The enforcers are very much affected by this concept; they would rather not enforce anything against somebody occupying a position of power or influence.'[27]

However, this type of constraint is hardly unique to lower income countries. The main lesson must be that it is important to make a particular effort to understand contextual constrains in formulating objectives and actions. Frank, face-to-face and off-the-record discussions are a helpful means of considering issues which normally may not be discussed or committed to paper. This is another area in which a network is a valuable means of support for difficult areas in management.

Technology and Local Management

In Chapter 3 we noted the process by which apparently benign technologies, like the automobile, can become, by their very attractiveness, structural imperatives in societies and thus virtually impervious to social control. A related point is that, in many countries, imported Western industrial processes and technologies are tending to eclipse historical, indigenous environmental management skills, and social, cultural and legal control structures which will have developed over many generations.

This is not surprising, for technologies are not culture-free. For example, Ghana has a long history of small-scale agroforestry. Historically, trees were felled only after careful communal deliberation with the tribal chief and priest and a lengthy ceremony to mark the significance of the act. In the past few decades, with the importation of industrialized forestry, both the environmental knowledge and spiritual concern represented by this process are disappearing. Similarly, past agricultural practices in Ghana, based on shifting cultivation and sustainable agroforestry, have been replaced by the intensive, industrialized farming of monocrops which rely heavily on inputs of chemical fertilizers and pesticides. Soil erosion, eutrophication and chemical pollution are the by-products of such processes; these are rapidly and seriously degrading water supplies in the country.

In future, the successful integration of indigenous skills and knowledge with new technology will become even more important as other powerful technologies, such as biotechnology, hold out the promise of increasing the volume of food production, as well as improving food quality. Brenner, considering the question of technological innovation in agriculture, notes:

> *Technological change is inherently difficult to measure or evaluate, all the more so when technologies have pervasive or synergistic effects [id]. Technologies can be 'embodied' in physical products or in skills and people. They can also be, in the case of agricultural production, land-saving, labour-saving, cost-reducing, input-reducing or quality-enhancing. Institutions, decision-making processes and diffusion mechanisms also have an important bearing on technological change.*[28]

In all countries there is a pressing need to diffuse technologies to serve the needs of development. The questions are: how can societies ensure that technological change serves as a means to sustainable development, and how can management systems be devised which allow us the benefits of technology without our becoming its unwitting victims in the longer term?

8

Organizational Ecology and Innovative Management

To explain global environmental change it is necessary to examine the direct human actions which influence it, as well as the indirect human actions that set in motion complex chains of events which also affect the environment.

Roberta Balstad Miller[1]

The future is not written anywhere – it is still to be built. It is an uncertain, multiple and indeterminate future. In fact, without this uncertainty, human activity would lose its elements of freedom and its meaning – the hope of a desired future.

Michel Godet[2]

This book's Preface suggested expanding the definition of environment to include the interaction of human society with natural ecosystems, the combination of which is called human ecology. In this chapter, we examine an aspect of human ecology – organizational ecology. We also look at the challenge of planning for the future, which is essential for sustainable development, given the endemic uncertainty in the direction of events and organizational constraints. To do so, we draw on concepts from organizational analysis. These insights help to explain the limits to governance – that is, the inability of current management and planning systems to cope with the dynamics of rapid change and the interaction between numerous organizations and entrepreneurs and the environment.

Organization theorists use the term 'turbulent environment' to describe the conditions which give rise to the limits to governance. Here the term 'environment' includes interactions between the natural and the social worlds, and the interactions between organizations. In a 'full world' economy, these interactions increasingly impinge on, or even determine, the quality of the natural environment.

The Turbulent Environment

Previous chapters discussed the challenge of complex environmental problems. In the literature of organization theory these are sometimes called metaproblems. We have seen how metaproblems are really many-sided clusters of problems, with interrelated symptoms, that are beyond the capabilities of existing organizational arrangements to grasp and tackle. They have also been described as 'wicked problems' because they are hard to define and because, in pluralist societies, we lack objective definitions of equity from which to fashion consensual solutions to them.[3]

Metaproblems are not amenable either to simple cause-and-effect analysis or to one-dimensional responses. Such problems are not only bigger than any one organization acting alone, they are seldom the responsibility of any one body. It is common for governments to excuse inactivity on a metaproblem by arguing that not enough is known about it, or because it spans functional departments and political jurisdictions. The 'wickedness' of these metaproblems has been heightened by the increased pace of change since the oil price rise by the Organization of Petroleum Exporting Countries (OPEC) in 1973, which ended a period of relative stability and ushered in a period of increasing turbulence. Metaproblems both exist in, and are the result of, turbulent environments which compound uncertainty, the root of the world problematique.

The notion of the turbulent environment was first discussed by Emery and Trist.[4] In a condition of turbulence, systems of interrelated problems are exacerbated by the independent actions of many unrelated organizations or entrepreneurs, and change can be rapid and complex, and even bewildering or apparently chaotic. Organizations will often act in uncoordinated and dissonant ways in attempting to meet their individual objectives, typically externalizing as many of the costs and internalizing as many of the benefits of their actions as they can.[5] Trist has defined turbulence as 'a kind of contextual commotion that makes it seem as if the "the ground" were moving as well as the organizational actors'.[6]

A turbulent environment is characterized by:

- uncertainty;
- inconsistent and ill-defined needs, preferences and values;
- unclear understanding of the means, consequences or cumulative impacts of collective actions; and
- fluid participation in which multiple, partisan participants vary in the amount of resources they invest in resolving problems.

For our purposes, the turbulent environment is a socioecological system, which is defined as any system composed by a societal (or human) and ecological (or biophysical) subsystem.[7] The levels of aggregation may range from a local community and the surrounding environment with which it interacts directly, up to the system constituted by the whole of mankind and the ecosphere. The ability of managing organizations to plan in the face of turbulence is constrained, partly because turbulence grows as a result of the activities of individuals and organizations attempting to respond to it.[8]

As we have seen, at the same time as complexity in urban and regional systems is growing, the number and complexity of international and interregional linkages and dependencies associated with the world economy have never been greater, nor has the rate of technological change. These lead to more turbulence, further uncertainty and a loss of local control. This condition has been aptly called the loss of the stable state.[9] It is a characteristic of modern societies in conditions of global industrialization and makes it difficult for organizations, especially in the public sector, to deal with their environment. The only realistic response has been described as 'permanent innovation'.[10]

Organization and Environment: Legacy of General Systems Theory

The relationship between any organization and its wider environment, natural and social, has been described as one of the most powerful and pervasive metaphors in the language of organization theory. This can help us to understand the complex interrelationships between the environment and development.[11] The distinction first arose in the early 1960s as theorists began to examine economic and societal forces that were external to organizations, rather than focusing solely on their internal dynamics. Soon after, the theories of Bateson on learning in complex animal, family and wider social systems formed the basis for consideration of the role of learning in organizational systems.[12] At the same time influential concepts in general systems theory were subsequently applied to a range of social science disciplines, including the study of organizations. This step marked an important shift in many fields of enquiry.

Systems thinking contributed some basic concepts to organization theory:

- a more holistic viewpoint which encompassed the organization–environment relationship;
- the importance of the boundaries between the two;
- the idea of constructive feedback; and
- the concept of 'requisite variety' which suggested that environmental complexity needed to be matched by an equal sophistication in organizational response.

These concepts are helpful to understanding and deriving appropriate responses to environmental metaproblems.

Systems theory views an organization as an 'open' system, differentiated from its environment by some sort of boundary.[13] An open system tends towards a state of dynamic equilibrium with its environment through a continuous exchange of material, data and energy. Both system and environment can affect the exchange, giving rise to important interactions.

The boundaries of environmental problems

A basic tenet of the systems approach is that organizations are processes striving towards survival, which can be understood in terms of inputs, throughputs, outputs and feedback. Units within an organization are subsystems with their own systemic characteristics. Boundary transactions, by which inputs are altered into outputs, are critical organizational activities, both internally between subsystems and externally via the environment. Boundaries can be expanded to draw in more resources or participants, or tightened to strengthen existing participation.

This idea of bounding environmental problems is a fundamental one, for if a problem is defined too narrowly, relevant factors and connections will be excluded; too widely, and the problem will seem diffuse and incomprehensible. The appropriate boundary definition will change over time, depending on the problem itself and the changing competences of the organizations concerned. Continually bounding and rebounding (or redefining) any environmental problem is therefore a primary task of environmental management.

The process of continually rebounding problems runs counter to the normal working of bureaucracies which tend to define any problem as either within their own area of competence, and therefore 'their' problem, or outside their area of competence, and therefore not their responsibility. Once a problem is defined in a particular way, a superstructure of programmes, political and funding commitments and careers is usually built around that definition. But every environmental problem or problem of sustainable development has these characteristics:

- The problem will inevitably evolve according to changing circumstance and as a result of every interaction which has any effect, positive or negative. What a problem cannot do is remain the same and neither therefore can its definition.
- If a problem will not remain static, then neither can the adequate response to that problem or the team needed to develop and implement that response. In other words, responses must be as dynamic as problems.

Bounding the problem in the right way, for a particular point in time, is therefore a key factor in determining who are the right stakeholders to participate in a problem resolution network. Again, a list of too few stakeholders will exclude important participants; too many will dilute the process to the point of uselessness.

In systems terms, this redefinition process depends on feedback, which describes the process whereby information concerning the system is fed back as input, leading to alteration of the behaviour of the organization and thus the system. Feedback is a critical concept for organizational learning. This is a point to which we will return.

For the purposes of considering the role of organizations in environmental management, five concepts from organizational analysis are useful:

1 The sources of endemic uncertainty in environmental management.
2 The idea of the resource dependence of organizations.
3 The potential role of action networks in environmental management and how they differ from other kinds of networks.
4 The role of conflict and consensus in management.
5 The importance of organizational learning which gives rise to innovation in management and the contribution of action research to this innovation.

These are considered below.

The Sources of Uncertainty

A major concern revolves around the extent to which organizations are able to 'manage' in what is clearly an uncertain world. In this situation, the traditional rational planning model (study the problem, develop alternatives, choose one, implement, move on to something else) has proved to be of little use, since the environment is an interactive, dynamic phenomenon which cannot be manipulated by unilateral action:

> *Complexity cannot be managed, intellectually or practically, through increased control. We have to learn to understand and manage complex systems while respecting the autonomy of the processes and the elements within these systems.*[14]

Robins argues that this uncertainty is a classic problem of social order and integration in modern societies and that this has been close to the 'heart of social and economic theory since the Enlightenment'.[15] The intractable problem of uncertainty has led analysts to speak of the 'poverty of prediction' in public policy-making.[16]

The poverty of prediction

Each organization will have a definite impact on the environment, but it will be impossible to predict that impact precisely because all other organizations will be acting at the same time. Therefore, although organizations may influence what is called their environmental 'niche', the larger context of their actions will always include a full range of phenomena which are important but which cannot be controlled. This gives a dramatic twist to the notion of uncertainty:

> *Environmental uncertainty has roots that lie deeper than the problems of collecting and evaluating information, directing organizational activity, or any of the other features discussed in the analysis of strategic planning and control. An uncertain environment exists precisely because the consequences of organizational activity are not realized until after the activity has taken place.*[17]

Uncertainty, therefore, is not simply a lack of adequate information relevant to a problem or management task; there is no body of knowledge which, if acquired, would unlock solutions or dissolve uncertainty. Nor is dealing with uncertainty simply a matter of organizational restructuring or revised management direction. Uncertainty exists because the impact of human, organizational activity cannot be predicted in a way which allows those activities to be altered to control environmental effects. The human ecological environment is therefore by nature uncertain. While this uncertainty can be managed, it can never be overcome. Rather, management and planning organizations must be prepared to take maximum advantage of the resources available to them and to adapt continually as new information (feedback) from the environment becomes available. This is adaptive management which is concerned with the process of learning and continuous decision-making, rather than with plans and projects alone.

Resource Dependence in Organizations

All organizations must interact with others which control the resources required for their survival. Four propositions describe this dependence:

1 Any organization is dependent upon other organizations for resources.
2 In order to achieve their goals, organizations have to exchange resources.
3 Although decision-making within the organization is therefore constrained by other organizations, the dominant coalition in any organization retains discretion. The culture of the dominant coalition will influence which relationships are seen to present an opportunity to secure resources, and which resources will be sought.
4 The dominant coalition employs strategies within known rules to regulate the process of exchange.[18]

Organization theory argues that organizations experience power and dependence, success or failure in policy areas, or positive results in conflict and strategic bargaining, depending on their access to the following major types of resource: finance, political access and support, information and expertise, legal authority and organizational relationships. Of these, information (feedback) and expertise (human resources) are potent resources which can strengthen the power of management organizations even where they are subordinated in jurisdiction or administrative relationships. Conversely, a shortage of information and expertise can undermine formally delegated powers. In an increasingly interdependent world, a pool of new resources is offered by interorganizational relationships.[19]

Increasingly, therefore, innovative management organizations are prepared to devote resources to productive, if temporary, linkages with other agencies and other sectors: public with private sector, private with voluntary sector, and so on. These initiatives may be called partnerships, joint ventures or networking initiatives and they have become increasingly common in attempting to govern or manage difficult public problem areas. In the next section we look at some different kinds of networks before discussing the action network in some detail.

Interorganizational Networks

The expansion of responsibilities in the modern state has clearly caused a centralization of resource dependencies in many areas of life. It is usually the case that the more centralized the resources upon which organizations depend, the greater the degree of interaction in that field and the greater the degree of uncertainty likely to arise.[20] A consideration of resource dependence in a highly interactive field leads directly to the concept of interorganizational networks for the exchange of the resources needed for problem solving. In technical terms, networks are non-hierarchical social systems which constitute the basic social form that permits an interorganizational coalition to develop.[21]

The development of networks in any field involves four steps:

1. an increase in the level of interaction among organizations in a field;
2. an increase in the load of information on organizations;
3. the emergence of structures of domination or patterns of coalition; and
4. the development at the cultural level of a dominant ideology of the field, usually accompanied by competing, minority ideologies.

Rhodes suggests some key features of networks:[22]

1. Constellation of interests: the interests of participants in a network vary by service/economic function, territory, client-group and common expertise.
2. Membership: membership differs in terms of the balance between public and private sector; and between political-administrative élites, professions and clients.
3. Vertical interdependence: intra-network relationships vary in their degree of interdependence, especially the dependence of central government on subnational actors for the implementation of policies.
4. Horizontal interdependence: relationships between the networks vary in their degree of horizontal articulation: that is, in the extent to which a network is insulated from, or in conflict with, other networks.

5 Distribution of resources: actors control different types and amounts of resources and such variations affect the patterns of vertical and horizontal interdependence.

In the face of complex issues and a pressing need for action, networking has become commonplace. For example, in the environmental field, an intense structuring process has been binding organizations into a complex web of information flows, computer links (such as the environmental information network GREEN NET), interests and resource exchanges, all encouraged by the integrating force of world conferences, such as the 1992 UN Conference on Environment and Development in Brazil, and subsequent UN Conferences and negotiation sessions in Istanbul, Kyoto, and so on.

It is important to distinguish between a range of networks serving different functions. The following four types can be identified:

- Policy networks are based on the major functional interests in and of government (energy, transport, education, housing, and so on). They are characterized by stable relationships, continuity of restricted memberships, shared responsibilities for service delivery and insulation from other networks.[23]
- Issue networks are less integrated, with a large number of participants and a limited degree of interdependence. Some are based on the need to share technical information, such as the agricultural development network AGRONET; others are based on shared concern over issues, such as conservation of the rainforest.
- Professional networks cut across policy and issue networks. National professional associations, such as the United Kingdom's Royal Town Planning Institute, may periodically formalize professional opinion, disseminate professional practice and regulate entry into a field. Professional influence is exercised in lobbying and in institutionalized policy networks.

  Where a particular group of professionals has operational control in government or quasi-governmental agencies, their views may coalesce around some political or professional ideology. This is especially the case in authoritarian or totalitarian regimes where freedom to publish and lobby is severely curtailed or non-existent. In the former Soviet Union, for instance, the ideological professionalism of technological élites contributed greatly to the near-total failure to integrate ecological concerns into agricultural and engineering developments, even in the face of major public health problems (described in Chapter 1). In democratic systems too, the ideological assimilation of professionals may be harmful. For example, Dunlevy has argued that the concentration of nuclear engineers in regulatory bodies like the UK Atomic Energy Authority, which works closely with the nuclear industry, has distorted the operational conception of the public interest.[24] But professionalism can also work in the public interest. For example, it has been reported that Britain's Nuclear Installations Inspectorate agitated behind the scenes for tighter safety at the Sellafield Nuclear Reprocessing Facility when government ministers tried to block inspections for purely political reasons.[25]
- Producer networks are concerned with economic functions and the relationship between private and public sector. Here private industry, through links with government and trade associations such as the UK Chamber of Industry and Commerce, may exert an influence on policy. For example, private industry, through the Chemical Industries Association, has had a major influence on pesticide analysis and control policy in the UK. In both producer and professional

networks there have been particularly strong links between public and private sector.

If we accept the proposition advanced earlier that interorganizational activity itself generates unpredictable policy impacts, then the emergence of a complex web of networks with the growth of modern states helps to account for the notion of increasing turbulence. It also suggests why it is insufficient for environmentalists to be 'issue-oriented'. For example, it may not be enough to understand and argue the relative merits of nuclear power, hydroelectric dams and coal-fired power stations. Rather, what Vickers called a 'policy appreciation' may require an integrated perspective on an issue and the promotion of cross-cutting networks to provide a dynamic analysis of policy issues.[26]

There is also a strong core–periphery dimension to the growth of such networks:

> *The emergence of policy networks with the growth of the modern state could be interpreted as the triumph of functional over territorial politics. Thus, channels of communication between centre and locality are not based on territorial representation but on professional–bureaucratic contacts: dispensed territorial justice rivals the politics of place; uniform standards challenge local variety.*[27]

The functional orientation is also reinforced by the professional one, creating tension between the drive for centralization and the need for local service delivery. In any event, what it does suggest is that only interorganizational activity itself, which requires resources such as mandate, staff time and funding, can unravel policy problems which are interwoven and demand attention across departments and specialisms.

Action Networks

As we have seen, management organizations are forced increasingly by turbulence and complexity into a range of temporary alliances, formal or informal, with other organizations. The capacity to do this productively is 'connective' capacity, which results in collaborative problem-solving. These alliances are the 'administrative cadres', 'multi-disciplinary project teams' and 'flexible adjuncts to all manner of work organizations' described earlier as unconventional institutional frameworks for environmental management and development planning.

There is growing evidence that such interorganizational collaboration is emerging as a clear feature of successful management. This trend also fits theories of responses to turbulence in the early organizational analysis of Emery and Trist. Following that early work, Trist suggests that management will be undertaken increasingly by such task-oriented networks.[28] The possible functions of action or task-oriented networks are:

- regulation – of present relationships and activities, establishing ground rules and maintaining values;
- appreciation – of emergent trends and issues, developing a shared image of a desirable future;

- mutual problem solving – by tapping into the extended range of knowledge, expertise and experience available from members of the network;
- infrastructural support – resources, research, information sharing and support of innovation;
- mobilization – of resources, including finance, political access and support, information and expertise, legal authority and administrative relationships; and
- development – of a network of external relations for interactive planning and mutual support.

A key issue in any such network is the degree to which the partner or stakeholding organizations are loosely or tightly 'coupled'. Coupling can be defined in terms of the strength of vertical or horizontal ties between organizations, and whether relations are voluntary or mandated. The degree of coupling also depends in part on the degree of hierarchical control, if any, exercised by a central authority. Following a review of networks within social service delivery systems, Aldrich summarizes the position:

> *Advocates assert that a loosely coupled structure is most appropriate under conditions of environmental change where decisions must be taken rapidly and where a high degree of responsiveness is desired. Advocates of centralization attack these arguments on the grounds that a decentralised system caters to local interests at the expense of societal interests and is more costly to administer because of duplication of administrative overheads across many semi-autonomous organizations.*[29]

Role of a linking-pin organization in an action network

Action networks usually differ from less task-oriented networks in that there is a strong central focus to the network which serves as a centre of communication, co-ordination and 'drive'. In organizational analysis, this is a linking-pin. It may be an existing organization which gives birth to, and nurtures the network, or a dedicated organization can be established by network members who recognize the need for a central focus. The linking-pin organization will play an absolutely key role in integrating the loosely coupled system, even if it has no formal status.

Five functions of a linking-pin organization are:

1. It serves as a communication channel between nodes or stakeholders within the network and to the wider world;
2. It links third parties to one another by transferring resources, information or clients;
3. If it is a high status organization it secures resources for the network;
4. It can use the dependence of other organizations on it to direct network activities;
5. It serves as a catalyst to drive the network forward towards its task or objectives; and
6. it encourages different nodes within the network in the development of specialized expertise for the benefit of the network as a whole.

A linking-pin organization may also use its stature or authority to link more than one network, and it can help to prevent the isolation of smaller organizations within any network. Linking-pin organizations play an increasingly important role in difficult environmental management tasks. For example, the World Wide Fund For Nature (WWF) plays a linking-pin role in a number of different national and international networks. Internationally, WWF pioneered 'debt-for-nature' swaps that linked interest groups in tropical countries and wealthy industrialized countries. In Britain, WWF draws together a variety of organizations concerned with the loss of rural farmland to suburban development. In the case study in Chapter 10, the parent Groundwork Foundation provides a linking-pin function to the semi-autonomous offspring Trusts that it helps to establish. And in Chapter 14, we see how the organization Homeless International has an important linking-pin role for local, national and international action networks concerned with shelter and housing around the world.

A linking-pin function can also be pursued at the societal level. Trist, for example, calls for advances in institution-building at the level of interorganizational domains which occupy a position in social space between society as a whole and the single organization. Such domains manifest themselves in concrete organizations to reduce and regulate turbulence. For example, in Canada the regular interprovincial meetings among premiers and senior ministers constitute the framework of an interorganizational domain which attempts to regulate endemic turbulence in a political system so fractured that the future of the country is at risk. In Britain, the non-profit NGO, The Environment Council, works to establish linkages between campaigning environmental groups, business and government.

In lower income countries, where linking-pin institutions do not yet exist, an early step by government is to establish some kind of arms-length environment council to set the environmental agenda and to draw in the competences of other organizations, such as business or university, to the environmental management task. This is the approach of the Government of Ghana which saw the establishment of a national environment council as an early step towards developing support for a national environmental policy.

The remainder of this chapter considers how organizations, faced with difficult management tasks, can improve their corporate abilities, and their members' abilities, for fostering innovation in management. Within the term 'organization' we now explicitly include the action network, whether formal or informal. In the arguments over the meaning and method of sustainable development, we see the opportunity for organizations and their members to improve their abilities to manage conflict to mutual advantage through a generic process of organizational learning. The rest of this chapter sets out a rationale for organizational learning; the next chapter covers a set of practical steps for initiating organizational learning within any environmental action network.

Conflict as an Opportunity for Innovation

In defining and implementing sustainable development, 'conflict between organizations is an inevitable result of functional interdependence and scarcity of resources'.[30] In all action networks, therefore, bargaining to resolve conflicts is likely to be a central mode of political action. Organizational dynamics will involve a relationship between positional power and authority derived from possession of resources and their use in bargaining.[31] Bargaining in turn can be made more effective by the processes of organizational learning, facilitation and by types of mediation.

Conflict among organizations over resources, power and influence is inevitable. If we take, for example, organizations that are concerned with regional development and environmental conservation in Canada's northern territories, the following areas of interagency conflict can be found:

- between federal government departments with different mandates – for example, the Department of Indian Affairs and Northern Development, and the Department of Environment;
- between federal, territorial and municipal governments;
- between native organizations and all levels of government;
- between environmental pressure groups and government agencies; and
- between private industry and environmental groups.

In fact, the list could be longer for there is a strong measure of centre–periphery tension between Ottawa, the federal capital, which is 2000 miles from the region, and regional administrative centres, such as Yellowknife.

But it would be a mistake to take such situations as one of constant and evenly spread conflict among competing agencies. There is also a constant shift of organizational alliances among groups. A federal department with a mandate over environmental conservation, the Department of the Environment, falls naturally into an alliance with the similar Territorial Department of Renewable Resources against federal and territorial agencies aligned with private industry to promote industrial development. For example, native organizations found it in their interest to continually align themselves with central government against the aspirations for provincehood of the previous government of the Northwest Territories (NWT), with dramatic results, described below.

These situational alliances constantly alter as agencies make progress towards, or review, objectives against a background of:

- shifting world prices and preferences for the region's commodities (oil, gas, gold, furs, etc) which, in this case, means a 'boom and bust' economy;
- the long-term constitutional struggle over the region's future and the future of Canada itself; and
- the democratic aspirations of the majority of native people for an independent political entity within or even outside the Canadian federation.

In late 1991 the federal government announced that such a political entity, within the federation, would be carved out of the NWT. It is to be called 'Nunavut', and in this region 18,000 Innuit will have the unrestricted right to hunt, fish and trap, and presumably to fashion their own version of a sustainable, natural resource-based society.

Canadian political scientists have reviewed this complex melange in all its fascinating detail.[32] For the purposes of environmental management, there are two useful observations. First, if, as we have argued, conflict is inevitable in attempting to realize goals of sustainable development, the nature of conflict itself is worthy of study if organizations are to manage better. Second, many empirical studies of management find in conflict a beneficial opportunity to improve the effectiveness of interorganizational relations, provided managers accept that conflict cannot be eliminated. Rather,

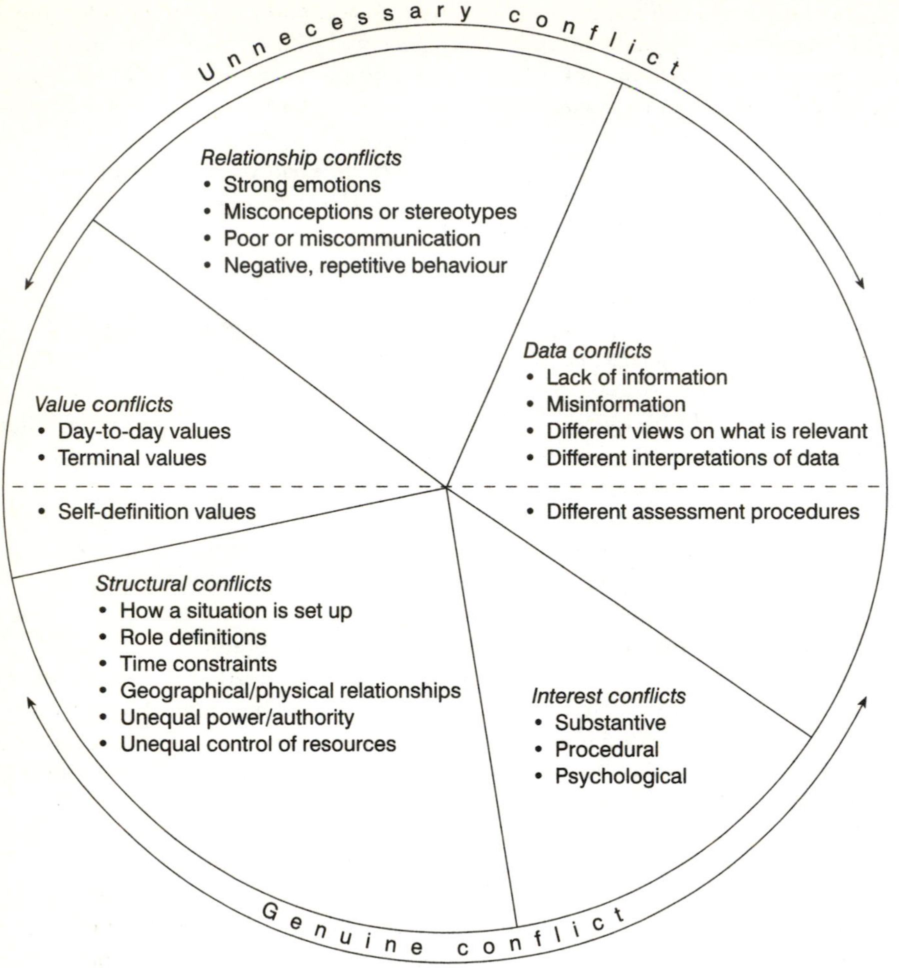

Source: CDR Associates, Boulder, Colorado[35]

Figure 8.1 *Types of conflict*

organizations may find in conflict the opportunity to redefine norms and identity, and to reassess ineffective structures. This view is echoed by Godet, who finds in system crisis both a threat and an opportunity for beneficial change.[33] Gemmill and Smith argue that it is at the point when there is a major thrust towards disorder within a system that genuine learning and transition can occur.[34]

Types of conflict

It would be a mistake to assume that all conflict over environmental policy is based on disagreement over substantive issues. Five types of conflict have been identified by CDR Associates during assisted environmental mediation processes in the United States and elsewhere (Figure 8.1), distinguishing between unnecessary and genuine, or unavoidable, conflict.

There are three types of conflict that are, on the whole, unnecessary and can be readily managed:

1 Relationship conflicts occur because of misperceptions or stereotypes, miscommunication or habitual negative behaviours which grate on other partners. These are unnecessary in that they may occur even when genuine conditions for conflict, such as limited resources or mutually exclusive goals, are not present.
2 Data conflicts occur when people lack information, are misinformed, disagree over the relevance of data, interpret information differently or have competing assessment procedures. Most can be resolved by better communication, although it is often the case in inegalitarian partnerships that dominant stakeholders hoard information to disadvantage other stakeholders and keep them in a subservient position. In Britain, for example, local government departments are often accused by community groups of hoarding information in this manner.
3 Value conflicts represent incompatible belief systems, but again these need not lead to genuine conflict unless people attempt to force one set of values on others or assert that divergent beliefs are not allowed. Conversely, people and organizations with quite different values systems can work together in relative harmony, unless their self-definition is threatened by conflict.

Two other types of conflict are genuine, inevitable and therefore difficult to avoid:

1 Structural conflicts are caused by oppressive patterns of human relationships, usually shaped by forces external to the participants in a dispute. Participants may be disadvantaged by economic arrangements, lack of political control, organizational or professional arrangements or spatial peripheralization.
2 Interest conflicts occur over substantive issues (the decision), procedural issues (how to arrive at the decision) and psychological issues (perceptions of trust, fairness, need for participation, etc). Conflict occurs when parties believe that the satisfaction of their interests is incompatible with the satisfaction of their opponents' interest: 'For an interest-based dispute to be resolved, all parties must have a significant number of their interests addressed or met…'.[36]

The best means of resolving conflict are usually best determined locally. However, the next chapter describes how procedures of facilitation and mediation are useful for identifying conflict and moving towards the resolution of disputes via the establishment of action networks. The case studies in Part V also follow up on these methods of conflict reduction.

Organizational and behavioural responses to conflict

In summary, conflict presents opportunities for positive action, particularly if types of conflict can be identified and addressed: to diffuse tension, to isolate genuine from unnecessary conflict and to meet as many of the interests of participants as possible. This is important for managers who constantly find themselves confronted with what seems to be one 'subsystem crisis' after another, sometimes called 'firefighting'.

Appropriate organizational responses to conflict may be institutional or behavioural. The former attempt to improve organizational effectiveness by changing organizational roles, mandates, legal obligations, communications systems, reward systems and other characteristics. It is equally important to engage in parallel behavioural change: of stakeholders' culture, attitudes, values, norms, and so on. This involves participants in a cycle of discovery–invention–production and evaluation of knowledge. The purpose is to increase human resource capability for managing conflict in a number of areas which are relevant to difficult tasks. These capabilities include:

- analytic: to formulate a view of the key problems facing the organization;
- target-setting: to have clear objectives in the sense of preferred future states of the operating environment;
- innovation: to devise appropriate strategies in non-traditional forms for the achievements of these futures;
- corporate: to be able to take an overall view of the resources and requirements for action in a given situation;
- functional: to develop and implement specific programmes within a corporate framework;
- monitoring: to evaluate changing conditions in the operating environment and the effects of interventions with a view to assessing their impact and further reviewing policies; and
- connective: to devise productive relationships with other bodies whose operations are relevant to the achievement or frustration of environmental goals.[37]

This list provides an agenda, focused on the innovation function, for improving skills within any organization, but it does not provide the method. At its simplest, the method is based on self-development through action-learning – by which we mean that participants or stakeholders engage in a self-directed, mutually supportive and iterative process of understanding organizational constraints and experiment with options for overcoming them.

The Path to Innovation: Organizations as Learning Systems

As we noted, organizations addressing environmental metaproblems cannot help being influenced by the activities of other organizations which are influencing the environment and each other. For this reason, organizations need to be aware of the changes which occur in their environment and to learn or adapt their behaviour to accommodate this flow of information. Such organizational learning is not mechanistic, as the cybernetic analogy might suggest, but must involve 'cultural change' – that is, accepting the possibility of altering what may be deeply held beliefs or entrenched patterns of organizational culture.[38] This gives rise to innovation:

> *Innovation involves new behaviour, new habits, new interlocking expectations which we call roles in social theory, and it even involves new interlocking patterns of roles, which we call institutions or practices. Innovation is collective action.*[39]

Organizations that do not engage in such cultural change remain immured in what have been called 'culturally programmed strategies'. These emphasize continuity, consistency and stability in order to maintain the status quo. However, when such an organization experiences turbulence it faces an array of internal and external disorders and is unable to deal effectively according to its accustomed patterns of operation. Bureaucracies, for example, are seldom structured for learning, adaptation and change, but rather to carry out a predetermined range of tasks.

Innovation: learning to learn

The essential definition of innovation involves the notion of learning to learn, what Bateson called higher-order learning.[40] The concept of organizations as learning systems is a valuable contribution of organization theory to innovation in management. For example, Argyris and Schon propose a 'theory of action' which describes a process of human learning in which knowledge is continually tested and reconstructed.[41] Morgan argues that the application of these insights has resulted in a major reorientation in organizations: goal-oriented rationality is superseded by an ethic which stresses the need to facilitate the creative interplay and development of contextual relationships, or action learning.[42]

Here the primary task of managers is to create the capacity for learning, which becomes a pre-eminent organizational function. Action learning strategies address three objectives:

1 Informed and effective decision-making through the changing of organizational culture.
2 The unification of theory (or systematic reflection) and practice through action research, which leads to replicable learning across a range of similar problem areas.
3 Professional development.

Action learning is the means by which organizations can deal with rapid and complex change which causes process outcomes and organizational objectives to be mismatched. Turbulent change can be seen as systems of problems or errors which need to be dealt with through learning and alteration of individual, professional and organizational beliefs. This is seldom easy, but the rewards are tangible in terms of enhanced management capacity and flexibility in the face of uncertainty, and in terms of personal and professional development:

> *Action learning strategies enable us to deal with systems of problems without having to solve them, and to do so in a continuous, adaptive and non-synoptic manner which meets the rapidity, complexity and uncertainty of turbulence.*[43]

Figure 8.2 summarizes the differences between traditional approaches and action learning strategies. This is, of course, a simplification: many agencies have other, often statutory, functions which do not demand innovation, and operate somewhere in the middle ground.

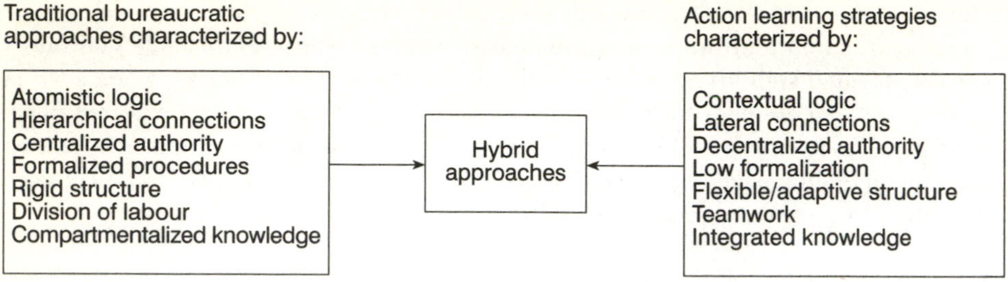

Figure 8.2 *Summary of the differences between traditional approaches and action*

The innovation process

Organizations generally do not adopt a specific blueprint for an innovative activity, but rather adopt a general concept, the operational meaning of which gradually unfolds in the management process. The stages in this process of unfolding have been identified by Rogers and Kim.[44]

Five steps are grouped into two main subprocesses – initiation and implementation. Initiation consists of all the information gathering, conceptualizing and planning. Implementation is action, from which the initiation process can restart.

Initiation

1 Agenda setting: a general organizational problem creates a perceived need for innovation as defined by members of the organization.
2 Matching: specific aspects of the problem are matched to alternative solutions (forms of innovation), and their fit is tested by members of the organization.

Implementation

3 Redefining: reinvention or modification of the innovation based on feedback about the fit.
4 Structuring: organizational structures may need to be altered to implement the innovation. For example, a new organizational unit may be created.
5 Interconnecting: relationships within and between organizations are clarified. As this happens the innovation may lose its separate identity and become institutionalized.

The process is not linear, of course, but circular, involving as many interior loops as necessary to ensure the fit of the innovation to the problem.

Innovation in government

Each partner in an action network makes a contribution of relevant expertise and enthusiasm to this innovation process, including representatives of government departments and agencies. But government also has an important overall societal role, which we can only begin to touch on in this book. This is a strategic role which Godet calls *la prospective*. It is not mathematical forecasting, nor is it reactive in the sense of attempting to respond to technological and economic imperatives thrown up by the marketplace. Rather, it is the proactive attempt to throw light on present action by

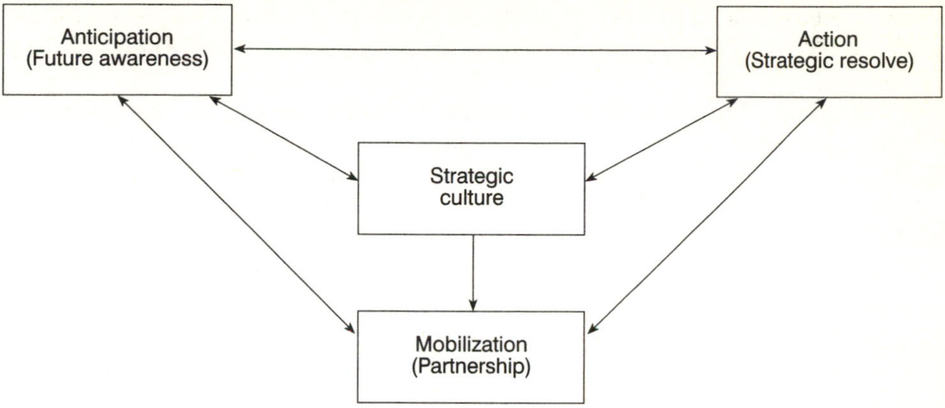

Source: After Godet[45]

Figure 8.3 *Anticipation – Action – Mobilization*

looking at possible positive futures. It begins with some sense of the possibilities of the future – call it vision – and uses this vision to initiate the subprocesses of innovation: the agenda of the future – what kind of society we might want to have; and commitment to implementation based on desire to realize this future and not some other, less satisfactory one.

First and foremost, *la prospective* is a way of thinking; it is reflected in the strategic vision a government communicates to society. Figure 8.3 shows how strategic culture is the pivot which links the 'Anticipation – Action – Mobilization' functions of a modernised society. Godet suggests why it is imperative:

1 The acceleration of technical, economic and social change necessitates long-term vision because 'the faster you drive, the further ahead your headlights must shine'; and
2 Factors of inertia inherent in structures and behaviour mean that we must sow today in order to be able to harvest tomorrow.

Prospective thinking involves two commitments by government, to be reinforced by organizational culture:

1 Commitment to strategic management, which involves monitoring major issues in society, including issues just appearing on the horizon, and making use of that information in planning for the future.
2 Commitment to partnership, recognizing that no agency of society can manage on its own, and that partnership, or networking, processes require and deserve support from public as well as private resources.

With all these terms – management, planning, partnership – it is the participation in the processes they represent which generates both policy innovation and the capacity to innovate. By promoting such innovation, government begins to define a new, sophisticated role for itself, beyond the failures of bureaucratic over-control and beyond the naïvety of *laissez-faire*. The experience of action networking is that the benefits of the process, in terms of new productive linkages in society and individual growth in the ability to take a wider perspective, continue after any particular aspect of the process is complete.

The Growth Management Consensus Project in California, described in Chapter 12, is a good example of this constructive role for government. This process of formal mediation, initiated (but not controlled) by the State of California, has been able to propose recommendations for policy and legislation based on consensus among many of the major stakeholding agencies in the state, ranging from environmentalists to property developers. This is reported to have brought forward the legislative programme, and the level of statewide debate over these issues by many years.

We now return to the concept of learning and show how a specific methodology of 'action research', arising out of the action learning perspective, can link anticipation and action in a single effective framework. This is also a methodology for policy-making and implementation which works well in the action-networking approach.

Action Research

Action learning is specifically concerned with integration: theory with practice, and research with action. Its underlying assumption is that there is an emergent quality to this process. It is not, therefore, either theoretical or anti-theoretical, but theory grounded in practical experience and experience directed by theoretical reflection. Action learning:

> *addresses head-on social inquiry's fundamental problems – the relation between theory and practice, between the general and the particular, between common-sense and academic expertise, between mundane action and critical reflection, and hence – ultimately – between ideology and understanding.*[46]

Action learning in organizations produces direct results in terms of innovation. It can also produce knowledge, or transferable learning, when linked to the parallel tool of action research. This new approach to research needs to be contrasted with traditional social science which requires that:

1 the primary objective of research remains unaltered during the research process;
2 there is precise and measurable control over dependent variables;
3 intervening variables be controlled or excluded from the research framework;
4 the researcher remains neutral and dispassionate throughout the process.

The problem is that (2) above is impossible in any dynamic policy situation characterized by turbulence, and that (1), (3) and (4) greatly reduce the value of social science research to real time-management problems because they negate the value of feedback and prohibit the researcher from contributing the benefits of experience and intuition to the process. All four criteria ensure that qualitative aspects of environmental problems will be ignored or undervalued. For these reasons, traditional approaches to research in the management field are often unrealistic, cumbersome, unresponsive and unable to bridge institutional barriers to understanding.

The action-research approach, on the other hand:

1 makes use of the social context of a specific environmental problem or development challenge to increase its own effects;
2 redefines the research process towards a rapid, interactive cycle of problem–discovery–reflection–response–problem redefinition;
3 replaces the neutral social scientist/observer with a multidisciplinary team of practitioners and researchers, all working together in a process of mutual education;
4 proposes that pluralistic evaluation replace static models of social processes. This is characterized by concern for: institutional functioning, continual monitoring of project implementation, the subjective views of major constituent groups and methodological 'triangulation' by which a variety of data sources are brought to bear for evaluation; and
5 generates replicable learning from the above elements which is constantly tested against both past experience and the results of current action.

Action research therefore differs substantially from research or action alone. It differs from research, in its avoidance of the static, controlled and contrived model and its emphasis on a fluid, on-going approach which generates conclusions at the most appropriate time in the process rather than waiting until the bitter end. It differs from action alone in the constant feeding back of evaluation, resulting in crucial shifts in the direction of action. It is fundamentally about collaboration and dialogue:

> *Action research is a collaborative endeavour in which groups of practitioners work together to understand better their own practice, to increase their awareness of the effects of their practice, and of their control over the situation in which they work.*[48]

There are personal and professional, as well as organizational, benefits. Participants in action research strategies and/or in action networks tend to become sensitized to the diversity of motivations for human action, and the constructive and sustainable means for altering them. The result is what Schon calls the 'reflective practitioner'.[49]

Conclusion

This chapter has argued that the context of environmental metaproblems is turbulence, which is characterized by uncertainty about the nature of complex problems and the consequences of collective action, by inconsistent and ill-defined preferences and values, and complex networks of participants with a varying interest in problem resolution. A mistaken belief in a stable state, in which planning can act as a buffer against change and uncertainty, gives rise to institutional dysfunctions caused by organizations attempting to fulfil individual objectives, while maximizing their own benefits and externalizing costs.

The main conclusion to be drawn is that complexity and fluidity are inevitable in the modern state, often reinforced by instability in the world's economy. Any organization faces not only system complexity but is dependent on other organizations in that environment, each of which is probably pursuing unrelated objectives. Such interdependence of organizations and the environment is compounded by political, economic, cultural and psychological changes. This has caused the range of governments' problems to increase dramatically, made it more difficult to respond appropriately, and is thus responsible for the limits to governance. This, in turn, is manifested in concern over poor management, deficiencies in service co-ordination, poor quality of service and an inability to establish a conception of the public good which commands confidence. The problem is exacerbated by a rise in pluralism and a changing value system which reduces willingness to cooperate with government.[50]

Here we arrive at the argument that the management of complexity is a continual process of innovation rather than a product. It is a journey which can be done poorly or well, but where each arrival is a point of departure. Managers must work towards a synthesis of knowledge and promote a common problem conception and an evolving consensus on a series of pressing issues. They must relish the rough and tumble of interorganizational negotiation and accept the indeterminate nature of their calling. Collaboration and a drive towards consensus, rather than subordination, is the preferred approach. The situation was summarized excellently by Whalen, writing 40 years ago:

> *The law of life is the law of change, social activities breed and transform social and political arrangements. The achieving of an acceptable balance between change and order involves a continuing tension between institutional effectiveness – interpreted as operational efficiency in relation to a matrix of communal skills, resources, demands and skills – and group images of institutional legitimacy. Given the complex, changing, independent and potentially unstable conditions common to most democratic states, and given the public measures required to secure social stability in such an environment, the condition of government may be described as a crisis of effectiveness.*[51]

The challenge is much the same whatever the field to be managed: natural environment, transport, land use, energy, resource consumption or any other. This supports Webber's contention that good management is about a 'cognitive style, not a substantive field'.[52] The next chapter suggests a distinctive organizational framework for nurturing that style in pursuit of sustainable development.

9

Developing Action Networks for Environmental Management

It is widely assumed that environmental issues can be dealt with in the same way as other government activities. But the complex inter-relationships demand holistic thinking and a new multi-level, multi-organizational approach – presenting a challenge to traditional government organizational and management structures.

J D Stewart[1]

The substitution of open communication for bureaucratic authority in informal groups and temporary or parallel organizations, encourages creative thinking. This may equip the organization to move from chaos to order as it needs to begin a new phase in its existence.

H P Knowles and B O Saxberg[2]

The inability of command and control bureaucracies, working on their own or vertically with international bureaucracies to deal with complex environment and development problems is a major concern worldwide. This calls for an examination of the processes of decision-making, including the organizational culture of governments, as well as the products of policy-making. Unfortunately, as noted in Chapter 7, process issues are of little interest to politicians and bureaucrats who already have power, and therefore a vested interest in maintaining the status quo.

Even in the face of continual inefficiency in government and governance, process issues are usually swept under the carpet because they are more difficult to conceptualize than substantive environmental issues. And, to be honest, process issues do not rank very high on many people's list of exciting things to talk about. None of this negates the need for a radical improvement of the processes of decision-making.

Fortunately, there is a growing concern among people who are addressing environmental and development challenges that good work is continually undone by lack of attention to process. There is much interest in the possibilities for interorganizational innovation in action networks, linking the public, private and voluntary sectors.

Alternatives to the existing situation have been suggested under many names, but they all boil down to innovation in what has been described as an evolving network that should be flexible, open and capable of restructuring itself over time.[3] Unlike the loose linkages in the more usual information-sharing networks, the action network is focused on the goals of its management and research tasks, and engages in a regular, critical review of its progress towards those goals. The networks function at a number of levels:

- as growing constituencies for sustainable development, fostering an ongoing political process of mediation and the building of consensus even where conflict is bound to be pervasive;
- as a vehicle for new partnerships between government, business and non-governmental and community groups;
- as groups of public administrators and natural and social scientists with a commitment to mutual learning to develop a new range of skills in environmental management; and
- in multilayered, 'nested' networks, as a means of integrating efforts at sustainable development from the local to the international level.

Increasingly, forward-thinking government officials are sanctioning the involvement of such task-oriented, less formal groups in environmental management. These groups define environmental problems in a more holistic and practical fashion, and work to develop consensus on the way forward. These kinds of innovation are not, however, a replacement for the traditional bureaucracy, as they do not carry out any routine functions of government. Rather, government will find it helpful to participate in such networks, as a partner with business and community groups in tackling problems in environmental management.

The characteristics of these parallel action networks are:

- flat, flexible organizational structures involving teamwork or partnerships;
- equality of relationships among all relevant stakeholders;
- vision and value-driven leadership;
- an emphasis on participation and organizational learning;
- undertaking continuous performance review and improvement; and
- a method of network development in which events progress at a pace which is politically and culturally sustainable given local conditions.

The action-network approach is concerned with both sustainable development and the sustainability of the innovations identified as necessary to improve environmental management, whether they originate in public administration, business management, community development, or wherever.[4] It addresses substantive and process issues simultaneously.

This chapter describes some of the fundamental principles and mechanisms involved. These are divided into underlying assumptions, operational tactics and methods of working, as listed in Figure 9.1. The case studies which follow each suggest a similar methodology for developing action networks at widely varying levels of decision-making.

Underlying Assumptions of Action Networks

Redefinition of environment

A basic premise is that common definitions of environment are often too narrow in their focus on biophysical factors, at the expense of the social environment and of environmental, economic and social objectives for human development. Such defini-

Major underlying assumptions
- Redefinition of environment
- Stakeholder equality
- Action learning
- Grounding in real problems

Operational tactics
- Enrolment of stakeholders
- Problem reiteration
- Interdisciplinary analysis
- Institutional and organizational development
- Role of key individuals
- Linkage between public and private sectors
- Linkage with non-governmental organizations

Methods of working
- Management as planning
- Role of consensus
- Facilitation and mediation procedures
- Concept of nested networks
- Generation of replicable learning
- Paying for networking

Figure 9.1 *The basic elements of action-centred networking*

tions also narrow the management task unacceptably and lead to failure because of the large number of uncontrolled intervening variables outside the working definition.

The action-network approach redefines environment, and thus the tasks of environmental management, in the context of national development, as a mediation process between economic/industrial needs and the maintenance of the biosphere, with the objective of an increased level of integration. In this way projects attempt to operationalize the concept of sustainable development in a practical manner as a dynamic process of good decision-making and management, not as a static product of policy or a distant vision of future policy.

Stakeholder equality

Underpinning the structure of these networks is the assumption that stakeholders are equal in terms of the validity of their values and perceptions, and in terms of their right to participation in, and power over, decision-making and implementation. This is a simple principle to articulate but one that is difficult to implement. As noted in Chapter 2, it implies that old hierarchical arrangements and patterns of paternalism or domination must be swept away in the new structure: for example, North over South, 'developed' over 'less developed', professionals over non-professionals, business over NGOs, men over women, rich over poor, urban over rural, government over community, and so on. There are many ethical reasons for doing this, but even pragmatically, there is little chance of progress unless stakeholders are strongly committed to 'ownership' of problems and solutions based on a feeling of genuine participation.

Implementing stakeholder equality is hard. In an unequal world, it is easiest to start with a limited task and to rely on progress on that task to promote change in other areas of life by 'good example'. It is important to note that equality is not to be equated with a lack of strong leadership. Network participants understand that challenging organizational culture and accomplishing difficult tasks requires leadership in terms of the resources offered by a linking-pin organization. Finally, government or other public sector officials tend to find it difficult to relinquish status and control; business and community groups may be less concerned about hierarchical distinctions and the status they confer, but are still likely to find it difficult to achieve a sense of equality.

Action learning

At a basic level, the action-network approach works in two ways: realistic environmental problem definition and redefinition as circumstances change; and individualized, adaptive responses designed to improve management capability that is relevant to specific tasks. In short, the network teams intervene in the process of management, learn about it and improve it, hands-on:

> *... combining past experience, organizational intelligence and future goals in a mode of action-oriented management which is intended to produce valid information, informed choice and, most importantly, a commitment to action based on consensual knowledge.*[5]

Grounding in real problems

The action-network approach grounds transferable learning about environmental management strategies in practical development challenges. This accords with Hirschman's advice that 'uniform solutions to development problems invariably lead us astray'.[6] In the IDEA programme (Innovations in Development for Environmental Action), for example (Chapter 11), the environmental problems first identified, such as river pollution, were redefined into a series of positive 'management and action' projects in watershed, waste and natural resources management, supported by a second-level network providing information services, environmental advisory services, and training and action research methodology.

This underlines the point that, although countries face many enormous environmental problems, most of these will only be resolved by the development of local skills and solutions. Problems may be analysed at a global or national scale, but the resolution of big problems will be the result of the aggregated results of smaller projects and initiatives. The process of local problem redefinition generates the necessary local commitment and an understanding of the skills needed to implement solutions. Even the partial implementation of more productive management approaches builds confidence in local abilities in environmental management.

Operational Tactics

Enrolment of stakeholders

An important aspect of the network approach is to address the range of identified constraints on good management more or less simultaneously. Some constraints will require institutional development, others the development of a new consensus as a basis for action. These are discussed below. Two fundamental constraints usually found in any environmental management task are lack of political commitment and a failure of integration.

One way of addressing political constraints is campaigning, such as that undertaken by NGOs like Friends of the Earth or Greenpeace. The action network takes a different, but complementary approach by gradually drawing in relevant stakeholders – affected interest groups, including politicians and government officials – thus building up a momentum and commitment to change in an emerging constituency for sustainable development. Some people will join the process because they recognize its potential in addressing a serious environmental problem; others would rather not join but will be afraid of being left out of something. Still others may need to be induced into coming along once because an important or expert speaker is addressing a topic of national or international significance. Some people will come because the minister is making a brief appearance, and for no other reason. Most people will have no idea what an action network is like, but once exposed to the stimulating discussion in a non-hierarchical setting, become attracted to the process.

How stakeholders are attracted is a tactical decision; the important point is that the right stakeholders are invited or even lured into the process. The IDEA projects tackled urgent problems of national significance and then used widespread media coverage, senior ministerial speeches, addresses by international experts, and invitations to a broad range of possible participants to convince people of the relevance of the approach and the urgent needs it was addressing.

Drawing in the right stakeholders tackles the problems of integration at the same time, assuming that participants are empowered to represent their organizations and report back to them. In the more formal mediation approach, described below, it is a requirement of the process that participants can commit their organizations to the solutions that emerge from discussion. This was the case in the Growth Management Consensus Project in California.

The major areas of integration which usually need to be addressed by drawing stakeholders into the team are between:

- different government departments;
- central and local government;
- public and private sectors;
- government and the academic/scientific community; and
- government policy level and community level, particularly smaller scale businesses, agriculture and community-based NGOs.

Problem reiteration

Policies seldom address comprehensively the problems they are intended to solve. This is because the initial problem assessment is faulty – often biased to fit into preconceptions or an existing party political programme, or because the nature of the problems changes while administrative responses do not, when too much is committed in the initial response. Problems change because circumstances change: the economy goes up or down, other organizations intervene for better or worse, or some progress is made on some aspects of the problem.

A simple but important tactic, therefore, is regularly to re-examine and redefine the nature of the problem, with the critical but constructive assistance of network members and other experts. There is no other way to ensure that the response is appropriate to the task. This is easier said than done – once we think we know what the problem is, we are not inclined to have this certainty disturbed. We will be loath to admit that a change of direction is required or that our responses have been inappropriate to the problem. We will be inclined to defend what we have done because we have done it – where is the reward for admitting failure? The solution lies in changing organizational culture within the network to make the admission of failure a positive, constructive act, as it surely is, and to make problem redefinition an exciting challenge. Incentives may be required. The network, because it carries little baggage of organizational history, can refashion its culture in the light of what works.

The main criterion in these decisions is to make progress in the task at hand rather than stick rigidly to a particular boundary definition. In particular, the informal, parallel organization has the flexibility to redefine its mandate in this way during an unfolding process of problem redefinition.

Interdisciplinary analysis

The scale and interactive causes and effects of most environmental problems require holistic analysis which can appreciate the complex interrelationships which define those problems. It is from these that damage and further risks arise; it is holistic thinking that can tease out the linkages which environmental policies need to recognize. Drawing in the right stakeholders, complemented by expert advisers to the network, ensures that an interdisciplinary team is assembled.

For example, the need to shift from an initial focus on pollution to the development of commitment to watershed or ecosystem management, and the institutional framework to accomplish this, means that tasks which originate from knowledge and expertise in the natural sciences – say, of water quality – soon require complementary knowledge and expertise from the social sciences, such as regional land use, urban planning and economic analysis.

Institutional and organizational development

Institutional development, broadly defined, addresses legal and organizational constraints and limitations in human resources. As with other constraints, improvements may need to be pursued more or less simultaneously by networks for maximum effectiveness.

Legal institutions underlie the fabric of development and environmental control. For example, the property system and land-use planning controls are a vital factor in any rural or agricultural development or conservation initiative, yet very often programmes are initiated without any analysis of these fundamental systems.[7] Legal systems include the necessary laws, regulations and environmental standards, and the framework of government to implement them. These are necessary but not sufficient conditions for successful management. The legal system also embodies formal arrangements for centralization or decentralization of planning and implementation – often a critical issue in development – and the institutional arrangements of government.

The term 'interorganizational development' covers the shaping of the new formal and informal linkages within government, and beyond government to business and the voluntary and community sectors. Investment in individual and team skills is the key to organizational innovation. This is crucial to improving the management process, both in terms of personal and professional development, and in terms of the development of all other organizational, institutional and legal structures of support.

We noted above the built-in bias of administrative systems towards maintaining the status quo. Those who favour innovation must therefore develop a reinforcement system which achieves three things:

- Rewards people who try innovations, whether they succeed or fail.
- Insures against losses, such as blame, if the innovation fails.
- Insures against losses even if the innovation succeeds.[8]

Incentives must therefore be given much more consideration as a means of generating commitment. At higher levels, the process of networking and achieving consensus must be made to be so stimulating and essential to good decision processes that senior officials feel that they would not like to be left out. They in turn can stimulate changes in organizational culture which can ripple throughout their organizations.

The role of key individuals

When initiating a network, there is a need to identify individuals who have the potential to mobilize people in a situation that is often characterized by tension, conflict and stalemate. A premise of the action-network approach, validated by case studies, is that senior people with the right outlook and human relations abilities, whether scientists or administrators, with the support of the network, can move beyond their normal professional boundaries and become important agents of change in the improvement of the quality of management. This understanding, and particularly the means to achieve it, is a major output of the network approach.

Linkage between public and private sectors

The waning of socialist ideology, and the obvious advantages of linkage between public and private sectors in economic development, have made this a challenging area for improved management. For example:

> *New forms of public–private relationship are sought to replace the traditions of techno-bureaucracy which grew up with the post-war welfare state. The state itself is struggling to restructure itself, ideologically and institutionally in response to these demands. This in turn destabilises the established practices of interest mediation through which claims in respect of land and environmental issues are recognised.*[9]

The result, as suggested in a review of the future of public administration and development in Tanzania, is:

> *For most economic activity, it will be an enabling administration, promoting private sector solutions or partnerships with the private sector, and only intervening where the market or the private sector will not carry the risks involved.*[10]

These changes are in keeping with the notion of sustainable development as a process of mediation between production needs and environmental goals. Such new linkages between government and the business sector, encompassing small-scale and medium enterprises as well as big business, will therefore be at the forefront of organizational challenges.

Linkages may prove somewhat easier to foster with multinational corporations eager to prove their environmental credentials, and their branch plants which are part of an international organizational culture; they may be more difficult to foster with heads of small businesses which may be suspicious of government. The task of working with, and developing, organizations of small-scale businesses is similar in many ways to tasks of community organization and requires similar skills of diplomacy and empathy. Equally, any government which hopes to pursue sustainable development objectives in any field will need to learn to work with the private sector.

Linkage with non-governmental organizations

In Chapter 7, the common failure to extend vertical integration downwards and upwards between policy-making levels of government and small-scale natural resource users, such as farmers or small businesses, was identified as a cause of failure in policy-making. The failure stems from governments' lack of knowledge of the motivations and constraints which need to be influenced, a lack of appreciation of the cumulative impacts of even small resource-using actions, and a failure to enlist these resource users in implementation. They are obvious candidates for network membership.

While organization of small-scale stakeholders can be difficult, it is important, and it will probably occur through either local government or non-governmental organizations. As with any other organization with a hand in development, the ability of NGOs to participate productively in development tasks depends on their organizational capacity. Strong NGOs can be active partners in development and environmental management to redress failures of vertical integration. In a discussion paper, the World Bank suggests:

> *People's propensity for organising is an immense development resource and NGOs are an adequate vehicle for tapping it. NGOs should not be regarded just as a conduit for funds or as a means of implementing programs, but as a resource in themselves, a type of development capital. Thus building them up is development.*[11]

It is helpful to distinguish between environmentalist NGOs and community-based NGOs. Environmentalist NGOs now engage in research, lobbying, public education, coordination of funding and protest actions at the international and subnational level. They can target specific issues, generate widespread public interest, lobby key politicians and pressure public agencies. Community-based NGOs are usually more local in orientation, but can have a wider brief than environmentalist NGOs in that their concerns will be more geared to the overall development of their locality.[12] In this sense they are 'people-oriented'. This is a major strength:

> *They organize people to make better use of their own local productive resources, to create new resources and services, to promote equity and alleviate poverty, to influence government actions towards these same objectives and to establish new institutional frameworks that will sustain people-centered development.*[13]

For the purposes of the action network, it is important that every effort is made to extend the partnership to encompass relevant community-based NGOs. In Britain and the US, for example, the 1990s have seen a flowering of the involvement of community groups in successful urban renewal efforts, of which Groundwork (Chapter 10) is only one example. These are all predicated on the realization that it is no good doing things 'to' or 'for' people, particularly in single-sector approaches, like housing renewal, which had failed so dismally in the past. The alternative is to build up networks that encompass community groups, government and business, and to focus on the overall improvement of the quality of life in the community, as well as on critical local issues, such as unemployment or fear of crime.[14]

The new partnership approaches, as they came to be called, recognized that local people, with appropriate assistance from a range of partners in government and business, could analyse their own problems and fashion their own solutions. These approaches, while difficult to build up, are potentially more relevant, more integrated and more sustainable than any which have gone before. They also generate multiplier effects, both for local people who have new confidence and new skills, and for neighbourhoods and cities at large, which become better places in which to live and do business, and which are better equipped to attract inward investment. Urban partnerships in the UK, which are clearly action networks, are a tremendous source of innovation but still face a struggle in recruiting private sector participants and in overcoming suspicions in local government and the voluntary sector over working alongside business.

The question of which NGOs to involve is a matter for local decision in any network. National or regional level NGOs, such as Friends of the Earth, could be expected to contribute to initiatives at that level, while community-based NGOs could initiate development at their own level. What is important is the understanding that local (or national) solutions are appropriate to local (or national) problems, and it is inconceivable that appropriate solutions would surface without partnership with the community through their NGOs.

Methods of Working in Networks

Management as planning

For reasons set out in Chapter 6, sustainable development is unlikely to be realized through initiatives based solely on the functional integration of the space economy. It is for this reason that network approaches are always grounded in some real, spatial or territorial concern, be it an urban neighbourhood or a watershed region, or some larger unit such as a state. With environmental issues too, the fundamental need for planning on a regional ecosystem basis is inescapable. Rowe argues that:

> *In practice sustainability has to be a regional concept. We used to call it land use planning. Fortunately we can substitute for its two-dimensional flatness a better, more inclusive concept, perceiving a world surfaced with three-dimensional ecosystems in which we are immersed. These creative spaces are the focus of regional planning, whose ecological aim is a sustainable earth.*[15]

In a similar vein, Fairclough argues:

> *Most countries have economic plans, forest plans, plans for tourism, industry, services, ranching etc – not to mention plans for rural agricultural development. All these plans and development efforts impact on one another, and can conflict with one another. My simple thesis is that, in any attempt to harmonize economic development with sectoral objectives, a land use planning overview is essential – a planning framework within which public bodies, the private sector and individuals can all operate.*[16]

Fairclough argues that only such a framework can provide the vehicle for mediation among competing objectives, such as economic development and environmental protection. The alternative, he says, is a recipe for 'continuing conflict'.

The role of consensus in the network

A key expected outcome of the network approach is an emerging consensus over the real nature and extent of the problem at hand, and a consensus about, and commitment to, the means of resolution. This drive towards consensus is quite different from the standard adversarial approach of parliamentary politics and law, which is based on simple majority rule and which invariably leaves a large minority, or even a majority, dissatisfied with the outcome of the process and alienated from the decision-making process. It is also different from the top-down administrative style of the traditional bureaucracy. Both can contribute to a lack of confidence in decision-making procedures and active or passive resistance at the stage of implementation.

However, the context of sustainable development is one of a pervasive conflict of interest, and therefore any shift towards consensus-building faces many challenges, for two reasons:

1. Issues raised in considering sustainable development question ways of living that have been established at the expense of the environment and will not be discarded easily.
2. Environmental issues raise questions of values that may be assumed to be absolutes and therefore cannot be 'traded off'.[17]

In spite of these constraints, there is ample evidence that a consensus-based approach is workable and practical, and, more important, that it delivers environmental policy decisions that are appropriate to sustainable development.

First and foremost, consensus-building approaches are based on face-to-face interaction, and informed and guided discussion. The purpose is to arrive at a resolution which meets the needs of all the participants, and during which stakeholders become committed to, and accept greater responsibility for the solution. Such consensus-building is a learned skill, either mutually learned by network members working with a facilitator who will be a member of the network or, more formally, in a process of mediation under professional guidance. In no case is a third-party decision-maker involved, as is common in the adversarial approach.

At the operational level, there are four broad requirements for achieving consensus:

1. Effective mobilization of organizational self-interest as a basis for bargaining and exchange.
2. Legitimation of wider interests in the goals of sustainable development.

3 The creation of a broad, rather than narrow, base for interorganizational relations.
4 Recognition of the role and dynamics of trust.

Webb argues that the mobilization of real, rather than apparent, self-interest is difficult and requires awareness, ability and skill, especially when those interests can best be maximized through bargaining and negotiation. Both self-interest and the interests of others have to be perceived and understood, and mutually satisfactory opportunities have to be sought:

> *Many in the public sector are not used to thinking in these terms and lack the necessary motivation and skills. The upshot is all too easily a failure to recognize the possibility of mutual gain or a failure to achieve it because relationships become one-sided, deteriorate and end in avoidance and conflict.*[18]

The legitimation of wider interests is also challenging, particularly as politicians and administrators have a tendency to pay lip-service to these without any real motivation to engage in processes that would lead to long-term societal change. Webb argues that the consistent involvement and leadership of senior administrators and politicians in shaping a more appropriate organizational culture must be supplemented by the direct mobilization of a wider public interest. Without this attendant pressure:

> *Inter-organizational and inter-professional collaboration may appear to be underpinned by a broad commitment to the wider good only to be shattered at the level of detail by divergent interpretations and priorities.*[19]

The facilitation and mediation procedures described in the next section, and in Chapters 11 and 12, are one way of beginning a process of generating commitment from politicians to longer-term strategic initiatives and policy changes.

Similarly, collaboration and interorganizational working at operational levels are likely to be undermined unless senior officials in departments, agencies and NGOs are committed to the process. Once again, consensus-building approaches set out at the onset to involve senior staff and politicians, to 'coopt' them to the cause of sustainable development, while recognizing that their time may be severely constrained. Here it is the case that top-down efforts are often required to generate a broad, sustainable framework for subsequent, more balanced efforts.

Finally, trust is the *sine qua non* of collaboration, and in its absence, conflict or avoidance are the likely outcome:

> *small successes in joint endeavours may be needed to generate a virtuous spiral of expanding trust. Regard therefore has to be given to group dynamics, to the symbolic importance of including particular interests and individuals, and to showing proper respect for the joint activity and all the partners involved in it (eg by avoiding an 'inner core' of the 'senior' parties).*[20]

The development of consensus, and subsequently joint implementation, is a challenging task. It cannot be treated as a peripheral activity. Fortunately, new skills and knowledge about the means of building consensus are becoming available every day, especially from trial-and-error field efforts, driven by the growing need for consensus on environmental issues. The next section outlines a 'facilitation' approach to networking and a more formal 'mediation' procedure. Both are gaining recognition as a practical means of achieving consensus, notably over problems of environmental management.

Facilitation and mediation

The recent history of formal approaches to consensus-building is described by Chapman:

> *In the United States, Australia, Canada, and a host of other nations, mediation approaches have permitted and encouraged traditional foes to work together to develop creative and more satisfying solutions to challenging environmental problems. Even where scientific data are uncertain and policy objectives are conflicting, mediation techniques help clarify the scope and sources of parties' disagreements, leading to more effective results. Disputes over the location of power plants, dam construction, water conservation and land use have all been mediated successfully.*[21]

Consensus-building by facilitation or mediation involves a dynamic process based on the realization of the broader nature of organizational self-interest and the potential for changing minds. The idea of changing perceptions is a key to the process: it assumes that most intelligent people are prepared to listen to reasonable arguments and to engage in an iterative cycle of learning which narrows the scope of disagreement and clarifies the difference between parties. The approach also assumes that a process of decision-making will need to be newly fashioned to fit the issue at hand, and that it is unlikely that the existing institutional framework will be appropriate. Consensus-building requires skill and perseverance, and is concerned with how things are done (process, thoughts and feelings), as well as what is done.

The following are guidelines for the types of issue which are amenable to facilitation/mediation techniques:

- A significant, visible environmental issue in which a response is needed and for which progress and resolution are possible.
- An issue which is of managable proportions related to the skills available for resolution.
- An issue which can generate commitment from participants with full decision-making powers in their organizations.
- The potential commitment of stakeholders to long-term participation and to the outcomes of the process.
- An issue with funding available to initiate the mediation or facilitation process.

There are basic differences between facilitation and mediation. Mediation is formal and carefully structured, focuses on clearly defined and contentious issues, and makes use of one or more trained mediators (as in the example discussed in Chapter 12). The facilitation approach is more useful when issues are ill-defined, when apparently smaller problems will need to be reappraised and linked to larger issues of development, or when stakeholders or politicians are likely to be suspicious of the implications of the consensus-building process. The approach is more subtle and less direct than mediation and takes longer in order to allow key features of local politics and culture to be accommodated fully within the process. It is usually built into a process of 'unfolding' the issue and of mutual self-discovery within a network, relying on one or more trusted, unbiased facilitators (as in the Chapter 11 case study).

One of the main tasks of the facilitator is to ensure equal participation among stakeholders. From this process, which may take some time, network members derive, through extended discussion, collaborative problem resolution which meets their individual and joint needs. The role of the facilitator is to:

> *act as a catalyst to stimulate awareness of common interests, to introduce communication techniques that facilitate analysis and to provide information on organizational strategies employed in similar circumstances elsewhere.*[22]

Mediation, on the other hand, is a form of assisted dispute resolution. While the facilitator generally assists parties in maintaining open and constructive dialogue, the mediator may challenge entrenched views, suggest alternatives and help parties to bargain more effectively. Participants in a mediation process:

> *learn to listen to each other's views and to communicate and identify their interests, sources of conflict and areas of agreement. The parties engage in joint fact-finding where appropriate, invent options for mutual gain, and reach voluntary, binding agreement based on trading or 'packaging' the options created.*[23]

Three examples of the growing interest in mediation initiatives that have contributed to environmental policy-making are given by Chapman.[24] One, in Louisiana, involved senior officials from local and federal government, business, industry, civic organizations and environmental groups who negotiated a 'consensus risk-based ranking' of the 33 main environmental issues confronting the state, based on scientific studies and public concern. The result is a 10-year action plan which commits the state to balance environmental protection and commercial development. In a second example, the Australian Resource Assessment Commission, charged with resolving resource use and environmental conflicts, has decided to use mediation to 'develop policies which meet the demands of sustainable development'.[25]

In the third example, the United States Environmental Protection Agency (EPA) has decided to make a major shift of resources from defending its regulations against industry or environmental groups' attacks in the courts to involving these groups in the formulation of policy. Recently the EPA used this new initiative to formulate provisions relating to the Clean Air Act, with the result that the parties in the mediation have agreed not to bring any lawsuits to upset the settlements they reach.

Whether by facilitation or mediation, the achievement of consensus is satisfying for participants and produces more sustainable decisions. The main outputs to be expected include:

Substantive outputs

- Incorporation of the maximum range of information into decisions.
- Politically realistic, practical and workable policies.
- A framework for further policy, legislation or judicial action.

Process outputs

- Legitimation by participants and their organizations, and a strong commitment to the implementation of policies and decisions.
- Increased cooperation, trust and collaboration among participants.
- Productive working relationships among participants in an action network.

Nested networks

When the benefits of action networking become apparent, layers of networks may begin to interlink or spawn new levels, in what we term 'nested networks'. By tapping the potential for vertical and horizontal integration these can contribute to sustainable development strategy and implementation, assist governments wrestling with questions about how best to allocate functions among jurisdictions, and help with the organization of administration, monitoring and pollution control for effective action at various levels. For example, Holdgate argues that any sustainable development strategy requires components on at least three levels:

1. International (trade, economic, aid).
2. National (economic policy, education and training policy, arrangement for the supply of commodities and marketing of goods; general infrastructure).
3. Local (resource survey and evaluation, resource development and management, training and support systems).[26]

This need for a linkage of levels of knowledge and action in the face of burgeoning complexity is, as yet, a largely unmet challenge of sustainable development. King and Schneider argue that the challenge posed by the emerging global environmental crisis requires that problems should be simultaneously and comprehensively addressed at many different levels, by engaging in many possible solutions and by monitoring their impacts on other initiatives for the purposes of feedback and learning.[27] This challenges us to devise far more sophisticated organizational and information systems:

1. Complex bodies of information are pared down to their essential, interactive effects so as to avoid contributing to the already overwhelming problem of information overload.
2. Technical and scientific language is translated so that the message is accessible to other disciplines, to politicians and to the public at large.

While this revolution in organization and information constitutes a major world project for the early 21st century and is part of the organization–environment paradigm change we have identified, we believe that the network approach can make a valuable contribution. The question is how to link initiatives at various levels and how to carry out objectives in the most effective and efficient manner while avoiding traditional bureaucratic pitfalls and constraints and wasteful duplication of effort. In political terms, this

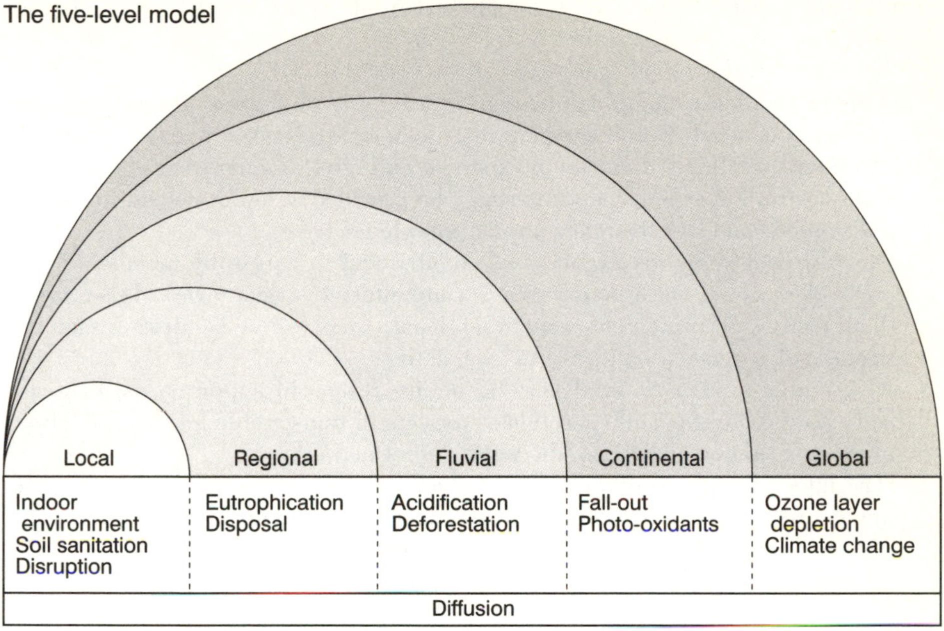

Source: National Environmental Policy Plan of The Netherlands[28]

Figure 9.2 *Linkage of levels in sustainable development tasks*

parallels the question of subsidiarity among different levels of government, extending it beyond the allocation of political functions to the linkages between science (or systematic knowledge) and action (governance, centralization and empowerment).

The need for nested networks arises not only from the nature of the problems we face in attempting to realize sustainable development, but also in the possibility of the increased effectiveness of management where networks reinforce one another at different levels. The five-level model from the Dutch National Environmental Policy Plan gives us an idea of the range of ecological tasks in a systematic framework towards sustainable development (Figure 9.2). The tasks cannot be isolated from one another as there are too many linkages and interactive effects. But nor can all the tasks, at all the levels, be undertaken by one organization or by one network – the law of requisite variety, as relevant to organizations as to biosystems, would be violated, and the complexity and challenges to control would result in management failure, even if political commitment did exist.

The notion of a series of nested, action-oriented networks provides an organizational framework for consensus-building, coordination and reinforcing organizational learning at many levels. The concept of nodes of excellence with the nested networks would further contribute to the required learning process. Among the world's advanced scientific organizations, such network formation is already occurring around the issue of global climate change. What has not been done, however, is to devise an effective means of linking scientific knowledge to integrated action at various levels.

The concept of the nested network has already been tested in the field in a modest way in a few of the case studies. The IDEA programme (Chapter 11) linked 7 'country tasks' in Africa, Asia and South America with 3 international support networks of natural and social scientists and legal advisers in about 35 countries. The following benefits were observed:

- Communication without organization in a hierarchical structure enhances the creativity of members and sharpens discussions to the task at hand.
- An interdisciplinary diversity of expertise and advice, often from senior people with a wealth of experience, can usually be provided at low or no cost to back up local efforts and link them into a wider knowledge base.
- Regular and supportive reviews of country task progress by members of the network results in constructive criticism and interactive peer review. This provides both motivation (which can wane when local teams feel isolated) and reinforcement, and generates confidence in local actions.
- Continuing systematic analysis (via action research) supports and critically reviews the projects and consolidates aspects of transferable learning which are disseminated to, and beyond, the wider parent networks.
- The international network, especially when members are on field visits, provides much credibility to the local team and enhances their status, thus contributing to the visibility of the environment problem or development task addressed and drawing new members into the local network.

Within the IDEA programme, the notion of nested networks also explained why local network members – say, in Guyana – could see themselves as members of the wider IDEA network of 7 countries with advisers and also with a parent network with members in about 35 countries. Each member and each network can call on the entire network for support, free advice and peer review. This support is not external to the management process as the more traditional consultant might be, but expands the team, addressing any particular task to include expertise from other countries.

The team in Guyana, for example, in developing the country's first national system for environmental management, was thus able to draw on field-tested information on environmental standards, impact assessment and training expertise from the Malaysian Government, national environmental reporting skills from the Zambian Government, private sector scientific expertise on chemical analysis from India, and legal expertise from London, all at little or no cost to the Guyanese. The international network also provides a means of diffusion of additional knowledge generated in areas such as environmental legislation, pollution control technology and environmental monitoring throughout the network.

Generation of replicable learning

A seminar in Washington on 'Improving Management in Developing Countries', hosted by the American Consortium for International Public Administration, noted:

> *There is a rapidly growing experience of institutional development. However, there is a great need to document such experience as a basis for in-depth analysis of both successes and those less successful. At present there is just not enough known to provide the kind of firm knowledge base necessary to approach new institutional development undertaking with confidence. There is no adequate kit of management tools for people-oriented projects.*[29]

As stated above, a corollary of action learning is action research, in which any case study generates not only direct action, but provides a field experiment for studying environmental management. The benefits to action researchers from attachment to active networks are obvious, and their key task is to generate transferable knowledge about the programme. This is done by recording the process as it develops, analysing the recording, making connections with other developments in the area, referring to the wider academic literature of institutional development and environmental management, and returning that information to the project teams and the wider network. The research team also provides the opportunity for members of the network to publish the results of their work in learned journals and to consider innovative means of dissemination. In all cases, unless we are to continue to reinvent the wheel, and thereby waste scarce resources, we must review what has been accomplished and assess the degree of success or failure.

Paying for networking

The case studies in Part V demonstrate the potential for cost-effective network support for national or regional action on environmental management tasks. However, it would be misleading to imply that successful, task-oriented networks do not require considerable nurturing and maintenance to survive and prosper, and therefore a source of outside funding. Any network made up of senior people from government, business and the community, and researchers, consultants and facilitators, requires administrative support, financial control and, most importantly, some central focus.

The networks reported in the case studies below are mainly supported by enlightened governments and agencies, including business in the case of the Groundwork Trusts. We cannot point to any examples of wholly self-funding management networks in the environment field. Part of the problem is that it is difficult to attract interest in process innovation, compared to more sympathetic causes. The charitable organizations know this well and gear their fund-raising campaigns accordingly.

In addition to government and multilateral funding, there is the potential to raise funds from business and from charitable foundations, or to put together consortia of funders. Multiple funding is increasingly common in research, but the experience is that a lot of resources can go on administering to the needs of the numerous funders themselves. Businesses may be sympathetic, but many have a strong interest in long-term strategic planning in their locale. They will need to have visible outputs, and it is possible to envision 'sponsored mediation' of serious environmental disputes. The California growth management project, for example (Chapter 12), received major financial and in-kind support from a consortium of funders, including the state assembly, a major bank, a large property developer, a charitable foundation, the California Housing Council and two universities. Additional support came from local government and public agencies, as well as from NGOs concerned about the environment, conservation and housing issues.

The whole question of financial support for sustainable network (and other process) initiatives requires much more consideration. One rule-of-thumb is to start with smaller, highly visible problems, and to earn credibility. Otherwise potential funders will be dubious about permitting the required degree of financial control.

Conclusion

The action network is an emerging participatory mechanism for environmental management in many different fields. The approach is an appropriate organizational tool for managing sustainable development because it fits the nature of the challenges posed by shifting to sustainable development paths. In the face of turbulent, shifting problems on many scales that cross administrative, political and disciplinary boundaries, it allows the construction of flexible teams, which also cross those boundaries. Such teams can generate new information and new ways of working, and pool resources that would otherwise not be brought together. The case studies in the next five chapters illustrate different forms of action networking, at scales of activity from the local community to the nation-state.

Part V

Case Studies in Innovative Management

Introduction

This section describes eight case studies of the use of action networks to promote sustainable development. All demonstrate major aspects of the action-network approach, particularly partnership between government, business and community groups, and consensus-building as a precondition for action on issues that are crucial to sustainable development.

The projects these case studies describe put the action network model into practice at different geographic levels and in very different ways. At the local or neighbourhood level, the Groundwork Foundation has established an extensive network of Groundwork Trusts in Britain and elsewhere in Europe to rehabilitate the environment in derelict industrial areas, to attract new businesses and to encourage local people to become involved in environmental action. Groundwork also mobilizes the private sector, locally and nationally, in new and innovative ways. The international nested network fostered by Homeless International supports community-level projects for people who describe themselves as 'shack dwellers' in Africa and 'slum dwellers' in Asia.

At a citywide or regional level, the IDEA (Innovations in Development for Environmental Action) Programme fostered organizational and human resource capacity in watershed management in Ghana, Zambia and Zimbabwe; in waste management in Nigeria and Malaysia; and in resource management in Mauritius and Guyana. These projects experimented in improving local management skills by the development of action networks, integrated internationally through a team within the Commonwealth Secretariat. IDEA projects began with specific environmental problems, such as water pollution, and then steadily built up interest and teamwork to the point of tackling real challenges in sustainable development, such as watershed management.

At the provincial or state level, in California the Growth Management Consensus Project is working to break a classic political deadlock between proponents of economic growth and environmentalists. The environmental risks are enormous – already pollution, water shortages, congestion and urban sprawl are engulfing large areas of this beautiful and prosperous state. By a highly structured and innovative process of mediation, the Legislature of the State of California is attempting to fashion a new consensus on the nature of sustainable development and the policies needed to prepare for it over the coming decade.

At the national level, a striking example of consensus-building and integrated environmental planning is provided by the progress through a number of iterations of the National Environment Policy Plan (NEPP) process in The Netherlands. This ambitious national sustainable development process involves formal, funded discussions between different environmental constituencies and different departments and tiers of government, considering short-, medium- and long-term prospects for the country, and the means of managing issues based on the development of consensus. The plan generated, although not without its problems, is as yet unmatched in the industrial world in its environmental goals, the degree of integration between areas of policy, and the level of consensus achieved and aspired to among interest groups and parties.

A final chapter looks at a variety of action networks focused on development and the environment. These case studies address the issues of:

- the needs of the homeless and for community housing around the world (Homeless International);
- household and community action on sustainable consumption (the Global Action Programme);
- African energy policy (African Energy Policy Research Network); and
- national sustainability policies which reflect global environmental limits and the need for equity between nations (the Sustainable Europe Campaign).

In particular, all demonstrate a kind of 'subsidiarity' or positive linkage between local, national and international initiative which recognizes that sustainable development can only come about from a chain of organization and action from the household level to the international level, including the key spatial levels in between. This 'chain' of sustainable development is only as strong as its weakest link.

10

Groundwork: Sustainable Regeneration for Local Communities and Environments

Local environmentalists ... are more likely to consider tangible environmental outcomes of greater importance than political points, enabling them to negotiate in good faith with business, seeking areas of common cause... People love the environment largely because they love particular places. The rivers they fish in, the forests they walk in, the parks they take their children to: all these add up to the natural surroundings that give people a spatial anchor in a world increasingly bereft of such real connections.

Steven Teles[1]

'The environment' can seem at times to be a remote concern from the perspective of economically disadvantaged citizens and communities. The language of sustainable development is abstract and hard to relate to the priorities and problems of people in places where the environment, economy and community have all suffered from neglect, industrial decline, unemployment and all the ills summed up in the policy-makers' jargon of 'social exclusion'. How do we connect people and places at the margins of the economy to a vision of environmentally friendly development which improves quality of life for all?

Some pointers to the answers can be found in the disadvantaged corners of England, Wales and Northern Ireland. A group of schoolchildren in the London inner city neighbourhood of Hackney gets involved in designing and making murals to brighten the housing estate where they live. A Welsh community hit by the closure of the coal-mining industry finds a way to revive its economic potential as well as its environment by developing new leisure enterprises based on the natural attractions of the area – and in the process creates Europe's largest indoor climbing centre. In Northern Ireland, a bridge is made between the divided communities of Catholics and Protestants by projects focusing on shared concerns for environmental and social regeneration. In the old industrial region of the West Midlands in England, a neighbourhood plagued by crime, poor health, lack of employment and bad housing begins to turn itself around through a programme of environmental renewal in which the local citizens have taken a leading role, creating new gardens, orchards and parkland in their estate. Across declining industrial districts, local people come together to help create brighter and greener environments for offices and factories, planting trees, landscaping derelict sites, restoring wildlife habitats on old manufacturing land. In the North West of England, derelict areas in and near the industrial town of St Helens have been transformed into new woodland.

What these and many other initiatives have in common is a partnership with a remarkable British action network – Groundwork. This federal organization, comprising a network of local trusts, is widely regarded as a highly effective initiative which connects environmental management and regeneration to economic and social renewal at the local level. Groundwork has evolved over two decades into an impressive network of local organizations which operate through multisector partnerships and make creative linkages between environmental, social and economic policy for disadvantaged neighbourhoods. Groundwork is a federation of local action networks whose impact commands attention as a potential model for application worldwide.

At the heart of its operations are three insights about sustainable development. First, that we cannot pursue environmental ends at the expense of social and economic development, but must seek wherever possible solutions which bring benefits in all three dimensions. Moreover, environmental action can be a catalyst for positive change by businesses and communities which might at first feel that it has little to offer them. Second, that sustainable development must not only be about new technologies, reform in affluent economies and lifestyles (see the chapters below on California and The Netherlands), and the protection of natural environments; it must also be about social equity, involving action to improve the prospects and quality of life for the worst-off communities, run-down industrial economies and urban environments. Third, that the old slogan 'Think global, act local' retains its power: the focus in much debate on the great global challenges of the environment and development can obscure the fact that delivering sustainable policies is about myriad *local* projects, and that people will be motivated to act more by local environmental change than by analysis of the global condition.

Groundwork has been at the forefront in the UK of attempts to make creative and positive connections between the environmental policy agenda, the sustainable development movement, and the economic and social policies designed to regenerate the industrial areas of the UK which have been hit by the decline of old manufacturing and extractive sectors, and experienced the social and economic ills summed up in the term 'social exclusion'. It has pioneered holistic project design and implementation, bringing economic, environmental and social policy issues together in the idea of sustainable regeneration, and working by bringing together interests from all sectors to work with the people closest to the problems on the ground.

The Groundwork Trust network began by developing projects for environmental improvement in run-down industrial areas and derelict urban land. This core activity remains important, but Groundwork is now increasingly operating as a networked enterprise which brings together sectoral interests and policy concerns to create projects designed and run in partnerships which aim to promote economic and social progress at local level via projects for environmental regeneration. Groundwork brings together companies, public agencies and community groups in partnership ventures which aim to integrate environmental action with local business development. It instigates measures to tackle crime, improvements in education and employment policies for people at risk of long-term unemployment.

Groundwork has over 40 operating trusts across the UK. The Groundwork approach is being introduced into continental Europe and it is set to be the model for similar developments in other European Union countries, and also beyond Europe. Groundwork is important because it is a successful and growing operation based on the principle of action-centred networking, partnership and improved mutual understanding between community groups, public agencies and business, and takes an integrated approach to environmental management and community development. Groundwork projects aim to improve the local quality of life, to foster links between companies and communities, and to involve all parties in the sustainable regeneration of local economies and environments, and in the design and management of local initiatives.

Organization and Aims of the Groundwork Trust

Development of the network

The Groundwork movement developed in the early 1980s from initiatives in environmental regeneration launched by the Countryside Commission, a public agency concerned with rural development in England and Wales. (This has since been absorbed in a new Countryside Agency.) The Commission devised Operation Groundwork, an experimental initiative in the renewal of run-down and derelict areas on the fringes of two towns in North West England, St Helens and Knowsley. The aim of this venture was to demonstrate how abandoned and neglected land could be regenerated for leisure, the encouragement of wildlife and flora, agriculture and the general benefit to local communities. The Commission's concern was to find ways of 'greening' the towns by rehabilitating wasteland. But the venture was also about innovations in ways of working on a complex policy problem, and especially about harnessing ideas and resources beyond the public sector agencies which had traditionally monopolized urban policy. The minister who backed the initiative, Michael Heseltine, said then that:

> *I was against creating just another public body. What I wanted was an entrepreneurial team which could act independently as an enabler to mobilise all the resources in the community – public, private and voluntary.*[2]

In other words, Groundwork was conceived as what we have termed in this book an 'action network' spanning sectors and diverse interests.

The problems that the initiative set out to tackle are well known and extensive in all industrialized countries, and are increasingly familiar in the newly industrializing countries: the degradation of urban environments as old manufacturing industry declines; the impoverished natural features of industrial areas; the low quality of life of communities in areas deprived of both green space and employers. The relentless post-war decline of British heavy industry accelerated in the 1970s with the oil price shocks, fierce competition from overseas and widespread failure to modernize plants dating from earlier phases of industrial development. The deep recession of 1980–81 in the UK saw factory closures and the abandonment of much industrial land; this added to long-standing problems of derelict land in the old manufacturing areas of the country. Since then, many coalfield communities have been badly hit by the closure of mines and the lack of alternative sources of employment and investment.

The original Operation Groundwork was managed by a 'Groundwork Trust' and the success of the project led to the establishment by 1983 of six trusts, all in the North West of England, a region that had suffered many factory closures and had large areas of derelict industrial land. By 1992 the network had grown to include 28 Groundwork trusts in England and Wales. As the trusts developed their role in 'greening' cities, towns and suburbs, sponsorship by the Countryside Commission became inappropriate and a new framework for funding was set up. Since 1985 the network has been coordinated nationally by a Groundwork National Office, based in Birmingham and supported by funding from the Department of the Environment and other sources. The network is especially extensive in the North of England, but Groundwork Trusts have been established in southern cities such as Plymouth, in the old mining valleys of South Wales, and during the 1990s in and around London. The network reorganized itself in the late 1990s as a federation of autonomous trusts, serviced by the National Office in Birmingham. The large areas of derelict land in Britain's cities and urban fringes provide considerable scope for continuing growth in the network. But the ambitions and activities of the Groundwork movement have expanded well beyond the recovery of fringe derelict land, as discussed below.

By 1999 over 40 trusts had been established, with more planned. In particular, Groundwork has expanded in recent years in London, focusing especially on projects to link environmental improvement to programmes of economic and social regeneration in the capital's poorer districts. The Groundwork movement is also poised to develop in other member states of the European Union, and to export its approach to the would-be EU members in the ex-Communist states of Europe. Groundwork-inspired initiatives can now be found also in the eastern US and Japan. The scope for exporting the Groundwork model to newly industrializing states such as South Africa and East Asian countries is immense.

Funding and organization

The funding of the network reflects the emphasis on partnership: at the centre, the federation's National Office receives around 40 per cent of its income (£42.5 million in 1997–98) from central government, principally through the Department of the Environment, Transport and the Regions (DETR). The DETR contributed £6.67 million in 1997–98, and this annual government sum is boosted by contributions to projects involving local trusts by business and local government bodies. Where does the money go? In 1997–98 Groundwork spent over £40 million, with nearly half allocated to physical environmental improvements around the country. Some 27 per cent was spent on projects concerned with youth, education and community regeneration; and 11 per cent was allocated to projects designed to integrate environmental improvements with local economic development.

A key aspect of Groundwork funding is the use of public sector funds to lever in resources from the private sector in the form of project funding and sponsorship deals. Groundwork trusts also receive funds from the European Commission. Large private and public sector employers provide management expertise through staff secondments. Funds are also generated through the trusts' professional commercial work in landscape design, business services and project management.

In 1997–99, under its new Chief Executive Tony Hawkhead, the Groundwork network was reorganized, moving from a system of a 'foundation', comprising the National Office coordinating the local bodies, to a federal system in which the centre services the trusts on the basis of a 'partnership agreement' and develops policy in partnership with them. This change was prompted by a number of concerns:

1 That despite many achievements at local level the movement was insufficiently recognized at regional and national level for its innovations and contribution to regeneration in the UK.
2 The need to strengthen the regional organization in response to the new UK Labour Government's establishment of Regional Development Agencies to promote economic, social and environmental development and regeneration.
3 The need to improve communications between the Trusts and between the local and national levels within Groundwork, in order to make the best use of resources and to make it easier to collaborate in projects, bids and learning.
4 The wish to strengthen Groundwork's capacity to contribute to national and regional debate and policy on indicators, targets and implementation of sustainable development, drawing on the network's long experience of linking environmental action to social and economic issues at the grassroots level.

The Groundwork federation's network now comprises the National Office, a set of regional offices and the local trusts, which are spread across England, Wales and Northern Ireland. The trusts, which develop and manage local projects and partnership networks, are all separate registered charities and limited companies with no share capital, and operate with considerable autonomy. The Groundwork National Office services the overall network, acts as a support system for the trusts, liaises at national level with government, industry and other partners, and negotiates the creation of new trusts. A key role for the National Office is to develop national initiatives that can be implemented locally by the trusts. The majority of the national board is made up of members elected by the trusts, which also help to set national policy and share in the resources generated by the National Office. The mutual relationship also applies at the local level: the National Office is represented on trust boards by nominated representatives. Overall, the National Office and the trusts employ over 750 staff, work with over 450 board members and recruit 60,000–100,000 volunteers annually for local environmental projects. Over 1 million schoolchildren have been involved in projects since Groundwork's inception, and the network is responsible for millions of hectares of improved land and pathways and for millions of new trees. Its impact on the environment and on volunteering in the UK has been substantial, although this is easy to underrate simply because the work of the trusts is spread over so many neighbourhoods.

The Groundwork Trusts are established in response to local demand, which can originate from local government agencies, businesses or other organizations. The process of setting up a trust may be lengthy, as the federation is concerned to ensure that a new Groundwork initiative receives a commitment to partnership from local government, key local businesses, public agencies, environmental groups and other voluntary bodies. Considerable negotiation may be required to overcome any initial suspicion – for instance, from established environmental groups and their funders that a new competitor for local resources is appearing. If such difficulties cannot be resolved, a trust will not be established. Trusts are designed to have a long-term role, so a special investment of time and effort is made at the outset to establish the partnership ethos among local stakeholders and to win support.

The trusts operate autonomously within the broad framework for development set out by the National Office and the partnership agreements they make with the centre to become part of the federation. Each trust has a board of directors composed of representatives from different sectors, typically from the relevant local government body or bodies, businesses and voluntary groups. A key aim is to ensure that the board reflects the range of interests in the area. The trusts have executive directors with a small team of professionals who are expert in fields such as landscape design and project management, and financial and administrative staff. Groundwork Trusts may be centred on a city or town, or on a wider area cutting across administrative boundaries. In London the trusts cover one or more boroughs (administrative districts) and can carry out project work extending into areas which do not yet have a Groundwork operation of their own.

Groundwork's partnership approach

The guiding principle of the Groundwork movement is the development of projects in partnership with business, public authorities and voluntary agencies, and community groups. The network's projects are all designed to foster developments that bring people together from different sectors in joint action that contributes not only to environmental improvement but also to enhanced quality of life and local prosperity. Environmental renewal and economic development are seen as complementary goals rather than as aims that are invariably in tension or conflict. The founding Chief Executive of Groundwork, John Davidson, has said that the aim of Groundwork activity in a community should be '... to encourage residents to take a pride in their surroundings once more, encourage industry to stay or move in, and gradually to renew environmental and economic prosperity'.[3]

Groundwork recognizes that, working alone, it cannot achieve the enormous changes that are needed to transform degraded environments and to give new purpose and direction to people in disadvantaged communities. None the less, Groundwork projects have a crucial role to play in demonstrating the potential for environmental improvement within relatively short timescales given cooperation from partners from business, public agencies and local communities. The practical demonstration of environmental regeneration can give confidence to communities that have suffered economic decline and ecological damage. It is also a key part of the long-term process of winning local commitment to sustainable environmental management.

Groundwork in Action

The range of Groundwork activity

The partnership approach means that a trust is concerned to act as a catalyst, facilitating the work of its partners as well as carrying out project work itself. Trust directors have a key role in raising sponsorship for projects and liaising with partners, and in contracting work in landscape regeneration to other voluntary bodies. There is particular emphasis on obtaining voluntary support from local residents and employees of sponsor companies. Trusts are essentially in the business of orchestrating environmental regeneration projects, securing a mix of national and local sponsorship from private and public sources, and deploying the physical and human resources of the private sector, voluntary groups and individual volunteers to blend with the expertise of local Groundwork staff.

The scale of the 'action network' activity of the Groundwork trusts is impressive. In 1998 Groundwork overall was engaged in projects with 2233 partners from the public sector, 2250 from business and 1956 from the voluntary sector; at any one point, some 3000 projects are in operation, in over 150 localities across the UK.[4] Groundwork measures its achievement of objectives against a set of performance indicators covering key areas of activity: improvement of the environment; education and community involvement; integration of the economy and environment; long-term management of projects; and a balance between the types of project undertaken. The performance indicators used by the trust place great emphasis on the impact on the benefits for people as well as on the changes made to the physical environment. The range of project work carried out by the Groundwork trusts and their local partners is very wide, covering the following areas:

- environmental improvement of derelict industrial sites and other run-down urban areas such as public sector housing estates in poor neighbourhoods;
- landscape improvement for industrial sites;
- development of urban fringe sites to encourage wildlife;
- consultancy to small businesses on environmental management and policies to reduce waste and energy consumption;
- the creation of leisure trails and parks on former industrial land;
- tree and flower planting schemes;
- consultancy on landscape design;
- development of urban farms;
- training courses in conservation skills and environmental management;
- assistance for voluntary bodies in developing local regeneration projects;
- environmental education projects in local schools;
- initiatives to harness the energies and motivation of young people who may be disaffected at school and home, and at risk of unemployment, delinquency, drug abuse or crime. The partnership scheme Youth Works, described below, has been instrumental in bringing 'excluded' young people into projects to improve both their own skills and self-esteem, and also their local environments.

Groundwork uses the network to transfer information about different projects and examples of good practice between the trusts, resulting in a continuous process of learning. All projects are implemented at the trust level, but the National Office also develops programmes that can be piloted locally and then implemented across the network. These are designed to attract private sector sponsorship: after an idea has been tried out successfully within the network, the National Office will seek financial support from sponsors such as major corporations. While funding from public sources is also sought, special emphasis is placed on bringing the private sector into initiatives in a significant way, backing schemes locally with money, expertise and publicity.

National and regional programmes are developed under three strategic headings:

1. Youth, community and education involvement.
2. Physical environmental improvements.
3. Integrating the economy and the environment.

Below we look at some of the major initiatives in each of these core areas.

Youth, community and education involvement: the Greenlink initiative

Groundwork is involved in many schemes which are designed to improve education and training in environmental management, and a key element of the network's strategy is to raise business and community awareness of environmental issues. The Greenlink initiative is a notably innovative example of this aspect of the network's activities. Greenlink is a Groundwork venture developed in partnership with the petroleum company Esso UK and with support from DETR. The scheme was launched in 1991 and aims to develop long-term partnerships between schools and local industry, built around a shared concern for the environment. Greenlink allows great flexibility in the choice of projects by schools and companies, but there is a common framework of activity. The partner school and company choose achievable aims connected with the company's environmental policies. These involve the development of a teaching plan by the school, including site visits and classroom work, and the integration of environmental issues affecting the plant in the agenda of both school and company. The aim is increased mutual understanding between schools and businesses, and the development of environmental education across the whole curriculum. The Greenlink initiative emphasizes the benefits to both partners. For schools, there is the opportunity to experiment with the methods of project work and new techniques for delivering the curriculum, and to give teachers more experience of industry. For the participating companies and other employers, there is the chance to improve their 'environmental friendliness', public relations and learning by employees. They can meet children face-to-face to explain what industry does and why, and in the process learn new skills and make new relationships with the education system and with environmental bodies that could enhance their capacity for innovation.

Youth, community and education involvement: the Youth Works initiative

Youth Works is a joint venture between Groundwork, the crime prevention organization Crime Concern and the famous retailer Marks & Spencer to foster the potential of young people and their communities to make a positive impact on their social and physical environment. The scheme works with children and young people aged between 8 and 25 in poor areas who could be at risk of failure at school, unemployment and eventual involvement in crime. Youth Works projects operate in the cities of Blackburn, Leeds and Sunderland in the North, in the London borough of Hackney, and in the city of Plymouth in the South West. All have in common neighbourhoods which have suffered from industrial decline, high unemployment, physical dereliction and the development of localities with a high level of crime, underachievement in schools and poor prospects for young people. Groundwork's trusts develop projects in partnership with local authorities, businesses and community organizations and specialize in ventures which encourage young people 'to play a creative role in their communities, creating new facilities, enhancing self-esteem and improving their employment prospects'.[5]

Work in Hackney has included making a mural and new garden in one housing estate, transforming a damaged wall into a community artwork at the heart of a leisure area for residents. Young people worked with local residents to design and paint the mural and to create the garden, making use of Groundwork's skills and experience in landscape design. The project has boosted local people's confidence and skills and has improved relationships on the estate between residents and young people.

The core idea of Youth Works is that connecting young people with projects to make a difference to their local environments can have social and economic pay-offs as well as environmental ones. Giving them the opportunity to take a lead in designing and delivering change to their neighbourhoods, rather than always being a passive recipient of change imposed from outside, will help to develop new skills. Crucially, it can also create new self-confidence and a sense of genuine contribution to the community. The hope and expectation of the initiative is that all these benefits to young people will feed through the community and lead to a reduction in crime and the propensity to get involved in delinquency and truanting. The evidence so far is that persistent and well-designed project work is able to deliver good results. Environmental action can play a significant part in overcoming the 'social exclusion' of the young and thus in preventing crime and disaffection – in short, it makes an impact on 'social sustainability'.

This is also a recognition underpinning Groundwork's involvement as a leading actor in delivery of the UK Labour Government's 'New Deal' programme for unemployed people. Groundwork is a partner in running the Environment Task Force, one of the several New Deal options for people seeking to move from the welfare roll into education or paid work. The Task Force offers unemployed people, especially young people, the chance to become involved in environmental regeneration projects managed by Groundwork and its local partners. This represents an experiment which could develop into a significant contribution to social as well as environmental sustainability across the UK, and Groundwork's involvement in influencing the design and delivery of such public programmes is an opportunity to reinforce the Government's commitment to making innovative connections between environmental and social policy.

Other Groundwork programmes under this general heading are imaginative and diverse. They include Green IT, a venture to help young people use information and communication technology to design new landscapes for business sites and their local community; Waste Savers, bringing young people into projects to help reduce waste in their schools and neighbourhoods; and SiteSavers, a major programme developed with Barclays Bank, a national clearing bank, and DETR. SiteSavers is an action network programme run by Groundwork in partnership not only with Barclays and the Government, but also with the conservation bodies, The Wildlife Trusts, Scottish Conservation Projects and the British Trust for Conservation Volunteers (BTCV). The initiative involves bringing residents living near neglected or derelict land into projects to design and create new environments such as wildlife reserves and community amenities (gardens, parks, playgrounds). Barclays staff, Groundwork teams and local volunteers have together worked with local people to initiate and run projects which have had many benefits for the communities concerned. These include a reduced fear of crime as unsightly and uncared for environments are cleaned up and improved, the development of new skills for the volunteers, and a greater sense in the community of belonging to and feeling proud of their local places. Again, the programme points to the potential for making connections between individual and community social 'inclusion' and environmental regeneration schemes.[6]

Integrating the economy and the environment

Groundwork has developed extensive relationships with business. Support from private enterprise for national, regional and local initiatives is the most visible aspect of this relationship. But the Groundwork movement has also developed schemes that are designed to raise the environmental awareness of business, in particular of small firms. The aim here is not only to reduce the impact of waste, pollution and energy use on the environment, but also to highlight to companies the benefits to business of effective environmental management and compliance with regulations.

Three schemes stand out. First, the Brightsite initiative, a major venture in Groundwork's development through the 1980s. Brightsite projects aimed to improve industrial sites, landscaping car parks, office and factory grounds, forecourts, approach roads, enhancing business environments and generating not only gains for the local environment but also for employers, employees and residents. This was the precursor of more ambitious programmes aiming to integrate local economic development with environmental regeneration and protection.

The expansion of Groundwork has led to more extensive projects to support environmental action by business, with special attention to the needs of small companies which may be ignorant of eco-regulations, apprehensive about the implications of 'going Green', or missing opportunities to benefit the bottom line through waste reduction or developing environmentally friendly products and services. Groundwork has collaborated with other partners in localities across the UK to develop Business Environment Associations, clubs for small and medium-sized firms as well as major employers. These associations offer information and advice to member companies on environmental policy issues, legislation, regulatory enquiries and the opportunities for gaining from more 'eco-efficiency' through waste minimization and energy saving. Many Groundwork trusts are also involved in providing advisory services to small- and medium-sized enterprises to improve their environmental management practices and to boost their competitiveness by exploiting their potential to improve quality in the company and along the supply chain. In many cases companies have been able to make substantial savings in spending on waste disposal and energy consumption, and to identify new opportunities to save money and raise product quality by cutting out waste. Overall, Groundwork has played a significant role in engaging with small business and raising awareness of environmental management, and has also commissioned research to improve understanding of how small firms can be assisted to improve their performance.[7]

Physical environmental improvements

Groundwork's original activity was the physical improvement of derelict and neglected land, and this remains at the heart of its expanding and ever more ambitious programmes for sustainable regeneration. Along with projects such as SiteSavers and Youth Works, which focus on helping individuals and whole communities to gain new skills and resources, two major Groundwork programmes have been established to promote the physical restoration and improvement of environments in and around industrial zones, towns and cities. The first, Changing Places, was funded by the UK's Millennium Commission as a celebration of the Millennium. The programme, worth over £50 million, focuses on derelict and underused industrial land, creating new landscapes which will be protected by a 99-year covenant, securing benefits for the public throughout the new century. The programme regenerates over 1000 hectares of derelict land and, as with the other initiatives mentioned above, brings people from local communities and numerous partner organizations into networks of action for environmental improvement which have many economic and social benefits – new jobs, skills, amenities and local pride. The programme includes the renovation of canals and their surroundings, of parks and paths; the creation of new parks, nature reserves, play areas, community facilities and artworks, where previously there were exhausted quarries or waste tips; and a recycling research programme, funded by energy utility companies, looking at alternatives to primary aggregates for road and pavement building.

The second major venture is Trees of Time and Place, a programme to involve people in gathering and cultivating seeds from trees that are distinctive to their locality, and ultimately in planting the new trees. The programme is intended to do more than simply create new woodland and urban tree cover; it aims to recover some of the local environmental distinctiveness lost in the increasingly homogenized economic and social development of the UK's countryside, towns and cities over the last half century.

Case study: the Groundwork Trust in Britain's 'Black Country'

How does a Groundwork Trust put the concepts of partnership and sustainable regeneration into action? Below, we examine the experience of one of the trusts, based in the so-called 'Black Country' in the English Midlands, the original heartland of the Industrial Revolution. The region is full of run-down inner city districts in need of greening and improved community leisure facilities; abandoned industrial land in need of rehabilitation and landscaping; degraded land in urban fringe areas capable of being converted into parkland or wildlife refuges; and functioning factory sites with derelict or ill-used land.

The origins of Groundwork Black Country (GBC) lie in the decline of the region's industrial base. The recession of the early 1980s led to a dramatic rate of closure of manufacturing plants and to widespread dereliction, with ensuing vandalism and pollution, and the reinforcement of an already poor environmental image for the region. The four boroughs that fall within the area have a combined population of some 9 million people and cover some 34,000 hectares. The region has been the object of numerous programmes funded by central government to stimulate local economic redevelopment and urban renewal.

The four boroughs have set up joint ventures to promote the area's potential to investors and to improve its public image through initiatives for new jobs and environmental regeneration. The Groundwork Trust was established after much local discussion and negotiation once senior officials in the boroughs became convinced that Groundwork could play a major role in facilitating partnerships for environmental renewal in the area, especially by securing private sector sponsorship for projects, helping to secure additional funds from central government and other public agencies, and bringing in new ideas from the experience of the nationwide Groundwork movement. A further consideration was that GBC could carry out projects that crossed local political boundaries in a way that would have been very difficult for the individual borough authorities to tackle in an integrated way. One example is the regeneration of environments in the valley of the River Stour, which runs across borough boundaries.

GBC was set up in 1988 with the backing of the local boroughs, private companies and voluntary agencies, and declared its aim to be the development of projects that would support the overall environmental strategy that had already been devised by the boroughs. A board was set up including representatives of the four boroughs, local business and local environmental groups. Board meetings are held alternately in each of the boroughs and board members are also involved in visits to project sites, though not in detailed project management. At the district level there are meetings involving local government officials to discuss the progress of individual projects and improve coordination and exchange of information.

GBC sees its mission as follows: 'To bring about sustainable improvement to the local environment through partnerships, and to contribute to economic and social regeneration'.[8] It aims to operate on the basis of three core values:

1 Sustainable improvements: engaging local people in finding solutions to problems and ensuring that they are fully involved in the design of solutions which must meet high standards of quality and tests of long-term viability.
2 Positive action: investing in the skills and motivation of local partners to secure 'sustainable change'.
3 Equality and accessibility: understanding the links between personal health, prosperity, economic development and the sustainability of the local environment, and opening up opportunities to everyone to improve their quality of life. A key part of this is developing the skills of people who are excluded from mainstream work and economic opportunity.

GBC committed itself at the outset to developing the established range of Groundwork activities and also to providing support and guidance to local community groups carrying out environmental projects. In addition, it planned to raise revenue from 'design and build' landscaping services for the private sector in order to supplement grants from the local sponsoring organizations. A crucial element in the approach developed by GBC has been the determination not to duplicate or compete with the work of other environmental bodies in the area. This involves subcontracting work to other voluntary agencies, passing ideas on to community groups, and taking up suggestions and ideas from them in turn.

In the 1990s GBC made a significant impact on the area. Over 3500 people worked with the trust as volunteers, receiving training and personal development opportunities. Over 240 hectares of derelict and neglected land was regenerated. Over 500 businesses received advice and support to improve their environmental management and their competitive position through better environmental performance. And the trust worked with nearly one-quarter of the area's schools to raise environmental awareness and provide volunteering opportunities to students and educators. In the decade following its inception in 1988, it completed projects worth £14 million.

The GBC programme at the end of the 1990s summed up Groundwork's shift since its foundation from concentrating on local physical improvements to a more ambitious and holistic vision of working in partnership to implement genuinely sustainable development, embracing environmental regeneration, social inclusion and economic renewal. GBC has positioned itself as a source of skills, knowledge, funding, business advice and project management for the region, able to work with organizations across all sectors and to make connections between all the dimensions of sustainable development. It is involved in five broad areas of activity:

- Local Agenda 21: supporting the network of LA21 projects in the area through projects on neighbourhood planning, building up local groups' capacity for project work, and connecting environmental schemes to community health and arts policies.
- Working with business: improving business parks; offering services to business to improve environmental management systems; and helping to manage the Black Country Business Environment Association, a club for businesses to share ideas and information on environmental performance.
- Training for employment: offering unemployed people training and placements on environmental projects in order to help them make the transition from welfare into paid work. The area has two Environment Centres which act as both education and training bases, and also as demonstrations of how environmentally sustainable design of new developments can transform derelict sites.
- Youth and education: school programmes and projects for personal development aimed at school students and young people at risk of crime or alienation.
- Greenways: projects to improve the environmental quality of the roads, paths, rivers, canals and corridors linking open spaces and other places in the area, and helping local schemes to fit together into wider strategies for environmental enhancement.

The GBC approach is perhaps most strikingly demonstrated in one place – the Wren's Nest, an area which combines a national nature reserve with a large and deprived public housing estate, home to some 4000 people. The Wren's Nest Estate has suffered all the ills of social exclusion: low income, high unemployment, poor health, vandalism and other crime, bad housing and a degraded physical environment. But a successful bid to the Government for regeneration funding in 1996, following a multi-sector Community Vision Conference to identify ways out of the decline of the estate, has begun to transform the area. Working with local people and many partner organizations from government, public services and business, and helping local residents to develop their own community associations and project teams, GBC has been a major force for regeneration, not only of the local environment but also of the community's trust in itself and in the organizations it now works with. The local council has focused on physical improvements to homes and gardens, while Groundwork has worked with residents to create new shared landscapes and facilities – a community orchard, new allotments, new community facilities and courses to encourage fitness, new skills and jobs, and projects with local children and their families to raise awareness of the scope for local food production and healthier eating. The Wren's Nest is a remarkable illustration of the overall Groundwork approach: working in an action network not only with business, public agencies and voluntary bodies, but also ensuring that local residents and children are brought into collective planning and decision-making, seeking to make connections between long-term environmental improvements and social and economic well-being.[9] Groundwork's capacity to bring long-overlooked local networks into productive relationships with public and private decision-makers to develop new projects is one of the keys to its successes.

Key Lessons from the Groundwork Experience

The main elements of the Groundwork approach comprise a model of objectives and values for networked multisector projects in environmental management.

National level:

- to develop policy to facilitate network growth;
- to develop national and network-wide initiatives;
- to provide support service to local trusts;
- to facilitate the transfer of information;
- to secure public and private sector finance;
- to form links with private sector, voluntary sector and public agencies;
- to attract and develop personnel.

Local level:

- to win trust and commitment from public, private and voluntary sector bodies;
- to attract private sector funding to add to public funds;
- to act as a catalyst for environmental projects linking business, public bodies and community groups;
- to implement local schemes based on national initiatives.

Key values:

- emphasis on multisector partnership;
- non-threatening to other voluntary sector interests;
- non-confrontational approach to business;
- long-term commitment to raising awareness in business, schools and the wider community of the need for sustainable environmental management.

What lessons about good practice can be gained from the progress of the Groundwork trusts? The Groundwork trusts' working method exemplifies what we have termed 'action-centred networking' – the cultivation of partnerships between local people, organizations and sectors, and the exchange of information with a view always to developing practical projects. The approach also emphasizes and facilitates learning between trusts and between them and their partners. Groundwork is itself an action-centred network. The trusts have great autonomy of action within a general strategic framework developed by the original foundation, and from 1999 part of a new Groundwork federation. National programmes are devised in partnership with trusts and others, and local piloting allows experiments and discoveries about good practice that can flow around the network. In funding and policy development Groundwork has created a fruitful blend of 'top-down' and 'bottom-up' approaches to environmental regeneration, and its links to policies for social and economic renewal.

Groundwork also practises an integrated approach to networking: its activities bring together urban regeneration, environmental education and community development in cohesive projects and programmes. Projects are never just about physical development or repair work: they are designed also to assist in achieving greater awareness in companies and communities of the importance of care for the environment. Groundwork has also been a builder of new relationships of trust between citizens and policy-making; it has been able to tap the skills and energies of people in disadvantaged areas who have been marginalized by private and public organizations alike, and who need to be brought back into dialogue with business and government via the brokerage of a trusted mediating organization. Groundwork has been able to make connections between citizens and sectors which would otherwise be hard to create.

The emphasis on bringing in private sector funding means that Groundwork tends not to be seen as 'confrontational' by the private sector. The approach to private sponsors is based on a commitment to businesslike partnership aimed at producing mutual benefits. This approach may draw criticism from environmental campaign groups on the basis that Groundwork does not challenge industry's values enough. However, there is clearly a need to encourage firms to take action in such a way as to increase the chances of making the experience popular with employees and local people. In this way, the 'cosmetic' projects of landscape improvement carried out by Groundwork trusts may create a bridgehead in companies for more radical ideas on involvement with the local community, redesign of production methods and product lines, and overall environmental responsibility.[10] Linked to this is the emphasis on the long-term development of the understanding of environmental issues in local communities: Groundwork is engaged, through its involvement in environmental education and volunteering schemes, in the business of 'winning hearts and minds' to the cause of taking the environment seriously.

The Groundwork experience reminds us that the city and the town are environments too – something often in danger of being forgotten as we debate the fate of the rainforests and other wildernesses. Initiatives to improve the urban environment are critical to sustainable development: we need to keep people in the cities in order to preserve the countryside and the dynamism of city centres, and this will only happen if the urban environment is enhanced. Groundwork's projects cannot 'green' whole cities and their regeneration strategies may focus on very long-range improvement, but what they achieve with specific projects is visible, valuable and accessible to large numbers of people: it brings tangible improvement to people's lives as well as to wildlife, flora and buildings, and it encourages widespread participation in environmental management. Again, in this respect Groundwork's activity provides a basis for long-term environmental education among individuals, community groups and companies.

An important aspect of the Groundwork approach to setting up trusts is the focus on careful preparation of the ground for networking in order to avoid, or at least to minimize, suspicions and jealousies on the part of other voluntary sector bodies and from local public agencies. This is a fundamental problem in partnership building in areas of policy where many voluntary and community groups exist and newcomers may be suspected of 'parachuting in' and trying to impose their patent solutions for the community's problems. The Groundwork experience offers many lessons and pointers to good practice for other action networks and partnerships, such as those based around Local Agenda 21 (LA21) and other programmes for environmental and social improvement.[11]

But an organization such as Groundwork, rooted in particular places and still identified with a particular bottom-up approach rather than broad strategic programmes for change, also needs to ensure that it continues to improve its own linkages to, and understanding of, the multifarious networks linked to LA21 in the UK and internationally through the International Centre for Local Environmental Initiatives (ICLEI). Groundwork and LA21 action networks have much to contribute to each other as Groundwork expands its operations and its policy horizons, and as LA21 networks in the UK and beyond push for greater recognition by mainstream policy-makers and by citizens. Groundwork and LA21 in the UK have to find ways of maintaining their core programme and ambitions while adapting their messages and methods to the changing policy environment, and this pattern is a common one across the world as the local interpretation of sustainable development is contested between environmental, social and economic priorities and timescales. One area in which bodies such as Groundwork and other actors in the LA21 movement will surely need to develop skills and exchange ideas and experience will be conflict resolution and consensus building, as tensions inevitably arise between the aims of long-term environmental regeneration and protection, and demands for social and economic development. The tools considered in Chapter 12 below on consensus-building in California will need to play a part in the development of more ambitious programmes for action networks which go beyond environmental management to embrace social justice and economic renewal.

The movement's evolution has seen it develop from a modest urban fringe charity focused on derelict land improvements to a major player in the urban regeneration world of the UK. Under John Davidson the network was steadily expanded and the programmes became more varied and ambitious, providing the basis for the movement's development in the late 1990s under Tony Hawkhead of a wide-ranging agenda for promoting sustainable development. The election of the Labour Government in 1997, in rhetoric and policy plans at least more committed to Local Agenda 21 and to 'joined up' holistic programmes to link environmental, social and economic policies than its predecessor was, opened up new opportunities for Groundwork. The Government talked ambitiously of promoting sustainable development, social inclusion and new economic development in the UK's poorest communities. Above all, it looked for creative connections between policy domains and practitioners, and for approaches to regeneration which could deliver practical solutions and gains in people's quality of life. Groundwork has been able to seize opportunities arising from this shift in the policy environment, emphasizing the connections it makes between places and people, the environment and the community, regenerating land and developing skills.[12]

Groundwork was able to present its entire experience and expertise as a practical demonstration of how to pursue the elusive goals of 'sustainability', 'inclusion' and 'regeneration' at once. Within Groundwork, the emphasis had always been on getting the detailed project work done, without much attention to the wider theoretical and political dimensions of its activities. The new national policy focus on sustainability and on connecting excluded communities to the economy and society, gave Groundwork a language in which to describe itself, its achievements and its mission anew to policy-makers and partners. Groundwork could claim, with justice, that it had been a pioneer in designing and implementing sustainable development, and in doing it through action networks linking sectors in 'joined up' or 'holistic' partnership projects. It can also claim to be at the forefront of fostering new relationships between people and their places, helping to regenerate trust and self-belief, and making links between policy domains which have been kept apart, such as housing and education, the environment and social justice, and public health and economic regeneration. As Ken Worpole notes, 'it is a long way to have travelled from site clearance schemes and topsoil replacement'.[13]

Entering the new century, Groundwork is well placed to pursue not only bottom-up projects for regeneration, but also to link them more ambitiously to top-down strategies for sustainable development, business support and social inclusion. This brings its own risks, however. Groundwork reorganized itself in 1997–99 not only to position itself for a new policy environment, but also to overcome problems that had become clear – a relative lack of success in gaining as much national attention and acclaim for its approach, despite considerable achievement at the grassroots; and a considerable variation in performance between trusts and project areas. It needs to ensure that the new structure works well and overcomes problems rapidly, so that the network can concentrate on maintaining its success in its difficult dual strategy – simultaneously delivering practical achievements at local level, literally down-to-earth, and promoting an ambitious development of a 'sustainable regeneration' programme, linking environmental improvement to social and economic renewal in poor neighbourhoods.

The challenges ahead are large and complex: to develop new indicators of achievement which reflect long-term outcomes and their relation to sustainability measures; to reconcile the pressure for short-term success in tackling social deprivation and business performance with the much longer timescales of sustainable environmental renewal; and to find ways to link the national aspirations for environmentally sustainable development with local ambitions which could be based on different priorities. Groundwork has unrivalled experience of the processes which, we have argued, are essential for managing sustainable development; but it has yet to link its activities to a rigorous set of outcome measures that reflect real impacts on ecological sustainability – reductions in an area's 'environmental footprint', for example. And the network has yet to enter fully into debate and policy in the disputed areas of sustainability, where environmental objectives can clash with economic and social ones. Not every environmental project produces 'win-win' results for economic and social demands as well as for the environment. Finally, will the greater focus on social inclusion and economic regeneration in Government funding at national level lead to a dilution of environmental initiatives, or can Groundwork succeed in integrating all the dimensions of its activity in a coherent model of sustainable development?[14]

So the challenges for the new century facing Groundwork are daunting. But the achievements to date suggest that the federation could rise to meet them. It is clear that the trust model has become a recognized pattern of good practice among policy-makers in central government and is capable of winning enthusiastic support from local government and business, and above all from local citizens. As mentioned above, the model is a prime contender for 'export' to the rest of the European Union and beyond. Several elements of the Groundwork approach stand out as good practice for other initiatives in sustainable regeneration.

The Groundwork experience offers one of the clearest and most impressive illustrations of an action network which is attempting to promote sustainable development in all its dimensions, going well beyond a focus on environmental management. It is a potential model for action networks internationally, as well as an expanding venture which will need to connect itself to wider networks and partnerships for sustainable development if it is to fulfil its ambitions to influence change on a larger canvas. The local work of the Groundwork movement is often of modest scope and is easily viewed as unspectacular and unglamorous, a mere scratch on the surface of our problems of unsustainable development. But the local projects add up to a major nationwide development in the regeneration of environments in decline and the reconnection of people to places they care about, and to real involvement in decision-making about their environments and communities.[15] This is essential to achieving a long-term change of heart: in business, in favour of the integration of commercial concerns with respect for the environment, both natural and urban; and in local communities, making clear linkages between environmental improvement and gains in the quality of life and in trust, self-confidence and a sense of local 'empowerment' for people left marginalized by the forces of economic change. Groundwork is a pioneer and exemplar of the action-network approach to managing sustainable development; it shows us what leading practice in 'doing sustainable development' actually looks like on the ground.

11

Innovations in Development for Environmental Action

In practice sustainability has to be a regional concept. We used to call it land use planning. Fortunately we can substitute for its two-dimensional flatness a better, more inclusive concept, perceiving a world surfaced with three-dimensional eco-systems in which we are immersed. These creative spaces are the focus of regional planning whose ecological aim is a sustainable earth.

J S Rowe[1]

A network is by definition non-hierarchical. It is a web of connections among equals. What holds it together is not force, obligation, material incentive, or social contract, but rather shared values and the understanding that some tasks can be accomplished together that could never be accomplished separately.

D Meadows et al[2]

This chapter describes an experimental programme to use action networks to enhance local management capability for addressing serious environmental problems in seven lower income countries. The IDEA programme – Innovations in Development for Environmental Action – developed networks led by senior scientists or public administrators in Malaysia, Mauritius, Zimbabwe, Zambia, Ghana, Nigeria and Guyana.[3] The seven local teams, with a small, worldwide interdisciplinary support team, constituted an international network. Much of the learning about action networks contained in this book was 'unlocked' by action research on innovation and constraints on organizational development and environmental achievement in the IDEA projects over a period of five years.

The IDEA programme itself, funded mainly by the (then) UK Overseas Development Administration, was wound up in the mid-1990s. But its action-network approach continues within the projects themselves and inspires the action networking of the larger parent network. This was orginally the Commonwealth Consultative Group for Technology Management, now called the Commonwealth Partnership for Technology Management (CPTM), which links 53 countries. This name change of the parent network reflects a shift of the network central coordinating body (or linking-pin organization) from the multilateral government sector to a non-profit but private sector organization. One reason for the shift in status of the parent network was to foster easier and more fruitful association between government and business in pursuit of the parent network's main aim, using technological advancement to foster development. This aim is set out by the Chair of CPTM:

> *CPTM harnesses the collective experience of both the private and public sectors, as well as the insights of gifted individuals, to identify and promote best practice in technology management to issues of current concern. We regard application of technology management as crucial to success in emerging economies to balance growth with sustainable development.*

The seven IDEA projects presented a cross-section of challenges to environmental management under three headings:

1 Watershed management: the development of mechanisms to reduce pollution and promote coordinated watershed management in the Densu River Basin and Weija Reservoir in Ghana; improved institutional coordination to reduce pollution in the Harare watershed, Zimbabwe; and improved management of the Copperbelt and lower reaches of the Kafue River in Zambia.
2 Waste management: the establishment of a cooperative arrangement for common waste-water treatment facilities among metal-finishing industries in the Klang Valley of Malaysia, and the development of policy guidelines and institutional arrangements to reduce unregulated waste disposal in Lagos State, Nigeria.
3 Resource management: the promotion of the use of replacement construction materials as an alternative to coral sand depletion in Mauritius, and the development of a legal and policy framework for the management of mineral exploitation in Guyana.

For each of these projects, management issues have been addressed at the policy, strategy and project levels by both direct and indirect action (Figure 11.1). Direct action includes, for example:

- the development of better policy and legislation to control the environmental effects of gold mining in Guyana;
- new institutional arrangements, such as the new cooperative of small-scale industrialists for pollution control in Malaysia; and
- direct links to community leaders and NGOs, as in the towns and villages of the Densu Basin in Ghana.

Indirect action includes, for example:

- building awareness in field visits and meetings of industrialists, local government officials and the IDEA teams;
- using various media such as newspaper articles, posters and slide presentations; and
- developing management and technical skills – for example, with the Science Council of Zimbabwe or the National Council for Oceanographic and Marine Research in Nigeria.

Within a project, action followed careful analysis of the problem and of potential constraints that could inhibit successful management. In keeping with the network approach, each IDEA project promoted new formal and informal linkages within government, and beyond government to the business, voluntary and community sectors. This

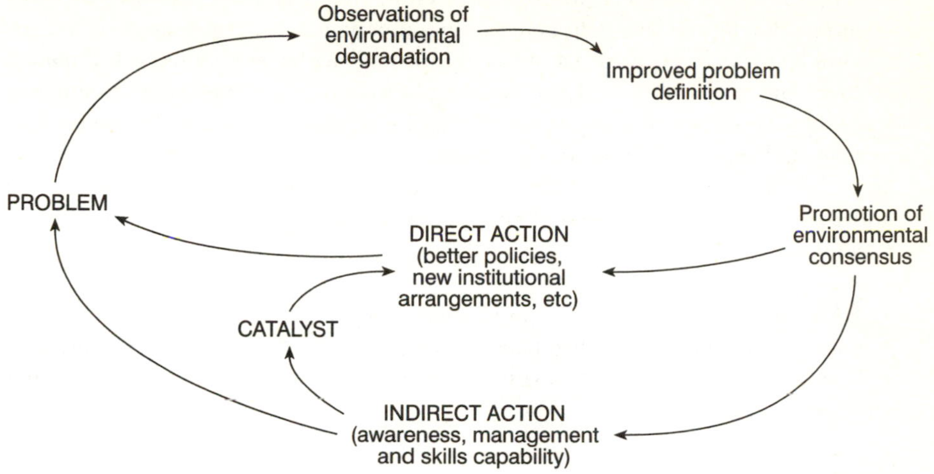

Source: Carley and Smith[4]

Figure 11.1 *Direct and indirect action in the IDEA programme*

structure was fostered by informal communication channels and working methods that were not always available to line departments and other government agencies.

The IDEA programme validated a number of the concepts described above for improving performance in the management of the environment and development planning. In particular, it provides an illustration of the value of non-hierarchical action networks as a complementary to traditional bureaucratic structures. Because of its grounding in topical environmental issues, IDEA contributed to an understanding of a practical methodology for generating these networks. IDEA also validated the usefulness of the action research methodology for learning about good management. The benefits of this learning proved relevant to:

- the pilot project countries which now have local nodes of professional experience in innovative problem assessment and management of the environment for development;
- other countries, which shared this knowledge and experience;
- the entire IDEA and CPTM network which provides the opportunity for diffusing this knowledge within and outside the Commonwealth, and which channels new knowledge back to the local nodes of professional experience; and
- funding and bilateral aid bodies who use the knowledge as part of the criteria to assess the degree of good management in the use of their funds for development.

The IDEA Programme

The objectives of the programme at the outset were:

1. To examine both the institutional frameworks, and the management strategies and techniques which constrain or enhance the implementation of development programmes with major environmental concerns.

2 To identify pilot projects in African, Asian and Caribbean Commonwealth countries. Each project was to be an example of a clear-cut, current environmental problem which requires institutional mechanisms for mediation at the policy, strategy and project levels. Each case study was to represent an environmental issue that was sufficiently important that failure to promote such mediation mechanisms could seriously hinder development.
3 To identify lessons at both country and overall generic levels for the management and assessment of development programmes which will assist in a review of current management practice.

The IDEA Programme took a broad view of the components of institutional frameworks as encompassing organizational, legal and human resources development. The areas of critical concern in institutional development as identified by many international agencies are relevant to IDEA:

- the host country policy environment;
- the potential of various forms of organization;
- the importance of institutional learning capacity;
- the problem of transferring knowledge, coordination and linkage among agencies;
- the improvement of management systems; and
- the role of local initiative and participation.

To this list, the IDEA team added the importance of parallel local and international networks to support initiatives in sustainable environmental management. Within IDEA, primary importance has been attached to local initiative and participation. IDEA addresses the organizational and human resource constraints which operate on government policy and implementation systems, in the specific context of the tasks identified.

The IDEA programme developed in three phases. Phase I, a period of six months, was initiated at a meeting at the Commonwealth Science Council in London, which identified themes for individual country tasks and a research team leader in each country. The agreement of the relevant authorities – for example, the Office of the Prime Minister or the main Financial Ministry – in each country was also secured during this period. This gave political credibility to each project at its initial stage, and encouraged (but did not ensure) a process of horizontal integration among relevant government departments.

It was also agreed by the first members of the network that no project would be selected which could be construed as destabilizing to the government of the host country. In one case, a project (to study the management of pig farm waste in Malaysia), which had religious and ethnic overtones, was rejected by the Office of the Prime Minister. This was accepted by the local team, and thus by the network, because the main aim of IDEA was to generate new skills in environmental management, rather than to solve any particular problem from an array of problem types.

Phase II, lasting a further three to four years of monitored experimentation, consisted of the implementation of each of the management and action projects identified, and a series of joint meetings of all the IDEA country team leaders and representatives to review the progress of the research teams and to offer guidance on possible future steps. In addition to the tangible outputs of each country task, reported

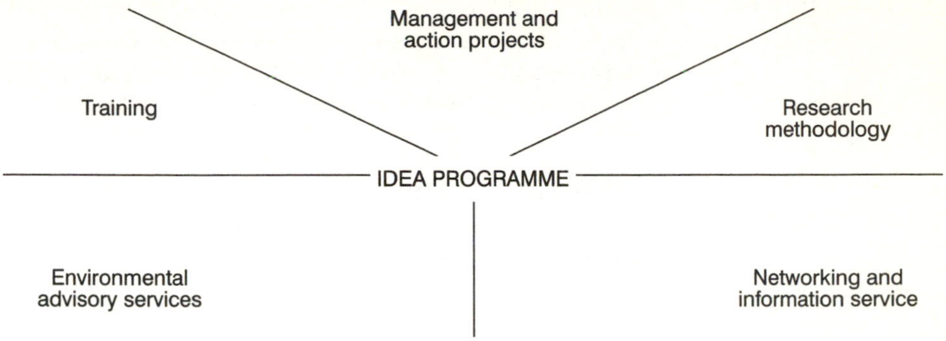

Figure 11.2 *Components of the IDEA programme*

below, the first two phases of IDEA were subject to formal monitoring and analysis. This provided both a vehicle for additional learning for IDEA teams and a means of generating transferable learning from the overall process, as reported here. Phase III of the project, continued implementation, followed formal bilateral funding.

One obvious strength of IDEA is that it grounded transferable learning about environmental management strategies in practical development activity, thus fulfilling a basic criterion of the action research methodology. Rather than attempting to adopt uniform solutions, the environmental problems identified as critical in the seven countries were redefined into a series of positive 'management and action' projects, supported by IDEA's network and information services, environmental advisory services, and training and research methodology (Figure 11.2).

Key concepts of the approach

1 An individual, called the team leader, served as a catalyst to the entire process. The team leader was invited to participate by the larger network and selected for his or her ability to take a broad, process-oriented perspective on local environmental problems. The team leader is usually a senior scientist, administrator or professor from a potential linking-pin organization.
2 The selection of a serious environmental problem proved crucial. The choice was made by the local team of a problem of national importance, which it is also possible to reduce or resolve. The problem provided a case study for learning about the environmental management process and for developing new skills.
3 A local project advisory group provided relevant stakeholding agencies and individuals with the opportunity for participation in the definition of the problem and in its resolution. Each group was typically 8–14 people.
4 An IDEA researcher was hired locally to develop the project under the guidance of the team leader and advisory group. These three, together, made up the local IDEA team.
5 The local team had a facilitating and/or mediating role among the various stakeholders as necessary. Iterative problem definition broadens the perspective of team members and gradually builds up consensus and commitment to the resolution of the problem.
6 As the local network developed, it received financial and administrative support, advice and peer review from the international component of the network.

7 Because any new organization could appear threatening to existing institutional arrangements and individuals in positions of power, IDEA local networks were developed only at a pace which is politically and culturally sustainable, by a process that is much akin to traditional community development, but at a regional scale.

The IDEA Projects

The IDEA projects have been extensively documented and the intention here is only to summarize the main points to arise from the case studies. It is also important to note that, although this is a report on a research project of limited duration, by the very nature of the networks, a dynamic process has been initiated which will continue, although not necessarily in its present form. This is true of all the case studies in this book and a general feature of the network approach. The projects are therefore mostly reported as ongoing.

Naturally the degree of progress for each country's task varies according to the severity of the original problem, the individual national characteristics and constraints that are relevant to problem resolution, and the success of the intervention team. The extent of the progress is reported below. However, it is within the methodological expectations of IDEA that this variety provides a cross-section of likely institutional constraints and thus contributes to learning within the programme.

Watershed management

Watershed management in the Densu River basin of Ghana

The original concern, arising out of the project leader's scientific studies, was with the long-term effects of pollution and siltation in the Weija Reservoir on the Densu River, which supplies about half the drinking water of Accra, as well as irrigation further downstream. The problem analysis of the project was described previously in Chapter 7. The project objectives were set out as:

- to rehabilitate the Densu River basin ecosystem and thereby improve the flow of the river, minimize flood risk, and improve the quality of the water in the river and Weija Reservoir;
- to document the methodology and findings of this study and to disseminate them to target audiences and communities via discussions, seminars, audiovisual presentations and field demonstrations; and
- to publish the results in an appropriate form and media for wider dissemination and possible application.

The main causes of pollution in the watershed arise from rapid urbanization as a result of rural to urban migration at Nsawam Township, and the intensification of agriculture and logging activities along the banks of the Densu River. Eleven agencies in central and local government have been identified by the project as having substantial control over the activities in the Densu basin, and their management structures and legal and institutional frameworks have been analysed. The project team also extended the initial boundaries of the study area to include the whole of the Densu Basin from its estuary to its source, a distance of 116km. This brought two more agencies, responsible for forestry and mining activities in the upper reaches, into the framework.

As water quality continued to deteriorate, the project team initiated a programme of awareness creation to alert people to the severity of the problem and the implications of their actions on water quality. This included visits to agencies and the use of newspaper articles to raise the level of problem acceptance. During year two of the project, the local team organized a seminar on the Densu River Basin Development. This was attended by 40 people, representing 26 agencies and organizations with an interest in the Densu basin. This seminar was described by the team leader as 'the first ever meeting of agencies involved in diverse developmental projects within a common ecological zone in Ghana'. Out of this seminar arose a series of recommendations, the foremost of which included the establishment of a river basin authority, a public awareness programme, agency actions to reduce environmental degradation, and the institutionalization of environmental impact assessment (EIA) procedures.

The project team was based in the Institute of Aquatic Biology, which continues to work in collaboration with other technical institutions and agencies, including the Water Resources Research Institute, the Institute of Renewable Natural Resources, the Forestry Department, the Ghana Water and Sewage Corporation, the Industrial Research Institute and the Environmental Protection Council. The IDEA team set itself a series of tasks stemming from the above recommendations and others that were more detailed. District administrations in the project area are now relying on the team to formulate guidelines for rehabilitation of the Densu basin.

The guidelines focus on the problems of sewage, industrial effluent and inappropriate landfill arrangements. To prevent siltation, agroforestry has been recommended in the context of locally accepted means of rehabilitating deforested areas in the river basin. The idea of dredging the river at Nsawam or channelling through canals is also being explored. It is proposed to measure the improvement in the quality and flavour of the water in the Weija Reservoir, the reduction in chemicals used in water production, and the reduced incidence of flooding in the basin as indicators of the success of the rehabilitation exercise.

The IDEA team also identified areas for which training is necessary to enable the continued successful implementation of environmental management strategies. These include river basin management, waste management, environmental impact assessment, urban systems management (with special reference to rapidly growing tropical townships) and environmental health.

The Ghana project has brought together institutions, agencies and the communities at risk through their district administrations in a broad-based network to tackle a watershed management problem. It created environmental awareness among local communities and, through the press and other media, highlighted nationally the urgent need to tackle environmental degradation in this and other river basins. In addition, the experience gained by the professionals involved widened their perspectives and improved the capability of their respective institutions. Following the conclusion of the supported, experimental phase of the intervention, the team faced the task of maintaining the coordinated relationship that was developed among the technical agencies on the one hand, and the eight district administrations on the other, during the next phase of implementing, monitoring and evaluating the rehabilitation programme.

The IDEA initiatives enabled the Ghanaian team to complement institutional development, and legal and formal environmental controls, with voluntary action at the local level. In this way motivation was devolved and local mechanisms evolved to maintain water quality as new development pressures arose. The main outcome of these efforts was to create a pool of personnel who were trained in river basin management and a parallel network of local action. The result is intended to be a prototypical river basin management system which will be transferable to other watersheds. As of 1998, substantially improved communication and a far more systematic watershed management were a tangible outcome of the IDEA effort.

Watershed management in the Harare region of Zimbabwe

This project arose out of the concern that the rapid growth in population and industrialization in the area of Harare degraded water quality in Lake Chivero, the main source of drinking water for Harare, although it is downstream of the city. In particular, the rapid spread of a blanket of water hyacinth over 1 metre thick across more than 40 per cent of the surface of the lake, generated much concern about the need to sustain water quality.

The overall objective of the project was to develop a well-coordinated institutional mechanism for the management of the Harare watershed which would lead to a reduction in the amount of pollutants entering the water system. To achieve this aim the team engaged in three complementary activities: information gathering and awareness raising; water quality monitoring; and generating participation in activities to reduce the water hyacinth problem.

The project team, recognizing that neither urbanization nor industrialization were likely to abate, decided to expand from a focus on water quality monitoring to the promotion of watershed management. They identified:

- the main agencies in central and local government with potential responsibility for watershed management;
- some of the major sources of pollution – domestic and sewage waste, and industrial effluents – from both public and private companies; and
- the trends in population and industrial growth that were likely to result in major environmental impacts.

Among the latter, for example, major concerns include pollution caused by the main fertilizer plant for the country (partly government-owned), and discharges from sewage works of a rapidly growing and poorly planned town with low-cost housing near Harare.

The team initiated a project advisory group representing eight main agencies with relevant responsibilities in the watershed area. They also reviewed the current legal and institutional framework for watershed management, and documented gaps between adequate policy and law, and inadequate implementation and enforcement. They developed a survey questionnaire that was piloted to senior agency officials. The main survey was immediately followed up with face-to-face interviews with key people in government and industry.

The occasion of an international IDEA programme meeting in Harare was used by the project team as a springboard to launch a major awareness campaign, including front page newspaper coverage, and to alert senior government officials in the industrial and financial departments to the need to reconcile industrialization with environmental quality. The meeting helped to forge new links between government officials and industrialists in the region.

The project team and advisory group then promoted a three-pronged effort: to encourage the enforcement of existing pollution control laws; to encourage the private sector to invest in pollution control and recycling technology and to develop a coordinated managerial system for water quality maintenance. Having initiated direct communication between the government, the research sector and the business community, the project team was in a position to help to establish interinstitutional collaboration. Within the context of improved watershed management, more stringent pollution control by industries within the water basin has been a main tangible outcome of IDEA.

Watershed management in the Kafue basin of Zambia

The original concern of the National Council for Scientific Research, base of the Zambian project team, was over declining water quality in the entire Kafue River basin, in spite of the existence of various laws for environmental protection and pollution control. The basin covers an estimated area of about 15,000 square kilometres. Although the problems of the entire watershed were well documented by the team, this proved unwieldy as a project owing to the great distances involved. With assistance from the team leaders from Ghana and Zimbabwe, the Zambian team decided to redefine the scope of their project to focus on problems on the lower Kafue River in the vicinity of Lusaka and in the mining area on the Copperbelt, where problems arise from pollution from inadequately treated raw sewage, industrial effluents and agricultural run-off, as well as poor practices in solid waste disposal.

One particular problem identified in these two areas is the failure of municipalities to maintain existing sewage treatment plants owing to financial constraints and the lack of skilled manpower arising from a long-term economic recession in the country. This problem has been exacerbated by high rates of urbanization, which is currently increasing at about 6.7 per cent annually, as well as lack of resources in the private sector for investment in pollution control technology and a lack of personnel in government agencies that are responsible for environmental monitoring.

Following detailed problem definition, the Zambian team established an advisory group of six relevant agencies, including government departments for agriculture, commerce and industry, local government, the National Commission for Development Planning, the National Council for Scientific Research and Zambia Consolidated Copper Mines. The first meeting identified the constraints on water quality improvement, including the inability of the relevant institutions to implement existing legislation on environmental protection and pollution control, and the lack of monitoring of industrial and sewage effluents.

The advisory committee then organized discussion meetings in both the lower and upper Kafue areas. These brought together representatives of industry, local authorities and central government agencies. The discussions focused on environmental concerns and pollution risks, and a number of recommendations for action were made.

In connection with the development of mechanisms for interinstitutional coordination, a main thrust of the project, the priorities identified were:

1 The establishment of a special committee of the National Environmental Council (currently being established under the Environmental Protection and Pollution Control Act of 1990) to deal specifically with policy issues of the basin's environment and development.

2 Promotion of the formation of community-based environmental action associations to address the issues of environmental quality at the grassroots level. For example, the Kafue Water Users Association has been established.
3 A requirement to generate a resources and environmental quality data base to facilitate periodic reviews of the state of the environment and environmental impact assessments of new development projects.
4 The need for investment in rehabilitation and expansion of the districts' systems for water treatment and distribution, sewage and solid waste collection and disposal; the training of skilled staff in local and national government; the installation of efficient treatment plant in industry; and the promotion of public awareness of environmental issues.

Waste management

Cooperative wastewater treatment in Malaysia
Since 1987, the manufacturing sector has been the leading economic sector in Malaysia, followed by the agricultural and mining sectors. The main manufactured products for export are electrical/electronic goods, textiles and rubber-based products. Small-scale, or 'backyard', industries play a major role in the industrialization process of the national economy and account for about 90 per cent of employment in the manufacturing sector. These industries include metal finishing, textiles and food processing.

Following the recognition of the need to enforce standards for the discharge of effluents under the existing environmental quality regulations, a survey indicated that metal finishers were a major source of toxic and hazardous wastes (acids and alkalis containing metals such as chromium, nickel and aluminium). The survey identified more than 100 small-scale operators employing less than 20 people, of which slightly more than half were located in the Klang Valley surrounding Kuala Lumpur. These metal finishers produce items such as nuts and bolts for the automotive industry, components for the electrical and electronic industries, as well as various household utensils. They play an important role in industrial development.

It was recognized early in the project that, although strict enforcement of pollution control legislation was desirable, simply putting the metal finishers out of business was not a viable option. A more sophisticated response was necessary. The IDEA team therefore redefined the problem as:

1 a pollution problem;
2 an economic problem, concerning the viability of the enterprises, their contribution to industrial growth, the costs of waste-metal removal from the effluent and the cost-effectiveness of communal treatment run cooperatively;
3 a land use problem in terms of the incompatibility of industrial and residential uses; and
4 a spatial problem of whether to relocate the businesses near a waste treatment facility or to transport the waste from the industries to a central facility.

Figure 11.3 illustrates the management problems involved. Failure to comply with stipulated effluent discharge standards and to install pollution control measures was generally linked with financial, technical and spatial constraints. The government,

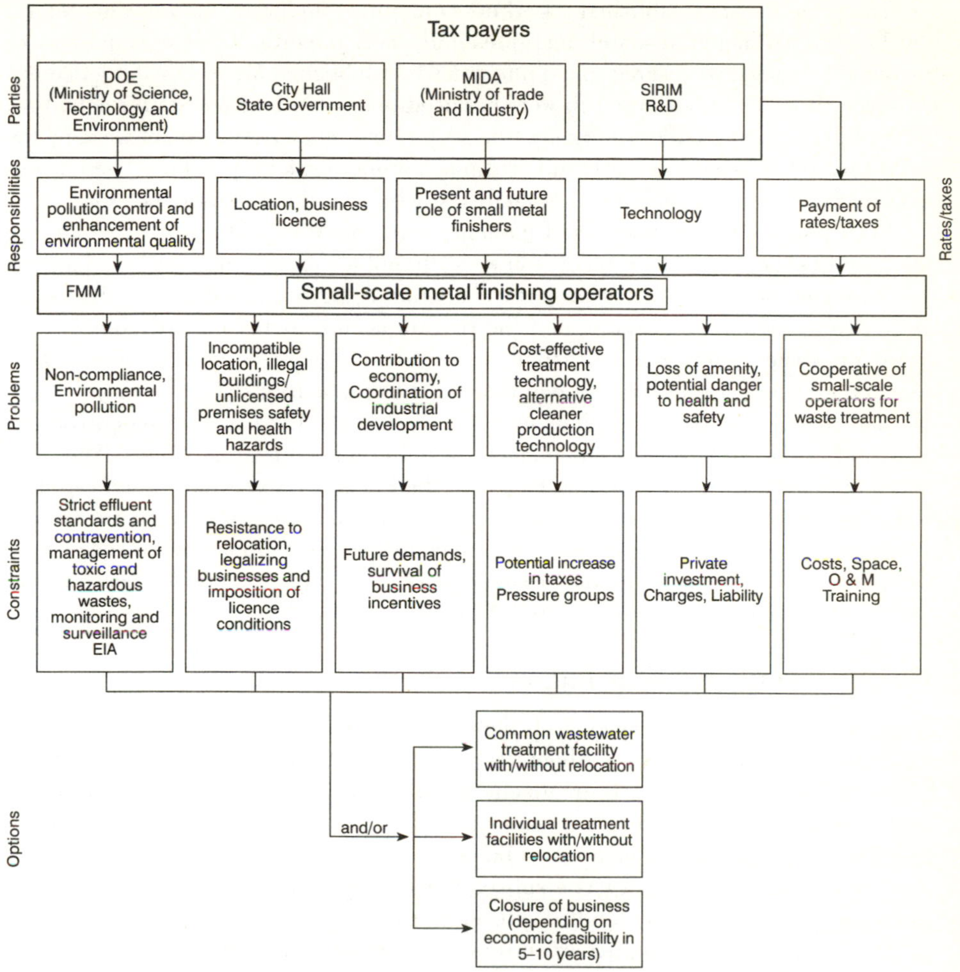

Source: Malaysian IDEA Team, Department of Environment, Malaysia

Figure 11.3 *Management problem chart in the establishment of common wastewater treatment facilities among small metal finishing industries in Malaysia*

through the IDEA project, decided on a common wastewater treatment facility, to be managed by a cooperative of metal finishers.

The objectives of the country's task were set out as follows:

- Short term: the identification of the wastewater characteristics of the industry as well as pollution load in the selected study area of the Klang Valley.
- Medium term: the development of a consensus over the measures that were acceptable to the metal finishers and the various government enforcement agencies in controlling pollution, managing toxic and hazardous wastes, and preventing nuisance to the adjacent areas.
- Long term: a proposal on the cooperative arrangements for a common wastewater treatment facility in the Klang Valley, and consequently an enforcement of the environmental quality standards.

The project team established a working committee, including the relevant central and local departments, research institutes and, most importantly, representatives of the metal finishers, who were formed into a newly established Metal Finishing Society. However, these small businessmen were not used to any kind of cooperative activities, particularly in conjunction with the public sector, and much development work by the project team has been necessary, and continues. From this, a proposal has been developed for cooperative waste treatment facilities, with or without plant relocation.

Like the projects in watershed management, the Malaysian project generated much interest because the problem of how to attempt to control small-scale industry is common to many countries. The project's cooperative approach, both among the industrialists and between the public and the private sector, is undoubtedly innovative. However, some of the metal finishers were decidedly uncooperative in the first instance, in keeping with their individualistic, entrepreneurial style. The project team has had to make delicate decisions over whether to use the carrot of incentive and dialogue, or the stick of legal enforcement of pollution control regulations. The most useful approach was to hold discussions with the uncooperative small-scale operators to explain to them the advantages of joining the metal finishing cooperative for mitigation of pollution. Despite these challenges to coordinated environmental management, the metal finishers' waste treatment cooperative is in business and successful, and constitutes a sound output from the IDEA project.

Waste management in Lagos

Lagos, a sprawling city of around 7 million people, is home to numerous domestic and multinational industrial firms. About 70 per cent of all industries in Nigeria are in Lagos, and very few have waste-treatment facililties. The IDEA project focused on the institutional arrangements for waste management in Lagos state. To bound the problem, initial research was further focused on Ikeja municipality, one of the four main industrial areas in the state. Ikeja has a substantial resident population of some 250,000 and also contains a major landfill site of the Lagos State Waste Disposal Board (LSWDB). Ikeja provided a pilot area within which to begin to understand the complex issues of waste disposal in the wider state.

The main governmental agencies with a responsibility for waste include the Federal Ministry of Science and Technology (FMST), the Federal Environmental Protection Agency (FEPA), and the state government, represented by the LSWDB. The complexity of evolving institutional arrangements initially caused delay in the implementation of the project. But by year two, a workshop was held to examine the need for improvements to the waste-management system for Lagos metropolis; various agencies' arrangements and responsibilities in this regard; and the possibilities for a new workable alliance among the agencies to tackle waste management efficiently.

The interinstitutional aspects of the project were developed considerably. The participants included a number of representatives of the FEPA, FMST and LSWDB, the Federal Ministry of Industry, the Federal Ministry of Education, the Municipality of Ikeja (Department of Health and Environmental Services), the business sector (including local representatives from multinational companies), the University of Lagos, the University of Calabar, the National Institute for Oceanography and Marine Research (NIOMR), the National Centre for Genetic Research and Biotechnology, and the Commonwealth Fund for Technical Cooperation. Many of these representatives joined an advisory group, along with the Manufacturers Association of Nigeria (MAN).

The first step of the advisory group was to identify the following requirements as critical to the improvement of waste management for the Lagos metropolis:

- additional landfill sites;
- a system for monitoring and controlling toxic, liquid industrial wastes in the Lagos area;
- more sewage treatment facilities, which were needed partly to keep up with the urban population growth;
- definitions and standards for various kinds of wastes and pollutants;
- cost-effective waste disposal, possibly including commercialization, joint treatment facilities, 'user pays' charging, and the local sourcing of supplies and replacement parts;
- the development of local managerial and technical capacity in all agencies, instead of relying on expensive outside consultants;
- the creation and/or rationalization of laboratory facilities for Lagos state;
- the minimization of waste production, including the exploration of recycling options;
- better organization among government agencies for factory inspection, and possibly more integrated pollution control; and
- forward planning to deal with the increasing proportions of inorganic wastes (mainly due to an increase in packaging).

In Nigeria as a whole, the policy and administrative systems for environmental management, and the relationship between the federal and state governments in this area, continue to evolve, albeit in difficult circumstances for public administration. As a result of the project's activities, it was determined that waste management arrangements in Lagos state, and their funding, could serve as a pilot for other states, especially those with large cities. The FEPA confirmed that analysis from the IDEA project was helpful to its primary task of establishing an environmental management structure for the country.

Resource management

Management of coral sand exploitation in Mauritius

Accelerated economic growth in Mauritius in the 1980s and early 1990s was accompanied by a construction boom in offices, hotels and residential developments. More than 35 major tourist hotels now ring the island and an 18-storey office block is one of a number of new offices under construction in the capital, Port Louis. Such developments have put enormous pressure on the supply of construction aggregates, both crushed basalt and natural coral sand. Inland coral sand deposits are virtually exhausted, resulting in an increased amount of coral sand being extracted from the lagoons inside the reefs – about 320,000 tons per year at present. This is having detrimental effects on the environment, including beach erosion, increased sea water turbidity and disruption of the food chain in the lagoons. The coral sand resource cannot be managed in any sustainable fashion, as the replacement time for a few years' extraction must be measured in centuries. The objective of the IDEA project was to encourage the use of replacement materials for coral sand in construction as a critical element in the sustainable management of coastal resources.

The environmental implications of the continued use of coral sand as a construction material are becoming known in Mauritius, but when the IDEA project began there was no consensus as to the nature or extent of the problem. Indeed some Members of Parliament were still urging an increased exploitation of the resource, which was considered necessary for economic growth. Although replacement construction materials are technically and economically feasible, as demonstrated at the University of Mauritius, there were no appropriate institutional arrangements for mediating the need for replacement construction material with the need for continuing economic growth and development. The IDEA project also noted conflicting interests within the government, and between government and the private sector. In so far as lagoonal mining causes beach erosion, the continued extraction of coral sand will have a negative impact on the tourist industry. This, along with the pollution of lagoons from hotel effluent, suggests the need to mediate conflicting uses within a systematic framework for management of the coastal zone.

The IDEA team have documented the institutional and technical aspects of the problem in great detail, and drawn together information from all the relevant published and ongoing studies. A project steering committee was established, including almost all the main government ministries, and representatives of important private sector firms and the academic community. The IDEA team, with the steering committee, embarked on a public awareness programme and a systematic assessment of the organizational and economic constraints on the outright banning of coral sand extraction. They have embarked on a programme to encourage the construction and aggregate industries to make use of replacements on a voluntary basis, and have assisted in the retraining of builders to adjust to using the new materials with the aid of video training packages, among other tools.

During the project, the government's Ministry of Lands and Environment established a technical committee for phasing out the use of coral sand, with very similar terms of reference to those of the project committee. This government committee invited the university to participate and used the report of the IDEA project as a working document. The IDEA Team Leader summarizes the relationship between the project and the new government committee:

> *The [IDEA] Steering Committee was viewed as having the task of making a study of the coral sand problem and making appropriate recommendations for alternatives, whereas the Ministry of Environment Committee has as a priority implementation and enforcement of recommendations.*

This institutionalization of the environmental problem, first addressed by the IDEA project in Mauritius, constitutes a most satisfactory outcome and indicates the effectiveness of the temporary 'parallel organization' focusing action on an important environmental issue.

Resource management and environmental control in Guyana

Guyana is under great pressure to exploit its natural resources, partly to meet the requirements of structural adjustment. This pressure extends to gold mining. Although a number of multinationals, mainly American and Canadian, are moving into the gold-mining sector in the country, much mining is carried out by individuals and small, mainly family groups. There are about 10,000 miners. The main method of gold extraction involves a technology called 'missile dredges' which is capable of mechanically dredging river banks and cutting into the foreshore.

Tailings from missile dredging form small islands which interfere with navigation, and the missiles often change the contour of the river bank and cause serious downstream turbidity. There are severe social impacts, including disruption of traditional food fishing activities of local, mainly Amerindian, residents of the areas, and the degradation of their drinking water.

Such disruption has been documented in the Pakaraima and Upper Mazaruni Mountains, a rainforest area which is home to the Akawaio Indians. Waterways provide the main thoroughfare in the area and many of these are already blocked. Fish are unable to spawn as their breeding grounds are destroyed by the dredgers, whose operations are reported to render water undrinkable 60km downstream. Recently in Guyana there has been increasing political and public awareness of the environmental damage caused by this form of mining, and a concern to exert control over this and all other environmentally damaging forms of gold mining. The new road from the Brazilian border to tidewater at the Guyanese capital, Georgetown, brings with it the grave danger that the near anarchy of the Brazilian goldfields will spill over into Guyana.

Against this background, the project team established the following objectives:

- National: to ensure that environmental considerations are an essential and integral part of sustainable national economic development objectives.
- Immediate: to promote greater cooperation among, and strengthen the institutional capability of, the agencies involved in the protection and development of natural resources through a study of gold-mining projects.

The project team, led by the head of the government's agency for the environment, decided that the project should first tackle the absence of any environmental legislation for Guyana which would give the government some authority for action. This attention to the problems of gold mining, and the need for interagency cooperation to address it, would then have benefits which would flow throughout the government's approach to environmental policy. To this end, both the Geology and Mines Commission and the Guyana Agency for Health Education, Environment and Food Policy (GAHEF) collaborated to address the problem.

The Guyana team leader drew up a draft environmental protection bill for the country. He then sought the assistance of the IDEA programme in refining that legislation and in assessing the many substantial institutional and administrative implications that flowed from it. The IDEA programme provided both general advice on environmental policy and legislation in member countries from members of the network, and specialist legal advice in drafting acceptable and useful legislation in a commonwealth context. As a result of these activities, a Guyana Environmental Protection Act was brought before the Guyanese Cabinet.

Having secured legislative authority for environmental protection and control, the project turned its attention to the difficult task of developing the necessary conditions for the successful implementation of environmental policy. Six key needs have been identified:

1 acceptable standards of environmental quality;
2 environmental monitoring staff and laboratory facilities;
3 guidelines and expertise in environmental impact assessment;
4 review of the institutional structure for pollution and environmental control;
5 training to meet the human resource requirements; and
6 winning financial resources within a severely constrained economy.

Through IDEA, the experiences of other countries in the setting of standards and in environmental monitoring were examined. In addition, linkages within Guyana were strengthened with an agency with competence in monitoring – the Mahaica–Mahaicony–Abary Agricultural Development Authority. This organization was funded for a number of years by the Inter-American Development Bank to develop environmental monitoring expertise that was relevant to that agricultural project. To this end, it initiated, through its Environmental Monitoring and Control Unit, on-the-job training of environmental field technicians. In this programme, secondary school graduates in relevant science disciplines have been trained in the various aspects of monitoring: water quality, wildlife, fisheries, vegetation and spatial monitoring. It is expected that the expertise developed through this programme will be shared with GAHEF.

Guidelines for environmental impact assessment in gold mining were developed by GAHEF for discussion with the Geology and Mines Commission and other appropriate agencies. A survey assessed the adequacy of the institutional structures for dealing with pollution control and of the legislative framework, and the types of regulations required. Finally, training needs were documented and priorities established prior to the attempt to secure the necessary resources. In considering the question of training and the broader issue of human resource capability in Guyana, the project also addressed the fundamental constraint on environmental management in that country, which is the long-standing 'brain drain' overseas of many of the country's skilled professionals and technicians.

Another area of achievement initiated by the project, but not necessarily intended when it was first framed, has been the self-organization of the various water users, many indigenous peoples of the region, into a more organized, collective pressure group. This puts water users on a more sound footing in negotiation with corporate players, such as the government and larger mining concerns, enabling them to enter more forcefully into negotiation to protect their right to water quality.

This evolution of the project's focus from the initial specific environmental problem to a generic institutional problem (gold mining to environmental legislation to implementation capability) is typical of the achievements of a number of IDEA projects in broadening their attention to major constraints on environmental management and sustainable development. By attempting to overcome those constraints the lessons and the achievements of the specific IDEA projects became replicable for other environmental problem areas.

Lessons from IDEA

IDEA was a practical, experimental effort to understand and resolve some of the complexities of environmental management in lower income countries, and to make that knowledge available for use in similar circumstances. A reasonable measure of success can be attributed to the programme, in terms of both project outputs and transferable learning. In addition, the knowledge base in the parent network has grown substantially. Through practical environmental management, the programme has been able to validate many of the propositions about management and organizations which lately have found favour in the academic literature on both private and public sector management and environmental mediation. In this sense, IDEA has been a successful empirical effort in developing organizational capacity for improved environmental management.

Views of the team leaders

Participants in IDEA reported that they found the action network methodology, which they themselves helped to develop, useful in addressing the serious environmental challenges identified at the beginning of the programmes. This is especially true of the team leaders, most of whom, although eminent scientists or administrators, had no particular background in environmental management or institutional development. In each project, tangible outputs in institutional development have resulted, and indicators of environmental improvement have been identified as the objectives or measures of the intended results. The views of the team leaders on the achievements and lessons of the IDEA methodology are given below.

Achievements

1 The approach resulted in a clear definition of the environmental problems, and the identification of the main participants or stakeholders with an interest in those problems.
2 The approach also served to identify the main constraints to good management as it related to the particular problem.
3 The process of mutual problem definition resulted in a shared appreciation of the problem as a basis for action.
4 The projects had a clear triggering effect, where inertia or uncoordinated action had previously held sway. In other words, the projects served as catalysts for local action.
5 The project advisory groups provided a forum for the resolution of conflict, and induced a logical synthesis of views and objectives towards practical solutions.
6 As the problem was redefined, the number of relevant stakeholders grew, but at a pace which was manageable for the existing group. This process served to focus attention on wider, more diverse perspectives.
7 The projects mobilized local skills for direct action on the problem and provided high value interventions at modest cost.
8 The projects led to the discovery of talented local people, linked them to the challenging tasks, provided an opportunity for further mutual learning, linkage and recognition, and thus developed a pool of local skills in environmental management.
9 The projects led to new linkages between people in diverse institutions and organizations concerned with development, some of which will be long-lasting.

Lessons

The process of evaluation also uncovered some other lessons, insights or 'confessions' from the participants, as follows:

1. Motivation at the grass-roots is an imperative for successful environmental action.
2. Solutions to environmental problems will invariably be found in a wider context than is at first apparent.
3. The provision and discussion of reliable information and data builds up trust among participants.
4. The mass media must be involved and cultivated to serve the purposes of environmental education.
5. Solutions usually involve a multiplicity of policy instruments, ranging from participatory mechanisms to financial inducements and penalties.
6. The process of developing a project team needs to be recorded and documented to avoid misunderstandings and to generate agreement on, and commitment to, intended actions.
7. Innovatory approaches, because they often risk upsetting the status quo, require the development of emotional as well as intellectual commitment.
8. The interactions between the project teams from various countries helped to motivate and mobilize local people as part of a wider international network.

Conclusion

The IDEA programme generated tangible outputs in environmental management and institutional development, and a methodology for enhancing local capacity to address serious environmental problems through building action networks. In particular, the challenge of problems of national concern, combined with the interactions of the diversely skilled professionals, administrators and community and business leaders in the interlinked international and local networks, generated more material for learning than we have been able to analyse and report here. Like the individual projects, the overall programme generated considerable value for money, and the lessons derived will continue to flow for some time.

12

Consensus-building and Collaborative Planning in California

> *... movement in the direction of inclusionary, collaborative planning should help to improve the quality of life for the many cultural communities in a place; to add material value not just to the companies in a place, but to those who share the experience of living there, and to work out how to act to sustain the critical biospheric capacities of a place. These benefits arise through the deliberative work of collaborative capacity-building, not through encouraging individualistic competitive behaviour.*
>
> Patsy Healey[1]

Like the South East of England, the Tokyo–Osaka region and an increasing number of intensively developed regions throughout the world, California is a victim of its own economic success on a grand scale. It is often noted that the GDP of California exceeds that of many countries in the world. The state is already the most populous in the US: it is set to become a good deal more crowded. Throughout the 1980s an economic boom and the attractions of the landscape and climate attracted record numbers of immigrants. During this decade, the state's population grew by 25 per cent, two-and-a-half times the national average. The rate of growth within the cities has been phenomenal: between 1970 and 1990, the regional population of the Greater Los Angeles region grew by 45 per cent, and the area of land used for development grew by 300 per cent. In Sacramento the population grew by over 40 per cent between 1980 and 1999. By 2020 California is forecast to be home to some 45 million people, 11 million more than at the end of the 1990s. And although the state covers a large area, it is mainly mountain and desert – the Californian cities are increasingly squeezed as more people arrive.

There are substantial environmental costs attached to this growth, and Californian politics is marked by an increasing dissatisfaction with the declining quality of life. This chapter explores the innovative network approaches that are intended to help the contending interests in the state to come to terms with that growth. In particular we describe one of the first attempts to mediate between competing interest groups and to achieve agreement on managing the demand for land and other resources – the California Growth Management Consensus Project (GMCP). This pioneering project grew out of the rising awareness in California of the links between environmental problems, land use and the clash of special interest lobbies over economic development issues. It is an attempt to overcome the blockages and conflicts in the policy development process caused by the entrenched positions of diverse and powerful lobbies, and to build consensus between key constituencies in environmental management. It offers important lessons – both inspirational and salutary – to the many similar initiatives in sustainable resource management and consensus-building on complex, contested issues now developing across the world.

We go on to look at subsequent initiatives and relate these to a wider movement in the developed world to experiment in new forms of deliberative, participatory planning as a key part of the shift towards more sustainable development. First, however, we look at the ecological costs of rapid growth in the already highly developed regions of California.

The Environmental Cost of Growth

The current population of California is some 44 million, mostly concentrated in southern California – in the Los Angeles/San Diego regional conurbation – and in central California around the San Francisco Bay area.

Southern California is home not only to tens of millions of people but also to millions of motor vehicles, which make the air some of the most polluted in the United States. In San Diego, 90 per cent of the water comes from sources outside the conurbation, principally from the Colorado River, which passes through the Grand Canyon. The water from the north travels through 500 miles of aqueducts and canals. Out of the Colorado River, 1 billion gallons of water per day is drawn for southern California, making up 70 per cent of the region's water supply; the river is so drained by this and other extractions that it disappears entirely before it reaches its outlet at the sea in Mexico. The entire estuarine ecosystem of the Colorado has simply disappeared. In the San Franciso Bay area, vast amounts of fresh water are taken by canal to the Central Valley and the southern cities, creating severe problems for the state's fisheries: Chinook salmon and the Bay delta smelt have become endangered species. The Colorado has been the focus for resource disputes between business interests and between California and the neighbouring states of Arizona and Nevada: in the mid-1990s California exceeded its allocated withdrawals from the river, leading to threats from the federal government to reduce its official allocations. The Colorado has been managed for decades as if it were an inexhaustible resource, rather than an essential and vulnerable lifeline that must be sustained if southern California is to survive as an urbanized region.[2]

Against this backdrop, there is a serious risk of water shortages. The coastal strip of southern California is located in semi-desert, receiving on average only 10–15 inches of rainfall per year. The years 1985–90 were marked by drought, with rainfall down to the lowest levels since recording began in the late 1880s. At the best of times, natural water supplies meet less than one-third of current needs in that region, and demand is certain to grow as the population continues to expand in coming decades. Already many of the state's 350 ground water basins are overdrawn, some critically so. The water situation is so severe that without new sources of water becoming available, there will be chronic shortages within the next two decades, according to the California Water Resources Board. The likelihood must be that new sources will not come on stream, making it essential to develop radical new approaches to demand management, water conservation and efficiency of use, and better management of aquifers.

California pioneered the car-based society, and the population continues to sprawl over vast areas, in part to escape rising land values in and near the major cities. To fill the current demand for housing by people working in southern California and the Bay area, developers have turned their sights on some of the most productive agricultural land in the United States. This is the vast Central Valley which accounts for two-thirds of the state's annual agricultural income. To find affordable housing, people are prepared to live hundreds of miles from their place of employment and drive two or even three hours to work. As a result, it is estimated that hundreds of thousands of acres of new suburban development could exist by the year 2010. There is also a social dimension to these problems: it is mainly the white population that is fleeing to the distant suburbs, leaving Latinos, Asians and African-Americans isolated in the inner cities. Ethnic minority incomes are 30 per cent below the median and few people in ethnic minority communities have access to home ownership.

The Central Valley is seen increasingly as the only large area left that can absorb the newcomers to California, given the extreme pressure on land and water in the South and the existing dense development around San Francisco Bay. But, as elsewhere in the US, the prevailing pattern of development of housing and retail has been to produce what environmental campaigners call 'dysfunctional sprawl',[3] an issue that is rapidly rising up the political agenda in turn-of-the-century America. Sprawl is the result of the deep-rooted preference for large family homes on big plots of land and for suburban living well away from the crime and violence of the big cities. For this and other reasons, particularly the dispersal of retailing and leisure activities to follow the affluent consumers and their families, the number of vehicle miles travelled on Californian roads has grown at twice the population rate, and the congestion of the highways has reached such a level that in the 1990s Californian policy-makers began to recognize the need for investment in mass urban transit systems. The writer Mike Davis claims that already by the 1970s more than one-third of the Los Angeles region's land surface had been colonized for freeways, parking, driveways and other roads.[4] Cars are California's biggest source of air pollution. Long a serious problem in urban regions, air pollution has also become a problem in agricultural areas.

The soil is also increasingly polluted. Agricultural production in the Central Valley is entirely dependent on irrigation and large areas of farmland are in danger of becoming unproductive because of salination. In the cities, a tremendous growth in the high technology industry, such as among the semiconductor and computer producers in Silicon Valley, has polluted water supplies with heavy metals. A shortage of treatment facilities means that untreated wastewater from both domestic and industrial sources is being discharged into the natural environment. This in turn raises the cost of treatment of drinking water.

All these problems highlight environmental and social limits to traditional patterns of growth. California has grown its population and economy almost as if resource constraints could be overcome indefinitely. But the population boom and the favoured forms of suburban development now pose real threats to water management and environmental quality. The supply of water and land cannot be extended to cope with new growth. This means that a new politics of consensual demand management needs to develop, allowing new forms of collective decision-making which will correct the problems arising from a mass of uncoordinated individual decisions to build and consume across the state by citizens, businesses and administrative units. The alternative to the further erosion of natural resources and amenities is more integrated planning of economic development and environmental management, and an acceptance of some constraints on consumption. This demands a new approach to governance and dialogue between citizens, business and the public sector.

Limits to Business-as-Usual in California

The weight of California's growth-related problems rests largely on local government, which is rapidly coming up against the limits to 'business-as-usual' in its governance. Cities, towns and counties are no longer able to provide the schools, transport infrastructure, sewage-treatment capacity and solid waste-disposal sites necessary to match the population boom. At the same time, the ability of local government to raise tax revenues is limited by fiscal constraints. In a desperate attempt to balance the books, many local governments are reported to be making land use and zoning decisions based primarily on the possibilities for revenue generation. The result of what in California is called the 'fiscalization' of land use has been:

> *... a growing imbalance between jobs and housing, a shortage of regional facilities to provide the services necessary for a complex society, and rising levels of air pollution, traffic congestion and social segregation. There is growing awareness among leaders throughout the state that these problems, if left unaddressed, threaten the very foundations of California as an economically powerful, democratic and socially cohesive society.*[5]

Additionally, the inequitable distribution of the benefits of growth limits the ability of lower income residents to 'purchase' public goods and services. For example, to get around taxation limitations, local governments increasingly rely on user fees for public services, which become less accessible to those on lower incomes. Similarly, fees on new homes pay for much of the new infrastructure supporting growth. But poorer residents are mostly priced out of the home ownership market, and are thus cut off from the infrastructure and services that are related to the new development.

The potential for innovative response to these problems within the existing institutional arrangements in California is limited. Local authorities do not have the statutory authority or the institutional capacity to address many of the problems which confront them. Against this background, in the late 1980s and early 1990s the mayors of the four largest cities in California convened 'growth management forums'. However, it became obvious that efforts at the city level could not unlock the solutions to what were clearly statewide problems. At the state level, the policy apparatus has been described as being 'near paralysis':

> *As diverse constituencies advocate on behalf of their own growth-related agendas before the Legislature and Governor's Office, they checkmate each other. Thus develops the political gridlock that so typifies growth management policy discussions at the state level.*[6]

Background papers prepared by the California Growth Management Consensus Project team identify some of the reasons for that paralysis: a 'state policy muddle', lack of clarity on issues, lack of leadership and strategic planning at the state level, dysfunctional planning, agencies working at cross-purposes, and the uncoordinated implementation of policies. The papers give the following examples:

- New infrastructure investments, such as motorways and sewer lines, or irrigation projects, which take no account of their tendency to induce growth and related problems such as urban sprawl, traffic congestion and pollution, or in the case of irrigation, salination.

- Major decisions taken, such as the location of a new university campus, without due regard for other policy considerations concerning transport, rural conservation and air quality.
- The failure of single sector agencies, such as Air Pollution Control Districts or Regional Transportation Planning Agencies, to come to grips with the multidimensional nature of growth management concerns.
- The failure of advisory regional coordination bodies, called Councils of Governments, to have any real impact on land use and development decisions.

These problems, common the world over, are the result of two broad issues addressed in this book: the failure to develop integrated, comprehensive policy in environmental management, as opposed to fragmented, sectoral vision and action; and the difficulty in achieving a balance between centralized, or strategic, decision-making and the decentralization of functions. In California and in the United States generally there is a strong bias towards local decision-making. In a sense, the US is overly decentralized, compared with, say, the UK which, although it began to devolve more power from national government in the late 1990s, remains an overcentralized system. In each case, new types of mediation and conflict resolution, and adequate and binding institutional arrangements, are required in order to deal with the complex issues of demand management which arise when the limits to traditional patterns of growth and consumption are reached.

The Need for Environmental Mediation

California, facing dramatic population growth and an increasing level of controversy over sprawl and water management, is on the threshold of critical decisions as to the limits of sustainable growth. These decisions, or the failure to make them, will affect the quality of life for decades to come. At the same time, differing perceptions of the benefits and costs of the surging population and economic growth have tended to polarize the society into 'pro' and 'anti' growth factions. The discussion is said to be framed 'almost exclusively by environmentalists on one side, developers and tax-hungry local officials on the other'.[7] By the early 1990s the power of polarized interest groups in the legislative process led to a situation in which elected representatives rarely made progress on environmental management. As is familiar in many democratic cultures, the interplay of entrenched interests creates a blockage in the legislature, and leads to stagnation in strategic policy-making. Specific measures are vetoed through the pressure of one group or another on legislators, and the inability to break the legislative impasse means that higher level policy-making is stymied.

To break out of this policy paralysis and meet the challenge of growth, the Legislature of the State of California, working with the Center for California Studies at the California State University at Sacramento, embarked on an innovative and fascinating project in growth management: one that pioneered a model for managing development through the fostering of consensus in an action network. The Growth Management Consensus Project (GMCP) sought to establish a basic consensus on a number of key issues and policies at the state level, and is a case study that is relevant to many of the exploding urban regions of the world. The team which devised and ran the GMCP later formed the California Center for Public Dispute Resolution, which has continued to innovate in deliberative processes for resolving policy 'gridlocks' in the state across a wide range of fields.

The general objective of the project was to:

> *... chart out the contours of those controversies in an attempt to initiate dialogue, find common ground, identify solutions that require state-level leadership, and develop policy agreements among the stakeholders that can provide a context for implementing solutions. The project's purpose is to explore the proper role of state government in managing growth.*[8]

Origins of the Growth Management Project

In an attempt to shed some light on a confused and politically contentious area of growth management, the policy research offices of the two houses of the California State Legislature decided to take joint action. These were the Senate Office of Research and the Assembly Office of Research. They approached the Center for California Studies at the California State University and asked for discussions to be convened that would explore, identify and articulate what they called 'bottom line' points of agreement or disagreement among the key stakeholders in the state on the growth management issue. The bottom line is the point where constructive discussion and formal mediation can get no further – where stakeholders agree, or agree to disagree. Where points of consensus could be reached by negotiation, they would be identified clearly in writing. This process would identify areas for action where widespread, all-party political support would be likely to emerge. Where agreement was impossible, the project's task would be to define precisely the points of contention and to try to generate alternative options for resolving these issues.

The project's objectives were summarized by the Center for California Studies:

1. To identify the four to five key growth management issues requiring state-level leadership.
2. To identify the key interests (needs or conditions) that participating constituencies consider to be an important part of a workable solution.
3. To develop specific and explicit agreements among the participating constituencies on the main policy issues to inform and guide state policy.
4. To identify the issues where there is disagreement and the basis for this; interests that need to be satisfied; and alternative settlement options that were discussed but not agreed.
5. To prepare a final report for the Legislature, the Governor, the press and the public.

Discussions would not attempt to suggest specific pieces of legislation, but rather provide an overall framework for the Legislature to address growth management questions. To meet the university's needs for autonomy and to reinforce the non-partisan nature of the effort, the project would be independent of government and the legislative process. The project was to inform the legislative process, but not to be influenced by it. Four components of the projects were identified:

1. Identification of the relevant stakeholders from major organizations with statewide constituencies and interests, their recruitment and orientation.
2. Preliminary identification of the key issues for discussion.
3. A series of statewide meetings of the participants selected by major stakeholder organizations with the specific purpose of identifying and negotiating policy agreements in writing to inform and guide policy; the discussions are professionally facilitated and/or mediated.
4. Publication and wide dissemination of the project's results.

At each stage in the process, substantive policy issues and procedural ground rules are identified, refined and clearly articulated so that the participants can focus their undivided attention on the central policy concerns.

Identifying Stakeholders

The first step in the development of the consensus-building work was to identify and recruit the key interest groups, or stakeholders. The university team selected organizations from four broad constituencies in California:

1. environmental protection lobbies;
2. local government;
3. business; and
4. land/infrastructure development interests.

The process of recruiting organizations from these constituencies was difficult and sensitive, as is the case whenever multisector partnerships or consultations are put together. The organizations in question needed careful persuasion that the initiative was worth supporting:

> *... most of these groups were cautious and protective, concerned that this endeavour could politically isolate them, weaken their strategic position vis-à-vis their legislative foes, or waste their organizational resources.*[9]

Once the agreement of the four constituencies had been secured concerning the principle of participation, the task was to select a group of stakeholder organizations that were representative of the broad constituencies, of the main sectors in the state economy and of the ethnic balance in California. Project workers collaborated with organizations from all the constituencies, which selected their official stakeholders who had to select a final list of bodies to be invited to participate. This group of invitees in itself represented a major success in consensus-building, since the final list had to be 'representative of California's body politic on the issue [of growth management], manageable in terms of the numbers of participants, and not so politically volatile as to cause an early collapse of the project'.[10]

The final list of 32 invited organizations comprised an assembly of interests of unprecedented breadth. Ethnic minority communities were formally represented in the debate on environmental management for the first time, and many of the invitees had never sat around the same negotiating table before. The list included representatives of local and regional governments, labour unions, agricultural interests, environmental lobbies, water suppliers, air-pollution control districts, Latino, African-American and Asian-Pacific organizations, regional voluntary sector initiatives, low and moderate income housing lobbies and business/development interests. All but the water suppliers chose to attend.

The process behind the interplay of stakeholders in mediation projects such as the Growth Management Consensus Project is elaborate, designed to build up confidence and minimize breakdowns in communication. Each stakeholder organization in turn selects a representative and an alternative. To keep the group manageable, only the representative takes part in the discussion. The alternative must attend all plenary sessions as an observer, and be prepared to take over in case of illness or other unforeseen event. This avoids the all-too-common situation where some participants always seem to be unavailable. All stakeholders taken together constitute a plenary, and all project ground rules, which are put out in writing, may be modified only by a full plenary session.

The list of stakeholder slots for statewide meetings (Table 12.1) gives a good idea of the range of organizations participating. Each organization is selected as a statewide constituency with a large membership. Representatives in turn are selected according to the following criteria:

- the ability to articulate and represent the interests of the stakeholder organization;
- a rapport and credibility with his or her own constituency;
- a grasp of, or willingness to learn about, the technical and policy issues involved;
- the ability to listen to, and openly discuss negotiation issues with, people holding diverse views; and
- a willingness to participate in cooperative problem-solving procedures to resolve differences.

The project team encouraged stakeholder organizations to appoint senior executives to the consensus-building exercise rather than to send lobbyists. Discussions were considered confidential within participating agencies, until such time as written agreements were entered into. This was to encourage participants to speak freely. Each stakeholder could also invite one or more staff to meetings as observers and advisers. One of these was designated formally as staff liaison officer to the project.

Identifying Issues

At the beginning of the project, it was decided that an issue-by-issue approach to the litany of problems (air pollution, shortage of affordable housing, etc) was not the most productive approach. In preparation for negotiation sessions, the project team, working with legislative staff, produced papers that identified a broad range of state-level policy issues and options. It was made clear that these background papers do not define issues for discussion at the meetings, but that they are information and discussion papers about major policy initiatives and implementation strategies. The latter were defined as governmental structure, institutional arrangements and the authority of agencies. In the space available here we can only summarize the main issues to arise in the GMCP discussion papers.

Table 12.1 *Stakeholders identified in the California Growth Management Consensus Project*

31 participants	*Selecting organizations*
1 city elected official	Leagure of California Cities
1 city planner	League/American Planning Association
2 county elected officials	County Supervisor Association of California
1 COG Representative	Californian Councils of Government
1 south coast air quality management district	South Coast Air Quality Management District
1 other air district	County Air Pollution Control Officers Association
1 local transportation agency	Selected by League/CSAC/Cal COG
1 residential developer	California Building Industry Association
1 non-residential developer	California Business Properties Association
1 community developer	California Housing Council
1 realtor	California Association of Realtors
1 broad-based business	California Chamber of Commerce
1 large employer	California Manufacturers Association
1 utility	Council for Environmental/Economic Balance
1 agriculture	California Farm Bureau
1 labor	California Labor Federation
5 environmentalists	Sierra Club California
	Green Belt Alliance
	Planning and Conservation League
	Natural Resources Defense Council
	Environmental Defense League
2 low-income affordable housing	Western Ctr. on Law and Poverty
	California Rural Legal Assistance
	California Homeless and Housing Coalition
5 community-based organizations	Mexican American Legal Defense and Education Federation
	Latino Issues Forum
	NAACP
	Coalition of Asian Pacific Americans
1 Bay Vision 2020	Bay Vision 2020
1 2000 Partnership	2000 Partnership

Source: Growth Management Consensus Project, California State University, Sacramento

Lack of certainty in conservation, development and social equity

The process of making land use decisions in California, as in many places, is based on unsystematic and varying criteria. In other words, there is a policy vacuum. In these circumstances, each individual major development tends to be fought out at a high level of political and legal confrontation.[11] No constituency, whether developers, low-cost housing advocates, environmentalists or government, has any assurance that their interests will be represented in decisions. The overall quality of decisions is bound to be poor in these circumstances, and the high cost of uncertainty disadvantages all parties and generates cynicism about the political process. The paper recommends that the state government should establish a more stable planning process that reconciles conflicts at the policy level rather than on a project-by-project basis.

The unsustainable development of urban sprawl

The paper recognizes that urban sprawl is the result of powerful market and cultural forces, but argues that it is an unsustainable land use pattern which assumes a limitless supply of land.[12] Sprawl increases demands on the infrastructure, wastes financial resources, wastes valuable agricultural land, results in air pollution and disadvantages existing urban areas, financially and socially. The paper recommends the creation of three types of public policy strategies:

1 Market strategies to reflect the ultimate scarcity of land and the true cost of infrastructure and resource use.
2 Regulatory strategies to establish common outcomes of planning and zoning statewide, and performance standards to ensure environmentally acceptable development.
3 Planning policies and strategies to direct the use of supporting market and regulatory strategies and to bring greater certainty to decisions about conservation and land use.

Public finance and growth management

This paper notes that land use decisions in California became increasingly influenced by public finance considerations in the 1980s – the process of 'fiscalization' mentioned above.[13] This is the result of three changes in policy. First, the disengagement of federal and state governments from funding public works projects, called 'fend-for-yourself federalism'. At the local level, the result has been that funds are shifted away from discretionary programmes, such as public works, and into areas of mandated expenditure.

Second, the 1980s was a period of major constraints on many areas of public expenditure in the US. The result in California, with its system of decision-by-referendum, has been voter-approved initiatives limiting local government revenues and expenditure (only one of which is the well-known proposition 13). These conditions force local officials to use development and land use decisions to raise the revenues necessary to support local government:

> *Under Proposition 13 property tax revenues only accrue to those communities where development occurs. The situs method [of tax allocation] profoundly influences land use decisions; local officials are enticed to approve only lucrative projects, regardless of the impacts on job/housing balance, air pollution, traffic congestion, sewer capacity, water supply, or open space.*[14]

The paper offered several strategies for making land use choices more fiscally neutral and for adjusting some property assessments to reflect key land use policies. The paper also reviewed ways of making more effective use of the the 'state's scarce public works dollars' through linking capital spending with land use policy.

Implementation: the role of the state

A final discussion paper looked at the direct and indirect influences the state has over land use, conservation and development, through its role in initiating projects (university campuses, water projects, etc), as a funder through public works grants, and as a regulator and source of legislation.

The Method of Consensus-Building

There were meetings of statewide stakeholders spread over 13 days in a 6-month period in 1991. These involved a substantial commitment from the participants. The main stakeholder representatives were expected to attend every day of the statewide meetings. The time devoted by participants to the process represented a very substantial investment. This level of commitment also was a departure from the usual pattern of token attendance by busy senior decision-makers at comparable events. The project provided one or more professional mediators to assist the stakeholders in their plenary discussions. The Project Director also assumed the role of facilitator or mediator as appropriate. Facilitators are expected to remain neutral and impartial towards the substance of the issues under discussion. Small working groups convened meetings between formal statewide stakeholder sessions in order to discuss particularly difficult issues and to carry out preliminary negotiations. The formal meetings were lengthy and could involve up to 70 participants working in a number of negotiating sessions. The structure of the discussions was shaped largely by the stakeholders themselves. Early in the process, the organizations with common interests formed 'caucuses' in order to discuss issues and to formulate their own consensus before moving into 'mixed interest' sessions. The negotiations thus moved from a 'caucus' phase to a 'cross-caucus' discussion, then to attempts at plenary, project-wide agreements. The stakeholders formed seven caucuses:

1 business and development;
2 local government;
3 environmental protection;
4 affordable housing;
5 air pollution district authorities;
6 social equity (ethnic minority groups);
7 civic organizations (NGO/voluntary sector groups).

Participants established a set of key issues for negotiation, concentrating on questions for statewide strategic thinking on environmental management, rather than on specific items for legislation:

- state policies in interrelated areas of environmental, economic and social policy;
- institutional reform to facilitate better strategic policy-making;
- fiscal restructuring to provide the resources needed for sustainable growth management.

The decision-making process within the project was based on consensus, not on majority voting. Consensus was defined as a settlement or solution with which all parties can agree. Consensus did not necessarily imply unanimity:

> *Some parties may strongly endorse a particular solution while others may accept it as a workable agreement. This instance still constitutes a consensus. Each party participates in the consensus without embracing each element of the agreement with the same fervor as the other parties, or necessarily having each of his or her constituency's interests satisfied to the fullest extent. However, given the combination of gains and trade-offs in the decision package, a consensus is the strongest agreement that the involved parties can make at this time given current circumstances and alternative options.*[15]

Tentative consensus agreements reached in plenary were referred to the stakeholders' constituent groups for discussion and final consultation, prior to final approval by the plenary and designation as a 'final agreement'. Once issues were agreed by consensus they could not be reopened; the process must move forward. Negotiations on many issues in this kind of process will not result in consensus. In that case, a stakeholder has a number of options:

1. to stand aside and allow the issue to be approved in the interest of overall progress;
2. to allow consensus but request a minority view to be included in the Final Report; or
3. to block the consensus, in which case the reasons for this would appear in the Final Report. (The Final Report was entirely subject to the approval of the plenary.)

Outcomes of the Project

The results of the GMCP were made public early in 1992 in a report that received wide coverage in the Californian media.[16] The project was never seen as a process likely to lead to overall consensus on a wide range of environmental management issues and, in the event, the areas of 100 per cent consensus were few. However, the process produced 'emerging agreements' – proposals enjoying majority support within each of the caucuses – on some 30 issues, although these do not necessarily reflect the official policy of the participants' organizations. On around 30 other issues, no consensus or 'emerging agreement' could be reached, but the negotiations clarified the nature and extent of the disagreements.

Consensus was achieved on the broad strategic objective of moving California towards 'compact, efficient and integrated urban development patterns' and away from the uncontrolled land use policies of recent decades. The issue of the design of urban areas was seen as fundamental in devising policies for growth management, and the consensus achieved represents a powerful boost for planning approaches based on higher density settlements with mixed housing and business, and the targeting of state infrastructure policy on 'compact urban form'[17] – there would be more use, for example, of apartment blocks and condominiums.

Emerging agreement rather than total consensus was arrived at on the broad outline of several areas of policy:

- The need to integrate the consideration of social and economic equity in policy-making on growth management: previous debates on economic development and environmental protection had unfolded with little attention being paid to the implications of policy for ethnic minority communities and low-income groups.
- The need for greater clarity in the designation of land for conservation or for development, although there was no consensus on the way in which an improved designation process should work or on the means of dealing with the impact of designations on land owners.
- 'Easy' consensus was reached on the need to reduce dependence on single-occupant vehicles, but not over measures to cut vehicle miles travelled – for example, through new transport pricing policies.
- Strong support was expressed for the improved coordination between state, regional and local performance standards in relation to growth management goals; the consistent implementation of planning policy across the different levels of government; the preservation of local control over planning when it is not inconsistent with policy at the state level; and the use of new procedures, including conflict resolution. Agreement did not emerge in relation to specific measures at the local level for deciding on development proposals; for institutional reform at the state level; and for mechanisms for the enforcement of local plans and performance standards.
- There was an emerging agreement on the necessity of more public expenditure to ensure the investments demanded by the policies and institutional reforms that most participants wished to see in pursuit of a new growth management strategy for California. Support for more public investment was made conditional upon increased cost-effectiveness in government spending and the careful matching of expenditures to priority areas.

Lessons from the GMCP

The emphasis in the California Growth Management Consensus Project on the far-reaching effects of traditional patterns of economic growth, and on the role of consensus in developing policy in environmental management, deserves close attention. In the 'hothouse' climate of a booming region, when there is money to be made from almost any kind of development in the short term, policy development for environmental protection and sustainable economic change becomes highly contentious. In this context, the achievement of consensus on long-term strategic goals is extremely difficult. In California, as in much of the democratic world, the power of special interest groups contributes substantially to blocking specific measures for sustainable environmental management and discouraging political debate and consensus on long-range strategy. Yet for sustainable development to be achieved, it must be possible to work out a vision and integrated policy framework for environmental management by government, and to achieve a consensus on the key goals for government, business and citizens.

Like our other case study initiatives, the California Growth Management Consensus Project represented a modest beginning in the process of building up a basic, multisector consensus on the issues in environmental management. The achievement of the venture may seem very low-key: a few areas of consensus, more of emerging agreement, and a number of areas in which no meeting of minds took place. However, the project needs to be judged as an initial attempt at building up a sense of potential partnership in strategic policy-making among a very wide range of interest groups whose mutual antagonisms were creating a severe blockage in the policy process. In the light of its experimental character and the widespread appreciation of its contribution to the debate on growth management in California, the project deserves to be seen as a success and a pioneering model for future exercises.

Much of the value of the project lay in the fact that so many of the stakeholders involved were required to deal face to face with adversaries and to acknowledge areas in which values and policies were held in common, and where consensus appeared to be possible. Even the acknowledgement of disagreements could be seen to be of some value, since they were now set against areas of perhaps unexpected agreement and potential progress, and the parties concerned had developed a far better appreciation of each other's point of view. As the project team noted in their report on the initiative, 'A grudging respect among even the unlikeliest of foes developed'.[18] The process succeeded in establishing new contacts and working relationships between groups, within and across constituencies; in this way, the project fostered the development of an action network based on shared problems, insights and the potential for collaborations.

The political neutrality of the university team as mediator and the existence of a set of ground rules that clearly specified the safeguards for the participants were crucial to the integration of so many diverse stakeholders into the process. This indicates that the mediation approach can achieve a level of participation and trust in negotiation that more traditional methods of resolving disputes cannot attain. The involvement of ethnic minority groups and low-income lobbies brought a new dimension to the debate on environmental management and raised all parties' awareness of the issue of social equity in relation to development in the state.

The lesson emerging from the initiative is that mediation techniques have the potential to play a highly valuable role in forging consensus and clarifying areas of dispute in environmental management. It is vital to emphasize that the approach is by no means a substitute for the legislative process or for traditional political debate and brokering. However, it does provide a method for bringing interests together and establishing mutual confidence in a way which complements established political procedures and gives them a more productive context in which to operate. With this experience behind them, the university team has since established a full service in mediation and conflict resolution to apply the method to other areas of policy in California in which many interests have reached an impasse and blocked the legislative process. There are economic benefits for the public sector here, and thus for taxpayers too. In the field of special education cases, the cost of a successful mediation is a mere 13 per cent of the cost of an administrative hearing in the courts. This factor is a powerful spin-off benefit to set alongside the process' achievements in bringing stakeholders in a policy conflict to discussion and agreement.

Clearly the Growth Management Consensus Project was a success in bringing antagonistic groups together, and in clarifying areas of agreement and dispute in environmental management. The process helped to inform the legislative debate and to begin to overcome 'policy paralysis'. The knowledge that so many special interests could agree on a number of key issues was a spur to elected representatives to introduce new measures in the state legislature. By early 1992, two legislators had included several of the project's emerging agreements into growth management bills.

The salutary lessons from the project are, however, as important as the positive ones from its pioneering design. The key problems for such initiatives lie in their novelty and lack of connection with the established policy-making process. The scale of the mobilization of people and the organizational resources needed for major consensus-building ventures are such that the participants may be inspired the first time around, but could lose motivation and face difficulties in justifying investment in subsequent rounds of deliberation unless clear results are achieved in the form of legislation or other action. If deliberative initiatives are perceived as 'talking networks' rather than action networks, their potential as catalysts for change is bound to be diminished.

In the case of the GMCP, the recommendations of the initiative could not be 'hooked up' to a clear policy-making process. It was up to legislators to take what action they could to build on the consensus achieved. The fundamental question is this: if conventional representative politics fails to deliver progress in policy-making in key areas, leading to gridlock and a decline in public confidence and trust in the process, what status should we confer on alternative participatory and deliberative techniques? If the stakeholders in a consensus project hand over their ideas to legislators who are a key part of the problem and nothing happens, it is possible that trust and confidence in the political process will worsen. Yet in a democracy, the decisions of elected representatives must take priority over deliberative stakeholders. How can the two be linked up? In California, the complex politics of growth management have ensured that the state enters the new century with many problems far from resolution, especially those of sprawl and lack of coordination between land use planning policies from county to county. In this context, the GMCP can be seen to have pioneered a process rather than to have acted as a catalyst for a radical change in policy. But later work by the Center for Public Dispute Resolution points to ways in which the consensus-building process can evolve and become more closely linked to real action.

The Sacramento Region Water Forum – Consensus-Building in Central California

In the introduction at the beginning of this chapter we reviewed the severe problems of water management facing California, and in particular the south of the state. In 1993 the experience of policy gridlock over water policy finally brought diverse interests in the Sacramento region to the point of seeking a mediated process to achieve some progress in decision-making and implementation to manage the American River watershed. Again, the Center for Public Dispute Resolution was brought in as a manager of a consensus-building process.

The interests involved comprised business and agricultural leaders, environmentalists, citizens' groups, water management authorities and local government representatives, and their aim was to reach agreement on a plan for sustainable water management across the Sacramento, Placer and El Dorado region of central California. As with the GMCP, the motivation was that of alarm and impatience at the stagnation of policy debate and decision-making through the normal channels. The group joined together as the Water Forum, having concluded that:

> *... unless we act now, the region is looking at a future with water shortages, environmental degradation, contamination, limits to economic prosperity, and stiff competition from other areas for our water.*[19]

The Water Forum made no bones about the need for a new approach to water governance. The stakeholders called for new collective solutions to overcome the failure of an excessively individualist approach to policy conflicts, leading to gridlock and high legal costs:

> *Here in the American River watershed, our biggest stumbling block to balanced water solutions is that individual groups – water purveyors, environmentalists, local governments, business groups, agriculturalists and citizen groups – have been independently pursuing their own water objectives – without much success. In many cases, competition among groups has generated protests, lawsuits and delay. Even though well over $10 million has been spent in the past decade pursuing single purpose solutions, there has been little to show for these fragmented efforts. Gridlock has hit our water solutions... In today's complex water environment there is no longer an option for 'I win–You lose' solutions. Either everyone with a stake in the outcome cooperates in the solution, or everyone faces stalemate.*[20]

The stakeholders in the process collectively spent over 18,000 hours identifying the problems, the causes of policy gridlock, commissioning expert studies on the technical issues, and drawing up a draft plan for long-term water resource management. The aims were to come up with a cooperative programme of action that would provide safe and reliable freshwater supplies to the region to 2030; and to preserve the fisheries, wildlife and amenity value of the Lower American River. In doing this the process had to tackle many thorny issues, such as sustainable amounts of water diversion from the Sacramento, American and Feather Rivers in the area; the resistance of a substantial minority of citizens to the retrofitting of water meters in existing properties; maintaining water supply reliability in drought years; and achieving equitable pricing policies in relation to low-income households.

The process was a long-term one: the consensus project began in the Sacramento area in 1993 and the final agreement was achieved in 1996. Agreements then needed approval in many cases from state and federal agencies, which were kept informed of the forum's deliberations and emerging ideas throughout the project to ensure that unworkable proposals were highlighted at an early stage and could be reconsidered. Like the GMCP, then, the forum represented a major investment of resources by the stakeholders.

The first step for the forum was to achieve consensus on its aims, and its mission statement and diagnosis of the problems it sought to deal with. This was done by early 1994 and was followed by a lengthy process of mutual education between the members of the coalition to identify positions, potential solutions and specific groups' key concerns. The GMCP methods described above were applied to build up mutual respect and trust and to help stakeholders 'leave their guns at the door', moving from a statement of their positions to a recognition of shared concerns and interests in solutions.

Having identified shared interests, the stakeholders made rapid progress in brainstorming about possible solutions to the water management crisis. By spring 1995, 65 draft principles were agreed as a framework within which the specific proposals could be developed. These were publicly aired, after which the great majority of stakeholder organizations agreed to proceed with detailed negotiations. Early in 1995 water suppliers and local agencies in adjacent counties to Sacramento joined the process. The deliberations involved taking proposals and brainstorming them iteratively in order to test assumptions and build up consensus as the suggested solutions were reframed and refined. In 1995 the full set of draft proposals was published, along with a detailed account of the process being used to reach consensus, and sent for consideration and comment by the stakeholders, and these were debated in public at a Water Summit conference in 1996. After this the final agreement was reviewed and agreed by stakeholders and the long-term process of implementation could begin. But the final stages of the process were time-consuming – only in 1999 was the agreement concluded by the stakeholders and a successor organization to oversee implementation established.

The Water Forum represented a further striking application of consensus-building in a political culture that is seemingly addicted to individualist recourse to litigation and fragmented local governance. Like the GMCP, it could hardly be expected to usher in a transformation of the policy-making culture. But it did succeed in bringing together diverse interests to tackle an issue that had clearly been poorly handled by the prevailing culture and institutions, opening up new routes to action, as well as better debate and public awareness of the trade-offs and the inescapability of change. It also succeeded in focusing attention on the long-term implications of current behaviour – something that representative democratic processes often fail to do as legislators are always constrained by the timescale of elections. This was encouraged by the lengthy processes of consultation and problem definition, and the commitment to frame proposals that could cope with change in the area over three decades or more.

Unlike the GMCP, the programme focused on a single, albeit highly complex, set of issues. Here, perhaps, is a pointer for future mediation programmes. Tackling a clearly defined problem or cluster of problems was the key to making more progress towards consensual solutions than was possible with the GMCP, which by comparison was less an action network than an invaluable mutual education and awareness-raising network.

The consensus-building, deliberative approach to environmental management problems and to intractable issues of public policy is becoming more popular. In part this reflects the dissatisfaction of Western electorates with the democratic process and the lack of confidence people say they have in their representatives, as expressed in many opinion polls across the OECD world in recent years. In part it reflects the problem that traditional political configurations and administrative arrangements in government have in dealing with 'cross-cutting' issues – novel problems that have no clear answer in ideological terms – for instance, those arising in relation to the ethics of bio-engineering and the classic questions of sustainable development, linking ecological limits to social equity, economic interests and technical innovation.

Above all, they are a way of opening up the debate on the long-term issues of demand management and limits to consumption as usual, such as managing the demand for health care or curbing the demand for car use in congested cities, which our 'short-termist' democratic systems fight shy of tackling for fear of losing key support from electors. New forms of 'deliberative democracy' are emerging: citizens' juries that offer deliberation by lay citizens on tough issues which policy-makers and politicians are wary of; deliberative polling exercises to develop public awareness of issues and to assess how opinion changes as more information and ideas are absorbed; 'visioning' conferences that focus citizens' attention on the future quality of life they would wish to see in the long term for their communities; 'round-table' forums that bring interests together on common problems where collective solutions have been elusive; and the ambitious mediation processes pioneered by the California Center for Public Dispute Resolution.

In the UK, there has been extensive experimentation with new processes.[21] There has been great interest in citizens' juries and consensus conferences, in which a jury of citizens learns about a complex issue over a number of days, is able to examine expert witnesses and (it is hoped) reaches a consensus on policy options. The low levels of public turnout for local elections have spurred efforts to devise innovations in the decision-making process in areas such as local land use planning, to give citizens more sense of 'ownership' and 'empowerment' in local democracy. There has also been the widespread use of community 'visioning' events, often as part of Local Agenda 21 initiatives at the district level of governance, to identify citizens' long-term concerns and priorities for their neighbourhoods. Citizens' juries and consensus conferences have been used to develop ideas about such complex issues as the rationing of public health care services, the disposal options for nuclear waste and the development of genetically modified foods.[22]

In Canada, the dissatisfaction with the existing 'business-as-usual' politics in resource management has led to the development of round-table processes at national, provincial and local levels. The round-tables are consensus-seeking mechanisms, bringing diverse interests together to debate key problems in moving towards sustainable development. Round-tables have focused on issues such as long-term visions for local and regional economies, on public health and quality of life, on waste-management problems, land use planning and water management. As in California and the UK, these processes have been popular with policy-makers and community stakeholders alike, opening up new forms of dialogue and building new trust and confidence, and above all creating a space for deliberation about long-term problems that have been ignored or mismanaged by the conventional processes for identifying policy issues and framing solutions.[23]

Conclusion

The Growth Management Consensus Project and the Water Forum explored issues that are of specific relevance to California, but the underlying process can be applied to many areas of environmental management in which the interplay of interest groups threatens to block all progress towards sustainable development and cohesive thinking on long-range policy options. This is an increasingly familiar situation in the advanced industrial countries, where powerful lobbies for economic development vie with the burgeoning environmental protection movement, and where the awareness of ecological and social limits to growth raises many problems of social equity. It will become more familiar in the newly industrializing world as environmental debates open up and unrestrained development comes into question. The great potential of techniques for mediation and consensus-building will surely be explored by many other states, north and south, as the conflicts of interest mount in the debate on sustainable development.

All of these initiatives are likely to be seen in increasing numbers across the OECD, and perhaps especially in the Anglo-American cultures which have traditionally operated on the basis of a confrontational winner-take-all approach to representative democracy and clashes between interests. But even the 'consensual' democracies of continental Europe, which are more concerned than the US and UK with procedures for bringing diverse stakeholders into national deliberation on economic policy and the environment (see The Netherlands case study in Chapter 13), are experiencing a decline in public trust in political business as usual. The affluent world is entering a period in which the limits to growth of public services, welfare spending, energy and water consumption, and car use are becoming apparent. Growth in the quality of life needs to be based on a reorientation of demand as well as innovations in supply, and this poses huge problems to conventional political processes that are geared to satisfying demand and treating natural resources as indefinitely expandable. New deliberative processes offer a way to refashion politics in the light of sustainable development pressures, discontent with political processes, and the need to win consensus on the complex and controversial issues of demand management. The benefits of deliberative processes are clear:

- They offer a way to involve dissatisfied citizens in the process of framing problems and seeking solutions.
- They offer a new route to public education about the responsibilities as well as the rights of citizens, and to better awareness of trade-offs and compromises in balancing short-term economic demands with long-term environmental and social sustainability.
- They open up citizens and politicians to a process of 'revelation' – learning experiences which can help to change values and transform perspectives on problems.[24]
- They represent an attempt to create a 'highest common denominator' in disputes between different communities and commercial or policy interests, overcoming the fragmentation and scepticism towards transcultural values and empathy between cultures which haunt modern multicultural societies. The German philosopher Jürgen Habermas has sought to theorize ways in which different groups can transcend difference and resolve issues on a universal basis, not through a new common ideology but through a shared process of unconstrained dialogue in an 'ideal speech situation'.[25] The tools of mediation and consensus-building used in processes such as the GMCP can be seen as techniques to make a much-needed reality of this ideal.
- They allow politicians to spread and share responsibility – and political 'heat' – for decisions on potentially unpopular measures.
- They offer a route towards action based on consensus rather than the policy gridlocks that are characteristic of the representative systems faced with complex and politically combustible issues of demand management such as restraining car use.

But the development of action networks using deliberative consensus-building techniques into mature systems in widespread use as a complement to representative democracy depends on wider systemic change. The great problem for the techniques currently in use is that they are not yet coherently connected to mainstream policy-making and implementation. Big issues arise:

- How binding should the decisions of consensus-based initiatives be on representative legislators who have avoided the issues for years, but whose legitimacy is founded on votes rather than on stakeholder voices?
- How should consensus-building systems be used to help to implement action as well as make recommendations? If they are not used, there is a risk of reluctance among stakeholders to get involved in mere 'talk networks'. If they are used, how should they be integrated with mainstream mechanisms for delivering change?
- Which issues are most suitable for deliberative processes and which are labour-intensive and costly, and thus cannot be used for every area of policy?
- Which issues are most suitable for lay citizens' juries, and which for large-scale consensus conferences and processes of mediation such as the Water Forum? What mechanisms of wider accountability to the public are required for deliberative processes?
- How can citizens be motivated to take part on a large scale, and what fiscal incentives or other measures can be used to encourage participation by individuals and organizations facing many other demands on their time?

Answering these questions means tackling complex issues about the relationship between what Tim O'Riordan calls 'informal governance' and the formal mechanisms of representative democracy.[26] The future of action networks for consensus-building depends in part on the continued experimentation and learning across sectors, policy domains and countries. But it also depends on reform in the processes of civic education, so that more citizens are aware of their responsibilities to engage in debate on sustainable development and other key issues for the future; and on changing the roles of local politicians and executive officers, as O'Riordan suggests, so that they have greater scope for sharing power and become more comfortable with partnerships with action networks, rather than seeing them as a parallel political culture uneasily connected to their own. This means that we need new forms of civic education not only for citizens but also for policy professionals, to equip them for a future in which mediation techniques, consensus-building systems and action networks are a familiar part of the policy-making landscape, drawn on for the resolution of intractable disputes and policy gridlocks.[27] The lesson is that the move towards sustainable development and the evolution of the action-network approach depend as much on innovation in the culture of democracy as on innovations in knowledge, technology and policy-making.[28]

13

The Netherlands National Environmental Policy Plan

> *Sustainable development should be regarded as a positive force. It has the potential to be the focus of a coherent, comprehensive agenda for the environment, as in the Netherlands. It is inherently long-term and all-encompassing, and so lends itself to establishing a social consensus, in a way which individual environmental problems cannot do because they can be 'solved' and so disappear from popular consciousness.*
>
> David Wallace[1]

> *Government should create the right conditions for target groups to fully exercise their own responsibility. As environmental policy evolves, the scope for the target groups to take their own responsibility will grow. This will allow government to limit its role in the longer term to the establishment of the framework and facilitation.*
>
> (from The Netherlands' National Environmental Policy Plan)

The Netherlands' National Environmental Policy Plan (NEPP), first published in 1989 and now in its third version, is perhaps the most striking example to date of long-range policy-making in environmental management at the national level. Inspired by the vision of sustainable development set out in the Brundtland Report, the successive NEPPs have analysed the challenges posed by environmental problems and set out policy goals for a three- to four-year cycle, working towards sustainable development objectives set for the years 2010 and 2020. The plans are intended to cut across administrative boundaries, economic sectors and levels of activity from the local to the international. Special attention is paid in NEPP3 to the integration of Dutch national policy with international policy efforts in recognition of the fact that:

> *... sustainable development can only be achieved in the Netherlands in an international context, recognising that the Netherlands forms part of a larger whole in social, economic and ecological terms.*[2]

The NEPP is of considerable interest as a model of public policy development in environmental management for a densely populated and heavily polluted industrial country. The process through which the plan is assembled and revised is also significant: the NEPP is the product of a process of action networking and consensus-building at the level of the nation state. It is not the work of any one political party or ideological movement, but rather the output of a process that shares the features of the network approach at the local and regional levels described in our other case studies in Chapter 11.

The NEPP is an example of good practice in policy integration and networking that is relevant to all industrialized countries, but it arises from distinctive features of Dutch political culture. As such, it must be understood against the background of Dutch traditions in physical planning and of the ecological pressures at work in The Netherlands.

The Netherlands Policy Background

Land use and industrial development

The Netherlands is a small country in which the taming and management of nature have been fundamental to the very existence of the nation. The land is almost entirely given over to intensive agriculture, industry, transport infrastructure and housing. Large areas are also, famously, the creation of environmental management: the coastal landscape has been for centuries the site of prodigious efforts at land reclamation and dike construction. The urban environment is no less striking, dominated by an enormous network of cities, including Amsterdam and Rotterdam, known as the 'Randstad' (urban ring). These pleasant and well-managed urban areas have some of Europe's highest population densities. The industrial base of The Netherlands is centred on intensive agriculture: the country is the world's third largest exporter of farm produce.

The institutional framework: planning and consensus-building

The need to control and reshape landscape, and the pressures on the country from population growth and industrialization have greatly influenced the institutional framework of policy-making in The Netherlands. The two decades after World War II saw the gradual development of a system of national physical planning as a means of managing industrialization and post-war reconstruction, and housing a growing population. The national system set out broad lines of development for land use, and more detailed planning was carried out by provincial and local government.[3]

The evolution of the planning system has reflected changes in ideas about the role of the state in economic development and social policy over recent years. The 'top-down' strategic planning approach of the immediate post-war period was modified by the 1970s, with greater efforts to consult the public, and elaborate systems for the coordination of land use plans between different sectors.[4] By the late 1980s, when the Fourth Physical Planning Report was produced, the ascendancy of free market liberalism in the West was reflected in the further downplaying of detailed strategic planning. Emphasis shifted to a facilitating role for central government and partnership between the public and private sectors, and the stimulation of voluntary action by companies and individuals:

> *The more rational approach to strategic planning, based on systems thinking, was set aside in favour of an approach characterised by negotiations with important agents of economic change; an orientation towards market forces; much more open-ended and broad policies combined with safeguards for the implementation of specific elements considered to be 'of*

> *national importance'; and a strong revival of design in spreading the message of planning.*[5]

The tendency to seek consensus is rooted in two other aspects of Dutch political culture. First, what Jamison et al call 'the segmentation of Dutch society into various religious or political blocs, which is known in Dutch as "Verzuiling"'.[6] This term means 'pillarization', indicating the existence of distinct social 'pillars' on which the political order rests. This concept stems from the religious divisions that characterized Dutch society from the formation of the nation state in the late 16th century, and which were modified by the process of early industrialization. The political process was dominated by bargaining between the élites representing each religious or ideological 'pillar':

> *Since the beginning of the twentieth century, these elites developed a policy of accommodation and pacification. This political attitude forms the basis of Dutch corporatism. Because each pillar represented a minority in Dutch society, none could make decisions without support from the others.*[7]

Second, this historical tendency towards consensus-building is reinforced by the nature of Dutch political institutions. The electoral system is based on proportional representation, and coalition government is the norm, with a consequent reliance for political stability on consensus-building and detailed negotiations between different political parties. The system is also characterized by considerable autonomy for ministers, who are directly responsible to Parliament rather than to the Prime Minister. As Faludi notes, in this context 'formulation of planning policy becomes a matter of interdepartmental negotiations. The advantage is that many planning documents are signed by all ministers responsible for policies set out therein'.[8] NEPP3, for example, is signed by six ministers, including the expected ministers for planning and the environment, agriculture and transport, but also by influential ministers for economic affairs, finance and foreign affairs.

Finally, the emphasis on consensus is also promoted by the highly decentralized nature of the Dutch state. There are 12 regional or provincial authorities and nearly 800 local authorities or municipalities. Although central government has a considerable amount of control over finances, the provinces and municipalities play a significant role in land use planning and the implementation of environmental management laws, such as in the field of water management. The decentralized structure leads to 'interlocking of policy-making processes on all three levels of public administration' and to considerable 'bargaining and negotiation' between them over their respective roles in implementing policy.[9]

Pollution and the rise of environmental politics

The geography of The Netherlands and its success in developing intensive and highly productive agricultural industries have been the source of the country's severe environmental problems. It receives large loads of airborne pollution from neighbouring countries as well as from domestic sources. The Rhine and Meuse Rivers drain large industrial areas of North Western Europe and collect many pollutants from factories and agricultural run-off; the build-up of pollutants in the rivers damages drinking water and ultimately affects the North Sea. River pollution has also led to the accumulation of toxic chemicals in the Rhine estuary, making costly special storage necessary for sediments dredged from the delta area.[10]

The Netherlands also suffers from the effects of acid rain, to which domestic and neighbouring countries' sulphur dioxide and nitrogen oxide emissions contribute.[11] The first version of the NEPP envisaged an action plan on acid rain to the year 2000 that would protect only 20 per cent of the country's forests; given the scale of the problem, it was thought that only such a modest interim target was feasible.[12] In fact, reasonable progress in reduction in the four main contributors to acidification had been made by 1995. Substantial additional reductions, to around half of 1990 levels, are proposed for 2010. The situation is not positive, however, with regard to greenhouse gases, with a rising emission of all greenhouse gases between 1985 and 1995, including a 23 per cent increase for CO_2. In part this reflects a growth in road traffic, especially for freight, which is expected to continue to bedevil greenhouse gas targets. NEPP3, written just before the Kyoto Conference on greenhouse gas control, devotes many pages to considering how transport emissions can be controlled without damaging the economy.

Other serious environmental problems for the Dutch include the loss of habitats for wildlife; the subsequent loss of animal and plant species; and the disposal of household and industrial waste. An overriding problem is the pollution generated by the country's spectacularly productive agricultural sector. Two issues dominate this area of policy: the 'manure mountain' produced by the enormous livestock population (over 100 million animals), and the pollution of soils, ground water and surface water by the pesticides and fertilizers hitherto essential to the great gains in agricultural productivity.[13] The quantity of manure produced by livestock is such that ammonia pollution of soils and air is a serious problem; the tonnage of manure greatly exceeds that which can be spread safely on farmland and recycled as fertilizer pellets. Moreover, the leaching of pesticides and chemical fertilizers from fields into ground water and surface water is facilitated by the network of canals and drainage ditches.

Public awareness of these problems has risen steadily since the initial stirring of environmental consciousness in the 1960s. This has been paralleled by the development of a strong and diverse environmentalist movement, and by the gradual recognition of environmental policy as a priority by political parties.[14] The 1970s saw the establishment of a Ministry of Health and Environmental Hygiene, and the passage of numerous laws to control pollution. In the 1980s there was a strong surge in support of determined action on environmental crises as awareness grew of the effects of acid rain, the problem of ozone depletion and the potential threat of global warming and sea-level rises that would be disastrous for The Netherlands. This phase culminated in the publication in 1988 of a report entitled *Concern for Tomorrow* by the National Institute of Public Health and Environmental Hygiene, which publicized the scale of the emerging global environmental problems. This report produced a new sense of urgency among the public and political organizations, and was an important input to the first National Environmental Policy Plan.[15]

Origins of the NEPP: Towards an Integrated Environmental Policy

The environmental policy measures adopted in The Netherlands during the 1970s were typically 'media-oriented', with different pieces of legislation focusing on specific problems, such as air pollution and soil contamination, all requiring different consultation and licensing procedures.[16] The rise of awareness of international pollution problems and of linkages between different problems led to a gradual shift in the 1980s towards integrated policy-making in environmental management. The move was also prompted by the need to deal with inconsistency in standard-setting and policy-making between government departments.[17]

The first concrete steps towards integrated environmental management in The Netherlands came in 1984, with a workshop held in collaboration with the United States Environmental Protection Agency (EPA) in order to develop ideas for a new policy framework. The outcome was the preparation of a four-year programme for environmental policy across government departments, presented to Parliament at the end of 1984. Between 1984 and 1989 several more multiyear programmes were published. Meanwhile, an earlier administrative reorganization had contributed to the process of integration: the General Directorate for the Environment was detached from the Health and Environment Ministry in 1982 and was merged with the Ministry for Housing and Physical Planning. The new department allowed for the improved integration of environmental management into 'mainstream' policy-making, and the new Minister brought environmental issues directly to Cabinet discussion for the first time – previously they had been the province of junior ministers.[18]

The key elements of the emerging integrated approach to environmental management were:

- the identification of environmental themes as the basis for policy;
- the identification of target groups as partners in policy development and implementation; and
- the process of internal integration in environmental policy-making.[19]

The focus on environmental 'themes' (such as acidification or waste disposal) replaces the traditional compartmentalization of problems on the basis of 'media' (air, soil, ground water, sea water). Instead, policy-makers are to work with cross-cutting concepts that allow all aspects of an ecological issue to be addressed. The basis for this approach is the recognition, now widespread, that a problem such as acidification is not simply a threat to air quality, but also to soil and water quality. Policy must therefore acknowledge the linkages between environmental media and analyse pollution flows 'in the round'.[20]

Target groups

The need to identify, work with and drive towards consensus within target groups (or action networks) is fundamental to the Dutch approach. The list of target groups, expanded in NEPP3, now includes consumers, farmers and the agricultural industry, manufacturers, refineries, energy companies, retailers, members of the transport sector, the construction industry, waste processing companies and 'actors in the water cycle'. The cooperation of all these constituencies is seen as essential to the successful implementation of policies for the reduction of emissions and for the achievement of sustainable development. As NEPP3 notes:

> *The successes of environmental policy are related to the willingness and receptiveness on the part of industry (the target groups), regional and local government (also internationally), interest groups and the general public to shoulder their responsibilities and to contribute to resolving environmental problems.*

The identification of these groups is carried out on the basis of the various themes: problems and proposed solutions are elaborated and the sectors of the economy involved in implementing the changes become apparent. The target groups are seen as negotiating partners who are involved in the development of environmental management plans, rather than as obstacles or groups on which policies are to be imposed. The approach is underpinned in central government by the appointment of group managers within the Ministry of Housing, Physical Planning and the Environment who have a dual mediating role as 'translators', conveying the demands of environmental management to the target groups and relaying the concerns of the target groups back to central government.[21]

Finally, the process of internal integration concerns the continuing attempt to ensure that environmental management becomes a priority throughout government and industry, and among all citizens, rather than being seen as an 'external' issue to be dealt with only by the relevant ministries and specialist agencies. The 'internalization' strategy involves:

- new lines of communication on environmental issues between public agencies and the three levels of government;
- the elimination or reduction of emissions at source rather than at the end of production processes;
- an emphasis on developing 'closed loop' management of industrial processes to minimize waste and emissions and reduce energy needs; and
- public education programmes to raise awareness of companies' and individuals' responsibility for cleaning up the environment – as the NEPP says, 'The private citizen is a de facto manager of the environment'.[22]

Integration is a long-term process, as yet only partially complete even within the Dutch government.[23] The process was accompanied by new funds for research programmes and for environmental organizations to develop public education schemes.[24]

In summary, the approach developed in the mid-1980s involved the systematic analysis of pollution flows in order to develop the environmental 'themes' and set priorities and standards for the reduction of emissions, and then seeking to work with target groups and convince them of the need to take greater responsibility for managing their impact on the environment. The focus on partnership with the target groups, the formation of linkages between the different sectors and tiers of government, and the use of mediating target group managers all indicate the initial development of an action-network approach at the national level.

Although the strategy of internalization and working with target groups was seen as successful by the ministry, there was a recognition that a more comprehensive approach to planning for long-range environmental management was needed. De Jongh sets out the main reasons for the decision to embark on the development of what became the NEPP:

- the need for a long-term strategy based on environmental forecasts;
- the need to give a clear indication to Dutch industry of exactly what environmental policy would imply for its operations over the long term;
- the need to secure the wider cooperation of other government departments with interests in aspects of environmental policy, such as the Ministries of Agriculture, Transport and Economic Affairs;
- the desire to enhance public understanding of the demands of environmental management, and in particular to emphasize the positive features of new policies rather than to associate environmental planning always with the analysis of ecological threats; and
- the impetus to sustainable development provided by the publication of the Brundtland Report.[25, 26]

As noted, the NEPP process was sparked by the report *Concern for Tomorrow* which made a considerable public impact. It concluded that a sustainable development path could only be reached by The Netherlands if emission and waste reductions of 70–90 per cent were made by 2010. The required reductions could only be made either through cutting the volume of emission sources or through 'structural changes' in production and consumption patterns – for example, by reducing car journeys and implementing new forms of industrial process to minimize waste.

According to de Jongh, the message of the report had a profound effect on the officials working on the NEPP:

> *the positive element we were looking for was found: to avoid volume-reduction measures, structural changes in consumption and production patterns should be prepared. But such changes can be a challenge, not only for policy makers, but also for developers and technology innovators.*[27]

In line with the requirements of sustainable development, the NEPP was to set out a vision of opportunities for economic development and improved quality of life, as well as to analyse problems.

Key Elements of the NEPP

The first NEPP was submitted to Parliament in May 1989 by the Minister of Housing, Physical Planning and Environment on behalf of his department and of the Ministries of Economic Affairs, Agriculture and Fisheries, and Transport and Public Works. It was a substantial report, with the stark title in its English translation of *To Choose or to Lose*.

Multiple timescales for action and policy development

The preface of the first NEPP stated that the NEPP 'contains the strategy for environmental policy in the medium term directed at the attainment of sustainable development. The long term objectives in this NEPP are intended to provide tentative direction to this process'. All NEPPs make use of distinct timescales, setting out short-term policy proposals, medium-term strategic goals, and long-term aspirations to 2010 and now 2020.

The intention is to produce a new NEPP every four to five years. This approach recognizes 'lag times' in the understanding of environmental problems and the development and implementation of policies, a factor that requires policy-makers to think in terms of decades for the solution of many problems. This integration of a short-, medium- and long-term analysis and objectives is an important aspect of the NEPP. The Government supports this integration with funding for research and public participation to consider issues within the timescales.

Review of successive NEPPs indicates both the value of iteration in the review of the achievement of goals and objectives, and that not all objectives are realized within the timeframe suggested. Greenhouse gas emissions, control of road traffic levels and agricultural wastes are problematic. The NEPPs are forthright about their failures to achieve targets, generally proposing a redoubling of effort with new policy implements.

Multilevel analysis of environmental issues

Successive NEPPs, drawing on *Concern for Tomorrow*, identify five spatial scales on which ecological problems develop and must be tackled:

1. Local: the built environment, soil contamination, local air pollution, noise pollution.
2. Regional: waste disposal, eutrophication, landscape degradation, changes in soil balance.
3. Fluvial: eutrophication, deforestation, soil erosion, pollution of ground waters, rivers and coasts, accumulations of chemicals in soils.
4. Continental: acidification, photochemical airborne pollution.
5. Global: enhanced greenhouse effect, depletion of the ozone layer, pollution of oceans, loss of biodiversity.

Figure 9.2 showed this. The levels, of course, are not independent – problems overlap and increasingly they are occurring at higher levels as industrialization spreads around the planet. At the fluvial level the policies of any one country must typically be accompanied by concerted action by its neighbours; at the continental and global levels joint action by many countries is essential.

Emphasis on integrated policy

The NEPP identifies the main problems facing environmental policy-makers: the externalization or 'roll-off' of problems by producers and consumers, the displacement of environmental problems by inadequate coordination of abatement measures, excessive energy and resource consumption, the neglect of recycling and waste minimization, and the failure to manage feedback of damaging emissions and waste streams. The solution proposed is to focus on integrated pollution control. This is to be achieved not only through application of the best available technology, the well-known 'polluter pays' principle and the principle of reducing pollution at source rather than at the 'end of the pipe', but also through structural measures and the process of internalization.

Structural measures include the radical modification of production processes to cut energy consumption, enhance quality of output, and close product life-cycles as far as possible by recycling and minimizing waste. 'Internalization', mentioned above, involves the encouragement of producers and consumers to take on responsibilities in environmental management and the development of environmental policy as an integral part of the business of all government bodies and industrial organizations. The NEPP speaks of 'external integration' as the process through which environmental considerations enter the main stream of policy-making in all government agencies. Links are also to be developed between central and local government in order to improve the enforcement of environmental regulations.

Policy development based on environmental themes

The NEPP identifies a number of themes for the elaboration of specific policies:

- climate change and the need for the reduction of greenhouse gas emissions, especially of carbon dioxide and CFCs;
- acidification;
- eutrophication;
- the diffusion of harmful chemicals;
- waste management;
- disturbance (noise pollution, odour and local air pollution);
- dehydration of soils relating to the need to reduce household and industrial consumption of water to restore a balance between consumption and ground water and surface water sources);
- 'squandering' (relating to the need to prevent waste by developing measures that will indicate the value of environmental resources and reward behaviour that is compatible with sustainable development; policies include the development of environmental accounts, product life-cycle analyses and corporate environmental programmes).

Cooperation with target groups

A further continuation from the programmes of the mid-1980s is the involvement of target groups for consultation and cooperation in the development and implementation of policies flowing from the various themes listed above. The NEPP makes it clear that the long-term goals will only be reached if there is extensive and intensive collaboration between government and the different interests represented by the target groups.[28] Target groups specified in NEPP3 were listed above.

For each group the NEPP indicates the implications of the measures required under each of the environmental themes, the contributions required of organizations and individuals over the next three- to four-year policy period and longer term, and what role the government expects to play in helping to meet the objectives. The measures envisaged place major demands on the target groups and imply a move towards radical change in the existing patterns of consumption and production. A sample of the main policies set out in NEPP3, for various target groups, are given below to give the flavour of the NEPP.

The public at large
The use of education and information to secure the modification of citizens' behaviour, reinforced by increasing the inclusion of environmental costs in the prices of goods and services, and life-cycle analysis of products, services and household activities to highlight environmental costs and benefits.

Agriculture
The control of manure and ammonia; a 70 per cent reduction in ammonia emissions from 1980 levels by the year 2005 had been proposed in NEPP1 but NEPP3 notes that this may not be feasible and proposes instead additional technological control to reduce the impacts of emissions; a 50 per cent cut in the use of pesticides, with the elimination of harmful substances, now requires the accelerated introduction of more stringent standards; the introduction of nutrient accounting systems for all livestock farms to be achieved by the year 2000 and for all arable farms and horticultural businesses by 2002.

Refineries
NEPP1 proposed sulphur dioxide emissions to be cut by 80 per cent by 2000, with a 60 per cent achievement by 1996; complete life-cycle analyses for new products and the replacement of harmful chemicals are now proposed; the replacement of the need for liquid fuels in refineries to be achieved by 2010.

Retail sector
The adoption of an environmentally friendly stocking policy; the use of environmental management systems and sustainable building principles for shopping areas.

Construction sector
The continued implementation of the Declaration of Environmental Targets for Construction and Housing 1995, signed by representatives of the construction industry; a sustainable building action plan to be continued; NEPP3 reports good progress on most targets, including, by 1996, that the total volume of building and demolition waste offered for end processing (landfill or incineration) had been reduced by 80 per cent since 1985, and the target for 90 per cent recycling for building and demolition waste had been achieved in 1996.

Transport
The main elements of policy are to limit the growth of road transport; to improve alternatives to road transport for passengers and freight, including public transport, car-pooling, cycling, rail and inland waterways; exhaust pollution from passenger cars to be cut by 75 per cent from 1980 levels by 2010; a 10 per cent reduction in carbon dioxide emissions from vehicles by 2010; the use of cleaner technologies for vehicles; structural measures such as increased taxes on fuel, road-pricing and new public transport investment to reduce single-passenger car journeys in favour of public transport; structural measures in land use planning to reduce the need for travel.

Consumers
Domestic energy consumption in 2000 to be at 1985 levels; limited growth only in passenger miles per car, and more use of transport modes other than private cars; by 2000, all used batteries, small chemical waste, tin, glass and paper to be collected separately for disposal and recycling.

Environmental protection sector
Waste-processing companies to ensure the improvement of the disposal system to minimize landfill site dumping, to incinerate more waste and use the heat generated,

and to promote recycling; drinking water suppliers to develop a role as all-round 'environmental firms', signalling problems and improving public information; environmental technology producers to be given a key role in developing clean integrated processes and helping to introduce the major policy changes in industry.

Environmental organizations, trade unions, voluntary bodies
Special emphasis is laid on the 'indispensable' role of environmental interest groups and campaigners in highlighting environmental problems, raising public awareness, disseminating information and promoting environmental consciousness among all the various target groups.

Evolution of the NEPP, 1989–99

The NEPP represents an ambitious statement of governmental intent and presents a remarkable challenge to the different sectors of Dutch society and economy. However, in the short time since the original publication it has become both more ambitious in its goals and more realistic about its achievements, as described below.

NEPP1 to NEPP Plus

Ironically, given its origins in a process of consensus-building and mediation, NEPP1 attracted most attention abroad for apparently causing the fall of the then Dutch coalition government in 1989 – the first time a government had been toppled by an environmental issue, according to many commentators. In fact, the political developments in question demonstrate the remarkable level of consensus across party lines achieved in the evolution of the NEPP.[29] The coalition government that prepared the NEPP1 comprised the centrist conservative Christian Democrats and the centre-right free market Liberals. The radical nature of the NEPP is all the more striking for being the product of an administration that is essentially fiscally conservative and pro-business in character. The coalition was an uneasy one, and in the debates over the NEPP the Liberals seized on a single proposal – the abolition of tax relief for commuters – and opposed it to the point of bringing down the coalition.

The notion that this was a case of an environmental issue bringing down an administration was a simplistic view of the situation. The dispute over the commuter tax relief was more a pretext for the eruption of long-standing rivalries within the Liberal Party and the coalition; the NEPP was by contrast a matter of near-total cross-party consensus, and in the subsequent elections all the main parties have continued to support the NEPP, albeit with variations.[30]

The outcome of the 1989 elections was the formation of a new coalition, this time between Christian Democrats and the social democratic Labour Party. The change of government led to changes in the NEPP. A revised version appeared in June 1990, known as the National Environmental Policy Plan Plus (NEPP Plus). Continued consensus on environmental issues ensured continuity of policy on sustainable development. NEPP Plus differed from its precursor mainly in calling for the more rapid implementation of many policies and for more ambitious targets for the reduction of emissions over the 1990–94 period and to the end of the century.

NEPP Plus retained all the key features of the original NEPP in relation to environmental themes, and the principle of dialogue and partnership with target groups. Overall it represented a strengthening of many of NEPP1's proposals. However, NEPP Plus came in for considerable criticism from environmental campaigners and politicians on the grounds that the revision of the first plan had meant a year lost in the struggle against pollution;[31] and the revision of the NEPP unleashed controversy over the timescale for stabilizing carbon dioxide emissions,[32] still the most problematic area of policy at NEPP3. With NEPP Plus, consensus on the need to move towards radical 'structural change' in the pursuit of sustainable development seems to have become firmly established not only among political parties, but also among industry and the general public. This is the result in part of substantial efforts to develop consultative networks and mediating systems to assist in policy formation.

NEPP2

NEPP2, called *Environment: Today's Touchstone*, which was published and debated in 1994, began almost immediately by focusing on the achievements of NEPP1 targets by various target groups. It notes a strong relationship between progress and the nature of various target groups. The greatest progress had been made by target groups:

> *... relatively easy to reach, for example, some sections of industry, the refineries, the construction industry and agriculture. In these cases it proved possible to convert the NEPP1 objectives rapidly into clear targets, adequate technology and facilities. Clear agreements could be made with them regarding implementation, thus reducing uncertainty about the role of the authorities in the long term.*

Conversely less progress was achieved by target groups labelled 'more difficult to reach', such as consumers and small and medium-sized enterprises (SMEs). The main reasons suggested are that these groups have so little insight into the environmental pollution they cause that it is not feasible to enter into formal agreements with them and that they are not subject to licensing procedures. For these groups, it was now recognized that broader economic and social instruments, such as consumer education and green taxes, would be required. The difficulty of reaching a greater number of smaller polluters – say, car drivers or small firms – compared with dealing with large point sources of pollution – say, power stations or large factories – is one which continues to dog efforts at pollution control and sustainable development.

Three main themes are identified to drive forward NEPP2:

1 strengthened implementation of objectives;
2 additional measures where objectives will not be met with existing policy; and
3 sustainable production and consumption.

In discussion of the latter, NEPP2 introduces the concept of 'environmental space' or 'ecospace' which is defined as:

> *the capacity of the environment, including all its natural resources and ecosystems, to provide for man's needs. This capacity is circumscribed by physical limits in relation to provision of raw materials and energy and by the resilience and regenerative capacity of the environment.*

It proposes that the idea of environmental space in all its aspects should be explored further in a broad social and international forum. The evolution of this forum is decribed in Chapter 14 under discussion of the action network, the Sustainable Europe Campaign.

During the period covered by NEPP2, a dialogue was initiated between the public and the government about the development of an environmental policy. Detailed discussions were held in many towns within the framework of Agenda 21 initiatives, about the objectives of sustainable development.

NEPP3

NEPP3, already discussed in terms of its target groups, builds on the environmental space approach which complements environmental management initiatives with tangible objectives to work towards the achievement of sustainable production and consumption. It proposes the concept of 'decoupling', which is defined as improved living standards (economic growth), while at the same time reducing environmental pressure. A distinction is made between relative and absolute decoupling:

- Relative decoupling occurs when environmental pressures continue to rise, albeit at a slower rate than the growth of economic activity – that is, environmental pressures grow more slowly than the economy as a whole.
- Absolute decoupling occurs when environmental pressure reduces while economic growth increases – that is, economic growth with falling levels of environmental pressure.

NEPP3 notes that while the term 'decoupling' may be new, the idea has always been present within the NEPP philosophy:

> *In other words, the NEPP1 and the NEPP2 also aimed to achieve decoupling. The objectives were set, de facto, to reduce emissions per unit of GNP by a factor of between 2 and 10.*

NEPP3 records achievement of absolute decoupling in a number of areas, such as construction, relative decoupling in others, as in some aspects of agriculture, and the failure to achieve either in aspects of transport and for CO_2 emissions. The concept of decoupling is now firmly embedded in the NEPP:

> *Based on the lessons learned from the policy of NEPP1 and NEPP2, the government concludes that in important respects environmental policy is entering a new phase, that of 'environmental management'. After a period in which the focus was on clean-up (tackling existing environmental problems) the main job is now shifting more towards ensuring an absolute decoupling of economic growth and environmental pressure and the sustainable use of natural resources.*

Like the previous NEPPs, NEPP3 goes on to list the achievement, or lack of it, on 14 key indicators within the original environmental themes (climate change, acidification, eutrophication, etc) and then focuses the main body of attention on target groups (now called 'The Actors' and 'Partner Organizations'). The point is brought home repeatedly that it is not the government alone that is responsible, but government establishing the systematic framework for sustainable development and then working with specified actors, such as business, regional and municipal government, the refinery sector, and so on. For each of the actors, their contribution to environmental degradation is estimated prior to policy proposals, to bring home the specific extent of their responsibility. The agriculture target group, for example, is held to be responsible for 12 per cent of the country's contribution to climate change, 35 per cent of acidification, 64 per cent of water eutrophication by nitrates, 38 per cent of water eutrophication by phosphates, 60 per cent of ground water depletion and 2 per cent of emissions of volutile organic compounds (VOCs).

NEPP3 then goes to record developments in interactions between actors, using reporting headings that are indicative of the nature of the process, such as dialogue, good cooperation, regulation, price incentive, provincial barriers dismantled, changes in behaviour, and a continuous improvement plan. The description of the process is followed by a discussion of the policy plan for the next four-year period. NEPP3 concludes with its focus on the requirements for European and international efforts at environmental control.

The NEPP Process: Networking, Mediation and Iteration

The acceptance of environmental issues as a high priority for policy by the main political parties in The Netherlands was accompanied by a new openness towards the environmental movement, at least in comparison with most other countries. Increasingly, government agencies have sought the opinions and advice of lobby groups, and the latter gained in professionalism and scientific expertise.[33] A new pragmatism developed among many environmentalists about collaboration with the political and industrial establishment in pursuit of environmental goals and, despite tensions among some campaigning groups over the danger of being coopted into the mainstream political culture, the lines of communication between environmental organizations, business and public agencies remain more open and productive in The Netherlands than elsewhere.

The spirit of consensus-building and cooperation between different interest groups has been basic to the development of the NEPP. De Jongh notes that:

> *The process of preparation of the NEPP was founded on the idea of 'open planning': industry and interest-groups should be involved in the process of preparation and should not be confronted with final decisions.*[34]

The development of the NEPP has taken place in an atmosphere of heightened concern over ecological threats and intense public discussion:

> *A substantial part of the Dutch population was confronted repeatedly with drafts of the NEPP. The battles among the various ministries – tiresome enough even when fought behind closed doors – came out into the open*

> *... environmental policy was one of the major topics being handled by the media.*[35]

The participative process of compiling the original NEPP, which sowed the seeds for all subsequent NEPPs, is described by de Jongh.[36] This began with a workshop involving representatives of industry, local and provincial authorities, environmental organizations and the Ministry of Housing, Physical Planning and Environment. This meeting established an agenda of the key issues and concepts for policy development. This was followed by the creation of an interministerial group to elaborate the plan. In addition, a high-level steering group was established, along with 'circles' of officials focusing on specific themes and concepts. Theme coordinators were required to provide reports on the quality standards to be aimed for in the long term and the measures needed to achieve them. Consultations went on meanwhile with industry and environmental organizations.

Subsequently, a wider round of consultation assessed the response of representatives of the target groups and of local and provincial government to the analysis and proposed targets. This set of discussions was managed by professional facilitators and sought to answer the question, 'What can your target group contribute to meeting the challenge of the required reductions in emissions?' De Jongh notes that the outcome of the consultation was important not so much for its effect on the content of the NEPP draft as for its effect on the target groups: minds were concentrated on the urgency of the demands of environmental management, and a major contribution was made to 'agenda-building' within the target groups as well as within government.

The process thus involved the creation of action networks designed to produce improvements in subsequent drafts of the plan, changes to the internal agendas of government agencies and target groups, and qualitative responses to the concepts and objectives set out in the plan. The process was relatively open – de Jongh stresses the importance of strategic planning for environmental management to bring in ideas from interest groups, and in particular of people not 'heavily involved in day-to-day policy making on one aspect' of environmental policy. This process of active consultation with target groups has been repeated in subsequent NEPPs, thus establishing a long-term process that is intended to foster continual improvement of the plan in the light of environmental, technological and economic change.

Successive NEPPs have strengthened the networks linking public agencies, governmental tiers and target groups. NEPP2 emphasized agreements between central government and other formal networks such as the Interprovincial Consultation Forum, the Association of Netherlands Municipalities and the Association of Water Boards. NEPP3 proposes that NGOs and interest groups should be supported to play an increasing role in mobilizing public opinion in support of objectives.

The implementation of the NEPP also involves an extensive process of networking and mediation in relation to the technical means of implementation and the timimg of specific measures. This involves both formal environmental assessment and policy and planning mechanisms, and linkage with networks within target groups to promote implementation. Environmental assessments and screening for all significant developments are required by the Environmental Management Act, and there are numerous appropriate policy frameworks, from national and regional land use plans to more specific initiatives, such as the Multi-Year Crop Protection Plan or the Policy Plan for Domestic and Industrial Water Supply. On the organizational side, efforts are supported by networks within target groups, such as the Association of Energy Producers. Both strategic policy and networking initiatives reflect strong support within Dutch political culture for national and local planning, and subsidiary and formal participative mechanisms that lead towards social consensus – yet within the context of one of Europe's most successful economies and prosperous countries.

The NEPPs also make considerable use where feasible of voluntary agreements or 'covenants' which substitute for government regulation where they can achieve effective results. NEPP3 continues this. An example of the approach is the use of covenants between government and industrial sectors on energy saving: agreements can be signed after joint investigation of the scope for investments in pursuit of the NEPP's objectives, and this arrangement allows a 'customized' setting of targets for industries instead of top-down regulation.[37]

Conclusion

In the NEPP process, there are many areas of achievement, but also some major areas of lack of progress, particularly in the achievement of major reductions in carbon dioxide emissions, road traffic levels, agricultural wastes and domestic energy consumption. In the words of the Director of Vereniging Milieudefensie (Friends of the Earth Netherlands):

> *... the good thing about NEPP is the system, the worrying thing is the content.*[38]

Despite these limitations, there is no doubt that the NEPP represents one of the most thorough and systematic approaches to environmental management and national sustainable development. Its achievements include:

- A complete, systematic national overview of the major challenges to national sustainable development in the short, medium and long term.
- A genuinely participative system, led but not dominated by central government, in which all major stakeholders from local government, business and voluntary organizations play a valid role in a national network which drives towards consensus.
- A thematic approach, such as for acidification, combined with a focus on target groups that are in a position to influence the outcomes of development processes.
- A rigorous, legally mandated monitoring system which involves the annual review of target achievements and a four-yearly broad review by a national environmental planning agency funded by, but independent of, government.
- Regular updated NEPPs which represent the consensual, political response to the monitoring process.

What are the constraints on this process and why are achievements in some areas not matched by achievements in all areas? At the most basic level, any process based on consensus is more likely to be an incremental rather than a radical process, making the most achievement in areas which are less politically sensitive and in which there are fewer, larger stakeholders in the target groups. In areas which are politically sensitive, which involve many, many stakeholders – such as car users – or which involve large expenditures by target groups – the consensual solution may tend to the 'too little, too late'.[39]

This is why the NEPP has proved successful in tackling industrial pollution from large point sources, but has been unable, as yet, to secure environmental improvements for air pollution which outstrip the growth of car use itself. As in California's debate on growth management, it is relatively easy to agree on the need to reduce car dependence, but specific measures produce marked nervousness on the part of the politicians about putting these into practice. The importance of the car in consumer culture poses major challenges to consensus-building on environmental policy in The Netherlands, as it does in virtually all other industrial countries.

Of course, The Netherlands is hardly alone in facing these problems where the solution lies in structural change beyond the parameters of change set by the status quo. Current discussions towards NEPP4 are focusing on radical, but market-led, solutions such as national, or EU-wide, ecotaxes and tradable permits for carbon dioxide emissions. It is still, however, an open question of how The Netherlands, or any other country, will control road traffic growth, but increasingly stringent 'road pricing' must be the 'stick' part of the 'carrot and the stick solution'. The solution may also lie in government-led setting of radical targets which 'redefine the rules' of capitalist endeavour, but within the bounds of dampening the basic workings of the market. This is the approach of 'environmental or eco-space' pioneered in The Netherlands within the NEPP process, and now finding its way into NEPP3. The environmental space approach is discussed under the Sustainable Europe Campaign in the next chapter.

There are other, less fundamental constraints on the NEPP. First, there is the need for still better integration and coordination within government. The Dutch system has generated a large number of plans and memoranda since the mid-1980s, and it is important that coherent linkages should be established between long-range plans in areas such as land use and nature conservation in NEPP3 and its successors.

Second, and crucially, the NEPP will be put under pressure if the Dutch government's commitment to sustainable development is not matched by its partners in the European Union and the OECD. NEPP3 recognized this explicitly. Many of the problems analysed in the plan are continental in nature and require coordinated policies in several countries. If The Netherlands' European partners do not join in a cohesive and ambitious strategy for moving towards sustainable development, and if the plan's stringent environmental measures prove to be disadvantageous for Dutch industry, especially for agricultural producers, there will be a clamour for a slow-down in the implementation of the plan or a modification of its targets. Finally, new policies at the European Community level, economic and technical change, and new information on ecological problems from the local to the global level all need to be factored into account as medium- and long-term goals are set.

Despite these constraints, there is clearly a deep-seated consensus within the political system and industry on the inescapability of radical policies for managing sustainable development. Moreover, it is unlikely that The Netherlands' European Community partners will be able to argue for long against the adoption of similar objectives, given the build-up of common problems of emission reduction, energy inefficiency and waste disposal.

Although it would be foolish to imagine that the NEPP approach could be exported without problems to countries with different traditions and institutional frameworks, it surely has lessons for other countries. These relate to the implications for environmental management to recognize the linkages between environmental problems that are traditionally dealt with on a fragmented basis, and between different levels of a geographical scale. The Dutch approach recognizes that multilevel, long-lasting and multidimensional environmental problems demand long-range, holistic solutions. This implies the need to reorganize policy responses on the basis of environmental themes, the analysis of which in turn indicates the need to involve key target groups in designing and implementing solutions. The target groups must also be mobilized over the long term in an iterative process of mediation, consultation and evaluation, in order to keep up with dynamic changes in the environment.

Finally, the need for long-term continuity demands a top-level commitment to the overall goals of sustainable environmental management among political parties and target groups, even if opinions differ widely on specific measures. The Dutch experience provides a model of action networking and mediation at the level of the nation state that cannot be ignored by other democracies facing the demands that the imperative of sustainable development will place on their institutions and capacity for consensus-building for the year 2000 and beyond.

14

Action Networks for Sustainable Development Around the World

In Mumbai, a new arrangement has been entered into with Citibank. The agreement will release financing for a major slum rehabilitation project in Dharavi – reputedly Asia's largest slum. The scheme has been developed in partnership with a wide range of agencies. SPARC, the National Slum Dwellers Federation, participating co-operatives, Citibank, the Slum Rehabilitation Authority… It's a good example of the kind of partnerships that Homeless International is likely to become involved in – linking private sector and community resources with a public sector policy framework that we are increasingly seeking to influence with our partners. The challenge remains the same – helping communities to develop the capacity and access the resources they need to create solutions that make sense to them.

Ruth McLeod[1]

During the 1990s the usefulness of the action-network approach to sustainable development became readily apparent. More organizations are building formal and informal networks: to foster a larger political constituency around positive social and environmental progress; to link South and North, top-down and bottom-up, and to join government, community and business in a common, driven, action-oriented agenda; and to marshal the broad-based expertise and experience that is necessary to tackle the complex, dynamic challenges of sustainable development.

These reflect the fact that at the same time as current and historic overconsumption of the world's resources, including the atmosphere itself, by the richest one-fifth of the world's population continues, another one-fifth of the world's population lacks the basic needs for a decent life or even survival. In terms of overconsumption, the 20 per cent of the world's population in the rich countries have generated almost three-quarters of carbon dioxide emissions, a primary cause of global climate change. Many other global resources, from metals to timber, are consumed in about the same proportion, with about one-fifth of the world's population consuming four-fifths of the resources annually, many of which are non-renewable.

On a global basis, overconsumption by some countries means a reduced resource base for the future development of others. The gap between the world's rich and poor is constantly widening, with the richest one-fifth now having 85 per cent of the world's income. In 2010 there will still be more than 800 million chronically undernourished people in the developing world while, perversely, obesity causing ill-health is becoming endemic in the wealthy countries. Poverty is both a cause and effect of environmental degradation. It is indicated by the lack of basic needs, such as food, water, shelter and access to primary education, health services and energy resources.[2]

The challenge, of course, is not just to reduce consumption by the rich and to help low-income communities meet their just basic needs, but equally importantly, to work towards a sophisticated, equitable and ecologically sound development framework which generates prosperity without environmental degradation or social marginalization. This must encompass the diverse economic and social needs of South and North in a common framework: for development, amelioration of poverty and concern for the health of societies. Otherwise the poorest countries will remain poor, while newly industrializing countries will follow the OECD countries' unsustainable industrial path.

There is a strong organizational dimension to these challenges, for we will only move towards sustainability by organizing ourselves, locally, nationally and internationally, to do so. It is also clear that no government, or any level of government, acting on its own can address these challenges. Partnership between government, business and citizens' organizations is the key, as are creative, enabling linkages between top-down and bottom-up initiatives. New means of forging partnerships in action networks to accomplish and monitor practical development tasks is a new and positive way of working. This implies a rethink of organizational relationships within the market framework, a basic level of embedded human rights, and the empowerment of local communities and regions within the national structure.

This chapter describes some recent advances in action networks as a point of inspiration for everyone concerned with organizing themselves around these issues. Each of the networks described here is addressing, in its sphere of influence, these fundamental challenges.

The case studies address the issues of:

- the needs of the homeless and for community housing around the world (Homeless International);
- household and community action on sustainable consumption (the Global Action Programme);
- African energy policy (African Energy Policy Research Network); and
- national sustainability policies which reflect global environmental limits and the need for equity between nations (the Sustainable Europe Campaign).

Many other cases might have been selected, but those above both demonstrate the principles of action networking set out in earlier chapters and represent long-standing – that is, in operation five years or more – diverse networks of which the authors have first hand knowledge. In particular, as we noted in the introduction to Part V, all demonstrate positive linkage between local, national and international initiative – a kind of 'subsidiarity' which recognizes that sustainable development can only come about from a chain of organization, and action from the household and community level to the international level, including the key levels in between of the city, bioregion and the nation. In each case, it should be noted that the all-too-brief description here does not do justice to the full range of activities and linkages represented by these networks. The purpose is as much inspiration as description and the interested reader will follow up on the references given.

Homeless International

One of the most pressing challenges to sustainability is to assist disadvantaged households and communities around the world to provide for themselves access to decent, adequate shelter. This is the mission of Homeless International, which is a worldwide action network coordinated by a UK registered charity of the same name. Its purposes are twofold:

- To provide financial and technical support to NGOs working to assist housing-related community projects and the development of self-help housing for low-income families in Asia, Africa, Latin America, the Caribbean and Europe.
- To support the exchange of ideas, experience and information on homelessness and self-help housing between these communities and also with professionals, communities and young people in the UK.

The housing projects are all initiated, developed and managed by local community groups. All the projects 'focus on long term, sustainable solutions actively involving women'.[3]

The primary activity of Homeless International in 1997–98 was to support, in partnership, 30 organizations in 13 countries. Other activities include support for community-based savings and loans to organizations through a Homeless International Guarantee Fund; a website to share ideas on housing and homelessness; and fund-raising to support development. Some examples of the work of Homeless International are given below.

South Africa

Many of the partnership projects of Homeless International are within the context of large, community-based networks in their home country, making the organization a good example of the strength of working within what we have termed 'a network of networks'.

An example is Homeless International's support for the South Africa Homeless People's Federation (SAHPF), itself a network of over 1100 savings and credit collectives for self-help housing development involving 50,000 households in 200 communities throughout the country.[4] SAHPF's work is based on the recognition that, in a country where there are over 15 million people squatting in shacks, only 92,000 new housing units had been constructed by the new government by 1997. This suggests that the existing policy approach of government subsidy of the commercial property developers is not responding quickly enough to the magnitude of the problem and subsidies are not therefore being applied efficiently. The SAHPF have sought to develop an alternative housing delivery mechanism to the current arrangement, based on direct access by households to subsidy through savings and credit collectives to fund self-build housing initiatives.

Bolivia

In Bolivia, Homeless International is working with Pro-Habitat, a Bolivian housing NGO. One of Pro-Habitat's primary activities is to curtail the spread of Chagas' disease, a potentially fatal illness which has infected 1.3 million Bolivians, with another 2.1 million low-income residents at risk of the disease because of the poor quality of their housing conditions. The disease is spread by beetles which live in the walls of mud houses above 1000 metres in altitude. The best way to deal with the disease is to improve houses – by a modest subsidy combined with communities renovating their own houses using local materials. By the year 2000, 9000 houses will have been improved, benefiting 45,000 people.

Pro-Habitat complements housing improvements with training programmes for children and adults – for example, training women on the management of small business loans, and training teachers to educate children about how to avoid Chagas' disease. The Director of Pro-Habitat describes the training initiative:

> *We have trained communities that have learned how to manage themselves. They learn a trade – many of these people become masons then work for other communities. We have over 250 teachers trained. We're going to have the capitalization of the fund, a validated credit model and we have obtained regional coverage. And what's most important is that local government is becoming increasingly interested in what we are doing and want to replicate this in other areas of the country.*[5]

The Guarantee Fund

Homeless International's Guarantee Fund provides a good example of the value of innovative linkages within an international action network. The Guarantee Fund links top-down and bottom-up, South and North, and the private and voluntary sector, to enhance the financing available for development.[6]

For example, in Bolivia, Pro-Habitat, in partnership with Homeless International, is developing a new model of funding for local housing investment based on the Guarantee Fund. Homeless International provides a financial loan guarantee and Pro-Habitat uses that guarantee to leverage funds from a Bolivian mutual lending institution to increase the available amounts of housing investment for local communities. In India, because of the fund's guarantee, Citibank has agreed to provide financing to the Rajiv Indira Housing Co-operative.

Other linkages in the Homeless International network

As in the IDEA projects described in Chapter 11, one of the great strengths of an international action network can be in fostering South to South and South to North linkages, thus breaking away from the frequent but misguided assumption that expertise must flow from North to South because donor agencies are organized that way. On the contrary, action networks and the NGO sector in many less well-off countries are highly developed, and sharing ideas can be extremely productive.[7]

Within Homeless International's network, for example, the Indian Slum Dwellers Federation has been helping Cambodians, living on some of the most marginal land around Phnom Penh, to organize a network of over 50 settlements into the Solidarity for the Urban Poor Federation. The Director of Homeless International describes the situation:

> *A loan fund for financing the planned housing has been established with help from federations of slum dwellers in India, South Africa and Thailand. However, the fund currently only has US$175,000 at its disposal which is clearly inadequate to provide the financing needed for the many thousands of people who need the chance to build decent housing. While Homeless International has provided a grant so that a secretariat can be established to manage the existing fund we also want to contribute additional capital to the fund itself so that at least three communities can construct new housing over the next 18 months.*[8]

Other Homeless International linkages exist between networks in Pakistan, Chile, Peru. Finally, Homeless International also encourages South–North linkage. For example, Southern partners are assisting development work by the UK's National Homeless Alliance through Groundswell, which promotes self-help, user-led initiatives with people who are homeless, landless or socially excluded. At a recent Groundswell Forum, Homeless International helped to arrange visits from community leaders from South Africa and India to grass-roots projects across Britain.[9]

GAP International – the Global Action Plan

Global Action Plan (GAP), an international non-profit organization, was founded in 1989 to develop a structured support network for people wishing to modify consciously their way of life towards a more sustainable lifestyle. This support network is called the EcoTeam programme. The presumption of EcoTeam is that the modest amounts of information and incentives currently on offer for encouraging more sustainable household consumption patterns are not sufficient to the task.

Sustainable consumption is particularly challenging in the face of the global expansion of television and print advertising that encourage excessive consumption and social pressure on individual households to conform to the levels of consumption that exist in the wider community, or what Americans call 'keeping up with the Joneses'.[10] This means that any significant shift to sustainable consumption needs to be the result of a mutually supportive effort by many households in a neighbourhood, rather than just a few attempting to 'go it alone'.

Instead of households being faced with the dilemma of how to go it alone towards sustainable consumption, EcoTeams offer a programme of structured support. EcoTeams are a group of households, usually neighbours, who meet over a period of months and, with the help of a trained 'coach' and the national GAP network, examine and modify their consumption patterns.

The primary role of GAP in each country is to help to build these local community campaign groups. The groups achieve synergy and diffusion effects by recruiting and supporting a significant proportion of the population (a target of 5–10 per cent of all households in the neighbourhood) through the EcoTeam programme. The enabling role of the international network, combined with the strength of the community level initiative has also encouraged lead governments and the United Nations Development Programme (UNDP) to endorse the programme.

Organization of GAP

GAP has focused the majority of its action to date on the most affluent countries of the North, because the high levels of consumption in those countries is the main driving force behind most global environmental problems.

GAP sees itself as 'actively experimenting with new organizational forms ... at one point we came up with the metaphor of a spider plant putting out runners and establishing new clones'.[11] The nearest business equivalent might be franchising. Each national organization is autonomous in traditional terms, but committed to the purpose of adapting and disseminating GAP programmes, and contributing to further development in collaboration with other countries. One of the functions of GAP's international coordination is to ensure 'quality control' of the local initiatives, both for effectiveness and to maintain the reputation of GAP.

GAP's international coordinating body is registered as a charitable foundation in the US, but with its Secretariat located in Stockholm. The Secretariat services a Board and a Council and had start-up funding from the Dutch Government. The reasoning of the Dutch Government is that GAP represents a new type of policy instrument for national and local governments, which they have termed an 'empowerment instrument'.

All GAP country organizations are represented on the GAP Council, the highest decision-making body in the network. The Council meets twice a year to exchange experience and innovation. The Council has no legal status, but its decisions are said to 'carry a lot of weight' with the board of GAP International.

The primary purpose of the Secretariat is to:

- facilitate learning between countries, and transfer experience to other countries;
- introduce new countries and significantly reduce the time they need to become operational;
- support development and diffusion of additional GAP programmes;
- represent household consumption issues in the international fora;
- implement Board and Council decisions; and
- foster quality assurance of GAP programmes and research on household consumption.

Organizationally, in keeping with the characteristics of an action network, GAP sees a close relationship between similar sets of 'inner-oriented' and 'outer-oriented' activities at local, national and international levels. Inner-oriented tasks include getting the programmes going, enrolling EcoTeams, ensuring programme quality and monitoring and reporting results. Outer-oriented tasks include building alliances with other networks and organizations, fund-raising, strategy development in the light of the external organizational environment, management, coordination and dissemination of learning good practice throughout the network.

The GAP household programme

GAP household programmes are active in many countries, including Denmark, Finland, The Netherlands, Sweden, Switzerland, the UK, US, Belgium, Germany, Norway, Canada and others. Recent additions include Russia, Poland, Costa Rica, Kenya, Korea and Japan. Local and international financing for an initial three years must be secured before EcoTeams can be initiated.

A new project is initiated with the recruitment of a project leader and their subsequent recruitment of a project group, followed by what is termed 'first level training' comprising the principles of the Global Action Plan philosophy and empowerment, EcoTeam coach training and the programme adaptation process. This training is conducted on site in the host country, making use of GAP International staff and visiting participants from other GAP country teams. Using a locally adapted and translated version of the *Household EcoTeam Workbook*, EcoTeams address the following questions:

- How do we begin the process of the rethinking consumption patterns?
- What actions are important and how should priorities be established?
- How are the principles of GAP International best adapted to suit local requirements?
- How do we set about implementing change?
- Will this really make a difference?

The initiation period lasts around nine months, to be followed by 'second level training'. This comprises a review of the project; follow-up coach training; training for coach trainers ('teaching the teachers') and an introduction to the programme for schoolchildren in the 11- to 13-year group – Journey for the Planet. At this stage the new workbook is finalized using a professional author and layout/design personnel.

Over a number of months Team members focus on different aspects of consumption – waste, water, energy, transport, shopping, and so on. Regular flows of information from other EcoTeams in this and other countries are fed into discussions. During the life of the local GAP programme, GAP International provides support, guidance and information as required.

The GAP community campaign

GAP places considerable store in monitoring its activities, both to evaluate the effectiveness of its programmes in terms of the tangible outputs of sustainability and to marshal the lessons of good practice to improve effectiveness and inspire good practice elsewhere. In terms of tangible output, early research indicated that the combined EcoTeams in 12 countries had resulted in the following resource savings: a 40 per cent reduction in household waste sent for disposal, 12 per cent less energy consumption, 15 per cent less water consumption and an 18 per cent fall in household carbon dioxide emissions.

A more detailed longitudinal analysis of the Dutch EcoTeams after two years of participation has been carried out for the Dutch Ministry of the Environment.[12] The purpose of the study was to compare the original extent of behavioural change resulting in the saving of resources by households with their record of achievement two years hence (the durability of behavioural change), and to compare this with the behaviour of people who did not participate in an EcoTeam. Compared to other types of interventions, the research team found that changes initiated within EcoTeams continued and in some cases improved after participation ended. Factors which continued to have a beneficial effect included the reduction of household waste, lowered use of natural gas, electricity and water, and the use of environmentally friendly transport.

During 1997 and 1998, GAP International focused on three aspects of network improvement. First, GAP International has supported its local network at a global level by international lobbying on sustainable consumption issues, particularly of the UNDP, the UNEP and the UN Commission for Sustainable Development (CSD). Second, the international network has been expanded to take in new countries including Poland, Denmark and Russia.

GAP St Petersburg, for example, is a project funded by the EU's Tacis Environmental Awareness programme and the Swedish International Development Agency. The first stage of the project involved recruiting a project director with an established effective network in order to initiate a project group. First-level training was given in St Petersburg by GAP International with the assistance of GAP Finland. This training included the principles behind GAP and the EcoTeam approach; the principles of empowerment; coach training and the workbook adaption process. The Swedish workbook was used as a model. The project group formed three EcoTeams. For mutual support these run in parallel with the Swedish programme.

A second element in the St Petersburg project is an EcoHouse. The prototype is a large collective dwelling house of over 200 apartments where, through the human development aspect of the EcoTeam programme, a sustainable collective housing unit has been created. This will include such elements as rooftop gardening, recycling and composting. The project will also create job opportunities in the production of vegetables and flowers, in producing soil from household and the rooftop garden waste for compost, and in recycling.

Finally, GAP's third area of initiative, building on the experience of the original 14 countries, is to refine its training and support package for new countries. This has resulted in a dramatic fall in the amount of time taken to get EcoTeams up and running in new countries and to provide the necessary national support – from around one to four years. The continuous learning-by-doing which characterizes GAP is a basic aspect of most action networks.

African Energy Policy Research Network

Sub-Saharan Africa is caught on the horns of an energy dilemma. On the one hand it is endowed with abundant energy resources, including the potential of renewable energy in a wealth of biomass, solar and wind resources, and substantial unexploited hydro, geothermal and fossil fuel reserves.[13] On the other hand, the region's deep-seated economic problems have made it difficult to develop a modern energy sector. Insecure energy supplies and population growth put stresses on the traditional energy sector and low-income communities, now overly reliant on fuel wood, giving rise to serious environmental problems, such as deforestation, which in turn retard development. Access to electricity in many African countries is restricted to less than 10 per cent of the population and even this supply is not reliable. For national economies, and despite low world oil market prices, fossil fuel imports routinely account for up to a third of the export earnings of many sub-Saharan African countries.

Against this background, the African Energy Policy Research Network (AFREPEN) was launched in 1989 to link energy, environment and sustainable development issues for sub-Saharan Africa, with support from the Norwegian and Swedish development agencies. AFREPEN's overall goal is described by its Director:

> *Although the limited progress registered by the energy sector in Africa can appear discouraging, the low level of development in the modern energy sector paradoxically presents a window of opportunity. Once Africa has attained a threshold level of energy supply and consumption, it could eschew the traditional fossil fuel dependent, capital intensive, environmentally harmful and inequitable modernization path of industrialized countries and develop an ecologically and socially sound path to sustainable development of its energy sector.*[14]

The purpose of AFREPEN is to assist energy policy makers to realize this vision and to fashion strategies which strengthen the short and long term performance and sustainability of the region's energy sector.

The AFREPEN network

AFREPEN represents a collective regional response to the energy challenges of sub-Saharan Africa. It links academic and agency researchers, NGO representatives and energy policy-makers in 18 countries in eastern and southern Africa, with less formal collaborative arrangements with 5 additional countries in West Africa. The key objective of the network is to strengthen local research, policy analysis and institutional capacity in the service of energy policy-making and planning. To this end it prepares analyses on diverse topics such institutional reform in the power sector, performance of public sector energy institutions and the mitigation of Southern Africa's greenhouse gas emissions.[15]

AFREPEN has launched 18 major regional research projects in thematic areas such as renewable energy technologies, biomass, coal and gasification, electricity and institutional development and planning. The research is carried out by multicountry teams. Issues are discussed in a regular series of regional workshops and in a large number of publications.

For national level analysis and to encourage policy implementation, AFREPEN establishes country teams which, wherever possible, are led by 'paired' researchers, one from a university, independent institute or NGO, and the other from the government sector responsible for implementing policy. As of 1996, there were six country teams for Botswana, Kenya, Lesotho, Sudan, Uganda and Zimbabwe, with more paired teams proposed for the developing programme. Karekezi comments:

> *The pairing approach effectively ensures that the policy maker who is the primary target of the findings of the AFREPEN research programme is involved in all aspects of the Network... The advantage of pairing has been demonstrated in terms of the quality of research findings (compared with research projects carried out by researchers only or by policy makers only) and linking of research work to active and ongoing policy formulation and implementation.*[16]

A related benefit realized by AFREPEN has been the contribution of the research programme to institutional development by the establishment of independent energy policy centres by most of the country teams. Country teams prepare country profiles as the basis for policy.

Karekezi documents the limitations of this interdisciplinary research network. First is the difficulty of bringing together academics and policy-makers in the thematic, regional analyses. There can be a tension between the geographic diversity of the network representatives and the focus of the subject matter. Geographic diversity, on the whole, strengthens research findings by providing a comparative framework for policy review and analysis, and fosters the wide dissemination of AFREPEN's findings.[17] However, thematic reviews often demand specialization in a subject area – say, of the electricity industry – requiring technical specialists with engineering or scientific backgrounds who are not always available from each country.

If a research team is predominantly scientific in orientation, then practical policy and institutional analysis may suffer. This is critical because the past experience of energy sector analysis is that being overly technical in orientation often means the failure of downstream implementation owing to a lack of appreciation of the overriding political, economic and social factors, and the powerful effects of institutional constraints on what was earlier termed integrated management. For example, the establishment of a Ministry of Energy often has not resolved the 'administrative trap' discussed in Chapter 7, when vertical integration (usually heavily reinforced by North–South linkages) is confined to energy supply subsectors – say, in the petroleum industry or the electricity supply industry. Similarly, the good intentions of national energy policies are often undermined by the failure to appreciate the rational motivations of individual consumers, including residents of disadvantaged communities. Overcoming such constraints on energy policy requires sophisticated institutional and administrative analysis, and close attention to the practical day-to-day implications of policy implementation.

AFREPEN is now redoubling its efforts to attract social scientists and economists into the network. A related problem is the difficulty of achieving gender balance within the network, with just over 10 per cent of its members being women. Priority is being given to attracting women into the network, and to complementing the technical capabilities of all members with training in the necessary institutional, economic, social and environmental analysis to give a well-rounded perspective on African energy options.

AFREPEN must also wrestle with short-termism in the energy development process for sub-Saharan Africa, This often takes the form of 'projectitis', by which external donor agencies prefer to fund narrowly focused, short-term, technical projects with a defined completion date a few years hence, rather than broad development strategies linking projects, policies and economic sectors, and top-down and bottom-up initiatives. Thus 'the energy sector in the region is dominated by a multiplicity of project packages which are poorly co-ordinated'.[18] This in turn highlights a fundamental challenge to AFREPEN – to overcome a chronic dependence in the region on North to South flows of finance and expertise which characterizes energy initiatives:

> *The chronic dependency is demonstrated by the fact that in spite of constant complaints pertaining to the undue influence of external consultants and experts, their grip on policy initiatives continues to grow.*

To compound the problem, a South–North 'brain drain' depletes the existing human resources and research capacity in the region. AFREPEN's response is to redouble its efforts to strengthen its existing policy, institutional and regulatory frameworks and to build a critical mass of trained energy managers, professionals and entrepreneurs prior to the point when technical and economic instruments, such as new energy policies and pricing structures, are implemented. Developing the local capacity for self-assessment and self-management as a basis for action is very often a primary task of an action network.

Evaluation and reorientation of AFREPEN

In 1993, AFREPEN was subject to evaluation by one of its external funding sources. This found that the network itself was falling into something like the 'administrative trap' by orienting its research programme along conventional supply-side lines: biomass, oil and gas, electricity, coal, and institutions and planning, and so on. This meant that demand-side and environmental issues were not receiving appropriate attention.

This evaluation caused the network's research programme to be reoriented, with greater stress on developing a cost-effective demand-side approach to energy issues and greater emphasis on 'end-user' approaches, such as integrated resources planning, decentralized energy development and energy efficiency. A more intense focus on environmental issues, many of which are transborder issues, reinforces the value of the perspective of the regional network to national policy processes. Six major clusters of issues were identified in a relaunch of the research programme for the period 1995–98:[19]

1. Institutional issues, including an equitable access to energy, and the opportunities and pitfalls of privatization and deregulation in the industry.
2. Management issues, including the methods for improved management and increasingly efficient use of the existing assets.
3. Capacity building for effective policy formulation, analysis and implementation, with special emphasis on human resource development and training.
4. Finance and markets, particularly combining external and local finance, on terms not inimical to the interests of the region.
5. Local and regional environmental impacts, both existing and in terms of energy development options.
6. Climate change, both in terms of implementation options for the African energy community and a realistic and practical negotiating stance in international deliberations.

This type of honest, critical and constructive evaluation, which has benefited AFREPEN, is vital to the continued development of healthy, policy-useful networks.

The Sustainable Europe Campaign Network

The Sustainable Europe network, organized by Friends of the Earth Europe, links 30 countries across greater Europe, from Ireland to Russia and Georgia, and from Scandinavia to Malta, in action research and campaigning to promote sustainable production and consumption. A threefold focus is on international and European Union policy, national strategies and local action. A parallel South–North project brings a further eight countries from Asia, Africa and South America into the framework of dialogue and analysis.

The purpose of the Sustainable Europe Campaign (SEC), begun in 1992, is to assess what sustainable development means in practical terms and how it can be achieved. To do this, Sustainable Europe proposes the concept of fair shares in environmental space, based on three principles:

1 the need for measurable progress towards sustainable production and consumption – that is, living within the earth's carrying capacity;
2 balanced opportunities for development among all countries, including equal access to the world's resources; and
3 total quality of life rather than just materialism as a guiding force in public policy and values.[20]

The environmental space approach has its origins in the pioneering *Action Plan Sustainable Netherlands*, published by Friends of the Earth Netherlands (Vereniging Milieudefensie) as a contribution to the 1992 United Nations Conference on Environment and Development in Rio. The *Action Plan* maintained that sustainability can only be achieved if the use of natural resources is limited and more equally distributed throughout the world. The *Action Plan* also influenced the NEPP process in The Netherlands, described in Chapter 13.

Within the context of environmental space, the message of the campaign is intended not only to alter local and national practice but also to reach a worldwide audience, both in the other consumer societies of the North, such as in North America and Japan, and in the societies of the South, and Central and Eastern Europe, and the former Soviet Union, which are seen to have an equally important and influential stake in sustainable development in the 21st century.

Organization of the network

Sustainable Europe is a project of Friends of the Earth Europe, headquartered in Brussels, with Milieudefensie in Amsterdam as the coordinating group. Scientific analysis and methodological development have been carried out by a German research institute, the Wuppertal Institute for Climate, Environment and Energy. An international Steering Committee of sustainable development experts from the various regions of Europe met regularly to serve as a think-tank for the project, on both scientific content and policy impact. The message of environmental space is now spreading globally through the new Sustainable Societies Programme of Friends of the Earth International, which links around 60 member organizations on all populated continents.

In each of the 38 countries participating in the campaign, there is a designated action research team, of varying size, drawn from academia, research institutes, environmental organizations including, but not at all confined to, Friends of the Earth organizations, and government. Some members of the team have analytic capabilities, others may have skills for outreach to the key stakeholders outside the network. Each action research team has in turn its own advisory or steering group to oversee the programme and also, importantly, to foster linkages between the action research team and agencies and departments which can help it to undertake the quantitative aspects of the analysis and which should benefit from the dissemination of the reports and material prepared.

The action research team and advisory group identified target groups and key stakeholders within society for organized dialogue, such as within the energy, transport, agricultural, industrial and media sectors; relevant government department officials; and organizations in civil society, including churches, trade unions, poverty and development organizations and consumers groups. The intention was that dialogue over the concept and principles of environmental space would expand the national constituency for sustainable production and consumption, and broaden the membership of the network and its influence.

During its initial four years the network was able to attract substantial funding which provided for a small secretariat, biannual meetings of the Advisory Group and annual meetings of representatives of the national action research groups. During this period, the Sustainable Europe Campaign was funded by the Commission of the European Communities; the governments of The Netherlands, Norway and Germany; the Wuppertal Institute; the United Nations Environment Programme, and other organizations which provided help in cash and in kind.

Phases of the campaign

The main goal of the first phase of the campaign, completed in 1994, was to develop a more thorough understanding of the requirements for sustainable production and consumption at the continental level of Europe for an interim target date of 2010. During this phase, the Wuppertal Institute was responsible for scientific input and the development of a common methodology for assessing environmental space at both European and national levels, building on the approach pioneered in the Sustainable Netherlands project.

This first phase of analysis resulted in the published study *Towards Sustainable Europe* and a methodological handbook providing national groups with guidelines to analyse the current and sustainable use of environmental space in their country.[21] The report was produced as a discussion document for the campaign and translated into most European languages. Several summaries and audio-visual material were also produced.

During the second phase, from 1995 to 1997, studies were made by the action research teams at national level using the common methodology, set out in the handbook, which ensured a degree of methodological consistency across 30 national reports. Studies were also carried out within the eight South–North countries, but at a pace that was appropriate to those teams, given their differing circumstances and the difficulty of assembling data for quantitative analysis.

In each country parallel discussions were initiated to allow national groups to hold debates with key figures from relevant target groups. During this phase, these key stakeholders considered the problems and possibilities of closing the 'sustainability gap' in different economic sectors – the sustainability gap being the difference between present usage and the sustainable usage of resources in their country, the latter derived from environmental space analysis. At the conclusion of this phase, national reports on environmental space were made available in 26 languages, including French, Spanish, Portuguese, German, Croatian, Italian, Dutch, Greek, Polish, Russian, Norwegian, Japanese, Mandarin, and many others. A separate report combining the analysis and conclusions from the South–North project was also prepared.[22]

Action in Germany provides a good example of the work of the network at national level. There, Friends of the Earth (BUND) teamed up with a Christian human aid organization (Misereor) to undertake the environmental space analysis, to hold debates with various target groups (such as political parties, trade unions, religious organizations and business groups) and to present the finding as a basis for discussion at more than 100 meetings around the country. More than 95,000 copies of the long or short version of the report *Sustainable Germany* have been sold and 350 articles have appeared in the print media discussing environmental space. The German Federal Environment Minister said that the report is 'endowed with the breath of what is manageable'. The most important German news magazine called the study 'the green bible of the millennium transition'.

The third phase of Sustainable Europe, beginning in 1997, consists of project integration of national findings at a European level, further widening the debates in all countries, and preparation for follow-up campaigning activities by national groups and Friends of the Earth Europe and International to promote consensus around the way forward to sustainable development. The action research teams have moved to foster local action around sustainable production and consumption as well as influencing national policy.

The relevance of the environment space methodology is demonstrated by its now tested applicability the length and breadth of Europe. But it is also important to note that quantitative calculations are of little use without the qualitative process of dialogue and debate within the network and the gradual expansion of the membership of the network to build a Europe-wide and a South–North constituency around the environmental space approach. This final section touches on this key objective of the network.

Participation process within the network

All the Sustainable Europe teams organized a participative process in which literally thousands of representatives of governments, businesses and NGOs across Europe are discussing in an open-minded manner the sustainability targets and distance-to-sustainability measures for their countries. Debate was carried on in face-to-face seminars and in the media. In the Republic of Macedonia (former Yugoslavia), for example, Sustainable Macedonia researchers debated in a constructive manner with the Minister for the Environment on prime-time television. This is important in a country which is already living, in many areas, within the bounds of environmental space, but is under pressure to 'modernize' the economy.

Often contact led to further constructive outcomes. In Italy, the Sustainable Italy team has been asked to assess the National Environmental Policy from an environmental space point of view. Similarly, the Sustainable Slovakia report has become a supplement in the Government's Strategic Environmental Assessment manual. In Estonia, the study was influential in the Estonian Parliament passing an 'Act on Sustainable Development' which sets out a legal basis for the sustainable use of natural resources and establishes guidelines for environmental protection.

Although there was surprisingly widespread agreement in most countries on the appropriate nature of the environmental space approach and its three underlying assumptions, as would be expected, not everyone in the network agreed wholeheartedly with the assumptions or the calculations. Some people found the calculations too absolute and not sufficiently reflective of scientific uncertainties. The national action research groups themselves did not always agree with the common methodology which guided them in calculating distance-to-sustainability figures for the various resources, suggesting in some cases that the common methodology did not always reflect their particular national and local requirements.

On the other hand, there was very little contention about the absolute need for major reductions in excessive consumption. It was almost unanimously agreed by stakeholders that, whatever disagreement might exist over long-term targets, the directional guidance provided by environmental space analysis was clear and correct, and that present trends towards more and more unsustainable production and consumption must be altered. During debates it was indicated that setting an objective of a 50 per cent reduction in the use of primary raw materials and energy, for example, is seen as highly feasible as far as the design and development of new products is concerned. It became apparent that such an objective could be helpful in starting a process of developing and producing radically different products and services, which could offer equal levels of utility with greatly reduced environmental impacts.

Despite various reservations, the majority of network participants in Sustainable Europe see the value of the environmental space approach. In particular, gaining an insight into independent policy, long-term objectives appealed to many who participated in national fora. Furthermore, the need was expressed for long-term sustainability objectives to be converted into short-term financial and economic reforms.

15

Conclusions

Politics is no longer a clash of titans, a life and death struggle between rival ideologies or economic systems, but a matter of understanding the sheer complexity of the economic and social ecologies of the societies in which we live... Reflexivity, feedback, self-regulating and self-correcting loops of information and process, provisionality and cautionary optimism, now seem the hallmarks of successful political activity and change. Small is beautiful, but cautionary self-correction is best.

Ken Worpole[1]

... by concentrating on the generation of trust through careful experimentation with different structures and procedures, humanity at least stands a chance of coping with the challenges of global environmental change.

Steve Rayner and Tim O'Riordan[2]

This book has developed ideas about the forms of organization for environmental management which are suited to the challenges posed by the pressing need for sustainable development. We have argued that organizational innovation is critical to the task of managing the entire process of industrial and post-industrial development. A vital innovation is the development of the action network, a flexible, non-hierarchical, democratic and consensus-seeking partnership between different interests, spanning sectors, localities, regions, whole countries, and even the globe.

The action-network approach can be implemented both in developed and in industrializing countries, and at all levels of environmental management from the local to the international. It is being taken up in many cities, regions and national forums; it is beginning to make its mark in the new debates on the governance of the processes known collectively as globalization. Like the problems it addresses, action networks cut across policy compartments and counter the fragmentation which undermines so many efforts at environmental management and development planning. Action networks foster policy integration and the consensus required in societies if structural change in the direction of genuine sustainability is to be achieved. This concluding chapter sums up this argument.

Industrialism Becomes a Global System

The post-war period has seen a spectacular development in international trade and production. Industrialism is becoming a global system and the dramatic expansion in the reach of telecommunications and transport reinforces globalization, taking the messages of consumer culture into every village and town of every country. In this context, the newly industrialized countries and lower income countries aspire to a high degree of industrialization, even if some also wish to opt out of the 'Westernizing' aspects of the package of modernity. The ex-Communist states, on the other hand, generally aspire to achieve Western-style economic, cultural and political modernization, although the rapid penetration of mafia-style crime in the 1990s is highly disturbing. It is practically impossible to drop out of the globalizing industrial system, unless it is through despotic autarky or social disintegration, as witnessed in some parts of Africa and Asia in the 1990s. Despite some benefits, industrialization of the entire planet may also bring environmental disruption on a hitherto unimagined scale.

The rapid development of new industrial economies and the acceleration of technological change in the West generate complex and dynamic forces in the international economy. Great structural inequalities divide the high-income world from the poor South; the pressure of new competition generates tensions within the West; and the collapse of Communist economies has unleashed a wave of free-market capitalism in the former Soviet bloc and in the developing world. These forces intensify global stresses on the environment. The interactions between the global economy and ecosystems are only dimly understood, but are known to be of vast complexity and dynamism. The world of global modernity is thus immensely turbulent. While the US and Western Europe may often have acted since the end of the Cold War as if Fukuyama's forecast of international convergence on free markets and liberal democracy were already coming true, by the close of the 1990s it is clear that democracy and capitalism have many struggles ahead, with competing political systems and with their own contradictions – ecological, social, economic, cultural. The old ideological conflicts of the 20th century have passed, but new fault lines now become salient. These are less to do with the stand-offs between different civilizations and world views – although such clashes could arise again in the new century – than to do with the contradictions and tensions that are inherent in the various forms of capitalism now dominating the world and in individuals' aspirations for both material advancement and wider social and environmental well-being.[3]

Limits to Modernity

As modernity becomes a global condition, it is becoming clear that there are limits to industrial development as the West has known it and as the rest of the world would like to know it. Industrialism has conquered the globe, bringing for billions undeniable material benefits and advances in understanding. But it is increasingly clear that industrialism as we have known it is unsustainable. Limits to modernity are becoming evident in a number of areas.

Political culture and environmental management

In Parts I and II it was argued that the challenges posed by environmental crises place severe constraints on long-established elements of political culture in industrial societies. The two great models of industrialism – socialist centralized planning and liberal capitalism – are both inadequate. The removal of the Communist model from much of the world demonstrates the failure of centralized planning rather than the ultimate success of liberal capitalism. The latter system, especially in its *laissez-faire* conservative form, cannot yet deal adequately with the emerging regional, continental and global environmental problems through its favoured mechanism, the decentralized free market.

The challenge of ecologically and socially sustainable globalization raises old problems about the relationship between democracy and capitalism, which for decades has been maintained harmoniously through the process of economic growth, widely shared affluence and a social welfare safety-net of varying quality in Western societies. Globalization as we have seen it since the 1970s challenges the autonomy of nation states and the viability of generous welfare systems, and is speeding the degradation of many environments; but it is not inevitable that it should take the form it has done. We can imagine the emergence of a global framework of regulation and governance which will redirect globalizing processes towards sustainable development. This is already happening: as we argued in Chapter 5, globalization on the free-market model cannot be treated any longer as some kind of 'inevitable' and politically neutral process, but demands political management at the international level to deal with its social and environmental implications. In this area, as in others, planning for sustainability is an intensely political process, involving continuous mediation between environmental values and socioeconomic goals. It is inescapably bound up with trade-offs between competing interests, and between decentralized and centralized action. It calls for new forms of consensus-building between the state, market institutions and the groupings of 'civil society'.[4]

Science and sustainability

In Part II it was argued that the emergence of global environmental problems poses profound challenges to the rationality that has dominated Western science and technology since the Enlightenment. Key features of this model of scientific understanding include a split between human observers/actors and 'nature', and between facts and values; and a view that systems can best be understood through analysing their components. We have gained vast knowledge through the application of this model, but its limitations are revealed by global environmental change. The environment is not separate from humanity; rather, human activity is a fundamental feature of the ecosystems in the new global environment.

The need to achieve sustainability means that the technologies generated from scientific understanding cannot be seen as value-free, but must be assessed on the basis of social goals and values affecting the environment. Finally, the immense complexity of the ecosystems and global systems such as the atmosphere challenges the traditional analytic approach; the science of global environmental change is marked by uncertainty and the need for holistic understanding of the dynamic systems. We need not only traditional scientific analysis, but also an approach which recognizes our embeddedness, and that of our values, in the problems under scrutiny. The science of global environmental problems is bound up with political issues, the need for action in the face of uncertainty, and the fact that traditional scientific analysis is not sufficient to provide solutions.

Social and ecological limits

While many physical limits to growth may be distant, social and ecological limits apply to the growth of consumerism in industrial societies. The ecological limits are set by the emergence of global environmental threats. The social limits derive from the inherently self-defeating character of much 'positional' consumption and the element of pointlessness in what Ernest Gellner calls the 'perpetual potlatch' culture of consumerism: 'Affluent society simply chases its own tail'.[5] Global environmental threats also draw attention to the unsustainable inequalities between the rich industrial countries and the poor South; in particular, the gross disparities between energy consumption and resource use by the West, and the low-income countries in which the mass of the world's population lives. The ecological threats are exacerbated by key features of the global economic order such as the debt burden on the Third World. There has been a failure to integrate sustainability as a basic concern in the global policy-making bodies – the IMF, the World Bank, the GATT and transnational corporations.

The implications of these limits are as yet unclear. There is no prospect of a renunciation of industrialism, even if that were desirable; and there can be no denying the aspirations of the lower income countries to improved standards of living and a greater share of the world's energy consumption. Given these constraints, we must try to reconcile industrialism with the maintenance of the global commons; in short, to aim for a sustainable 'eco-industrial' society. The nature of a sustainable system is poorly understood, and we are unlikely to arrive soon at a conception of sustainability as an 'end product'. Rather, we need to manage our economies in ways that will bring closer the various goals that we can associate with sustainability and that take us away as fast as possible from the patterns of clearly unsustainable behaviour – in other words, we should consider sustainable development as a process that we can improve by continuous learning, wider debate about the ends of economic activity and ways of assessing progress, and the adaptation of organizational forms and policies.[6]

Managing in Turbulent Environments: the Action Network

In Part III we examined the main institutional constraints on managing for sustainable development: the fragmented nature of policy-making in key institutions; failure to promote organizational learning; the lack of policy integration in economic management; the massive complexity of environmental problems; the difficulty in balancing 'top-down' and 'bottom-up' initiatives in environmental management and planning; and the great turbulence of the world as industrialism becomes a global condition.

Part IV argued for innovative organizational forms for promoting environmental management and strategic planning for sustainability – action networks. These are designed to overcome the constraints afflicting traditional systems and methods, and to fit the nature of the problems of environmental change. In the face of dynamic, complex, interconnected problems, we need flexible, experimental organizations spanning disciplines, bridging policy compartments and social sectors. These organizational forms are capable of rapid learning, using all available knowledge (including 'local' skills and knowledge, not just those deemed 'expert' or 'scientific'). They are based on the ideal of equal partnership between different sectors, and foster consensus and increased levels of trust between them wherever possible, since environmental change causes major conflicts of interest between environmental, economic and social goals. They seek to develop flexible initiatives, with a continual process of problem specification, action, feedback and revision of policy.

Action networks are developing the world over, at various scales of activity from the local to the national. They reflect an emerging consensus among environmental campaigners and international bodies for environmental protection on the organizational mechanisms for promoting sustainable development. In Part V we considered examples ranging from the local to the global level. These diverse initiatives are all affected by various constraints and weaknesses, and all must be regarded as a modest beginning rather than a definitive achievement. But they represent striking examples of good practice and fruitful experimentation, and deserve attention from decision-makers.

At the local level, the Groundwork trusts in the UK demonstrate how the action-network approach can be used to encourage business to enter partnerships with government, public agencies and community organizations to carry out environmental regeneration in urban areas. The Groundwork initiative offers business a way in to deeper commitment to environmental management and wider partnership with local communities.

At the fluvial, regional level, the IDEA programme shows the benefits of action networks for analysing and tackling the problems of environmental management in low-income countries. IDEA allows stakeholders from different sectors to work together and learn from each other to identify problems, develop ways of overcoming conflicts, and mobilize local skills in areas such as watershed management and waste disposal. Elsewhere, projects to help resolve conflicts and build up consensus between different interest groups have grown in influence and popularity, and are often inspired by environmental problems. Initiatives in consensus-building, such as the Californian Growth Management Consensus Project, have helped often antagonistic interest groups to identify areas of actual and emerging consensus.

At the national level The Netherlands National Environmental Policy Plan (NEPP) represents the most ambitious attempt to date by an industrial country to devise a strategy for movement towards sustainable development. The NEPP is a dynamic process: a set of goals subject to revision in the light of new circumstances and evaluation of achievements. The creation of a consultative network of 'target groups' is fundamental to this: the NEPP and its successors are to be developed on the basis of discussion and consensus throughout Dutch society. As the NEPP notes, we are all de facto environmental managers; progress towards sustainable development depends on the understanding and acceptance of responsibility by all groups and individual citizens. For this to be developed, the policy process cannot be wholly 'top-down' in design; instead, it must be based on mediation, partnership and the fostering of consensus where possible.

At the global level, action networks have begun to emerge in the course of the past decade. The rise of the Internet and the personal and institutional links made through the Rio Summit and its follow-ups are among the factors promoting the growth of international action networks. Some are networks within particular sectors, such as environmental NGOs. But others span sectors, linking NGOs in different fields and countries, such as alliances between social justice NGOs and Green campaigners in the debates over the Multilateral Agreement on Investment or the relief of developing countries' debt burdens. Still others bring together businesses that are concerned with positive responses to the sustainability agenda, and new alliances are developing between businesses and NGOs, such as the Forestry and Marine Stewardship Councils established by the WWF and major corporations.[7]

These new global action networks have engaged in multidisciplinary research, in campaigning, in mutual learning, and in experiments in voluntary self-regulation. They can be seen as efforts to 'civilize' the raw processes of globalization, to develop patterns of sustainable management and more 'transparent' governance of the international economy in the absence of a truly global tier of democratic regulation and accountability for the new world economic order.[8]

Conclusion: the Future of the Action Network Model

Since the first edition of this book was published in 1992, examples of the multisector action network have begun to develop at the international level. It is hard to see what other form of organization can begin to make real progress in forging and then implementing agreements between nation states, international agencies and transnational corporations on the threats to the global environment. Global warming, appropriate technology transfer and the loss of biodiversity are matters of intense controversy between nation states, and rapid progress towards meaningful international treaties is unlikely, even though time is not on our side to cope with ecological degradation.

In such a context, the worldwide development of multisector partnerships for environmental management and planning for sustainability at all levels is a powerful innovation. Already, as we have shown, there are extensive networks linking NGOs around the world, and the UNCED Conference in Rio de Janeiro in 1992 stimulated more networking among campaigning bodies. Many transnational corporations have taken part in a high-powered Business Council for Sustainable Development to promote debate in business on sustainability issues. There are myriad multinational governmental bodies in need of improved coordination and better integration of environmental policy, which would benefit from greater exposure to multisector action networks.[9]

How can these international networks be developed further and brought into cooperative ventures? How could the values and techniques of the action-network approach be diffused? One initiative often mentioned in the context of global environmental change is the Marshall Plan. Many argue that only a Marshall-scale transfer of money and technology from the West to the ex-Communist countries and the industrializing world can hope to make a reality of sustainable development in countries seeking to emulate Western forms of industrialism.[10] Large transfers of financial and technological resources are crucial, but organizational skills and institutional design are also fundamental to realizing sustainable development. The action network is a necessary feature of the organizational basis for sustainable environmental management, and its techniques need to be diffused (in the West as well as in the rest of the world) as do the clean technologies and payments for the conservation of critical ecological resources such as the rainforests.

The rich Western powers, so far reluctant to contemplate a massive transfer of money and technology or to write off the debts of the poorest countries, could well afford to finance a Marshall Plan for environmental management and sustainability planning. This would take the form of a programme of diverse initiatives to build up international multisector networks for action on key problems. For example, it could empower NGOs to work closely on project assessment with international business groups and bodies such as the World Bank, the IMF and the GATT, in pursuit of a better integration of environmental concerns into mainstream policy. This idea, taken up by the UN Human Development Report in 1999, links the action network to emerging thinking on global governance and 'cosmopolitan democracy' – the extension of democratic processes to the global level to match the spread of corporate economic powers across the planet.

The initiative would also seek to transfer skills in environmental management and mediation; to generate new ideas for environmental management at all levels from the local to the global; and to allow mutual learning between organizations of all kinds. An international network drawing on the experience of Groundwork in the UK could disseminate the techniques of local partnerships in urban environmental improvement; an international Growth Management Consensus Project could spread techniques of environmental dispute resolution and mediation; and the IDEA system, already an international network in the Commonwealth, is well placed for wider dissemination in the developing world.

Such a programme would seek to transfer the best practice in environmental management, including the expertise of voluntary agencies and local communities, not only from the West to the ex-Communist world and the developing countries, but also between developing countries within the industrialized world, and from low-income countries to the West. Such a programme is far from Utopian and would be relatively inexpensive; it would also stimulate innovations and provide the essential managerial underpinning for the effective transfers of resources and technology.

The action network as a tool for consensus-building is also a vital ingredient in the process of negotiating burden-sharing deals between the rich nations and the rest of the world in relation to the greatest controversies we face in moving towards sustainable development. How do we foster trust and cooperation and the transfer of ideas and skills in relation to greenhouse gas reduction targets, or the tensions between free trade and environmental, cultural and social safeguards for countries, regions and localities? If we see negotiation at the global level solely as a matter for national governments, we will achieve only slow and painful progress, and we face great problems of negotiation between democracies and authoritarian regimes which cannot be held readily accountable for their implementation of sustainability agreements. The action network can make a contribution to accelerating progress by making linkages between sectors 'beneath' the level of the state, and promoting initiatives for learning, investment, social welfare and environmental regeneration and protection which do not depend on state agreement. Alliances between global NGOs and multinationals, which in turn collaborate with local and regional NGOs, firms and public authorities, can be a force for promoting bottom-up change and putting positive pressure on national governments which are paying lip-service to sustainable development. Such processes can be envisaged in industrializing countries where civil society is gradually being loosened from the grip of the state, and where local and regional autonomy is likely to grow as, for example, in China, Indonesia and much of the ex-Soviet world.

At the dawn of the 21st century the action network is poised to become a still stronger element in the tortuous process of shifting our societies, at all levels from the local to the global, in the direction of sustainable development. It remains to be seen how far it will succeed as a force for effecting real change directly as well as indirectly through its role as a tool for awareness-raising, consensus-building and mutual learning between sectors. For the action network to become a still more significant force requires more willingness from governments and corporations to shift from traditional modes of policy-making and implementation towards an embrace of more direct forms of participatory democracy – new forms of democratic dialogue and accountability, drawing diverse 'stakeholders' into deliberation on complex choices about how to bring about the sustainable and holistic regeneration of communities and local economies, and to move towards sustainable production and consumption.[11] It also demands a process of public education and genuine 'empowerment' of citizens on a large scale to motivate more people to take up the opportunities for a more direct engagement in decision-making.

Will governments and corporations take this path? Will citizens be motivated to become more active democrats as a result? And if they are, will they inevitably choose the sustainable course of action? We can be fairly optimistic about the first question. The concern in the West at the decline of public trust in central government and in the process of politics is now high, and experiments in a more direct, participatory democracy are proliferating. And increasingly corporations are moving towards more dialogue with NGOs and local communities, and reporting on their environmental and social impact. Slowly, a critical mass is being built up; we can envisage a time in the new century when all transnational corporations and many lesser corporations will feel that it is in their interest, or that they are legally required, to account for their contribution to sustainable development and to engage in dialogue with diverse 'stakeholders'.[12] Will citizens, however, rise to the challenge of a more participatory and deliberative democracy where it emerges? There can be no guarantees that a more active citizenry will be a greener and more socially responsible one. But it is a reasonable hope that a much wider public engagement in democratic decision-making, underpinned by civic education and a more extensive debate about sustainability as more evidence of ecological degradation and the social costs of globalization emerges, will lead to pressure for more sustainable policies and to more individual commitment to sustainable consumption. At the very least, the wider application of tools such as the action network to the renewal of democratic processes will help to give us the information and exposure to ideas and the evidence to make decisions with our eyes more open to the long-term impacts of our choices. As Michael Jacobs has said:[13]

> *We do not know what it would take to encourage people to value the quality of life more highly; to give more weight to the interests of future generations and distant people and wildlife; to appreciate less materialistic forms of consumption. But that is not the point. For those concerned about the environmental crisis, the task is surely to find out.*

The action-network approach to environmental management and sustainability planning is no panacea. The approach will not always succeed. Not all problems are amenable to consensus-building. The path to sustainability will be marked by clashes of values which will not be resolved by mediation and stakeholder consultations, but by determined leadership and tough regulation and self-regulation. The approach is not a substitute for campaigning, regulation, market-based incentives or technological innovation, and other means through which environmental and social problems are addressed and resolved. But it is an essential complement to them, promoting the political and cultural changes which must accompany the vital supply-side innovations in technology and product design.

On an industrialized planet, faced with mounting ecological problems and massive political and economic turbulence, the old institutional forms and management approaches can no longer analyse adequately the environmental and social challenges of globalization, devise solutions that fit the multifaceted and complex problems, and mobilize diverse social groups in a democratic framework to implement them. The action network offers a solution that fits the nature of our most daunting 21st-century problems. It can make a vital contribution to managing the process of sustainable development.

Notes and References

Preface

1 World Commission on Environment and Development, *Our Common Future*, New York, 1987

Chapter 1

1 Swanson, T and Barbier, E, 'The end of wildlands and wildlife?', in Swanson, T and Barbier, E (eds) *Economics for the Wilds: Wildlife, Wildlands, Diversity and Development*, Earthscan, London, 1992

2 There are many overviews of global environmental change and ecological damage. See, for example: United Nations Environment Programme (UNEP), *Global Environment Outlook 2000*, UNEP/Earthscan, London, 1999; Mannion, A M, *Global Environmental Change: A Natural and Cultural Environmental History*, Longman Scientific and Technical, London, 1991 (co-published in the US with John Wiley & Sons, New York); Myers, N, *Gaia: an Atlas of Planet Management*, Doubleday, New York, 1993; Schnelling, T C, 'Global environmental forces', *Technological Forecasting and Social Change*, vol 38, pp257–64, 1990; Holdgate, M, *The Environment of Tomorrow's World*, The David Davies Memorial Institute of International Studies, London, 1991; Defries, R S and Malone, T (eds), *Global Environmental Change and Our Common Future: Papers from a Forum*, National Academy of Sciences, Washington, 1989; Turner, B L, Clark, W C, Kates, R W, Richards, J F, Mathews, J T and Mayer, W B (eds), *The Earth as Transformed by Human Action*, Cambridge University Press, Cambridge, 1990; Arthur, W, *The Green Machine: Ecology and the Balance of Nature*, Basil Blackwell, Oxford, 1990; Calder, N, *Spaceship Earth*, Penguin, London, 1991; Grubb, M et al, *The Earth Summit Agreements: a guide and assessment*, RIIA/Earthscan, 1993; Easterbrook, G, *A Moment on the Earth: the coming age of environmental optimism*, Viking Penguin, New York, 1995; Brown, L et al (ed), *Vital Signs 1997–98*, Earthscan, London, 1997; Athanasiou, T, *Slow Reckoning: the ecology of a divided planet*, Secker and Warburg, London, 1997; WWF/NEF/WCMC, *Living Planet Report 1998*, Worldwide Fund For Nature, Gland, Switzerland, 1998; Hertsgaard, M, *Earth Odyssey*, Abacus, London, 1999. Accessible statistical and factual overviews on pollution, resource use, biodiversity, global consumption and production and sectoral trends are given in sources such as: UNEP, 1999, op cit; Brown, L and Flavin, C (ed) *State of the World 1999*, Earthscan, London, 1999 (annual series); Brown, L et al (ed) *Vital Signs 1999–2000*, Earthscan, London, 1999 (annual series); Seager, J *The State of the Environment Atlas: the international visual survey*, Penguin, London, 1995; Daily, G C, *Nature's Services: societal dependence on natural ecosystems*, Island Press, Washington, DC, 1997. New ideas on human pressure on the environment are given in WWF/NEF/WCMC, *Living Planet Report 1998*, WWF, Gland, Switzerland, 1998; *World Bank Atlas 1999*, World Bank, Washington, DC, 1999

3 For detailed arguments in favour of the 'technocentric' view of global environmental change and a positive view of the impacts of rising population, see Simon, J and Kahn, H (ed), *The Resourceful Earth*, Basil Blackwell, Oxford, 1984. See also Repetto, R (ed), *The Global Possible*, Yale University Press, 1985. An environmentalist variation on this 'cornucopian' perspective is provided by the vision of vastly increased resource productivity in von Weizsäcker, E, Lovins, A, and Lovins, L, *Factor Four: doubling wealth, halving resource use*, Earthscan, London, 1997. Easterbrook (op cit) also presents an 'eco-optimist' perspective on the tractability of environmental problems and the capacity of technological innovation to help solve them. See also Hawken, P, Lovins, A and Lovins, L, *Natural Capitalism*, Earthscan, London

4 O'Meara, M, 'Exploring a new vision for cities', in Brown et al (ed) *State of the World 1999*, Earthscan/Worldwatch Institute, London, 1999, p130

5 WWF, *Living Planet Report*, WWF, Gland, Switzerland, 1998
6 Brown, L and Flavin, C, 'A new economy for a new century', in Brown et al, 1999, op cit, p9
7 Brown, L, 'Feeding Nine Billion', in Brown et al, 1999, op cit, pp120–123; see also Conway, G, *The Doubly Green Revolution: food for all in the 21st century*, Penguin, London, 1997
8 Brown, L, op cit; WWF, op cit; Conway, G, op cit, Chapters 1–2
9 Tickell, C, 'Environmental refugees: the human impact of global climate change', *NERC News*, July 1989, pp14–20
10 Abramowitz, J and Matton, A, 'Reorienting the forest products economy', in Brown, L and Flavin, C, op cit, 1999
11 Mannion, op cit, pp237–41
12 Edberg, R, *Vart Hotade Hem*, Bra Bocker, Hoganas, 1982
13 Tickell, C, 'Timber and Destruction', *New Scientist*, 31 August 1991, pp47–8
14 WWF, 1998, op cit, p6
15 Mannion, op cit, p238
16 Brown, L and Flavin, C, 1999, op cit, pp12–13
17 Prance, G, 'Future of the Amazonian Rainforest', *Futures*, pp891–903, November 1990. See also Walker, G, 'Slash and Grow' and 'Kinder Cuts', *New Scientist*, no 2048, 21 September 1996; World Resources Institute, *World Resources 1994–95*, Oxford University Press, 1994; WWF, 1999, op cit; Abramovitz and Mattoon, 1999, op cit
18 Repetto, R, *The Forest for the Trees? Government Policies and the Misuse of Forest Resources*, World Resources Institute, Washington, 1988
19 Pearce, F, 'Beyond hope', *New Scientist*, 31 October 1998
20 Abramovitz, J and Mattoon, A, op cit, 1999
21 Daniel, J, 'The unkindest cut of all', *Nature Canada*, vol 18, pp37–44, 1989
22 Abramowitz and Matton, op cit, 1999; see also OECD, *Market and Government Failures in Environment Management*, OECD, Paris, 1992; Jones, T and Wibe, S (eds), *Forests: Market and Intervention Failures*, Earthscan, London, 1992
23 Calder, op cit, p119; see also Conway, G, op cit, Chapter 13; Dyson, T, *Population and Food*, Routledge, London, 1996; Leach, M and Mearns, R (eds), *The Lie of the Land*, James Currey, Oxford, 1996
24 Mannion, op cit, pp224–6
25 Conway, G, op cit, p244
26 Ibid, p253; see also Brown, L, op cit, pp 23–125
27 French, H, 'Restoring the East European and Soviet environments', in Brown, L (ed), *State of the World 1991*, Earthscan/Worldwatch Institute, London, 1991
28 Carley, P M, 'The price of the plan: perceptions of cotton and health in Uzbekistan and Turkmenistan', *Central Asian Survey*, vol 8, pp1–38, 1989. Carley reports that poisonous chemicals are applied to the cotton crop in Uzbekistan at the rate of 54.5kg per hectare compared to the average of 1kg per hectare in the former USSR. See also the special issue of *Post-Soviet Geography* on 'The Aral Crisis', May 1992; Feshbach, M and Friendly, A, *Ecocide in the USSR*, Basic Books, New York, 1992; Postel, S, *Last Oasis*, Norton, New York, 1997
29 Carley, ibid, pp14–15
30 Turner, K and Jones, T (eds), *Wetlands: Market and Intervention Failures*, Earthscan, London, 1991. See also Dugan, P (ed), *Wetlands in Danger*, Oxford University Press, New York, 1993
31 *The Virginian Pilot*, 'Environmentalists raise the red flags', 27 August 1991; Dalyell, T, 'Wetlands caught in the tourist trap', *New Scientist*, 22–9 December 1990; Seager, op cit, 1995; Starke, L (ed), *Vital Signs 1997–98*, Earthscan/Worldwatch Institute, London, 1997
32 Pearce, F, 'A dammed fine mess', *New Scientist*, 4 May, pp36–9, 1991. See also Gleick, P (ed), *Water in Crisis: a guide to the world's fresh water resources*, Oxford University Press, New York, 1993
33 Seager, op cit, 1995
34 Pearce, op cit, 1991
35 ibid
36 Seager, op cit, 1995
37 Theys, J, '21st century: environment and resources', *European Environment Review*, vol 1, pp2–7, 1987
38 O'Meara, op cit, 1999, pp135–6

39 Ibid; on the potential for sustainability as well as the problems of modern cities see also UN, *Report of the UN Conference on Human Settlements*, United Nations, New York, 1996; Worpole, K and Greenhalgh, L, *The Richness of Cities*, Comedia/Demos, London, 1999; Murray, R and Collins, K, *Reinventing Waste*, Ecologika, London, 1998; McLaren et al, op cit; Hall, P, *Cities of Tomorrow*, Blackwell, Oxford, 1996; Hall, P and Ward, C, *Sociable Cities*, John Wiley, Chichester, 1998; Levett, R and Christie, I, *Towards the Ecopolis: sustainable development and urban governance*, Comedia/Demos, London, 1999

40 On Thailand's explosive growth and Bangkok's problems of pollution and congestion, see Hertsgaard, M, *Earth Odyssey*, Abacus, London, 1999

41 O'Meara, op cit, 1999, pp134

42 Ibid; Hardoy, J and Satterthwaite, D, *Environmental Problems in Third World Cities: A Global Problem Ignored?* IIED Publications, London, 1990; Hertsgaard, op cit, 1999

43 Mannion, op cit, p240

44 McGee, T G, 'Asia's Growing Urban Rings', *Work in Progress*, vol 13, p9, United Nations University, Tokyo. See also Kenworthy, J, 'Automobile Dependence in Bangkok: an international comparison with implications for planning policies', *World Transport Policy & Practice*, vol 1, no 3, 1995

45 Orski, C K, 'Managing suburban traffic congestion: a strategy for suburban mobility', *Transportation Quarterly*, vol 41, no 4, pp457–76, 1987

46 O'Meara, op cit, pp143–145; Newman, P and Kenworthy, J, *Sustainability and Cities: overcoming automobile dependence*, Island Press, Washington, DC, 1999; Nadis, S and MacKenzie, J, *Car Trouble*, Beacon Press, Boston, 1993

47 See, for example, Barde, J-P, and Button, K (eds), *Transport Policy and the Environment*, Earthscan, London, 1990; Pearce, D et al (ed), *Blueprint 5: the True Costs of Road Transport*, Earthscan, London, 1995

48 Orski, op cit, p464

49 Robertson, J T, 'Assessing our second(hand) America', *American Planning Association Journal*, pp271–6, Spring, 1987

50 Starke, L (ed), *Vital Signs 1997–98*, Earthscan/Worldwatch Institute, London, 1997; Hertsgaard, op cit, Chapter 3, 1999; O'Meara, op cit, 1999

51 Hertsgaard, op cit, 1999

52 See, for example, Tengstrom, E, *Automobility – Is It Approaching a Global Crisis?*, paper presented to the conference on Human Responsibility and Global Change, University of Goteborg, Sweden, 1991

53 Seager, op cit, 1995; Hertsgaard, op cit, 1999; Starke, op cit, 1997; Elsom, D, *Atmospheric Pollution*, Blackwell, Oxford, 1993

54 Grubb, M, *The Greenhouse Effect: Negotiating Targets*, The Royal Institute of International Affairs (RIIA), Energy and Environmental Programme, London, second edition, 1992; see also WWF, op cit, 1998; Starke, op cit, 1997; Grubb, M et al, *Energy Policies and the Greenhouse Effect, vol 1, Policy Appraisal*, RIIA, London, 1990. See also *United Nations Framework Convention on Climate Change: Text*, UNEP, Geneva, 1992; International Energy Agency, *Climate Change Policy Initiatives, vol 1: OECD Countries*, OECD, Paris, 1994. On the policy issues raised by the Kyoto Summit agreements see Grubb, M et al, *The Kyoto Protocol*, Earthscan, London, 1999

55 On the scientific analysis of global warming, see International Panel on Climate Change (IPCC), *The IPCC Assessment of Knowledge Relevant to the Interpretation of Article 2 of the UN Framework Convention on Climate Change*, Geneva, 1996; IPCC, *The Scientific Assessment of Climate Change: Policymakers' Summary*, Cambridge University Press, Cambridge, 1990; Leggett, J (ed), *Global Warming: the Greenpeace Report*, Oxford University Press, Oxford, 1990; Schneider, S H, *Global Warming*, Sierra Club, San Francisco, 1989; Schneider, S H, *Laboratory Earth*, Phoenix, London, 1987; Flavin, C, 'Facing up to the Risks of Climate Change', in Brown, L et al (ed), *State of the World 1996*, Earthscan, London, 1996; Houghton, J, *Global Warming: the complete briefing*, Cambridge University Press, Cambridge, 1997, second edition

56 Tickell, op cit, p15

57 Schnelling, op cit, p257

58 Grubb, op cit, p22

59 Ibid. See also Christie, I, 'Social and political aspects of global warming', *Futures*, January/February 1992, and the essays in the special edition on global warming of *Town and Country Planning* journal, vol 67, no 9, London, October 1998

60 Arizpe, L, 'The Global Cube', *International Social Science Journal*, no 130, pp599–608, 1991
61 Robinson, J B, 'Modelling the interactions between human and natural systems', *International Social Science Journal*, no 130, pp629–48, 1991; see also International Federation of Institutes of Advanced Study, *The Human Dimensions of Global Change: An International Programme on Human Interactions with the Earth. Report of a Symposium*, Tokyo, 1988, IFIAS, Toronto, 1989
62 Theys, op cit, 1987, p7; Brown and Flavin (ed), op cit, 1999
63 See Turner, R K, Kelly, M and Kay, R, *Cities at Risk*, BNA International, London, 1990; McCulloch, J (ed), *Cities and Global Change*, Climate Institute, Washington DC, 1991; Pugh, C (ed), *Sustainability, the Environment and Urbanisation*, Earthscan, London, 1996
64 See Pearce, D W (ed), *Blueprint 2: Greening the World Economy*, Earthscan, London, 1991
65 See Schramm, G and Warford, J (eds), *Environmental Management and Economic Development*, World Bank/Johns Hopkins University Press, Baltimore, 1989; Bhaskar, V and Glyn, A (ed), *The North, the South and the Environment: ecological constraints and the global economy*, Earthscan, London, 1995

Chapter 2

1 Sen, A, 'What did you learn in the world today?', *American Behavioral Scientist*, vol 34, pp530–48, 1991
2 Rahman, M A, 'Towards an alternative development paradigm', *IFDA Dossier*, no 81, pp7–28, 1991
3 Korten, D, *Getting to the 21st Century: Voluntary Action and the Global Agenda*, Kumarian Press, West Hartford, CT, 1990
4 IUCN, *World Conservation Strategy: Living Resource Conservation for Sustainable Development*, IUCN/UNEP/WWF, Gland, Switzerland, 1980
5 World Commission on Environment and Development, *Our Common Future*, Oxford University Press, Oxford, 1987, p89
6 Ibid, p213
7 Mathews, J T, 'Environment, development and security', *Bulletin of the American Academy of Arts and Sciences*, vol xliii, pp10–26, 1990
8 Rees, W T, 'The Ecology of Sustainable Development' in Daysh, Z, Carley, M, Ekehorn, E, Phillips-Howard, K and Waller, R (eds), *Human Ecology, Environmental Education and Sustainable Development*, CHEC and Centre for Human Ecology, University of Edinburgh, 1991. See also Rees, W T, 'Atmospheric change: human ecology in disequilibrium', *International Journal of Environmental Studies*, vol 36, pp103–24, 1990
9 Rees, op cit
10 On the concept of sustainability and its operationalization, there is now an immense literature. For fundamental analyses of the conceptual underpinning of sustainable development, see, for example: Daly, H E, 'Towards some operational principles of sustainable development', *Ecological Economics*, vol 2, pp1–6, 1990; Daly, H E and Commoner, J B, *For the Common Good: Redirecting the Economy toward Community, the Environment and a Sustainable Future*, Green Print, London, 1990; Pearce, D W, 'Economics, equity and sustainable development', *Futures*, vol 20, pp598–605, 1988; Pearce, D W and Turner, R K, *Economics of Natural Resources and the Environment*, Harvester Wheatsheaf, Hemel Hempstead, 1990; Jacobs, M, *The Green Economy: Environment, Sustainable Development and the Politics of the Future*, Pluto Press, London, 1991; Clayton, A M and Radcliffe, N J, *Sustainability: a systems approach*, Earthscan, London, 1996; Kirkby, J et al (ed), *The Earthscan Reader in Sustainable Development*, Earthscan, London, 1995; Redclift, M, *Sustainable Development: exploring the contradictions*, Routledge, London, 1987

On measuring and securing progress towards sustainability, see Jackson, T, Marks, N, Ralls, J and Stymne, S, *Sustainable Economic Welfare in the UK 1950–1996*, New Economics Foundation/University of Surrey Centre for Environmental Strategy, London, 1998; IIED/IUCN, *Strategies for National Sustainable Development*, Earthscan, London, 1994; Trzyna, T (ed), *A Sustainable World: defining and measuring sustainable development*, IUCN/Earthscan, London, 1995; Carley, M and Spapens, P, *Sharing the World: sustainable living and global equity in the 21st century*, Earthscan, London, 1997; McLaren, D, Bullock, S and Yousuf, N, *Tomorrow's World: Britain's share in a sustainable future*, Earthscan/Friends of the Earth, London, 1998

On the application of sustainability concepts to industrial innovation and business strategy, see: Hawken, P, *The Ecology of Commerce*, HarperCollins, New York, 1993; Elkington, J, *Cannibals with Forks: the triple bottom line of 21st century business*, Capstone, Oxford, 1997; Christie, I and Rolfe, H, *Cleaner Production in Industry*, Policy Studies Institute, London, 1995; Roberts, P, *Environmentally Sustainable Business: a local and regional perspective*, Paul Chapman, London, 1995; Wallace, D, *Sustainable Industrialisation*, RIIA/Earthscan, 1996; Welford, R and Starkey, R (ed), *The Earthscan Reader in Business and the Environment*, Earthscan, London, 1996; Welford, R, *Hijacking Environmentalism: corporate responses to sustainable development*, Earthscan, 1997; Howes, R, Skea, J and Whelan, B, (ed), *Clean and Competitive? Motivating environmental performance in industry*, Earthscan, London, 1997; von Weizsäcker, E, Lovins, A, and Lovins, L, *Factor Four: doubling wealth, halving resource use*, Earthscan, London, 1997; Murphy, D and Bendell, J, *In the Company of Partners: business, environmental groups and sustainable development post-Rio*, Policy Press, Bristol, 1997

11 On market and intervention failures in transport, see Barde, J-P and Button, K (eds), *Transport and the Environment*, Earthscan, London, 1990; Pearce, D et al (ed), *Blueprint 5: the True Costs of Road Transport*, Earthscan, London, 1995

12 See Pearce, D W et al, *Blueprint for a Green Economy*, Earthscan, London, 1989; Pearce, D W and Turner, R K, 1990, op cit.; Pearce, D (ed), *Blueprint 3: Measuring Sustainable Development*, Earthscan, London, 1993; Pearce, D, *Blueprint 4: sustaining the Earth*, Earthscan, London, 1995

13 See Pearce, D W (ed), *Blueprint 2: Greening the World Economy*, Earthscan, London, 1991; OECD, *Applying Economic Instruments to Environmental Policies in OECD and Dynamic Non-member Economies*, OECD, Paris, 1994; OECD, *Environmental Taxes in OECD Countries*, OECD, Paris, 1995; Tindale, S and Holtham, G, *Green Tax Reform: pollution payments and labour tax cuts*, IPPR, London, 1996; O'Riordan, T (ed), *Ecotaxation*, Earthscan, London, 1997

14 See, for example, Swanson, T and Barbier, E (eds), *Economics for the Wilds*, Earthscan, London, 1992; Turner, R K and Jones, T (eds), *Wetlands: Market and Intervention Failures*, Earthscan, London, 1991

15 See Pearce et al, 1989, op cit; Pearce (ed), 1991, op cit

16 Anderson, V, *Alternative Economic Indicators*, New Economics Foundation, London, 1990. Anderson notes that GNP is similar to GDP but includes income (such as profits and dividends) resulting from property located in other countries and excludes property income flowing overseas. In the case of the UK, for example, there is little difference between the two figures

17 Sartari, G, 'Rethinking democracy: bad polity and bad politics', *International Social Science Journal*, vol 129, pp437–50, 1990; on the potential for renewal and extension of democratic processes in relation to environmental sustainability, see also Norgaard, R, *Development Betrayed: the end of progress and a coevolutionary revisioning of the future*, Routledge, London, 1994

18 On discounting, see Pearce and Turner, 1990, op cit, Chapter 14. See also Jacobs, 1991, op cit

19 Agarwal, A and Narain, S, *Towards Green Villages*, Centre for Science and Environment, New Delhi, 1990. See also the UN Development Programme's Human Development Index, presented in the UNDP's annual reports

20 See Pearce (ed), 1991, op cit

21 Daly, 1990, op cit

22 Rees, 1991, op cit

23 Daly, 1990, op cit

24 Thring, M, personal communication

25 Georgescu-Roegen, N, *Energy and Economic Myths: Institutional and Analytical Economic Essays*, Pergamon, Oxford, 1976

26 Daly, 1990, op cit. See also Daly, H E, *Steady-State Economics*, second edition, Earthscan, London, 1992

27 Alexander, W, 'A Sustainable Human Ecology', paper delivered to the Conference on Human Responsibility and Global Change, Göteborg, 1991

28 This is a modification of a definition in Rees, W T, *Defining Sustainable Development*, Research Bulletin, UBC Centre for Human Settlements, Vancouver, May 1989

29 Dator, J, 'It's only a paper moon', *Futures*, pp1084–102, December 1990; see also Swanson and Barbier, 1992, op cit

30 Anderson, W T, *To Govern Evolution*, Harcourt Brace Jovanovich, Dallas, 1987, cited in Dator, ibid
31 Carley, M and Spapens, P, *Sharing the World: Sustainable Living and Global Equity in the 21st Century*, Earthscan, London, 1998
32 Vandergeest, P, 'Peasant strategies in a world context: contingencies in the transformation of rice and sugar palm economies in Thailand', *Human Organization*, vol 48, p117, 1989
33 Ablin, R, 'The shrinking realm of *laissez-faire*', *Challenge*, March/April, p24, 1989
34 UNDP, *Human Development Report 1996*, New York, 1996, cited in Carley and Spapens, op cit, p14
35 Alexander, 1991, op cit
36 Carley and Spapens, op cit
37 Egero, B, 'No longer North and South – the New Challenges of Demographic-Economic Interrelations', paper presented at the International Conference on Human Ecology, Göteborg, 1991
38 Tabah, L, 1990, 'The world's population: a look ahead', paper presented to a DAC meeting on population and development, Paris, cited in Egero, 1991, op cit
39 Fukuyama, F, 'The end of history', *The Independent*, 20–21 September 1989, reprinted from *The National Interest*
40 Heilbroner, R L, *The Nature and Logic of Capitalism*, W W Norton, New York, 1985
41 Fukuyama, op cit. See also Fukuyama's elaboration of his thesis in *The End of History and the Last Man*, Hamish Hamilton, London, 1992
42 Sacks, J, 'The environment of faith', *The Listener*, 15 November 1990
43 Hirst, P, 'New ideals that follow "the end of history"', *The Independent*, 25 September 1989
44 Sacks, 1990, op cit
45 Leiss, W, *The Limits to Satisfaction*, University of Toronto Press, Toronto, 1986
46 *IFDA Dossier*, 'Indonesia: the Institute for Philosophy and the future of humanity', no 81, p113, 1991
47 Egero, 1991, op cit, p5
48 Bell, D, 'American exceptionalism revisited: the role of civil society', *The Public Interest*, no 95, pp38–58, 1989
49 Sen, A, 'The moral standing of the market', *Social Philosophy and Policy*, vol 2, no 2, 1985
50 Weale, A, 'The end of society?', *The Times Higher Education Supplement*, December 1988
51 Ibid. The quotation is in part from Marquand, D, *The Unprincipled Society*, Jonathan Cape, London, 1988
52 Bell, 1989, op cit

Chapter 3

1 Collingwood, R G, *The Idea of Nature*, Clarendon Press, Oxford, 1945
2 Owens, S, 'Interpreting sustainable development', in Jacobs, M (ed), *Greening the Millennium? The new politics of the environment*, Blackwell/Political Quarterly, Oxford, 1997
3 Yearly, S, 'Greens and science: a doomed affair?', *New Scientist*, 13 July 1999, pp37–40
4 Cited in Yearly, op cit
5 Dwivedi, O P, 'Political science and the environment', *International Social Science Journal*, no 109, pp377–90, 1986
6 Putnam, C, 'Do it again, Sam', *New Scientist*, 14 April 1988
7 Pearce, F, 'A dammed fine mess', *New Scientist*, 4 May 1991
8 Keller, K H, 'Science and technology', *Sea-Changes: American Foreign Policy in a World Transformed*, Council on Foreign Relations, Washington, 1989
9 Grove-White, R, 'Mysteries in the Global Laboratory', *The Times Higher Educational Supplement*, 26 October, p15, 1990
10 Grove-White, op cit
11 Robertson, J T, 'Assessing our second(hand) America', *American Planning Association Journal*, Spring, pp271–6, 1987
12 Hillman, M, Adams, J and Whitelegg, J, *One False Step: a Study of Children's Independent Mobility*, Policy Studies Institute, London, 1991
13 Collingwood, op cit, p9

14 Cited in Collingwood, op cit, p102

15 Jones, A, 'From fragmentation to wholeness: a green approach to science and society', *The Ecologist*, vol 17, pp236–40, 1987; see also Kumar, S, 'Green Spirit', *Demos Quarterly*, no.11, Demos London, May 1997

16 Jones, op cit, p236

17 Capra, F, *The Turning Point*, Wildwood House, London, 1982, p50

18 Capra, op cit, p66

19 Jones, op cit, p240

20 Cited in Jones, ibid; see also Bohm, D, *Wholeness and the Implicate Order*, Routledge & Kegan Paul, London, 1980

21 Jones, op cit, p237

22 Oltneau, J, 'Between globalism and fragmentation', *Institute for the Humanities Newsletter*, vol 3, no 2, Simon Fraser University, Vancouver, 1990

23 van Steenbergen, B, 'Potential influence of the holistic paradigm on the social sciences', *Futures*, December 1990, pp1071–83; on the development of a holistic and pluralistic approach to knowledge and assessment of environmental problems and their social and economic roots, see also Norgaard, R, *Development Betrayed: the end of progress and a coevolutionary revisioning of the future*, Routledge, London, 1994

24 Giddens, A, *Modernity and Self-Identity*, Cambridge University Press, Cambridge, 1991

25 Held, D, 'Central perspectives on the modern state', Held, D et al (eds), *States and Societies*, Martin Robertson, Oxford, 1984, p33

26 Held, op cit, p42

27 Wallerstein, I, 'Marxism as utopias: evolving ideologies', *American Journal of Sociology*, vol 91, pp1295–308, 1986

28 Benton, T, *Philosophical Foundations of the Three Sociologies*, Routledge & Kegan Paul, London, 1977

29 Giddens, A, *Studies in Social and Political Theory*, Hutchinson, London, 1977, p29

30 Goldberg, M A, 'The irrationality of rational planning', in Breheny, M and Hooper, A (eds), *Rationality in Planning*, Psion, London, 1985

31 Carley, M, *Rational Techniques in Policy Analysis*, Heinemann Educational Books, London, 1980

32 Simey, T S, *Social Science and Social Purpose*, Constable, London, 1968

33 Lanza, R, 'The past needs its people', *New Scientist*, 12 January 1991

34 See Gleick, J, *Chaos: Making a New Science*, Cardinal, London, 1988; *The New Scientist Guide to Chaos*, Penguin, London, 1992; Gell-Mann, M, *The Quark and the Jaguar*, W H Freeman, New York, 1994; Coveney, P and Highfield, R, *Frontiers of Complexity*, Fawcett Columbine, New York, 1995

35 See, for example, Davies, P, *The Cosmic Blueprint*, Touchstone Press, New York, 1988; Horgan, J, *The End of Science*, Little, Brown, London, 1997

36 Inayatullah, S, 'Rethinking Science', *IFDA Dossier*, no 81, pp5–16

37 van Steenbergen, op cit

38 Ibid

39 See Goldstein, W and Mohnen, V V, 'Global warming debate in the USA: the clash between scientists on policy projections', *Futures*, vol 24, no 1, January/February 1992

40 See Funtowicz, S and Ravetz, J, *Global Environmental Issues and the Emergence of Second Order Science*, Council for Science and Society Occasional Paper no 1, London, 1990; in the same series, Rayner, S and O'Riordan, T, *Chasing a Spectre: Risk Management for Global Environmental Change*, Council for Science and Society, London, 1990.

On the new sociology of risk, scientific knowledge and the limitations of mainstream 'expertise' in environmental risk analysis, see Beck, U (1992), *Risk Society*, Sage, London; Beck, U, *Ecological Politics in an Age of Risk*, Polity Press, Cambridge, 1995; Lash, S et al (ed), *Risk, Environment and Modernity*, Sage, London; Goldblatt, D, *Social Theory and the Environment*, Polity Press, Cambridge, 1996, chapter 5; Norgaard, R, *Development Betrayed: the end of progress and a coevolutionary revisioning of the future*, Routledge, London, 1994; Jacobs, M (ed), *Greening the Millennium? The new politics of the environment*, Blackwell/Political Quarterly, Oxford, 1997. There are powerful fictional reflections on the risks and uncertainties related to science, technology, pollution and waste management in advanced consumer societies in Don DeLillo's novels *White Noise*, Viking Penguin, New York, 1984, and *Underworld*, Scribner, New York, 1997

41 Derived from O'Riordan, T and Turner, R K, *An Annotated Reader in Environmental Planning and Management*, Pergamon Press, Oxford, 1983. See also Pearce, D W and Turner, R K, *Economics of Natural Resources and the Environment*, Harvester Wheatsheaf, Hemel Hempstead, 1990, pp13–15 and Chapter 15. On concepts in environmental ethics, see Hargrove, E C, *Foundations of Environmental Ethics*, Prentice-Hall, New Jersey, 1989; Sagoff, M, *The Economy of the Earth: philosophy, law and the environment*, Cambridge University Press, Cambridge, 1988; O'Neill, J, *Ecology, Policy and Politics: human well-being and the natural world*, Routledge, London, 1993
42 Pearce and Turner, 1990, op cit, p234
43 Ibid, Chapter 15

Chapter 4

1 Mulgan, G, *Connexity: how to live in a connected world*, Chatto & Windus, London, 1997, p56
2 Jacobs, M, *The Green Economy*, Pluto Press, London, 1991, pp128–9
3 Heilbroner, R L, *The Nature and Logic of Capitalism*, W W Norton, New York, 1985
4 Held, D, 'Central perspectives on the modern state' and 'Future directions for the state' in Held et al (eds), *States and Societies*, Martin Robertson, Oxford, 1984
5 Spragins, T A, *Understanding Political Theory*, St Martin's Press, New York, 1976
6 Lane, L M, 'Individualism, civic virtue and public administration', *Administration and Society*, vol 20, pp30–45, 1988; for a critique of individualism in the context of ecologically sustainable development, see Norgaard, R, *Development Betrayed: the end of progress and a coevolutionary revisioning of the future*, Routledge, London, 1994; on the limits to liberal individualism in an interdependent global system, see Mulgan, G, *Connexity: how to live in a connected world*, Chatto & Windus, London, 1997
7 Chandler, W U, *The Changing Role of the Market in National Economies*, Paper 72, Worldwatch, Washington, 1986
8 Lane, op cit, p32
9 Lane, op cit, p36
10 Hobbes, T, *Leviathan or the Matter, Forme and Power of a Commonwealth Ecclesiastical and Civil*, Macmillan, New York, 1977 (originally 1651)
11 Hobbes, op cit, p132
12 Held, op cit, p41
13 Spragins, op cit, p34
14 Held, op cit
15 Held, op cit
16 Rousseau, J L, *The Social Contract and Discourses*, Everyman, London, 1927
17 Rousseau, J L, Social Contract, Book 4, Chapter 2, cited in Dahl, R A, *Democracy and its Critics*, Yale University Press, New Haven, 1989, p355
18 Chandler, op cit, p7
19 Moss, L S, 'Power and value relationships in "The Wealth of Nations"', O'Driscoll, G P (ed), *Adam Smith and Modern Political Economy*, Iowa State University Press, Ames, 1979
20 Mill, J S, *On Liberty*, Dent, London, 1931 (originally 1859)
21 Moss, op cit
22 Held, op cit, p62
23 Schapiro, J S, *Movements of Social Dissent in Modern Europe*, Princeton: D Van Nostrand, 1962
24 Badie, B, 'Democracy and religion: logics of culture and logics of action', *International Social Science Journal*, no 129, pp511–22, 1991
25 Kleiman, M A R, 'Liberalism and vice control', *Journal of Policy Analysis and Management*, vol 6, pp87–98, 1987
26 Hayek, F A, *The Road to Serfdom*, Routledge & Kegan Paul, London, 1976 (originally 1944)
27 Ablin, R, 'The shrinking realm of laissez-faire', *Challenge*, March/April 1989, pp23–5
28 Scully, G W, 'The institutional framework and economic development', *Journal of Political Economy*, vol 96, pp652–64, 1988; Norgaard, R, *Development Betrayed: the end of progress and a coevolutionary revisioning of the future*, Routledge, London, 1994
29 Skolimowski, H, *Eco-Philosophy*, Marion Boyars, Boston and London, 1981

30 Bell, D, 'American exceptionalism revisited: the role of civil society', *The Public Interest*, no 95, pp38–56, 1989
31 Gellner, E, 'Civil society in historical context', *International Social Science Journal*, no 129, pp495–510, 1991. See also Gellner, E, *Conditions of Liberty: civil society and its rivals*, Hamish Hamilton, London, 1994
32 Keane, J, 'Democracy and the media', *International Social Science Journal*, no 129, pp523–40

Chapter 5

1 Seuss, Dr, *The Lorax*, Collins, London, 1972
2 Athanasiou, T, *Slow Reckoning: the ecology of a divided planet*, Secker and Warburg, London, 1997, p301
3 Neville, R, 'Howl '97', *New Statesman*, London, 12 September 1997
4 Held, D et al, *Globalization*, Foreign Policy Centre, London, 1999; Held, D et al, *Global Transformations: politics, economics and culture*, Polity Press, Cambridge, UK, 1999. On globalization, see also: World Bank, *Global Economic Prospects and Developing Countries*, World Bank, Washington DC, 1994; OECD, *New Dimensions of Market Access in a Globalising World Economy*, OECD, Paris, 1995; Miller, M, 'Where is Globalisation taking us?', *Futures*, vol 27, no 2, 1995; Michie, J and Grieve Smith, J (ed), *Managing the Global Economy*, Oxford University Press, Oxford, 1995; Falconer, C and Sauve, P, 'Globalisation, Trade and Competition', OECD *Observer*, no 201, August/September 1996; for powerful critiques of 'Washington consensus' globalization, see Soros, G, *The Crisis of Global Capitalism*, Little, Brown, London, 1998, and Gray, J, *False Dawn: the delusions of global capitalism*, Granta, London, 1998
5 Personal communication. The analysis here also draws on Christie, I, *Sustaining Europe*, Demos/Green Alliance, London, 1999
6 Short, C, 'The challenge of our age', *New Statesman*, London, 16 August 1999
7 Brown, L, 'The new world order', in Brown, L et al, *State of the World 1991*, Earthscan, London, 1991, p6. See also French, H, 'Forging a new global partnership', in Brown, L et al (eds), *State of the World 1995*, Earthscan, London, 1995
8 Brown, L et al, *Vital Signs 1999–2000*, Earthscan, London, 1999
9 Ibid
10 Ibid. See also Runyan, C, 'The Third Force: NGOs', *World Watch*, vol 12, no 6, November/December 1999
11 United Nations, *Global Outlook 2000*, UN, New York,1990
12 World Bank, *World Bank Atlas 1999*, Washington DC, 1999
13 Held et al, op cit
14 Ibid
15 World Bank, *World Development Report 1991*, World Bank, Washington DC, 1991
16 World Bank, *World Bank Atlas 1999*, op cit; World Bank, *Annual Report 1999*, Washington DC, 1999
17 Ibid
18 Ibid
19 See, for example, Chase-Dunn, Christopher, *Global Formation*, Blackwell, Oxford, 1989
20 French, H F, 'Restoring the East European and Soviet environments' in Brown et al, 1991, op cit, Chapter 6
21 *The Guardian*, 16 October 1991
22 Gray, J, 1998, op cit, Chapter 6
23 See Dahrendorf, Ralf, *Reflections on the Revolution in Europe*, Chatto & Windus, London, 1990; Glenny, Misha, *The Rebirth of History: Eastern Europe in the Age of Democracy*, Penguin, Harmondsworth, 1990; Garton Ash, T, *History of the Present*, Penguin, Harmondsworth, 1999
24 Cited in George, Susan, *A Fate Worse than Debt*, Penguin, Harmondsworth, 1988
25 Durning, A, 'Asking how much is enough', in Brown et al, 1991, op cit, Chapter 9. See also Schor, J, 'Can the North stop Consumption Growth?', in Bhaskar, V and Glyn, A (ed), *The North, the South and the Environment: ecological constraints and the global economy*, Earthscan, London, 1995; Goodwin, N et al (eds), *The Consumer Society*, Earthscan/Island Press, London, 1997; Ryan, J and Durning, A, *Stuff: the secret life of everyday things*, Northwest Environment

Watch, Seattle, 1998; Christie, I and Nash, L (eds), *The Good Life*, Demos, London, 1998; Redclift, M, *Wasted: counting the cost of global consumption*, Earthscan, 1996; Myers, N, 'Consumption in relation to population, environment and development', *The Environmentalist*, no 17, 1997; Noorman, K J and Uiterkamp, T S, *Green Households? Domestic consumers, environment and sustainability*, Earthscan, London, 1998

On the efforts to develop a model of 'sustainable consumption', see Robins, N and Roberts, S, *Consumption in a Sustainable World*, IIED, London, 1998; Carley, M. and Spapens, P, *Sharing the World: sustainable living and global equity in the 21st century*, Earthscan, London, 1997; McLaren, D, Bullock, S and Yousuf, N, *Tomorrow's World: Britain's share in a sustainable future*, Earthscan/Friends of the Earth, London, 1998; Zadek, S et al, *Purchasing Power: civil action for sustainable consumption*, New Economics Foundation, London, 1998; Ghazi, P and Jones, J, *Getting a Life: the downshifter's guide to happier, simpler living*, Hodder & Stoughton, London, 1997

26 Durning, op cit, p154; UNEP, *Global Environmental Outlook 2000*, Earthscan/UNEP, London, 1999

27 Durning, 1991, op cit

28 Brown et al, *Vital Signs 1999–2000*, op cit

29 Ibid

30 Meadows, D H et al, *The Limits to Growth*, Universe Books, New York, 1972

31 Durning, 1991, op cit, p162; Worcester, R, 'More than money', and Jackson, T and Marks, N, 'Found wanting', in Christie, I and Nash, L, *The Good Life*, op cit

32 See Giddens, Anthony, *Modernity and Self-Identity: self and society in the late modern age*, Polity Press, Cambridge, 1991, Chapter 6

33 DeLillo, Don, *Mao II*, Jonathan Cape, London, 1991. See also DeLillo's brilliant dark comedy examining high-tech consumer society, *White Noise*, Viking, New York, 1984

34 Hirsch, Fred, *Social Limits to Growth*, Routledge & Kegan Paul, London, 1977

35 Ibid, p109

36 Herstgaard, M, *Earth Odyssey*, Abacus, London, 1999, Chapter 3

37 Pucher, John, 'Capitalism, socialism and urban transportation: policies and travel behaviour in the East and West', in *APA Journal*, summer 1990. On the changing agenda in transport policy, see OECD, *Urban Transport and Sustainable Development*, OECD, Paris, 1995; Johansson, O et al, *Blueprint 5: the true costs of road transport*, Earthscan, London, 1996

38 'Betting big is better', *Time*, 21 June 1999. See also France, L, (ed), *The Earthscan Reader in Sustainable Tourism*, Earthscan, London, 1997

39 French, 1991, op cit.; Athanasiou, T, *Slow Reckoning*, Secker and Warburg, London, 1997, Chapter 3

40 World Bank, 1991, op cit, p105

41 George, S, 'The problem isn't beef, bananas, cultural diversity or the patenting of life. The problem is the WTO', *The Guardian*, London, 24 November 1999

42 Jackson, Ben, *Poverty and the Planet*, Penguin, Harmondsworth, 2nd edition, 1995. See also Goldin, J et al, *Trade Liberalisation: global economic implications*, OECD/World Bank, Paris, 1993; Watkins, K, *The Oxfam Poverty Report*, Oxfam, Oxford, 1995; Jacobs, M, *The Politics of the Real World*, Earthscan/Real World Coalition, London, 1996

43 Jackson, 1995, op cit

44 Ibid, Chapters 3 and 4

45 See WCED, *Our Common Future*, Oxford University Press: Oxford, 1987; IUCN/UNEP/WWF, *Caring for the Earth: A Strategy for Sustainable Living*, Gland, Switzerland; published in the UK by Earthscan, London, 1991

46 Christian Aid, *Who owes who? Climate change, debt equity and survival*, London, 1999. See also Barbier (ed), 'Tropical deforestation', and Swanson, Tim, 'Conserving biological diversity', both in Pearce, D W (ed), *Blueprint 2: Greening the World Economy*, Earthscan, London, 1991

47 Bown, William, 'Trade deals a blow to the environment', *New Scientist*, 10 November 1990; Ward, H, 'Trade and the Environment in the Round – and after', *Journal of Environmental Law*, vol 6, no 2, 1994; Elliott, L, 'Dream club that costs the Earth', and Zadek, S, 'Free trade is far from the perfect goal it is held to be', both in *The Guardian*, London, 16 December 1996; Elliott, L, 'Good for Monsanto, bad for the world', *The Guardian*, London, 30 August 1999

48 Shrybman, Stephen, 'International trade and the environment', *Alternatives*, vol 17, no 2, 1990. See also Ritchie, Mark, 'GATT, agriculture and the environment', *The Ecologist*, vol 20, no 6,

November/December 1990; Sen, P, 'Environmental Policies and North–South Trade Issues: a selected survey of the issues', in Bhaskar, V and Glyn, A (ed), 1995, op cit

49 See George, S, 1999, op cit; Elliott, L, 'For richer, for poorer', *The Guardian*, London, 25 November 1999; Vidal, J, 'Real battle for Seattle', *The Observer*, London, 5 December 1999

On the reform of the trade policy regime, see also Brack, D (ed), *Trade and the Environment*, Earthscan/RIIA, London, 1998; Ekins, P, 'World Trade and the Environment', *European Environment*, vol 4, part 2, April 1994; FIELD/NRDC, *Environmental Priorities for the World Trading System: recommendations to the WTO Committee on Trade and Environment*, Natural Resources Defense Council/Foundation for International Environmental Law and Development, Washington DC, January 1995; WWF, *Sustainable Prosperity? making trade and investment support sustainable development*, WWF, Godalming, Surrey, UK, 1997. Case studies of progressive developments in exporting sustainable products from South to North are provided in IIED, *Unlocking Trade Opportunities*, International Institute for Environment and Development/United Nations, London, 1997

50 See OECD, *The Multilateral Agreement on Investment*, OECD, Paris, May 1998. On the MAI and sustainable development issues, see Worldwide Fund for Nature, *The MAI and Developing Countries*, WWF, London, January 1998, and *The OECD Multilateral Agreement on Investment*, WWF, London, April 1998. See also the revealing and highly critical UK parliamentary report on the failures of the MAI process to be transparent and to take account of international agreements on environmental sustainability: House of Commons Environmental Audit Committee, *The Multilateral Agreement on Investment*, Volume 1, report and proceedings, The Stationery Office, London, January 1999

51 Shrybman, 1990, op cit

52 CEC Task Force, *1992: The Environmental Dimension*, Commission of the European Communities, Brussels, 1990. On EU environmental policy and approaches to sustainable development, see also CEC, *Towards Sustainability: 5th Action Programme on the Environment*, Commission of the European Communities, Luxembourg, 1993; European Environment Agency, *Environment in the European Union at the turn of the century*, EEA, Copenhagen, 1999; O'Riordan, T and Voisey, H (ed), *The Transition to Sustainability*, Earthscan, London, 1998; Christie, I, *Sustaining Europe*, Demos/Green Alliance, London, 1999

53 Shrybman, 1990, op cit

54 Brown, L et al, 1999, *Vital Signs 1999–2000*, op cit

55 Ibid

56 Ibid

57 George, S, 1988, op cit; Adams, Patricia, *Odious Debts*, Earthscan, London, 1991

58 Postel, S and Flavin, C, 'Reshaping the global economy', in Brown et al, 1991, op cit, Chapter 10, p171

59 See Jamie, R, 'The Politics of Forgiveness', *South*, July 1996; Bourgignon, François and Morrisson, Christian, *Adjustment and Equity in Developing Countries*, OECD, Paris, 1991; Reed, D (ed), *Structural Adjustment: the Environment and Sustainable Development*, Earthscan, London, 1996; OECD, *Assessing Structural Reform: lessons for the future*, OECD, Paris, 1994; Athanasiou, T, 1996, op cit, Chapters 3–4; Adams, 1991, op cit

60 See Athanasiou, T, 1996, op cit, Chapter 3; Hammond, R and McGowan, L A, *The Other Side of the Story: the real impact of World Bank and IMF structural adjustment programs*, Development GAP, Washington DC, 1993; George, S and Sabelli, F, *Faith and Credit: the World Bank's secular empire*, Westview, Boulder, 1994

61 Killick, T, *Making Adjustment Work for the Poor*, ODI Poverty Briefing, Overseas Development Institute, London, May 1999

62 Aid statistics are drawn from Brown, L et al, *Vital Signs 1997–98*, Earthscan/Worldwatch Institute, London, 1997; UNEP, *Global Environment Outlook 2000*, Earthscan/UNEP, London, 1999; OECD, *1998 DAC Report*, OECD, Paris, 1998

63 George, S, 1988, op cit, Chapter 7

64 See, for example, UN Development Programme, *Human Development Report 1999*, UNDP, New York, 1999; World Bank, *Annual Report 1999*, World Bank, Washington DC, 1999; World Bank, *World Development Report 1997: the State in a Changing World*, World Bank/Oxford University Press, New York, 1997; World Bank, *Making Development Sustainable*, World Bank, Washington DC, 1994

65 See in particular World Bank, *World Development Report 1997*, op cit

66 Sagasti, F, 'Cooperation in a fractured global order', *New Scientist*, 14 July 1990
67 World Bank, *Annual Report 1999*, op cit, p17
68 See Vidal, J, 'Modem warfare', *The Guardian*, London, 13 January 1999; de Jonquieres, G, 'Network guerillas', *Financial Times*, London, 30 April 1998
69 From a statement by the UK Chancellor of the Exchequer Gordon Brown on the need for new approaches to debt relief: see Brown, G, 'Smash the chains', *The Guardian*, London, 21 December 1999
70 See proposals for structural reform on these lines in: UNEP, *Global Environmental Outlook 2000*, 1999, op cit; Commission on Global Governance, *Our Global Neighbourhood*, Oxford University Press, Oxford, 1995; Kaul, I et al, *Global Public Goods: international cooperation in the 21st century*, Oxford University Press, Oxford, 1999; Jacobs, M, *The Politics of the Real World*, Earthscan/Real World, London, 1996; Carley and Spapens, *Sharing the World*, 1997, op cit; WWF, *Sustainable Prosperity?*, 1997, op cit; Robins, N and Roberts, S, *Consumption in a Sustainable World*, 1998, op cit; Zadek, S et al, *Purchasing Power*, 1998, op cit; Roodman, D M, 'Building a Sustainable Society', in Brown, L and Flavin, C (ed), *State of the World 1999*, Earthscan/Worldwatch Institute, London, 1999; French, H, 1995, op cit; Henderson, H, 'New Markets and New Commons: opportunities in the global casino', *Futures*, vol 27, no 2, 1995; Sachs, A, 'Upholding Human Rights and Environmental Justice', in Brown, L et al (ed), *State of the World 1996*, Earthscan, London, 1996; Washington, S, 'Globalisation and Governance', *OECD Observer*, no 199, April/May 1997. A radical perspective on cooperation between institutions and local, regional and dispersed communities of stakeholders is presented in Norgaard, R, *Development Betrayed: the end of progress and a coevolutionary revisioning of the future*, Routledge, London, 1994
71 Sachs, J, 'Helping the world's poorest', *The Economist*, 14 August 1999
72 See Tuxhill, J, 'Appreciating the benefits of plant biodiversity', in Brown, L and Flavin, C (ed), *State of the World 1999*, op cit; Tripp, R, *The debate on genetically modified organisms: relevance for the South*, Overseas Development Institute, London, January 1999; Tudge, C, 'Why we don't need GM foods', *New Statesman*, London, 19 February 1999
73 Sachs, J, op cit
74 See Brown, L et al, *Vital Signs 1999–2000*, op cit; Held et al, *Global Transformations*, op cit. For a powerful critique of TNCs and their role in globalization, see Korten, D, *When Corporations Rule the World*, Earthscan, London, 1996. See also Bryan, L and Farrell, D, *Market Unbound*, John Wiley, New York, 1996; Thurow, L, *The Future of Capitalism*, Nicholas Brealey, London, 1996
75 UN Centre on Transnational Corporations, *Benchmark Corporate Environmental Survey*, UN, New York, 1991
76 See Enderle, G and Peters, G, *A Strange Affair? The emerging relationship between NGOs and TNCs*, Price Waterhouse/University of Notre Dame, London, 1998; Murphy, D and Bendell, J, *In the Company of Partners*, Policy Press, Bristol, 1997
77 On the potential for and barriers to cultural change and systemic reform from within by corporations in the direction of sustainable enterprise, see Wallace, D, *Sustainable Industrialisation*, RIIA/Earthscan, London, 1996; Schmidheiny, S/Business Council for Sustainable Development, *Changing Course*, MIT Press, Boston MA, 1992; Hawken, P, *The Ecology of Commerce*, Harper Collins, New York, 1993; Elkington, J, *Cannibals with Forks: the triple bottom line of 21st century business*, Capstone, Oxford, 1997; Welford, R, *Hijacking Environmentalism: corporate responses to sustainable development*, Earthscan, 1997; Hopkins, M, *The Planetary Bargain: corporate social responsibility comes of age*, Macmillan, Basingstoke, UK, 1999; SustainAbility Ltd, *Engaging Stakeholders* report series, SustainAbility, London: see in particular *Benchmark Survey*, 1997; *The CEO Agenda*, 1998; *The Non-Reporting Report*, 1998

Chapter 6

1 Friedmann, J, 'Policy, planning and the environment', *Journal of the American Planning Association*, vol 56, pp334–46, 1989
2 Agarwal, A and Narain, S, *Towards Green Villages: A Strategy for Environmentally Sound and Participatory Rural Development*, Centre for Science and Environment, New Delhi, 1991; see

also Norgaard, R, *Development Betrayed: the end of progress and a coevolutionary revisioning of the future*, Routledge, London, 1994; Pye-Smith, C et al, *The Wealth of Communities*, Earthscan, London, 1994
3 Mill, J S, *On Liberty*, Dent, London, 1931 (originally 1859)
4 Smith, B C, 'The justification of local government' in Feldman, L D and Goldrick, M D (eds), *Politics and Government of Urban Canada*, Methuen, Toronto, 1969
5 Giddens, A, *Modernity and Self-Identity*, Cambridge University Press, Cambridge, 1991
6 Miles, I, *Social Indicators for Human Development*, Francis Pinter, London, 1985
7 Rhodes, R A W, *The National World of Local Government*, George Allen & Unwin, London, 1985
8 Jenkins, P, 'Squeezing democracy in liberty's name', *The Independent*, 7 May 1987
9 Eversley, D, *Regional Devolution and Social Policy*, Methuen, London, 1975
10 Sharpe, L J, 'Central co-ordination and the policy network', *Political Studies*, vol 28, pp27–46, 1985
11 Smith, B C, *Decentralisation: The Territorial Dimension of the State*, George Allen & Unwin, London, 1985
12 Frenkel, M, 'The distribution of legal powers in pluricentral systems' in Morgan, R (ed), *Regionalism in European Politics*, Policy Studies Institute, London, 1986
13 Bogdanor, V, 'Federalism and devolution: some juridical and political problems' in Morgan, ibid
14 Rondinelli, D A and Nellis, J R, 'Assessing decentralisation policies in developing countries', *Development Policy Review*, vol 4, pp3–23, 1986
15 Ibid, p5
16 Frenkel, op cit
17 Frenkel, op cit
18 Bedi, R, 'The imperial island', *Indian Express*, 17 April 1988
19 'Deadly effects of Delhi's power', *The Independent*, 25 May 1991
20 *Independent on Sunday*, 1 September 1991
21 Agarwal and Narain, op cit
22 Sattaur, O, 'The green solution for India's poor', *New Scientist*, 15 September 1990
23 Laitin, D, 'Political culture and political preferences', *American Political Science Review*, vol 82, pp589–97, 1988
24 Peeters, Y J D, 'Constitutional remedies for government overload', *Government and Policy*, vol 5, pp219–24, 1987
25 Weaver, C, *Regional Development and the Local Community*, John Wiley, Chichester, 1984
26 Gottman, J (ed), *Centre and Periphery: Spatial Variation in Politics*, Sage, Beverly Hills, 1980; Wellhofer, E S, 'Core and periphery: territorial dimensions', *Urban Studies*, vol 26, pp340–55, 1989; Wallerstein, I, 'Semi-peripheral countries and the contemporary world crisis', *Theory and Society*, vol 3, pp461–83, 1976; Wallerstein, I, *The Capitalist World Economy*, Cambridge University Press, Cambridge, 1980
27 Hebbert, M, 'The new decentralism – a critique of the territorial approach', in Healey, P et al (eds), *Planning Theory: Prospects for the 1980s*, Pergamon, Oxford, 1982
28 Friedmann, J, 1989, op cit
29 Lewis, D, 'The rape of the rainforest', *The Guardian*, 1 November 1991
30 Friedmann, op cit
31 Friedmann, J, *Retracking America: A Theory of Transactive Planning*, Doubleday Anchor, Garden City, NJ, 1973; Friedmann, J and Arbonyi, G, 'Social learning: a model for policy research', *Environment and Planning A*, vol 8, pp927–40, 1976; see also Norgaard, R, *Development Betrayed: the end of progress and a coevolutionary revisioning of the future*, Routledge, London, 1994, Chapters 12 and 13
32 Friedmann, J and Weaver, C, *Territory and Function*, Edward Arnold, London, 1979; see also Friedmann, J, *Basic Needs, Agropolitan Development and Planning from Below: the Construction of Political Communities*, University of California, Los Angeles, Urban Planning Program Paper, 1978; 'Development from above or below?', *Journal of the American Institute of Planners*, vol 48, pp249–60, 1982; 'Regional development in industrialized countries: endogenous or self-reliant?' in *Selected Writings*, University of California Academic Publishing, Los Angeles, pp237–60, 1984; 'Political and technical movements in development: agropolitan development revisited', *Environment and Planning D: Society and Space*, vol 8, pp927–40, 1985
33 Friedmann, 1989, op cit

34 Kohr, L, *The Breakdown of Nations*, Dutton, New York, 1978 (second edition)
35 Mawhood, P (ed), *Local Government in the Third World: the Experience of Tropical Africa*, Wiley, New York, 1983
36 Bogdanor, op cit
37 Frankel, op cit, p21

Introduction to Part IV

1 Self, P, 'What's wrong with public administration?', *Public Administration and Development*, vol 6, pp329–38, 1986
2 Kerrigan, J E and Luke, J S, *Management Training Strategies for Developing Countries*, Rienner, Boulder and London, 1987

Chapter 7

1 Gow, D D and Morss, E R, 'The notorious nine: critical problems in project implementation', *World Development*, vol 16, pp1399–418, 1988
2 King, A and Schneider, B, *The First Global Revolution*, Simon and Schuster, London, 1991
3 Dassah, A L, 'Man and the River Densu and its Basin', *Institutional Development for Environmental Action – the Accra Workshop Report*, Carley, M and Smith, M (eds), Commonwealth Consultative Group on Technology Management, London, 1991. Figure 7.1 appears in the Institute of Aquatic Biology, 1990 *Annual Report*, CSIR Ghana, Accra
4 Reisat, J E, 'Administrative reform in developing countries: a comparative perspective', *Public Administration and Development*, vol 8, pp85–97, 1988
5 Ibid
6 Regan, D, 'British administrative reform: the need for incentives', *Public Administration Review*, vol 44, pp545–50, 1984
7 Dichter, S F, 'The organisation of the '90s', *The McKinsey Quarterly*, no 1, pp145–55, 1991
8 Coulson, A, 'Feasible planning in a poor country: a utopian postscript to a country case study', *World Development*, vol 18, pp13–19, 1990
9 Tampoe, M, 'Driving organisational change through the effective use of multi-disciplinary project teams', *European Management Journal*, vol 8, pp346–54, 1990
10 Honadle, G and Cooper, L, 'Beyond coordination and control: an interorganizational approach to structural adjustment, service delivery and natural resource management', *World Development*, vol 17, pp1531–41, 1989
11 Knowles, H P and Saxberg, B O, 'Organisational leadership of planned and unplanned change: a systems approach to organisational viability', *Futures*, vol 20, pp252–65, 1988
12 Haas, P M, 'Intergovernmental institutions', paper presented to the Annual Meeting of the American Association for the Advancement of Science, 1991
13 Knowles and Saxberg, op cit
14 Zand, D E, 'Collateral organization: a new strategy', *Journal of Applied Behavioural Science*, vol 10, pp63–9, 1974
15 Knowles and Saxberg, op cit
16 Sagasti, F R, 'National development planning in turbulent times: new approaches and criteria for institutional design', *World Development*, p16, pp431–48, 1988
17 Rahmin, A, 'The interaction between science, technology and society', *International Social Science Journal*, vol 33, pp508–21, 1981
18 Baker, R, 'Institutional innovation, development and environmental management: an administrative trap revisited. Part I', *Public Administration and Development*, vol 9, pp29–47, 1989. 'Part II', vol 9, pp159–67, 1989
19 American Consortium for International Public Administration, *Institutional Development: Improving Management in Developing Countries*, Washington, 1986
20 Whittington, D and Calhoun, C, 'Who really wants donor co-ordination?', *Development Policy Review*, vol 6, pp295–309, 1988

21 Montgomery, J D, 'Environmental management as a Third World problem', *Policy Sciences*, vol 23, pp163–76, 1990
22 Cited in Carley and Smith (eds), op cit
23 Brandl, J, 'On politics and policy analysis as the design and assessment of institutions', *Journal of Policy Analysis and Management*, vol 7, pp419–24, 1988
24 Baker, op cit
25 Hulme, D, 'Learning and not learning from experience in rural project planning', *Public Administration and Development*, vol 9. pp1–16
26 Baker, op cit
27 Cited in Carley and Smith (eds), op cit
28 Brenner, C, *Technological Change, Structural Adjustment and Liberalisation in Developing Country Agriculture*, OECD Development Centre paper, 1990

Chapter 8

1 Miller, R B, 'Human dimensions of global environmental change' in DeFries and Malone, T (eds), *Global Change and Our Common Future*, National Academy Press, Washington, 1989
2 Godet, M, 'Effective strategic management: the prospective approach', *Technology Analysis and Strategic Management*, vol 1, pp45–5, 1989
3 Rittel, H W J and Webber, M M, 'Dilemmas in a general theory of planning', *Policy Sciences*, vol 4, pp325–33, 1973
4 Emery, F E and Trist, E L, 'The causal texture of organizational environments', *Human Relations*, vol 18, pp21–32, 1965; and *Towards a Social Ecology*, Plenum Press, New York, 1973
5 Ramirez, R, 'Action learning: a strategic approach for organizations facing turbulent conditions', *Human Relations*, vol 36, pp725–42, 1983
6 Trist, E, 'Collaboration in work settings: a personal perspective', *Journal of Applied Behavioural Science*, vol 13, p271, 1977
7 Gallopin, G C, 'Human dimensions of global change: linking the global and local processes', *International Social Science Journal*, no 130, pp707–18, 1991
8 Trist, E, 'The environment and systems response capability: a futures perspective', *Futures*, vol 12, pp113–27, 1980
9 Schon, D A, *Beyond the Stable State*, W W Norton, New York, 1971
10 Hoggart, P, 'A new management in the public sector?', *Policy and Politics*, vol 19, pp243–56, 1991
11 Robins, J A, 'Ecology and society: a lesson for organisation theory from the logic of economics', *Organization Studies*, vol 6, pp335–48, 1985
12 Bateson, G, *Steps to an Ecology of Mind*, Chandler, San Francisco, 1972
13 von Bertalanffy, L, *General System Theory*, Penguin, Harmondsworth, 1968
14 Kirby, M, 'Complexity, democracy and governance', *United Nations University Newsletter*, vol 8, p9, 1985
15 Robins, op cit, pp339–40
16 Miles, I, *The Poverty of Prediction*, D C Heath, Farnborough, 1975
17 Robins, op cit, p336
18 Rhodes, R A W, *Control and Power in Central-Local Government Relations*, Gower, Farnborough, 1981
19 Rhodes, R A W, *Public Administration and Policy Analysis*, Saxon House, Farnborough, 1979
20 DiMaggio, P, 'State expansion and organizational fields', Hall, R H and Quinn, R E (eds), *Organizational Theory and Public Policy*, Sage, Beverly Hills and London, 1983
21 Trist, E, 'Referent organizations and the development of inter-organizational domains', *Human Relations*, vol 36, pp269–84, 1983
22 Rhodes, R A W, 'Power dependence, policy communities, and inter-governmental networks', *Public Administration Bulletin*, no 49, pp 4–31, 1985
23 Rhodes, op cit, p15
24 Dunlevy, P, 'Professions and policy changes', *Public Administration Bulletin*, no 36, 1981; 'The architecture of the British central state', *Public Administration*, vol 67, pp391–417, 1989
25 Wilkie, T, 'Ministers barred Sellafield inquiry', *Independent on Sunday*, 1 December 1991

26 Vickers, G, *The Art of Judgment: a Study of Policy Making*, Basic Books, New York, 1965
27 Rhodes, R A W, *The National World of Local Government*, George Allen and Unwin, London, 1985, p39
28 Trist, 1983, op cit
29 Aldrich, H, *Organizations and Environments*, Prentice-Hall, Englewood Cliffs, 1979
30 Assael, H, 'Constructive role for interorganizational conflict', *Administrative Science Quarterly*, vol 14, pp573–81, 1979
31 Barrett, S and Hill, M, 'Policy, bargaining and structure in implementation theory', Goldsmith, M (ed), *New Research in Central-Local Relations*, Gower, Aldershot, 1986
32 Dacks, G, *A Choice of Futures: Politics in the Canadian North*, Methuen, Toronto, 1981
33 Godet, M, *Crises are Opportunities*, Gamma Institute Press, Montreal, 1985
34 Gemmill, G and Smith, C, 'A dissipative structure model of organization transformation', *Human Relations*, vol 38, pp295–316, 1985
35 CDR Associates, *Decision Making and Conflict Management: An Overview*, Boulder, Colorado, 1989
36 Young, K, 'Economic development in Britain', *Environment and Planning C*, vol 4, pp439–50, 1986
37 Hoggart, op cit
38 Hoggart, op cit. It has long been recognized that organizations, like societies, have distinctive cultures or patterns of basic assumptions, and this concept has been much studied by sociologists, anthropologists and organization theorists. Ouchi and Wilkins provide an overview of the sociological literature, and Allaire and Firsirotu of the anthropological approaches. Franks analyses the relationship between organizational culture and development. Ouchi, W G and Wilkins, A L, 'Organizational culture', *Annual Review of Sociology*, 457–83, 1985; Allaire, Y and Firsirotu, M, 'Theories of organizational culture', *Organisation Studies*, vol 5: 194–226, 1984; Franks, T, 'Bureaucracy, organization culture and development', *Public Administration and Development*, vol 9: 357–68, 1989; see also Norgaard, R, *Development Betrayed: the end of progress and a coevolutionary revisioning of the future*, Routledge, London, 1994
39 Merritt, R L and Merritt, A J, *Innovation in the Public Sector*, Sage, Beverly Hills, London, New Delhi, 1985
40 Bateson, op cit, p18
41 Argyris, C and Schon, D, *Organizational Learning*, Addison-Wesley, Reading, Mass, 1978
42 Morgan, G, 'Cybernetics and organization theory', *Human Relations*, vol 35, pp521–37, 1982
43 Ramirez, op cit, pp738–9
44 Rogers, E and Kim, P, 'Diffusion of innovations' in Merritt and Merritt, op cit, p102
45 Godet, op cit (no 2)
46 Ibid
47 Winter, R, *Action Research and the Nature of Social Inquiry*, Avebury, Aldershot, 1987, pviii
48 Brown, L, 'Action research' in *Action Research for Professional Development*, Elliot, J and Whitehead, D (eds), Institute of Education, Cambridge, 1982
49 Schon, D A, *The Reflective Practitioner: How Professionals Think in Action*, Maurice Temple-Smith, London, 1983
50 Kirby, op cit
51 Whalen, H, 'Ideology, democracy and the foundations of local self-government', in Feldman and Goldrick, op cit
52 Webber, M, 'A difference paradigm for planning' in Burchell, R W and Sternlieb, G (eds), *Planning Theory in the 1980s*, Center for Urban Policy Research, New Brunswick, NJ, 1978

Chapter 9

1 Stewart, J D, 'The environment – no respecter of organisational boundaries', *Town and Country Planning*, pp170–2, June 1991
2 Knowles, H P and Saxberg, B O, 'Organisational leadership of planned and unplanned change', *Futures*, pp252–65, June 1988
3 Sagasti, F R, 'National development planning in turbulent times; new approaches and criteria for institutional design', *World Development*, vol 16, pp431–48, 1988

4 See, for example, Peters, T J and Waterman, R H, *In Search of Excellence*, Harper and Collins, New York, 1982

5 Comfort, L, 'Action research: a model for organisational learning', *Journal of Policy Analysis and Management*, vol 5, pp100–18, 1985

6 Hirschman, A O, 'The case against one thing at a time', *World Development*, vol 18, pp1119–22, 1990

7 American Consortium for Public Administration, *Institutional Development in Developing Countries*, report of a series of seminars, 1986, p108

8 McGrath, J E, 'Groups and the innovation process' in Merritt, R L and Merritt, A J (eds), *Innovation in the Public Sector*, Sage Publications, Beverly Hills, London and New Delhi, 1985

9 Healey, P, 'The future of local planning and development control', *Planning Outlook*, vol 30, pp30–40, 1987

10 Coulson, A, 'Feasible planning in a poor country: a utopian postscript to a country case study', *World Development*, vol 18: pp143–19, 1990

11 Cernea, M M, *Nongovernmental Organizations and Local Development*, Discussion Paper No 40, World Bank, Washington, 1988

12 See, for example, *International Exposition of Rural Development, Approaches That Work*, Institute of Cultural Affairs, Brussels, 1988

13 Cernea, op cit

14 On partnerships in theory and practice and the role of socially responsible business in multi-sector networks, see Carley, M and Kirk, K *Sustainable by 2020? A strategic approach to urban regeneration for Britain's cities*, Bristol University Press, Bristol, 1998; Christie, I et al, *Profitable Partnerships: a Report on Business Investment in the Community*, Policy Studies Institute, London, 1991; Hopkins, M, *The Planetary Bargain: corporate social responsibility comes of age*, Macmillan, London, 1999; Audit Commission, *A Fruitful Partnership*, Audit Commission, London, 1998; Goyder, M, *Living Tomorrow's Company*, Gower, Aldershot, UK, 1998; Wheeler, D and Sillanpää, M, *The Stakeholder Corporation*, Pitman, London, 1997

15 Rowe, J S, 'Implementing Sustainable Development', unpublished paper, Department of Crop Science and Plant Ecology, University of Saskatchewan, 1990

16 Fairclough, T, 'The environmental reflex: policies, procedures and people', *The Courier* (ACP European Community), no 118, pp88–91, 1989

17 Stewart, op cit

18 Webb, A, 'Coordination: A problem in public sector management', *Policy and Politics*, vol 19, pp229–41, 1991

19 Webb, op cit, p238

20 Webb, op cit, p239

21 Chapman, M, 'Building consensus on environmental policy: a new approach', *Policy Studies*, vol 12, pp1–10, 1991; on mediation, facilitation and consensus-building methods in environmental and social policy, see also Susskind, L and Cruickshank, J, *Breaking the Impasse: Consensual Approaches to Resolving Public Disputes*, Basic Books, New York, 1987; Healey, P, *Collaborative Planning: shaping places in fragmented societies*, Macmillan, London, 1997; Weisbord, M et al, *Discovering Common Ground*, Berrett-Koehler, San Francisco, 1992; Schon, D, and Rein, M, *Frame Reflection: toward the resolution of intractable policy controversies*, Basic Books, New York, 1994; Bishop, J, 'Collaboration and Consensus', *Town and Country Planning*, vol 67, no 3, April 1998; Williams, L, 'Resolving planning conflicts', *Town and Country Planning*, vol 64, no 10, October 1995; Gordon, J, *Canadian Roundtables – and other mechanisms for sustainable development in Canada*, Local Government Management Board, London, UK, 1994; Norgaard, R, *Development Betrayed: the end of progress and a coevolutionary revisioning of the future*, Routledge, London, 1994, Chapter 13

22 Castellano, M, 'Collective wisdom: participatory research and Canada's native people', *IDRC Reports*, vol 15, pp24–5, 1986

23 CDR Associates, *Decision Making and Conflict Management: An Overview*, CDR, Boulder, Colorado, 1989

24 Chapman, op cit, p5–6

25 Ibid

26 Holdgate, M, 'Practical targets for sustainability and development', *Maintenance of the Biosphere*, Polunin, N and Burnett, J H (eds), Edinburgh University Press, Edinburgh, 1990

27 King, A and Schneider, B, *The First Global Revolution*, Simon & Schuster, London, 1991

28 Ministry of Housing, Physical Planning and the Environment, *A Clean Environment: Choose It or Lose It. Highlights of the National Environmental Policy Plan*, Den Haag, no date

29 American Consortium for Public Administration, op cit

Chapter 10

1 Teles, S, 'Think local, act local', *New Statesman*, London, 22 August 1997

2 Quoted in Worpole, K, *Regenerating Communities, Groundwork National Office*, Birmingham, UK, 1999

3 Davidson, J, 'Groundwork – a partnership veteran', in *Partnership Review*, Nature Conservancy Council, Peterborough, UK, September 1989

4 Christie, I, *This is your life: Groundwork Annual Review 1998*, Groundwork National Office, Birmingham, UK, 1999

5 Ibid. This account draws on case studies of projects to reduce young people's involvement in crime in Leadbeater, C and Christie, I, *To Our Mutual Advantage*, Demos, London, 1999

6 See Worpole, K, *Regenerating Communities*, op cit; Groundwork, *A new vision for Barclays SiteSavers in 1999*, Groundwork internal document, 1998

7 See Smith, A and Kemp, R, *Small Firms and the Environment*, Groundwork National Office, Birmingham, 1998

8 *A Green Future for the New Millennium*, Groundwork Black Country, Tipton, UK, 1998

9 See Worpole, K, *Regenerating Communities*, op cit; *Wren's Nest Agenda for the 21st Century*, Groundwork Black Country, Willenhall, UK

10 See Forrester, Susan, *Business and Environmental Groups – a natural partnership?*, Directory of Social Change, London, 1990

11 On Local Agenda 21 and its network of partnerships in the UK, see *Sustainable local communities for the 21st century*, LGA/Department of the Environment, Transport and the Regions, London, 1997; Local Government Management Board (LGMB), *Local Agenda 21: the first five years*, LGMB, London, 1997; Selman, P, 'A real local agenda for the 21st century?', *Town and Country Planning*, vol 67, no 1, London, January/February 1998; LGMB, *Sustainable Local Communities: some model approaches to strategy development*, LGMB, London, 1998

12 Worpole, K, *Regenerating Communities*, op cit; Christie, I, *This is your life: Groundwork Annual Review 1998*, op cit. On the Labour Government's visions for sustainable development and 'joined up' policies for regenerating poor localities, see DETR, *A better quality of life: a strategy for sustainable development for the UK*, The Stationery Office, London, 1999; Social Exclusion Unit, *Bringing Britain together: a national strategy for neighbourhood renewal*, The Stationery Office, London, 1998

13 Worpole, K, 'Bottle Banks in Arcadia? Environmental campaigning and social justice', in Warburton, D (ed), *Community and Sustainable Development*, Earthscan, London, 1998

14 Jones, P 'Groundwork – changing places and agendas', *Town and Country Planning*, vol 68, no 10, London, October 1999

15 On the links between community regeneration, local democracy and sustainability, see Worpole, K, *Regenerating Communities*, op cit; Carley, M and Kirk, K, *Sustainable by 2020? A strategic approach to urban regeneration for Britain's cities*, Policy Press, Bristol, 1998; Levett, R and Christie, I, *Towards the Ecopolis: urban governance and sustainable development*, Comedia/Demos, London, 1999; Worpole, K and Greenhalgh, L, *The Richness of Cities*, Comedia/Demos, London, 1999; Warburton, D (ed), *Community and Sustainable Development*, op cit; Local Futures Group, *A Strategy and Action Plan for London*, Association of London Government, London, 1998

Chapter 11

1 Rowe J.S, 'Implementing Sustainable Development', paper, Department of Crop Science and Plant Ecology, University of Saskatchewan, Saskatoon, 1990

2 Meadows, D et al, *Beyond the Limits*, Earthscan/WWF, London, 1992, p227

3 See, for example, Carley, M, Smith, M and Odei, M, 'Production, human resources and environmental management: resolving conflicts in the process of integration' forthcoming in *Humankind in Global Change*, Proceedings of the Symposium of the 1991 Annual Meeting of the American Association for the Advancement of Science, Washington; Carley, M and Smith, M (eds), *Institutional Development for Environmental Action: Kuala Lumpur Report* (1989), *Harare Report* (1990), *Georgetown Report* (1991), *Accra Report* (1991), Commonwealth Consultative Group for Technology Management, London; Carley, M, Smith, M and Varadarajan, S, 'A network approach to enhanced environmental management', *Project Appraisal*, vol 6, pp66–74, 1991

4 Carley, M and Smith, M, *Innovation in Development for Environmental Action*, Commonwealth Secretariat, London, 1992

Chapter 12

This chapter draws extensively on unpublished and published material provided by the California Center for Public Dispute Resolution, a joint programme of California State University, Sacramento, and McGeorge School of Law at the University of the Pacific; and on material prepared by CDR Associates, Boulder, Colorado, the professional mediators to the Californa Growth Management Consensus Project (GMCP). We are very grateful for their assistance

1 Healey, P, *Collaborative Planning: shaping places in fragmented societies*, Macmillan, London, 1997, p313

2 See Parkes, C, 'From dust to dust', *Financial Times*, London, 9 November 1997; Wyatt, D, *Five Fires: race, catastrophe and the shaping of California*, Addison-Wesley, 1997

3 'People want a place of their own', *The Economist*, 7 August 1999

4 Davis, M, *Ecology of Fear: Los Angeles and the imagination of disaster*, Picador, London, 1999

5 GMCP, Overview to Policy Background Papers, January 1991

6 GMCP, Project Summary, unpublished, no date

7 Delsohn, G, 'Is consensus on growth possible?', *Sacramento Bee*, 21 July 1991

8 GMCP, Project Summary, op cit

9 Sherry, S, 'Growth Management Consensus Project', *The Land Use Forum: a Journal of Law*, February 1992, published by California State Bar Association

10 Ibid

11 GMCP, *Achieving Certainty for Conservation, Development, and Social Equity*, no date

12 GMCP, *Achieving Compactness in Land Use*, no date

13 GMCP, *Growth Management and Public Finance*, no date

14 Ibid

15 GMCP, *The Implementation Role of the State*, no date

16 GMCP, *Ground Rules*, draft, 14 January 1991; parts of this document are cited as based on *Procedural Guidelines for Principled Negotiation and Cooperative Problem Solving for use in Contract Negotiations and Public Policy Dialogues*, developed by CDR Associates, Boulder; and Carpenter, S and Kennedy, W J D, *Managing Public Disputes*, Jossey-Bass, San Francisco and London, 1988

17 GMCP, *Summary of Findings*, Center for California Studies, California State University, Sacramento, January 1992

18 Ibid

19 Ibid

20 Water Forum, *Progress toward a regional water agreement*, Sacramento Area Water Forum, Sacramento, 1995

21 Ibid

22 See, for example, Stewart, J, *Innovations in democratic practice*, INLOGOV, University of Birmingham, UK, 1995; Stewart, J, *Further innovations in democratic practice*, INLOGOV, University of Birmingham, UK, 1996; Coote, A and Lenaghan, J, *Citizens' Juries: theory into practice*, IPPR, London, 1997

23 See, for example, the papers in UK CEED Bulletin, special issue on Public Participation, Issue 55, winter 1998–99, UK CEED, Cambridge, UK; Coote, A and Lenaghan, J, op cit; UK CEED, *Radioactive Waste Management: UK National Consensus Conference Report*, UK CEED, Cambridge, UK, 1999

24 See Doering, R, *Canadian Round Tables on the Environment and the Economy*, NRTEE Working Paper, Ottawa, 1993; Gordon, J, *Canadian Roundtables and other mechanisms for sustainable development in Canada*, Local Government Management Board, London, UK, 1994
25 See Habermas, J, *The Theory of Communicative Action*, Beacon, Boston, 1984–87
26 O'Riordan, T, 'On linking formal and informal governance', paper presented to seminar on deliberative and inclusive processes in environmental management, University College, London, UK, 17 December 1998
27 Ibid; see also Healy, P, op cit; Stewart, J, op cit
28 See Schön, D and Rein, M, *Frame Reflection: toward the resolution of intractable policy controversies*, Basic Books, New York, 1994, Chapter 8

Chapter 13

1 Wallace, D, *Environmental Policy and Industrial Innovation*, Earthscan/RIIA, London, 1995. Chapter 4 of this comparative study offers a good analysis of NEPP as an innovation in regulatory policy
2 Minister of Housing, Spatial Planning and the Environment; Minister of Economic Affairs; Minister of Agriculture, Nature Management and Fisheries; Minister of Transport, Public Works and Water Management; State Secretary for Finance; and Minister for Development Cooperation; *National Environmental Policy Plan 3*, full report and summary report, Den Haag, 1998. See also *National Environmental Policy Plan 2 The Environment: Today's Touchstone*, 1994
3 Mastop, H, Postuma, R, 'Key notions underlying Dutch strategic planning', *Built Environment*, vol 17, no 1, 1991
4 Faludi, A, 'Fifty years of Dutch national physical planning: introduction', *Built Environment*, vol 17, no 1, 1991
5 Ibid, p57
6 Jamison, A, Eyerman, R, Cramer, J, *The Making of the New Environmental Consciousness*, Edinburgh University Press, Edinburgh, 1990
7 Ibid, p123
8 Faludi, 1991, op cit, p8
9 Gijswijt, A J, 'The Kingdom of the Netherlands', in Enyedi, G, Gijswijt, A J and Rhode, B (eds), *Environmental Policies in East and West*, Taylor Graham, London, 1987
10 Stigliani, W M, Anderberg, S, 'Industrial metabolism and the Rhine Basin', *Options*, September 1991, published by International Institute for Applied Systems Analysis (IIASA), Laxenberg, Austria
11 National Environmental Policy Plan (NEPP), *To Choose or to Lose*, SDU Uitgeverij, 's-Gravenhage, The Netherlands, 1989, p194
12 Ibid, p133
13 Ibid
14 Jamison et al, 1990, op cit
15 Ibid
16 Gijswijt, 1987, op cit
17 de Jongh, P E, 1989a, 'A Short History of Integrated Environmental Policy in The Netherlands', paper prepared for Centre for Environmental and Economic Development workshop, London, 12 October 1989
18 Gijswijt, 1987, op cit
19 de Jongh, 1989a, op cit
20 See Weale, A, O'Riordan, T and Kramme, L, *Controlling Pollution in the Round*, Anglo-German Foundation, London, 1991
21 de Jongh, 1989a, op cit
22 NEPP, 1989, op cit, p115
23 de Jongh, 1989a, op cit
24 Jamison et al, 1990, op cit
25 de Jongh, 1989a, op cit
26 World Commission on Environment and Development (WCED), *Our Common Future*, Oxford University Press, Oxford, 1987

27 de Jongh, 1989a, op cit
28 NEPP, 1989, op cit, p179
29 Rogaly, J, 'Voters can take a lot more greening', *Financial Times*, 25 August 1989; see also Lenstra, W J, 'The role of the Netherlands National Environmental Policy Plan (NEPP) in energy policy', in Barker, T (ed), *Green Futures for Economic Growth*, Cambridge Econometrics, 1991
30 Association for the Conservation of Energy (ACE), *Lessons from the Netherlands*, ACE, London, 1991
31 See *Environmental News from the Netherlands*, no 1, November 1990, pp5–7
32 Lenstra, 1991, op cit
33 Jamison et al, op cit
34 de Jongh, P E, 1989b, 'The Process of Preparation of the National Environmental Policy Plan in The Netherlands', paper prepared for Centre for Environmental and Economic Development workshop, London, 12 October 1989; also Wintle, M and R Reeve, *Rhetoric and Reality in Environmental Policy – The case of the Netherlands in comparison with Britain*, Avebury, Aldershot, 1994
35 Lenstra, 1991, op cit
36 de Jongh, 1989b, op cit
37 Lenstra, 1991, op cit
38 Personal communication with Teo Wams, Director, Milieudefensie, 1999
39 Voogd, H 'NEPP–3 weighty but no clout?' *Town and Country Planning*, April 1999, p142

Chapter 14

1 Homeless International *1998/99 Annual Review*, Coventry, 1999
2 Carley, M and Spapens, P, *Sharing the World: Sustainable Living and Global Equity in the 21st Century*, Earthscan, London, 1998
3 Homeless International *1997/98 Annual Review*, Coventry 1998; see also http://www.homeless-international.org
4 For a description of this and other initiatives, see *Introducing the Shack-Dwellers International (S.D.I.)*, no date, from Homeless International
5 'Interview with Ernesto Vilaplana (Director of Pro-Habitat)', ibid
6 Homeless International (1998), *The Homeless International Guarantee Fund*, Final report to the Department for International Development
7 Patel, S, *From the Slums of Bombay to the Housing Estates of Britain*, Centre for Innovation in Voluntary Action with Oxfam, London
8 Ruth McLeod, ibid
9 Groundswell Project and National Homeless Alliance, *The Groundswell DIY Forum 1997*, London, 1997
10 Carley and Spapens, op cit
11 Personal communication from Marilyn Mehlmann, Director, GAP International, 1999; for further information contact GAP International, Stjarnvagan 2, S-182 46, Enebyberg, Sweden
12 Harland P and Staats, H J, *Long Term Effects of the EcoTeam Program in the Netherlands*, Centre for Energy and Environmental Research, Faculty of Social and Behavioural Sciences, University of Leiden, 1997
13 Karekezi, S, 'Building a Policy Research Network: The Case of the African Energy Policy Research Network (AFREPEN)', paper, AFREPEN, Nairobi, 1996; for further information, contact AFREPREN, PO Box 30979, Nairobi, Kenya
14 Karekezi, ibid, p4
15 AFREPEN, *Newsletters* nos 16, 17, 20, 1996–97
16 Karekezi, op cit, p6
17 Ibid
18 Ibid
19 Karekezi, S, Mutiso, D, Njoroge, M and Ndambuki, D, *AFREPEN/FWD Latest Acquisition Listing*, Nairobi, August 1998
20 Carley and Spapens, op cit

21 Spangenberg, J (ed), *Towards Sustainable Europe: The Study*, Sustainable Europe Campaign, Brussels, 1995. For further information contact Friends of the Earth Europe, 29 rue Blanche, B-1060 Bruxelles, Belgium
22 Friends of the Earth Netherlands, *Sustainable Consumption – A Global Perspective*, Amsterdam, 1997

Chapter 15

1 Worpole, K, 'The Path Not (Yet) Taken: the politics of sustainability', in Worpole (ed), *Richer Futures: fashioning a new politics*, Earthscan, London, 1999
2 Rayner, S, O'Riordan, T, *Chasing A Spectre: Risk Management for Global Environmental Change*, Occasional Paper no 2, Council for Science and Society, London, April 1990
3 On the prospects and challenges for capitalist democracies in the world order of the new century, see Beedham, B, 'The Road to 2050: a survey of the new geopolitics', *The Economist*, 31 July 1999; Cooper, R, *The Post-Modern State and the World Order*, Demos, London, 1996; Kennedy, P, *Preparing for the Twenty-First Century*, HarperCollins, London, 1993; Mulgan, G, *Connexity*, Chatto & Windus, London, 1997; Gellner, E, *Conditions of Liberty*, Hamish Hamilton, London, 1994
4 Rayner and O'Riordan, op cit.; O'Riordan, T, 'Civic Science and the Sustainability Transition', in Warburton, D (ed), *Community and Sustainable Development*, Earthscan, London, 1998
5 Gellner, E, *Plough, Sword and Book*, Collins Harvill, London, 1988; Hirsch, F, *Social Limits to Growth*, Routledge & Kegan Paul, London, 1977
6 Warburton, D (ed), *Community and Sustainable Development*, Earthscan, London, 1998; Worpole, K (ed), *Richer Futures: fashioning a new politics*, Earthscan, London, 1999; Jacobs, M, *The Politics of the Real World*, Real World Coalition/Earthscan, London, 1996
7 See Murphy, D F and Bendell, J, *In the Company of Partners: business, environmental groups and sustainable development post-Rio*, Policy Press, Bristol, UK, 1997; Hopkins, M, *The Planetary Bargain: corporate social responsibility comes of age*, Macmillan, London, 1999; Hawken, P, *The Ecology of Commerce*, HarperCollins, New York, 1993; Elkington, J, *Cannibals with Forks: the triple bottom line of 21st century business*, Capstone, Oxford, 1997
8 See Roodman, D M, 'Building a Sustainable Society', in Brown, L and Flavin, C (eds), *State of the World 1999*, Earthscan/Worldwatch Institute, London, 1999; French, H F, 'Strengthening environmental governance', in Brown, L et al, *State of the World 1992*, Earthscan, London, 1992; French, H F, 'Forging a new global partnership', in Brown, L et al, *State of the World 1995*, Earthscan, London, 1995; Christie, I, 'Ecopolis: tomorrow's politics of the environment', in Hargreaves, I and Christie, I (eds), *Tomorrow's Politics*, Demos, London, 1998; Edwards, M, *Future Positive: international cooperation in the 21st century*, Earthscan, London, 1999
9 See Gore, A, *Earth in the Balance: Forging a New Common Purpose*, Earthscan, London, 1992
10 Archibugi, D and Held, D (eds), *Cosmopolitan Democracy: an agenda for a new world order*, Polity Press, Cambridge, UK, 1995
11 See, for example, Healey, P, *Collaborative Planning*, Macmillan, London, 1997; Jacobs, M, *The Politics of the Real World*, Real World Coalition/Earthscan, London, 1996; Giddens, A, *The Third Way: the renewal of social democracy*, Polity Press, Cambridge, UK, 1998; Stewart, J, *Innovations in democratic practice*, INLOGOV, University of Birmingham, UK, 1995; Stewart, J, *Further innovations in democratic practice*, INLOGOV, University of Birmingham, UK, 1996; Coote, A and Lenaghan, J, *Citizens' Juries: theory into practice*, IPPR, London, 1997; Hirst, P and Khilnani, S (ed), *Reinventing Democracy*, Blackwell, Oxford, 1996; Wilkinson, D and Appelbee, E, *Implementing Holistic Government: joined up action on the ground*, Policy Press/Demos, Bristol, UK, 1999
12 Elkington, J, *Cannibals with Forks: the triple bottom line of 21st century business*, op cit
13 Jacobs, M, *The Green Economy*, Pluto Press, London, 1991

Index

Page numbers in *italics* refer to tables, charts and illustrations